Puritan Legacies

ALSO BY KEITH W. F. STAVELY

The Politics of Milton's Prose Style

Puritan Legacies

Paradise Lost and the
New England Tradition, 1630–1890

Keith W. F. Stavely

Cornell University Press

ITHACA AND LONDON

Cornell University Press gratefully acknowledges
a grant from the Andrew W. Mellon Foundation
that aided in bringing this book to publication.

First published 1987 by Cornell University Press.

International Standard Book Number 0-8014-2016-4
Library of Congress Catalog Card Number 87-47551
Printed in the United States of America
*Librarians: Library of Congress cataloging information
appears on the last page of the book.*

*The paper in this book is acid-free and meets the guidelines for
permanence and durability of the Committee on Production Guidelines
for Book Longevity of the Council on Library Resources.*

For Kathleen Stavely Fitzgerald
and Elizabeth Williams Stavely,
relations dear

I write the *Wonders* of the CHRISTIAN RELIGION, flying from the Depravations of *Europe,* to the *American Strand.*

Cotton Mather, Magnalia Christi Americana (1702)

Mr. [R. W.] Griswold justly and wisely observes: "Milton is more emphatically *American* than any author who has lived in the United States." He is so because in him is expressed so much of the primitive vitality of that thought from which America is born, though at present disposed to forswear her lineage in so many ways. He is the purity of Puritanism. . . . He is one of the Fathers of this Age, of that new Idea which agitates the sleep of Europe, and of which America, if awake to the design of Heaven and her own duty, would become the principal exponent. But the Father is still far beyond the understanding of his child.

Margaret Fuller, Papers on Literature and Art (1846)

Contents

Contents

Preface

This book represents the convergence of my professional interests as a literary critic—in Milton and in the relationships between literary text and historical context—with research pursuits that were initially motivated by much more personal concerns. Having been intermittently apprised since boyhood that I was myself descended from generations of New Englanders (these communications form but a small part of my inheritance from the second of my two dedicatees), and having reached a point at which questions of identity and roots had become increasingly pressing, I had set out in search of the historical bearings of a self I had begun to suspect of being of New England provenance psychologically as well as genealogically. What were the social determinants and cultural forms, the "structure of feeling" (to anticipate a concept to be explained shortly), within which I might locate my own characteristic habits, impulses, and restraints? I proceeded to consult a wide range of New England materials—introductory historical surveys, anthologized sermons, pamphlets, diaries— but as I did so, the questions relating to my individual psyche to which I had thought I was seeking answers came to be superseded by other questions arising from the comparisons I found myself making, as a historically minded literary critic, between the New England Puritanism with which I was becoming acquainted and the English and Miltonic Puritanism I already knew. Or perhaps it would be more accurate to say, not that professional had taken precedence over personal inquiry, but rather that I had been lucky enough to stumble on a way to marry the personal and the professional, to speak analytically and objectively of matters that were also, for me, of emotional and subjective significance. At any rate, at some point in the course of my reading, my irrepressible urge to compare Milton's literary version of Puritanism with the lived-out version that was planted and took firm root in New England crystallized into the conviction that such comparisons systematically pursued would shed new light on Milton and New England alike. What then resulted is the combination of literary criticism and sociocultural history found in the following pages.

A scholar working without academic affiliation, and therefore to an unavoidable degree apart from the established channels of connection and communication, is particularly indebted to those who have assisted him. Not the least of these, in my case, are my colleagues at the Watertown Public Library—especially Jane Eastman, Lani Gerson, and Catherine Richmond—who have constituted themselves as an environment providing a cultural and intellectual worker with stimulations and supports in abundance. Other librarian colleagues— at the Boston, Marlborough, and Westborough public libraries, the Massachusetts State Library and State Archives, the Massachusetts Historical Society, and the American Antiquarian Society—satisfied my seemingly insatiable demands for material with efficiency and great good humor.

I quote from *The Diary of Ebenezer Parkman*, Parkman's *Commonplace Book*, and from several documents relating to the early history of Marlborough, Massachusetts, by permission of the Massachusetts Historical Society, Boston. Quotations from published and unpublished portions of Parkman's diary, from his miscellaneous papers, and from his December 30, 1774, statement to the Westborough, Massachusetts, Town Meeting are made respectively from the Parkman Family Papers and the United States Revolution Collection, both owned by the American Antiquarian Society, Worcester, Massachusetts. The originals of the Westborough *Church Records* form part of the Local History Collection at the Westborough (Mass.) Public Library, which has given me permission to quote from them. The Marlborough (Mass.) Public Library has granted permission to quote from archival materials in Folder 8, "First Parish, 1700–1703," of the library's collection of local history documents. I quote from the Marlborough Association Records by permission of the Office of the Historian, First Church Congregational, Marlborough.

As will be immediately apparent to every reader, my most massive intellectual obligations, incurred over the course of twenty years of finding in their works models of how to integrate literary and historical studies, are to Christopher Hill and Raymond Williams. I can only hope that this book is not the sort of child who proves to be an embarrassment to its parents. Closer to home, Bennett Tousley permitted me to involve him in this project from a very early stage, devoting many hours, during a period when time was especially precious to him, to reading and responding to my first crude formulations. The manuscript was also improved in numerous ways by the scrutiny of William Riggs, Boyd Berry, Judith Stanford, David Hall, and John Demos, the latter two of whom kindly agreed to look over the work of a complete stranger and saved him many blunders that would otherwise have been committed by an interloper into their field of American history and culture. Andrew Delbanco and Philip F. Gura cast a cold eye on the version submitted to Cornell University Press, insisting on further modifications that resulted in further improvements. From first to last, Bernhard Kendler's editorial ministrations could not have been more considerate and efficacious.

The writing of a book is an emotional as well as an intellectual process, and two people must be particularly acknowledged for their preeminent contributions in both respects. From Michael McKeon's attentions, both author and book have benefited in many more ways than can possibly be recounted here. He encouraged what merited encouraging and restrained what needed restraining with an unfailing discernment. Conversations with him dealt invaluably with every aspect of the book's content and structure and with all the vicissitudes of its author's psyche. The other person who has played this part, not only supportively but also with heroic patience, is the first of the "relations dear" named on the dedication page. She has been the daily human form of the convention that a work is not produced by its author, but rather given to him.

Keith W. F. Stavely

Cambridge, Massachusetts

Primary Texts and Documents, with Abbreviations

In quoting from Milton's poems, I have used *The Poems of John Milton,* ed. John Carey and Alistair Fowler (London: Longmans, 1968). To avoid repetition in the notes, I have not employed the phrase "quoted in" in those cases (principally Chapters 4 and 7) in which primary materials are quoted from secondary sources.

Abbreviations

CPW   *Complete Prose Works of John Milton,* ed. Don M. Wolfe et al., 8 vols. (New Haven, Conn.: Yale University Press, 1953–82).

MT   *Marlborough Times.* The files maintained at the Boston Public Library and the Massachusetts Historical Society are the ones consulted. With scattered exceptions, these are complete for the following years: BPL—1877–79, 1882–89; MHS—1880–92.

PD   The Diary of Ebenezer Parkman. Some portions have been published: the entries for February through April and October through November 1737 and November 1778 through December 1780 are contained in *The Diary of Ebenezer Parkman,* ed. Harriett M. Forbes (Westborough, Mass.: Westborough Historical Society, 1899); those for 1719, 1723–34, and 1737–55, edited by Francis G. Walett, appear serially in *Proceedings of the American Antiquarian Society* n.s. 71–76 (1961–66), and are gathered together as a book, *The Diary of Ebenezer Parkman, 1703–1782,* 3 vols. in 1 (Worcester, Mass.: American Antiquarian Society, 1974). The remainder (1756–61, 1764–69, 1771–78,

1781–82) has been consulted in manuscript at the American Antiquarian Society and the Massachusetts Historical Society. A microfilm copy is available at the Westborough Public Library. Parkman's orthography has been left intact, but his many abbreviations ("y^e, y^t," etc.) have been spelled out. For simplicity and convenience, all citations, whether of published or manuscript portions, are identified by date only.

PFP   Parkman Family Papers. Originals are housed at the American Antiquarian Society; a microfilm copy of portions of the collection is available at the Westborough Public Library. Those portions of PD owned by AAS form part of PFP.

Puritan Legacies

Introduction

"John Milton was both a Puritan poet and the poet of the Puritans. . . . In its inception and through the lives of six generations of its people, Massachusetts was the Puritan Commonwealth *par excellence*." It therefore seemed to President Charles Francis Adams, on the afternoon of December 9, 1908, "manifestly proper and altogether fitting" that the members of the Massachusetts Historical Society had gathered together in the First Church of Boston in honor of the 300th anniversary of Milton's birth.[1] As a man of the nineteenth century, Adams perhaps knew from direct cultural inheritance what the scholarly reconstructions of our own twentieth century have enabled us also to grasp: that both Milton and New England (Massachusetts is obviously not the only part of New England to which Adams's remarks are pertinent) were indeed "Puritan" in many essential respects. As a result of the flourishing of New England studies over the past fifty years inaugurated by the work of Perry Miller, we now know a great deal about the lives of the inhabitants of the Puritan commonwealth par excellence, and our knowledge continues to increase at what seems an exponential rate. Meanwhile, Milton's participation in seventeenth-century Puritan experience, first investigated with multivolume exhaustiveness by David Masson a hundred years ago, has become a dimension of the poet's life and work which

[1] *Proceedings of the Massachusetts Historical Society* 42 (1908–1909):49.

can no longer be ignored, particularly since it received the authoritative attention of Christopher Hill a decade ago.[2]

Yet despite the fact that it is perhaps even more platitudinous today than it was for Adams in 1908 to assert that Milton was the most distinctly Puritan literary figure and New England the most distinctly Puritan society, almost nothing has been done to explore the possibilities raised by this sharing of cultural identity. When critics of Milton have concerned themselves with their poet's relationship with New England and America, they have confined themselves to the relatively innocuous question of the ways in which Milton was explicitly known by Colonial Americans.[3] As for historians of New England, while we would not particularly expect them to have Milton much on their minds, their disinclination to consider the Puritanism found on these shores in the context of and by comparison with its close transatlantic relation is quite striking, at least to someone such as myself who comes to the study of New England from the study of English Puritanism and Milton's place in it. Although discussions of the first generations in New England often look with great care at premigration English Puritanism as essential background to the stories they are telling, there has been no systematic attempt to correlate the overall state of Puritan affairs in the Colonies with that in the Mother Country since Alan Simpson's now-outdated *Puritanism in Old and New England*.[4]

[2]David Masson, *The Life of John Milton*, 7 vols. (London: Macmillan, 1859–94); Christopher Hill, *Milton and the English Revolution* (New York: Viking, 1978); see also by the same author *The Experience of Defeat: Milton and Some Contemporaries* (New York: Viking, 1984). Other works that have sought to locate Milton within the context of seventeenth-century Puritanism include Don M. Wolfe, *Milton in the Puritan Revolution* (New York: Thomas Nelson, 1941); Arthur E. Barker, *Milton and the Puritan Dilemma, 1641–1660* (Toronto: University of Toronto Press, 1942); Michael Fixler, *Milton and the Kingdoms of God* (Evanston, Ill.: Northwestern University Press, 1964); William R. Parker, *Milton: A Biography*, 2 vols. (Oxford: Oxford University Press, 1968); Keith W. Stavely, *The Politics of Milton's Prose Style* (New Haven, Conn.: Yale University Press, 1975); Boyd M. Berry, *Process of Speech: Puritan Religious Writing and* Paradise Lost (Baltimore, Md.: Johns Hopkins University Press, 1976); Mary Ann Radzinowicz, *Toward* Samson Agonistes: *The Growth of Milton's Mind* (Princeton, N.J.: Princeton University Press, 1978); Andrew Milner, *John Milton and the English Revolution: A Study in the Sociology of Literature* (Totowa, N.J.: Barnes and Noble, 1981); David Aers, Bob Hodge, and Gunther Kress, *Literature, Language and Society in England, 1580–1680* (Totowa, N.J.: Barnes and Noble, 1981), chaps. 6–8; Jackie DiSalvo, *War of Titans: Blake's Critique of Milton and the Politics of Religion* (Pittsburgh, Pa.: University of Pittsburgh Press, 1983).

[3]Leon Howard, "Early American Copies of Milton," *Huntington Library Bulletin* 7 (1935):169–79; "The Influence of Milton on Colonial American Poetry," *Huntington Library Bulletin* 9 (1936):63–89; George F. Sensabaugh, *Milton in Early America* (Princeton, N.J.: Princeton University Press, 1964).

[4]Alan Simpson, *Puritanism in Old and New England* (Chicago: University of Chicago

With our knowledge of each term of such a correlation having been so greatly augmented and enhanced in recent decades, there is reason to believe we have reached the point at which the correlation itself would prove to be extremely illuminating indeed. And there is further reason to make this a correlation not just between English and American Puritanism in general, but in particular between the English Puritan poet and the American Puritan commonwealth. To begin with, it is clear that Milton's life and writings and the establishment of New England arose from the same set of cultural circumstances. The disaffection from the Stuart regime which, as Christopher Hill has shown, Milton imbibed in his childhood was the same disaffection that was by the 1620s forcing John Winthrop and others to consider exiling themselves from their native land. That Milton's childhood tutor, Thomas Young, found it necessary to flee to Germany in the same year, 1620, that the founders of Plymouth Plantation set sail in the *Mayflower* is one suggestive coincidence. Another is the fact that the commencement season of 1629 at Cambridge University witnessed both the conferring of a B.A. on Milton and an address by the Reverend John White to an assembly of divines, urging them to consider joining the impending migration to Massachusetts Bay.

In that same year, on the eve of his setting forth in leadership of that Great Migration, Winthrop expressed a sense of moral and spiritual crisis that was almost certainly shared by Milton and his friends:

> What means then the bleating of so many oppressed with wronge, that drink wormwood, for righteousnesse? why doe so many sely sheep that seeke shelter at the judgement seates returne without their fleeces? why meet we so many wandering ghostes in shape of men, so many spectacles of misery in all our streetes, our houses full of victuals, and our entryes of

---

Press, 1955). For English Puritanism as the backdrop to the planting of New England, see, e.g., David D. Hall, *The Faithful Shepherd: A History of the New England Ministry in the Seventeenth Century* (Chapel Hill: University of North Carolina Press, 1972), chaps. 1–3; Timothy H. Breen, *The Character of the Good Ruler: Puritan Political Ideas in New England, 1630–1730* (New Haven, Conn.: Yale University Press, 1970), pp. 15–29; Stephen Foster, "New England and the Challenge of Heresy, 1630–1660: The Puritan Crisis in Transatlantic Perspective," *William and Mary Quarterly*, 3d ser., 38 (1981):624–60; "English Puritanism and the Progress of New England Institutions, 1630–1660," in *Saints and Revolutionaries: Essays on Early American History*, ed. David D. Hall, John M. Murrin, and Thad W. Tate (New York: Norton, 1984), pp. 3–37. For a brief comparison of the social dislocations in New England which may have contributed to the mid-eighteenth-century Great Awakening, with those in old England which may have helped cause the mid-seventeenth-century English Revolution, see Philip J. Greven, Jr., *Four Generations: Population, Land, and Family in Colonial Andover, Massachusetts* (Ithaca, N.Y.: Cornell University Press, 1970), pp. 277–82.

hunger-starved Christians? our shoppes full of rich wares, and under our stalles lye our own fleshe in nakednesse. . . . Our people perish for want of sustenance and imployment; many others live miserably and not to the honor of so bountifull a housekeeper as the lord of heaven and earth is.

What was driving Winthrop and others "to forsake their dearest home" for "the savage deserts of *America*" was that same intense conviction Milton would later articulate in *Comus* and *Lycidas*—the conviction that judgment was about to be passed on an England that had fallen lamentably away from its providential role as an elect, covenanted latter-day Israel.[5]

By the time Milton came to write *Comus* and *Lycidas,* in the 1630s, he had had an experience that more directly paralleled that of many prominent early New Englanders. For the two generations prior to the 1620s and 1630s, English Puritanism had managed to subsist as a movement within the Church of England. In some parishes, the right of the congregation to a voice in the selection of the minister had become established. One such parish was All Hallows in London, to which the family of the young John Milton belonged. In another such London parish, the people had elected John Davenport as their minister. And in yet another, this one outside London in Boston, Lincolnshire, the congregation's choice had been John Cotton. Additionally, especially in cities and towns where, as Christopher Hill writes, "educational standards and demands were rising," well-to-do Puritan laymen financed lectureships as a way of gaining access to sermons that they and others of like mind would find more edifying than those dispensed by a seemingly apathetic parochial clergy. One of these lectureships, in the town of Chelmsford, Essex, was in 1626 bestowed on Thomas Hooker. By these and other means, English Puritans had by the first decades of the seventeenth century become accustomed to conducting their ecclesiastical and spiritual lives in considerable independence from the episcopal hierarchy, and accustomed in particular to worshiping together without observing various of the liturgical ceremonies that were prescribed for them by the bishops but that they regarded as unscriptural and all but popish.[6]

[5]Hill, *Milton,* pp. 13–32 (for Thomas Young's exile to Germany, see p. 26); Darrett B. Rutman, *Winthrop's Boston: Portrait of a Puritan Town* (Chapel Hill: University of North Carolina Press, 1965), pp. 5–6; *American Puritanism: Faith and Practice* (New York: Lippincott, 1970), p. 30; Breen, *Character of the Good Ruler,* pp. 15–22. The final quoted phrases are from one of Milton's two direct references to New England, in *Of Reformation* (1641), *CPW,* I, 585. The other is in *Animadversions* (1641), *CPW,* I, 668.

When Milton later declared, in *The Reason of Church Government* (1642), that he had always "by the intentions of my parents and friends [been] destin'd of a child, and in mine own resolutions" to enter the church as a minister (*CPW*, I, 822), he meant that he had been intended and destined to become what John Davenport, John Cotton, and Thomas Hooker each already were—a minister in this Puritan church-within-a-church of lay and congregational autonomy and deritualized, preaching-oriented worship. But the moment when Milton came to maturity in the late 1620s and early 1630s (he received his M.A. from Cambridge in 1632) was the precise moment when the dogmatically and determinedly High Church prelate William Laud became the de facto (in 1633 the de jure) leader of the Church of England. Laud was convinced that lecturers "by reason of their pay are the people's creatures and blow the bellows of their sedition," and he therefore set about either to bring them under his control or, failing that, to silence them. Concurrently, as a believer in "the beauty of holiness," Laud insisted upon a "revival of hieratic ritual and visual ornament, in ways which had not been seen for over sixty years. Communion tables were put back in the east end of churches, and protected by altar rails; the erection of organs and stained-glass windows was encouraged; the clergy were ordered to use the surplice and the laity to kneel at the altar rails to receive the sacrament."[7]

Laud was seeking to eliminate what he saw as a subversive alternative Puritan church that had unwisely been allowed to take root and flourish. In so doing, he plunged many a Puritan into a crisis of conscience, John Milton among them. Milton, "perceiving what tyranny had invaded the Church, that he who would take Orders must subscribe slave, and take an oath withall, which unlesse he took with a conscience that would retch, he must either strait perjure, or split his faith" (*CPW*, I, 823), chose not to become a minister after all, but rather to pour all his moral and spiritual energies into his poetry. And the same policies that "church-outed" Milton and drove him into a more exclusively literary vocation drove many of those of an earlier generation who had already opted for a Puritan form of ministry, such as Cotton, Davenport, and Hooker, across the Atlantic to New

[6]Christopher Hill, *The Century of Revolution, 1603–1714* (New York: Norton, 1966; orig. 1961), pp. 88–90; Hill, *Society and Puritanism in Pre-Revolutionary England*, 2d ed. (New York: Schocken, 1967), p. 80; Hill, *Milton*, p. 24; Hall, *Faithful Shepherd*, pp. 75, 76, 77.

[7]Hill, *Century of Revolution*, pp. 83, 90; Hill, *Society and Puritanism*, p. 80; Lawrence Stone, *The Causes of the English Revolution, 1529–1642* (New York: Harper Torchbooks, 1972), p. 119.

England. All three of these Puritan divines chose exile in response to being summoned before the ecclesiastical courts to explain their failure to observe the new, more ceremonious mode of worship. In short, those who were forced to move "further to the margins of the church" by the Laudian counterrevolution included both the future "Puritan poet and . . . poet of the Puritans" and the future spiritual guides and ecclesiastical leaders of the three major centers (Cotton of Boston, Davenport of New Haven, and Hooker of Hartford) of "the Puritan Commonwealth *par excellence.*"[8]

To say this much is to make Adams's juxtaposition of Milton and New England more specific and pointed, but it is not yet to indicate anything about what is to be learned from such a juxtaposition. We gain some preliminary glimpses of what this might be, however, when we consider just how astonishingly pregnant was the historical moment in which Milton produced his major works. In politics and social relations, the English Revolution of the mid-seventeenth century not only did away with monarchy and briefly established a limited form of Parliamentary democracy, it also generated significant discussion of much broader extensions of the franchise and of a less strictly hierarchical social order generally, giving to large numbers of ordinary English people a schooling in insubordination and autonomy not easily forgotten. In economics, the Revolution not only brought capitalist relations of production and distribution much closer to dominance, it also provoked a searching critique of emergent capitalist values and, for a short time, a socioeconomic movement, that of the Diggers, based on alternative communist values. It is as though entire generations and centuries of historical development were concentrated into two accelerated decades, as (to simplify for the sake of the underlying pattern) feudalism was destroyed, bourgeois capitalism was created, and democratic socialism was proposed and resisted.

The historian who has done the most to demonstrate the epochal significance of the English Revolution is Christopher Hill.[9] It is also Hill who, as we have already noted, has done the most to define the

---

[8]Hall, *Faithful Shepherd*, pp. 72–78. Even if Michael Fixler is correct in his view that Milton's recollection of having been "church-outed" by the prelates was a piece of "passionate self-deception," this hardly matters in the present context. In 1642 Milton chose to present himself in public as someone whose own crucial experiences had been virtually identical to those that had sent many others to New England. See Fixler, *Milton and the Kingdoms*, pp. 47–48. For additional views of the church-outed question, see the material cited in Richard Helgerson, *Self-Crowned Laureates: Spenser, Jonson, Milton and the Literary System* (Berkeley: University of California Press, 1983), pp. 247–48, n. 109.

[9]See in particular *Century of Revolution*, pp. 145–61, 188; *Puritanism and Revolution*

nature of Milton's participation in that revolution. Because the tradition of strictly literary criticism of Milton has paid scant attention to them, Hill devotes his book on Milton almost exclusively to demonstrating the strength and complexity of Milton's ties to the immediate mid-century revolutionary milieu. He speculates about the enduring significance of Miltonic Puritanism only in the most general terms. But if the mid-century revolution was itself replete with long-range foreshadowings and consequences, as Hill has shown that it was, then we may well expect that the most important literary works to emerge from the revolution will exist on a similar plane of broad historical significance, will consist neither of timeless truth nor of purely topical commentary, but rather of insight into overall and underlying historical tendencies. And if we are justified in expecting to find such farseeing historical vistas in the entire corpus of Milton's postrevolutionary writings, we may particularly expect to find them in *Paradise Lost*, the most ambitious and wide-ranging of them all. It is this possibility—that in *Paradise Lost* Milton imagined the broad course of modern Anglo-American development down to the verge of our own day, insofar as that development was crucially shaped by Puritan ideology and sensibility—which leads me to propose the juxtaposition of *Paradise Lost* and the New England tradition as the subject of the present study. In providing an analogue to the history of the Puritan commonwealth par excellence, the Puritan poet and poet of the Puritans may also have offered in advance a paradigm for it.

More specifically, I argue that the profound ambiguities and instabilities that Puritanism introduced into the traditional relations of superiors and inferiors—and that revealed themselves most dramatically in the revolutionary leaders' killing of the king, only to find themselves experiencing extreme difficulties in keeping their own Leveller, Digger, Ranter, and Quaker followers under control—are Milton's central concern in his portrayal of the relationship of Adam and Eve and his narrative of the Fall. Similarly, the emergence of "the Protestant ethic and the spirit of capitalism" into socioeconomic prominence during the revolutionary years, along with the scathing critique of it articulated by the Puritan left wing, constitutes the most relevant context for understanding Milton's presentation of the character of Satan. After Part One of this book describes the treatment of

---

(New York: Schocken, 1964; orig. 1958), pp. 153–96; *Reformation to Industrial Revolution* (Hammondsworth: Penguin Books, 1969; orig. 1967), pp. 146–79; *The World Turned Upside Down: Radical Ideas during the English Revolution* (New York: Viking, 1972).

these central Puritan themes in *Paradise Lost,* Parts Two and Three demonstrate the close correspondence between what the Puritan poet Milton imagined in the seventeenth century and what came to be the dominant cultural modes in the Puritan society of eighteenth- and nineteenth-century New England.

There is another, more theoretical set of considerations which leads me to expect much from a sustained comparison between the most definite imaginative and the most definite historical manifestations of Puritanism. One of the major developments in Anglo-American historiography over the past twenty-five years has been the emergence of an approach that initially called itself "the new social history." By statistical analysis of evidence drawn from such hitherto neglected sources as parish registers and local records of land acquisitions and transfers, the new social history aimed to provide more accurate and precise knowledge of the structure of past societies and the social experience of that great majority of the peoples of past times which was prevented from entering its testimony directly into the historical record by its lack of literary skills and resources. In the first flush of communicating their discoveries and results, practitioners of the new social history were wont to propound what now look like extravagant, naively positivistic epistemological dogmas. Peter Laslett spoke of the desirability of "preferring any set of facts which can be counted over all those which arise from impressions, literary, legal and otherwise" and invoked "that statistical expectation and caution which so clearly distinguishes the inquirer after truth from the creator of impressions." Kenneth Lockridge, a prominent laborer in the statistical vineyards of Colonial New England, declared that "the very variety which lends fascination also frustrates any attempt to characterize [a] whole society through individual histories. Ultimately the underlying patterns of society . . . can emerge only from a consideration of the dull samenesses which have ever dominated human existence," and which Lockridge was himself considering by quantitative analysis of the records of births, marriages, deaths, and property arrangements available for his chosen community of seventeenth- and eighteenth-century Dedham, Massachusetts.[10]

[10]Peter Laslett, *The World We Have Lost* (New York: Scribner's, 1965), pp. 235, 239; Kenneth A. Lockridge, *A New England Town—the First Hundred Years: Dedham, Massachusetts, 1636–1736* (New York: Norton, 1970), p. 63. There is a striking inverse symmetry between the self-aggrandizing notion of quantitative historians that historical truth is to be found in arithmetical calculations, and most definitely not in "literary impressions," and the similarly self-aggrandizing claims made by poststructuralist liter-

In more recent years, the tendency among social historians to disparage "literary evidence" has been greatly reduced. Such writers as Alan Dawley and John Demos have recognized that statistics and literature both ought to be utilized in the effort to tell the truth about the past.[11] Nevertheless, it still seems worthwhile to emphasize not only that literary evidence has something to contribute to historical knowledge when employed in conjunction with facts which can be counted, but also that it has something distinctive to contribute, something that cannot be contributed by quantitative material and may even be obscured by it. Lockridge's assumption that those facts pertaining to the large, unvarying, virtually abstract rhythms of human life and death are the most real and revealing ones suggests that quantitative historical evidence tends, by its very nature, to conform the life of the past to traditional norms of stability and continuity. Moreover, this tendency can only be exacerbated by the fact that it is largely in official sources that the record of the dull samenesses of past human existence is preserved. The new social history has given us information about people formerly concealed from our view, but it has given it to us in a certain form, one that meshes all too nicely with the official self-image of preindustrial societies, to the effect that such societies abided in a condition of equilibrium and tranquility.

What Lockridge calls the "variety which lends fascination" to individual human experience would be, to a writer proceeding from a different social ontology and epistemology, not a peripheral and ultimately irrelevant but rather an essential aspect of social reality. In such an alternative view, the manifest variegation of human communities is a sign that human reality consists not of static "formed wholes," but rather of dynamic "forming and formative processes," and that what is needed in social investigation is an analysis dealing not only in "fixed explicit forms," but also in the "living presence" that those forms codify and render coherent but that they also falsify to a greater or lesser degree. The quoted phrases are drawn from the work of Raymond Williams, and it is Williams who has developed the most satisfactory theoretical rationale for the central importance of literary materials in historical study. In pursuit of a methodology that

---

ary critics, to the effect that history is best regarded as a literary construct; see Hayden White, *Metahistory: The Historical Imagination in Nineteenth-Century Europe* (Baltimore, Md.: Johns Hopkins University Press, 1973); and Marshall Grossman, "Formalism, Structuralism, Marxism: Fredric Jameson's Critical Narrative," *Dispositio: Revista Hispanica de Semiotica Literaria* 4 (1979):268, 272.

[11] Alan Dawley, *Class and Community: The Industrial Revolution in Lynn* (Cambridge, Mass.: Harvard University Press, 1976); John Putnam Demos, *Entertaining Satan: Witchcraft and the Culture of Early New England* (New York: Oxford University Press, 1982).

would require as little abstraction as possible from the substance and the quick of lived social experience, but which would nevertheless enable us to perceive those patterns and coherences that do in reality exist, Williams formulated many years ago a category he called "structure of feeling." "Structure" suggests that any given culture is indeed a distinct entity and unity, manifests a "firm and definite" articulation and shape. Yet "feeling" acknowledges that analysis remains reductive and invalid until it incorporates "the most delicate and least tangible parts of our activity. In one sense, this structure of feeling is the culture of a period: it is the particular living result of all the elements in the general organization."[12]

In his more recent work, Williams has linked his emphasis on structure of feeling to Antonio Gramsci's concept of hegemony. The close connection in Williams's thought between structure of feeling and hegemony is evident in the way he distinguishes hegemony from ideology. Where ideology primarily denotes the "articulate and formal meanings, values and beliefs which a dominant class develops and propagates," hegemony functions in a way that is both socially more pervasive and psychically deeper. It amounts in effect to "a saturation of the whole process of living," so much so that "the pressures and limits of what can ultimately be seen as a specific economic, political, and cultural system seem to most of us the pressures and limits of simple experience and common sense." So within Williams's overall theoretical construct, hegemony constitutes his recognition that in any place and at any time, the structure of feeling is relative to the configurations of political, social, and cultural power. It is neither spontaneous expression nor imposed indoctrination, but rather a synthesis of the two. Additionally, the hegemonic structure of feeling will never encompass all the forms of consciousness and practice manifested in a particular society. Immersed in time as any society unavoidably is, it will always have within it, coexisting and dynamically interacting with the hegemonic mode, both "residual" and "emergent" modes. The residual consists of "meanings and values which cannot be expressed or substantially verified in terms of the dominant culture," but which "are nevertheless lived and practised on the basis of the residue . . . of some previous social and cultural institution or formation." The emergent is, as the term suggests, the totality of the "new meanings and values, new practices, new rela-

---

[12]Raymond Williams, *Marxism and Literature* (Oxford: Oxford University Press, 1977), p. 128; *The Long Revolution*, rev. ed. (New York: Harper Torchbooks, 1966), p. 48.

tionships, and kinds of relationship [which] are continually being created." The hegemonic mode will seek to incorporate (or co-opt, in the parlance of the American New Left of the 1960s) whichever portions or aspects of the residual and emergent modes are perceived to constitute substantial alternatives to it and/or to stand in postures of opposition to it. But these strategies can never completely eliminate cultural plurality. At any point in time, we will sense that the "living presence" of the culture we are analyzing is an elaborate constellation of relations among the available modes: "elements of persistence, adjustment, unconscious assimilation, active resistance, alternative effort, will all normally be present, in particular activities and in the whole organization."[13]

This brings us to Williams's estimate of the place and function of artistic and literary expression within a given society and culture. To repeat, Williams posits the idea of structure of feeling in response to the fact that "practical consciousness is almost always different from official consciousness." Practical consciousness is the level on which "meanings and values . . . are actively lived and felt." It is on this level that people must and do make their own nuanced adjustments and negotiations as the hegemonic, the residual, and the emergent jockey for position around them and within them: "We are talking about characteristic elements of impulse, restraint, and tone; specifically affective elements of consciousness and relationships: not feeling against thought, but thought as felt and feeling as thought: practical consciousness of a present kind, in a living and interrelating continuity." Art and literature then become for Williams "the articulation (often the only fully available articulation)" of exactly this present, practical consciousness of the densely interwoven fabric of past, present, and future, of formal belief and spontaneous impulse and intuition, of sociocultural complexity, contradiction, tension, and resolution. In other words, in Williams's theory artistic and literary "impressions" are indispensable to the sociocultural analyst because they constitute the medium in which the affective and cognitive intricacy of actual social experience and social relations is likely to be most fully registered and represented.[14]

An approach that stresses the centrality of literary evidence may well prove particularly fruitful when directed toward the study of Puritanism, a culture that in its heyday based itself on the Word and the Book and that in its secularized nineteenth-century form re-

---

[13]Williams, *Marxism and Literature*, pp. 109–10, 112, 122, 123; *Long Revolution*, p. 46.
[14]Williams, *Marxism and Literature*, pp. 130–33.

mained prolifically discursive and verbal. New England Puritanism in particular offers an intriguing combination of relative social homogeneity and stability and a population consisting to a disproportionate degree of highly articulate observers of themselves and their surroundings. Kenneth Lockridge's assertions to the contrary notwithstanding, it is not at all unlikely that we will be able to characterize the whole society of New England through individual histories, characterize it, indeed, in view of the aforementioned homogeneity and stability, not only as it was during a single generation, but as it was over the long term from the seventeenth through the nineteenth centuries. We must take great care, of course, in choosing our representative figures and our literary representations, focusing on those sorts of individuals and those forms of expression which seem most likely to divulge the central concerns and contradictions of the culture, as they were actively lived and felt.

For the Colonial era, a clergyman seems a prudent choice. This is not in the least because everyone in Colonial New England society assented uncritically to the version of Puritan values propounded by the clergy, but rather because in each community the clergyman was the acknowledged cultural leader and was therefore forced to deal constantly with the manifold tensions arising from precisely what was ambiguous and problematic in the hegemonic Puritan scheme. Of the two primary forms of Colonial New England literary expression, the sermon and the diary, it seems advisable to rely primarily on the latter, because in his diary the Puritan clergyman was more likely to portray the life of his community as it truly was, with all its irresolvable conflicts, not as the deferential and harmonious brotherhood that the reigning Winthropian ideology insisted it ought to be. With these considerations in mind, I have cast the Reverend Ebenezer Parkman of Westborough, Massachusetts, in the role of representing the structure of feeling of Colonial New England. Parkman served in the Westborough pulpit from 1724 until his death (on Milton's birthday!) in 1782, presiding over, struggling with, and recording in his diary in great detail the experiential consequences of those profound ambiguities of Puritan hierarchy which the seventeenth century had bequeathed to him and which were manifested most definitely and painfully in the two formative upheavals through which he and his people lived: the Great Awakening and the American Revolution.

To extend our story through the nineteenth century requires that we find someone who participated in the socioeconomic and cultural transformations that marked the era, who nevertheless continued to function under the influence of the Puritan heritage, and whose literary testimony exhibits a blend of ideological commitment and empirical candor similar to that found in the Puritan diary. In terms of sheer incarnation of hegemonic values, the owners and managers of the new manufacturing enterprises played a part in the society and culture of nineteenth-century New England comparable to that played by the clergy in Colonial times. But the manufacturers were for the most part an inarticulate lot, preoccupied as they were with their economic activities. Their need for literary stand-ins and surrogates may well have been one of the factors conducive to the emergence and flourishing of a secularized press in the nineteenth century. So if we can find someone who edited a newspaper in a community that experienced the industrial capitalist revolution to a significant degree; who, as a cultural leader, had substantial ties to the community's economic leaders; and who articulated the Puritan cultural tradition as it both persisted and altered under the impact of capitalism, then we will perhaps have found someone who can disclose to us the structure of feeling engendered by the nineteenth-century secularization process. Such a figure is Charles F. Morse, editor of the *Marlborough Times*. Marlborough, Massachusetts, was the town from which Ebenezer Parkman's Westborough had separated in 1717. From the 1830s to the 1890s, it was drastically altering itself from a typical New England farming village into a small industrial city. Morse's community thus involved itself to the fullest in the dialectics of the Protestant ethic and the spirit of capitalism, and Morse registered that involvement and those dialectics in his newspaper with an entertaining and inadvertently illuminating exuberance.

The present book, then, attempts to utilize the great variety of available Puritan literary evidence to construct an account of the development of Puritan culture sufficiently broad to take in the *longue durée,* sufficiently coherent to be recognized as a single, unified story, and sufficiently nuanced to remain as faithful as possible to the complexities of experience. For that is what literature, cautiously selected and meticulously analyzed, can make available to the historian: a combination of integral unity and inwardness of detail found in no other source. We can ourselves piece together a combination of this sort from relatively occasional literature such as a diary so rich in its report of psychic interactions as Reverend Parkman's, or a newspaper written with as much bluntness and élan as Editor Morse's *Times.* But when we turn to a major literary work such as *Paradise Lost,* we find the requisite synthesis of coherence and unity with subtlety of detail and nuance laid out for us as a matter of conscious purpose and design. That is, we find a paradigm that allows us to understand macrohistorical developments as lived experiences. In Part One, we outline the paradigm for New England and American development that is discernible in Milton's stories of the falls of humans and angels. In Parts Two and Three, we confirm the validity and justness of this Miltonic paradigm by telling comparable stories of representative New Englanders and Americans.

In one of his recent essays on the nuclear arms race, E. P. Thompson laments the fact that Americans have been led to believe "that America is not a race or nation at all but is the universal Future." Thompson goes on to identify this belief as the main ideological underpinning of American behavior in the world since World War II. We have, in his words, laid "arrogant claim to a universalism of virtues—an incantation of freedoms and rights—and [asserted] in this name a prerogative to blast in at every door and base [ourselves] in any part of the globe in the commission of those virtues." Thompson does not speculate about the sources of our imperial self-righteousness, but it is safe to say that one of the most significant of them is Puritan utopianism, most concisely and famously expressed in John Winthrop's anticipation that New England would be "as a citty upon a hill" for all the world to contemplate and emulate.[15]

So to propose Milton's tale of the Fall as a helpful framework for American history is to bring the Puritan tradition to bear against itself, to exchange the intoxications of Puritan election for a sobered Puritan consciousness of transgression. And from the point of view of understanding and appreciating Milton, there is a particular appropriateness in having his most important poem play such a role. For according to Christopher Hill, Milton came to believe that it was just such messianic aspirations as are expressed in Winthrop's well-known dictum that had caused the defeat of the mid-century revolution to which he had so energetically committed himself, and he attempted in *Paradise Lost* and his other major poems both to debunk Puritan revolutionary romanticism and to hand down to the future what remained viable in Puritan revolutionary idealism. For those of us who love

---

[15]E. P. Thompson, *The Heavy Dancers: Writings on War, Past and Future* (New York: Pantheon, 1985), p. 40. The utopian and apocalyptic dimension of New England Puritanism is one of the primary themes of Sacvan Bercovitch, *The Puritan Origins of the American Self* (New Haven, Conn.: Yale University Press, 1975); see esp. p. 108. See also Stephen J. Stein, "Transatlantic Extensions: Apocalyptic in Early New England," in *The Apocalypse in English Renaissance Thought and Literature: Patterns, Antecedents, and Repercussions*, ed. C. A. Patrides and Joseph Wittreich (Ithaca, N.Y.: Cornell University Press, 1984), pp. 266–98.

Milton's poetry and find comfort and wisdom in his vision, it is pleasing to imagine that *Paradise Lost* might yet function as it was intended to function at the time it was written, that it might serve to disabuse the successor Puritan empire to the one Milton's own Puritan revolution did so much to create of its mythology of transcendent exceptionalism among the peoples of the earth and lead it toward that genuine internationalism that, as Thompson and others have been insisting, has become indispensable to the survival of the species. Of course, to be told that one is not exceptional but, like everyone else, fallen, to learn to do without an "ideologically-confected self-image" and struggle toward "an authentic self-identity" will be extremely difficult and painful. Thompson urges our poets and historians to assist us in this much-needed work of maturation, but luckily for us, we have already been shown the way by the very greatest of poets, who, with his prescient understanding of Puritan culture, turns out also to have been among the very greatest of historians.[16]

[16]Hill, *Milton*, pp. 341–412; Thompson, *Heavy Dancers*, p. 41.

PART ONE

Prophetic Strain: The Representation of Puritan Culture in *Paradise Lost*

Till old experience do attain
To something like prophetic strain.

Milton, "Il Penseroso" (1631?)

Every honest man is a Prophet he utters his opinion both of private &
public matters Thus If you go on So the result is So He never says
such a thing Shall happen let you do what you will. a Prophet is a Seer
not an Arbitrary Dictator.

William Blake, annotations to Bishop R. Watson,
An Apology for the Bible (1797)

Chapter 1

Antinomianism and Arminianism

Among those literary critics and intellectual biographers who have been most explicit and systematic about situating Milton within the context of the mid-seventeenth-century revolution, there has developed over the past several generations of study a fundamental consensus regarding Milton's social temper. When Christopher Hill declares that Milton, unlike John Bunyan or Gerrard Winstanley, is an "elitist intellectual," he is echoing the conclusion Arthur E. Barker came to in 1942: that Milton's ultimate position on social structure was the subordination of the many who "do not achieve regeneration" to the few and fit who do, those few simultaneously constituting the Puritan "aristocracy of grace" and "the natural aristocracy described by the classical philosophers." The ingredient Hill and other recent analysts such as Andrew Milner, Jackie DiSalvo, and Herman Rapaport have added to the earlier descriptions of Miltonic elitism is a sense of Milton's place in the class dynamics of emergent modern society. In DiSalvo's phrase, Milton speaks throughout his writings for "the saintly elite of a reforming middle class." He is the bard of the great transformation of a feudal and aristocratic into a capitalist and bourgeois hegemony.[1]

Of course, Christopher Hill must be distinguished from the others

[1]Christopher Hill, *Milton and the English Revolution* (New York: Viking, 1978), p. 266; Arthur E. Barker, *Milton and the Puritan Dilemma, 1641–1660* (Toronto: University of Toronto Press, 1942), p. 326; Jackie DiSalvo, *War of Titans: Blake's Critique of Milton and the Politics of Religion* (Pittsburgh, Pa.: University of Pittsburgh Press, 1983), p. 37. See also Andrew Milner, *John Milton and the English Revolution: A Study in the Sociology of Literature* (Totowa, N.J.: Barnes and Noble, 1981), pp. 90–93, 136, 204; and Herman Rapaport, *Milton and the Postmodern* (Lincoln: University of Nebraska Press, 1983), pp. 168–99.

who have portrayed a Milton who is at bottom bourgeois. The major purpose of Hill's book on Milton is to bring out the hitherto unappreciated extent of Milton's affinities with the distinctly unbourgeois revolutionary left wing of Quakers, Ranters, Levellers, and even Diggers. Hill's Milton is a figure who lived "in a state of permanent dialogue with radical views which he could not wholly accept, yet some of which greatly attracted him. . . . If we think of two eccentric circles, one representing the ideas of traditional Puritanism, the other those of the radical milieu, Milton's ideas form a third circle, concentric to neither of these but overlapping both." We will remain permanently indebted to Hill for his having provided a rich and detailed encyclopedia of the radicalism of Milton's intellectual and cultural orientation. But what is missing from his presentation is a sense of how the parts of his Miltonic "third circle" add up to a whole and of what the larger significance might be of a vision that both participates in and remains detached from the major ideological and cultural groupings within revolutionary Puritanism. This chapter is an attempt to describe a visionary synthesis rooted in the experience of Milton's times, set forth most fully and generously in *Paradise Lost,* and constituting the vantage point of imaginative autonomy from which Milton comments with critical empathy upon both the radical and the hegemonic permutations of Anglo-American Protestantism.[2]

Most of what attracted Milton in the thinking of the Puritan ultra-left can be grouped together within the broad category of antinomianism. Antinomianism was but the emergence into discrete doctrine of the tendency of all Protestantism to affirm inner experience in defiance of external and traditional authority. It insisted that imposed rules and regulations were not binding on regenerate Christians, that, in the words of William Tyndale at the very outset of the Reformation in England, "to steal, rob and murder are holy, when God commandeth them." But this aspect of antinomianism, the one that made it a byword for wildness and lunacy, is less relevant to *Paradise Lost* (although it is quite relevant indeed to *Samson Agonistes*) than is that broader sense of immanence and vitalism it implied, which was, according to Geoffrey Nuttall, more widely diffused in mid-seventeenth-century revolutionary England than in any other place and at any other time in Christian history. If a radical such as the Digger Gerrard Winstanley could remind his followers that "you do not look for a God now, as formerly you did, to be [in] a place of

[2]Hill, *Milton,* pp. 113–15.

glory, beyond the sun, moon and stars, nor imagine a divine being you know not where, but you see him ruling within you," so also could a more moderate figure such as the Independent Francis Rous turn the apprehension of an indwelling God into an appreciation of natural process that verged upon pantheism:

> We see in natural things, how joyfully the young ones run to their Dams, yea, children with earnestness apply themselves to the brests of their mothers. Surely, Man hath but one true and very Father, but one true Cause and Creator; and how joyfully should Man run to this his Original, how earnestly should he suck from God by prayer, the nourishment and increase of that spiritual life, which himself hath begotten in us?
>
> The young Lamb knows her Dam by that instinct, and notion, which neither it, nor we, can understand or express. How much more should those that are begotten by God, own God for their Father, by a secret acknowledgment and [y]earning.

Rous's metaphors outlive his somewhat reductive doctrinal applications, conjuring up a universe of radical similarity and commingling. He pictures biological and emotional nurturance so vividly that his point is transformed into an experience of immanence. Just as the content of the passage overcomes distinctions between animals and humans, begetters and nurturers, fathers and mothers, so its form, interweaving natural vehicle with spiritual tenor, marries the divine and intellectual to the human, natural, and physical, imparting a measure of the vivacity of the latter to the former even as it extends the full spiritual citizenship of the former to the latter.[3]

Such an antinomian sensibility, a conviction that "every creature hath a beam of God's glory in it," is communicated at many points and in many ways throughout *Paradise Lost*. One thinks most immediately of the account of Creation in Book VII, with its splendid panorama in

---

[3]Christopher Hill, *Change and Continuity in Seventeenth-Century England* (Cambridge, Mass.: Harvard University Press, 1975), p. 90; Geoffrey F. Nuttall, *The Holy Spirit in Puritan Faith and Experience* (Oxford: Basil Blackwell, 1947), pp. viii, 136, 144–45. This aspect of radical antinomianism developed, like all others, from the taking of Protestant commonplaces more literally than they were perhaps intended to be taken. Meditation upon the phenomena of nature, the Book of Creatures, was a practice repeatedly recommended to seventeenth-century English Protestants; see Barbara Kiefer Lewalski, *Protestant Poetics and the Seventeenth-Century Religious Lyric* (Princeton, N.J.: Princeton University Press, 1979), pp. 162–65. Thus, Joan S. Bennett is mistaken in her claim that the Ranters were the only revolutionary group that "gave a material, pantheistic interpretation to the meaning of Christ's indwelling spirit." And she is therefore also mistaken in implying that such a material, pantheistic interpretation is irrelevant to *Paradise Lost*. See " 'Go': Milton's Antinomianism and the Separation Scene in *Paradise Lost*, Book IX," *PMLA* 98 (1983):394.

which "air, water, earth, / By fowl, fish, beast, was flown, was swam, was walked / Frequent" (502–4). But the poem's dignification of nature and natural experience is made available not only on the level of visionary cosmic prospect, but also in its representations of dailiness. Consider this metaphoric interruption of the narrative of the demonic debate in Book II:

> As when the mountain tops the dusky clouds
> Ascending, while the north wind sleeps, o'erspread
> Heaven's cheerful face, the louring element
> Scowls o'er the darkened landscape snow, or shower;
> If chance the radiant sun with farewell sweet
> Extend his evening beam, the fields revive,
> The birds their notes renew, and bleating herds
> Attest their joy, that hill and valley rings.
>
> (II, 488–95)

Geoffrey Nuttall informs us that images of light, particularly sunlight, were among those most commonly used by mid-seventeenth-century Puritans to represent the way in which the created order was pervaded and animated by the Holy Spirit, and the present passage is one of the most noteworthy of many such uses of the light and warmth of the sun in *Paradise Lost*. The more we contemplate this simile—which in its emergence from the gloom of Hell and devilish machination enacts what it describes—the more dubious do our usual distinctions between natural and spiritual, human and divine, everyday and extraordinary, begin to seem. The radiant sun clearing up a darkened, stormy landscape one evening reminds us of the venerable association between sun and Son and therefore makes us think of the Son of God and his redemptive mission, which Satan will shortly be grossly parodying, but not in such a way as to make us forget that we are still in the presence of the natural sun shining on our familiar, fallen world. The bleating herds attesting their joy constitute an equally venerable figure both for the flocks of Christian believers and for the Lamb of God who is the sacrificial Son of God, but they also endure as actual, literal lambs glad of a moment's light and warmth. Christ is then both the giver and the receiver of that light and warmth, is all at once the sun and the lambs and, if we so choose, ourselves. What Raphael later tells us about the angels' style of making love could also be applied to the behavior of all parties to this metaphoric moment: "Total they mix" (VIII, 627). Being out in the sunshine turns out to be radically equivalent to living "under hope / Of heavenly grace" (II, 498–99). That preposition, "under," has been made thoroughly tangible and accessible. At this and many other moments in *Paradise Lost,* we learn, *pace* William Empson, to view the concept of a God who "shall be all in all" (III, 341) neither as a "high mystery" that Milton borrowed from the Cambridge Platonists nor as an "extremely grand climax" postponed until the Apocalypse, but rather as something readily available and regularly to be experienced in the world as it is right now.[4]

The teaching of revolutionary antinomianism which provoked the most heated reaction from more orthodox Puritans was summed up by Richard Baxter in 1655 when he indignantly asked: "Is not he a Pagan and no Christian that thinks that the light which is in all the Indians, Americans, and other Pagans on earth, is sufficient without Scripture?" The Quaker exhorter and organizer George Fox was forthright in his reply: " 'The light which doth enlighten every man that cometh into the world,' by whom the world was made, was before natural conscience was, or natural light either, or the blurr'd light as thou cals it; And many of the Indians do shew forth more in their conversations of the light then you do."[5] In *Christian Doctrine* Milton likewise speaks up for the spiritual dignity of non-Christians. By virtue of the truth of antitrinitarianism, "there are a lot of Jews, and Gentiles too, who are saved although they believed or believe in God alone, either because they lived before Christ or because, even though they have lived after him, he has not been revealed to them" (*CPW,* VI, 475). But it is not only in his prose treatise, which he prudently chose not to publish, that Milton formulates his own version of heretical Quaker universalism. *Paradise Lost* also pays its respects to "the light which is in all the Indians, Americans, and other Pagans on earth."

To some extent, such respect is implicit in that density of proper names and cultural allusions which is one of the poem's most distinguishing features. In the very first extended epic simile, comparing Satan to various sea monsters (I, 194–209), there is a sense that truth is to be discovered not so much from Scripture alone as from the placement of our understanding of Scripture in relation to whatever can be learned from a multitude of other sources, such as the "fables" of pagan antiquity and popular lore of the sort found in the tales that "seamen tell." Of course, a disposition to make use of pagan and

---

[4]Nuttall, *Holy Spirit,* pp. 40–42; William Empson, *Milton's God* (Norfolk, Conn.: New Directions, 1961), pp. 130–43. Lewalski, *Protestant Poetics,* pp. 89–90, notes the widespread use in seventeenth-century English Protestant discourse of light as a metaphor for spiritual regeneration.

[5]Nuttall, *Holy Spirit,* p. 160.

secular materials in telling a sacred Christian story will not, in and of itself, suffice to establish any particular affiliation between *Paradise Lost* and the Quaker acceptance of the spiritual dignity of all humanity. Such practices were amply sanctioned by Protestant typology as well as by Renaissance Christian humanism. But what are we to make of the simile Milton fastens upon Satan when he first emerges from Chaos, in the course of his journey to Earth?

> As when a vulture on Imaus bred,
> Whose snowy ridge the roving Tartar bounds,
> Dislodging from a region scarce of prey
> To gorge the flesh of lambs or yeanling kids
> On hills where flocks are fed, flies toward the springs
> Of Ganges or Hydaspes, Indian streams;
> But in his way lights on the barren plains
> Of Sericana, where Chineses drive
> With sails and wind their cany wagons light.
>
> (III, 431–39)

Here is the same hallowed imagery of the Christian pastoral as we have examined in the great simile from Book II. The flocks of the faithful are depicted as menaced by a satanic bird of prey. Conventionally pious readers might expect such a demonic vulture in search of hills where flocks are fed to fly in the direction of Europe, where the great majority of lamblike Christian believers would be found. But this one proceeds instead "toward the springs / Of Ganges or Hydaspes, Indian streams." Apparently he can gorge himself on blessed lambs in heathen India as well as in Christian Europe. It is an oblique acknowledgment of the legitimacy of Indian spiritual traditions, which is strengthened somewhat when these lines are linked to the spiritual significance consistently attached in *Paradise Lost* to springs and fountains, streams and rivers. (Unfortunately, it cannot be definitely stated that the lines are referring to the central place of the Ganges in Hinduism.) This acceptance of the culture and religion of India is followed by a more open embrace of the other ancient civilization of Asia, that of China. The "Chineses" live not up on rich hills where flocks are fed, but down in barren plains. According to conventional Christian definitions, the Chinese are in all probability fallen and so are living exactly where they belong. Their uninviting habitat may even give the orthodox and respectable the temporary satisfaction of reminding them of the sinful Old Testament cities of the plain. But the Chinese clearly do not conduct themselves as though they were fatalistically trapped in the sin of non-Christianity. They have had the wit and ingenuity to devise a way of life in which they cooperate with the contingencies that have befallen them, as they "drive / With sails and wind their cany wagons light." Wind was as commonplace a figure as light for the empowering and inspiring antinomian Holy Spirit, and if we suspect that such is the significance of the winds that are helping these people to transport themselves in so pleasingly buoyant a manner, our suspicions will shortly be confirmed. The "bright sea" that Satan will within a hundred lines find flowing beneath the gate of Heaven will be the sea on which those "who after came from earth, sailing arrived, / Wafted by angels" (518–21). These later lines inevitably make us think that the "Chineses" are among those who, sailing, arrived at the gate of Heaven, wafted by angels, for they are the devotees of sailing existing in closest poetic proximity to this glimpse of salvation. These images of the dignity of Asian religious traditions are so impressive, so compelling, that they resolve the hue and cry over the Quaker doctrine of the salvation of the heathen into a calm, assured "of course."

Our final piece of evidence on the question of *Paradise Lost* and antinomian universalism is a much more extended representation of Indian culture. After the Fall, when Adam and Eve awaken from troubled sleep, Adam recommends that they "now, as in bad plight, devise / What best may for the present serve to hide / The parts of each from other, that seem most / To shame obnoxious, and unseemliest seen" (IX, 1091–94). They decide to make clothing for themselves by sewing together the leaves of

> The fig-tree, not that kind for fruit renowned,
> But such as at this day to Indians known
> In Malabar or Deccan spreads her arms
> Branching so broad and long, that in the ground
> The bended twigs take root, and daughters grow
> About the mother tree, a pillared shade
> High overarched, and echoing walks between;
> There oft the Indian herdsman shunning heat
> Shelters in cool, and tends his pasturing herds
> At loop-holes cut through thickest shade.
>
> (1101–10)

It would be difficult to do greater violence to the import and spirit of this passage than is done in such a strangely confident interpretation as: "The Indian herdsman is put in because he is primitive and pagan, and perhaps also because his work is connected with fallen man's non-vegetarian diet. . . . The proliferating tree is a tree of error: it is an objective correlative of the proliferating sin that will ramify through Adam's and Eve's descendants."[6] Hardly. Such mechanistic translation into dogmatic allegory willfully ignores the actual, present texture of the verse itself. If this is the Tree of the Knowledge of Good and Evil, which has now played its part in the Fall, it is also the Tree of Life, spreading its arms with the natural generosity of Mother Earth, continuing after the Fall to bring forth daughters, to nurture them, and to make it possible for human beings to enjoy such things as "echoing walks." As for the Indian herdsman, it should be unnecessary by this point to descant further on the far from recondite spiritual significance of a herdsman and his pasturing herds. This heathen shepherd shows the same adaptability as the Chinese in Book III, sheltering himself and his herd from excessive heat, while making ingenious provision by means of "loop-holes" for "fresh coole aire . . . as also for light."[7] Cool breezes and rays of light that "cut through thickest shade"—Milton's and mid-century Puritanism's most pervasive images for the Holy Spirit steal in once again. At a major narrative moment, in commentary on Adam's "civilized" way of coping with the Fall by covering it up, Milton chooses to come forward with his most detailed and empathetic representation of a fully civilized non-Western way of life. There could not be a more effective imaginative restatement of Fox's retort to Baxter: "And many of the Indians do shew forth more in their conversations of the light then you do."

Of course, if Milton depicts "Indians" in such implicitly laudatory terms, he also just a few lines later speaks of the Native Americans encountered by Columbus as representing the nadir of degeneration from "that first naked glory" of the human race, "girt / With feathered cincture, naked else and wild / Among the trees on isles and woody shores" (1115–18). The salvation of the heathen is held out as a distinct and desirable possibility in *Paradise Lost,* but evidently it is far from guaranteed. As elsewhere in the poem, Milton presents us here with a choice between contrasting options, which he quietly, covertly sets forth. Such poetic situations confront us with the task of deciding either to "value right / The good before" us, or to pervert "best things / To worst abuse, or to their meanest use" (IV, 202–4). In Milton's

[6]Carey/Fowler commentary. In what is for him an uncharacteristically reductive reading, Joseph Summers, *The Muse's Method: An Introduction to* Paradise Lost (New York: Norton, 1968; orig. 1962), p. 106, likewise sees the significance of the fig tree simile as primarily malign.

[7]Carey/Fowler commentary, quoting John Gerard, *Herball* (London, 1597).

scheme of things, the liberation inherent in antinomianism must be a liberation not from external restraint into an allegedly inspired spontaneity, but rather from external restraint into the self-restraint of responsible choice and good works. As explicit doctrine, this emphasis on choice and works takes the form of the extended argument for Arminianism presented in *Christian Doctrine*. Michael Fixler points out that Milton developed his Arminian views in great part in reaction against "the subjective claims for saintship which in the last ten years of the Revolution grew so exorbitant." Arminianism, the doctrine that not divine decree or inspiration but rather free and thoughtful human will and choice must be the decisive factor in "moral or religious concerns" (*CPW*, VI, 398), is what most fully expresses that side of Milton that, in Christopher Hill's words, "could not fully accept" those radical ideas that nevertheless "greatly attracted him."[8]

As with antinomianism, we are confronted with an embarrassment of riches when we attempt to describe the presence and significance of Arminianism in *Paradise Lost*. Perhaps the most revealing thing to look at will be the portrayal of Paradise in Book IV. Intriguingly enough, a book in which we might expect to find the most gratifying sense of antinomian abundance and vitality begins with words of caution: "O for that warning voice." Satan is approaching the place of human habitation, and the archangel Uriel, whom Satan has just successfully deceived, is the first to take timely warning: "[Satan] not enough had practised to deceive / Uriel once warned; whose eye pursued him down / The way he went, and on the Assyrian mount / Saw him disfigured, more than could befall / Spirit of happy sort" (IV, 124–28). This is not the first time readers of *Paradise Lost* have been advised to be on their guard against Satan,[9] but it may be that Milton wishes us to be particularly vigilant as we enter a place that invites us to relaxation and revelry:

> Yet higher than their tops
> The verdurous wall of Paradise up sprung:

[8]Michael Fixler, *Milton and the Kingdoms of God* (Evanston, Ill.: Northwestern University Press, 1964), p. 219. Arminianism takes its name from the Dutch Protestant theologian James Arminius, who opposed Calvinist doctrines of predestination, insisting that human beings retain a measure of free will. For a convenient summary of the sixteenth-century origins of Arminianism, and of essential Arminian doctrines, see Dennis Richard Danielson, *Milton's Good God: A Study in Literary Theodicy* (Cambridge: Cambridge University Press, 1982), pp. 66–75; and for a sorting out of the various schools of Arminianism in the seventeenth century, see Hill, *Milton*, pp. 268–78.

[9]The fullest discussion of this aspect of the poem is Stanley Eugene Fish, *Surprised by Sin: The Reader in* Paradise Lost (Berkeley: University of California Press, 1971; orig. 1967), chap. 1.

> Which to our general sire gave prospect large
> Into his nether empire neighbouring round.
> And higher than that wall a circling row
> Of goodliest trees loaden with fairest fruit,
> Blossoms and fruits at once of golden hue
> Appeared, with gay enamelled colours mixed:
> On which the sun more glad impressed his beams
> Than in fair evening cloud, or humid bow,
> When God hath showered the earth; so lovely seemed
> That landscape.   (142–53)

The old idea, now widely and effectively disputed, that the paradisal existence portrayed by Milton was essentially an abiding in static perfection may not have been so entirely mistaken after all.[10] For here is a vision of static perfection if there ever was one, the yearly cycle transcended in a perpetual synthesis of spring, summer, and autumn. Allegedly, the sun is "more glad" to impress itself upon this paradisal grove "than in fair evening cloud, or humid bow, / When God hath showered the earth."

Such testimony to the transcendent superiority of Paradise is entirely conventional. But are we to accept it at face value? Before we do so, we should acknowledge that the inferior term of the comparison, evoking the ordinary processes of nature, is decidedly attractive. It may well remind us of the simile in Book II (488–95) just discussed, except that it goes beyond even that splendid moment in one respect. Evening showers, there construed as menace or discouragement, are seen here as God's very own transitive gestures ("When God hath showered the earth"). Moreover, a rainbow ("humid bow") will be employed by God to indicate the renewal of his covenant with humanity after the Flood (XI, 864–66, 879–901). Thus, that which Paradise ostensibly outshines is not only very attractive; it is also dense with benign significance. In the course of working his will in and through "ordinary" nature, God has showered the earth not only with fertilizing rain, but also with the generosity of his providential design. By the time we come to the words "so lovely seemed / That landscape," it is

[10]See J. M. Evans, Paradise Lost *and the Genesis Tradition* (Oxford: Oxford University Press, 1968), pp. 242–71; Barbara Kiefer Lewalski, "Innocence and Experience in Milton's Eden," in *New Essays on* Paradise Lost, ed. Thomas Kranidas (Berkeley: University of California Press, 1971), pp. 86–117; William G. Riggs, *The Christian Poet in* Paradise Lost (Berkeley: University of California Press, 1972), pp. 46–56; Danielson, *Milton's Good God*, pp. 164–201; Diane Kelsey McColley, *Milton's Eve* (Urbana: University of Illinois Press, 1983), pp. 3–4, 13–14, 26, 29, 38, 110; Anthony Low, *The Georgic Revolution* (Princeton, N.J.: Princeton University Press, 1985), pp. 316–20.

by no means clear which landscape is being referred to and, thus, whether the conventional demarcation between Paradise and everything else is still being upheld.

But in that case, why bring the superiority of Paradise up at all? And what does any of this have to do with the presence of Satan? The very conventionality of the idea of the static perfection of Paradise, along with the suggestions of artifice in the phrase "with gay enamelled colours mixed" may point us toward some answers to these questions.[11] Milton wishes us to be aware, apparently, that this Paradise is a work of art, a mythic construct, that it belongs to the venerable tradition of our imagined forms of escape from vicissitude and struggle. Like any other human construct, it can begin to degenerate into satanism. For example, it may be conceived to entail the locking up of the real world in unrelieved barrenness and woe, in consequence of the willed removal of all vitality and happiness to imagined realms of gold. This is what may be beginning to occur, ever so slightly and subtly, when those timeless "blossoms and fruits at once of golden hue / Appeared." The enjambment makes us suspect for a second that the flora of Paradise constitute no more than an appearance—as opposed to a reality—an appearance, we may now wish to note, which is presented to the eyes of none other than Satan himself, in whose narrative company we are seeking here in the early part of Book IV to gain entrance into the home of our first parents. The idea that the sun took more pleasure in shining on Paradise than on an average evening scene could become a satanic falsehood, and this is what is warned against in the forthright insistence that in such a scene, it is God who has abundantly showered the earth.

On the other hand, it would be untrue to the delicacy and poise of the passage to say that the projection of Paradise, the longing for stasis, is being flatly rejected. Indeed, such rejection would only

[11]The Carey/Fowler commentary notes that "the simultaneous concurrence of all stages of growth" was a convention of many imaginings of paradise. As for the term "enamelled," these editors see fit to define it as "fresh, lustrous, bright; variegated. With no suggestion of hardness." This seems to be based on the Oxford English Dictionary (OED), "beautified with various colours," with the "lustrous" component deriving from OED, "having naturally a hard polished surface, resembling enamel." In ruling out hardness, the intent of Carey/Fowler is presumably to rule out artifice. The second OED definition can therefore no longer be made to hover in an indeterminate realm between art and nature, while OED's first and entirely artificial meaning— "ornamented or covered with enamel"—evidently has no bearing on the case whatsoever, even though it and the meaning that combines artificial and natural elements were both fully current in the sixteenth and seventeenth centuries. But it would be more in keeping with Milton's constant practice if he were here exploiting the entirety of the term's semantic capacities.

amount to another version of satanism, an idolizing of divine process and a constraining of its redemptive generosity by placement of the Paradise tradition in stagnant isolation from its currents. This pitfall is what is avoided by the ambiguity of the closing words. So lovely seemed both landscapes. Art and nature, art and grace, art and providence, human and divine creativity—all are mingled and married in our inability to discriminate among forms of loveliness. The act of projecting, in myths and works of art, a situation beyond process is necessary and fully desirable so long as care is taken, as Milton is taking it here, to implant the act itself within process, so long as alertness to the larger divine vitality and purpose is maintained.

The critical convention of speaking of the parts of poems selected for analysis as though they were self-contained wholes has caused more than the usual amount of distortion in the present instance. The process of entering Paradise is nowhere near completed as yet:

> so lovely seemed
> That landscape: and of pure now purer air
> Meets his approach, and to the heart inspires
> Vernal delight and joy, able to drive
> All sadness but despair: now gentle gales
> Fanning their odoriferous wings dispense
> Native perfumes, and whisper whence they stole
> Those balmy spoils.   (152–59)

Gentle gales are the successors to the sun impressing his beams—twinned images we have learned to recognize as manifestations of an antinomian sense of immanence. Yet despite the compassion for Satan which seems to be evinced in the first few lines, the gentle gales have evidently been altered for the worse as a result of his presence. Their whispering is caressing us into self-indulgent relaxation, perhaps. It seems more definitely and distinctly than before that "our own exotic imaginings" of Paradise may be doing violence to the bountiful world we actually live in. That world may have been robbed of perfumes that are native to it by the gentle paradisal gales. Such a "likeness to Satan's aims," emanating from within the paradisal longing itself, "brings out the constant possibility that one side, the worst side, of our nature can engulf the other and 'pervert best things / To worst abuse, or to their meanest use.'"[12]

---

[12]Paul J. Alpers, "The Milton Controversy," in *Harvard English Studies 2: Twentieth-Century Literature in Retrospect*, ed. Reuben A. Brower (Cambridge, Mass.: Harvard University Press, 1971), p. 295.

So despite the caveats entered just now concerning the satanic re-
ductiveness of inveighing against paradisal bliss in "puritanical" fashion, such is exactly the posture toward which the poem seems to be
nudging us. Paradise is beginning to look manifestly and treach-
erously languorous. But the passage that follows points us in a different direction:

> and of pure now purer air
> Meets his approach . . .
> As when to them who sail
> Beyond the Cape of Hope, and now are past
> Mozambic, off at sea north-east winds blow
> Sabean odours from the spicy shore
> Of Arabie the blest, with such delay
> Well pleased they slack their course, and many a league
> Cheered with the grateful smell old Ocean smiles.
>   (153–54, 159–65)

Two observations seem warranted: first, the air, which has been anything but pure, is cleared by northeast winds blowing Sabean odors
from vehicle to tenor and from theoretically false pagan to theoretically true Judeo-Christian Paradise. That is, the temptations to
escapist pleasure that may arise from paradisal art are not corrected
in the usual Puritan fashion, by ascetic repudiation of sensuous plen-
itude and of art itself. On the contrary, the movement from seductive,
whispering gales to fresh northeast winds is a movement into additional layers and levels of artifice, into metaphor and mythic tradition.
Second, if conventional Puritan asceticism is indeed beginning to
loom as the mistaken mirror image of a perverse sensuality and aes-
theticism, that tendency is checked by the simile's picture of industrious mariners, in all probability practitioners of the Protestant ethic,
gratefully slacking their course and receiving hope, refreshment, and
inspiration from pagan lands and legends.

Yet no sooner have we relaxed into a grateful receptivity to sensuous bounty, and to the artifice sometimes needed to convey it to us,
than we are propelled back in the direction of a strenuous Puritanism
by the next words, "So entertained those odorous sweets the fiend /
Who came their bane" (166–67), which introduce a summary of the
tale from the apocryphal Book of Tobit about how Tobit's son succeeded, with the help of an angel, in bringing the demonic spirit
Asmodeus under control. Now that we have finally arrived in Paradise, in other words, Milton seems determined to deprive us of the

opportunity to look around and enjoy ourselves. Instead of allowing us to do that, he makes us listen to one warning after another about the various postures that can be adopted with respect to the Paradise myth. Each time we correct for the flaws in one posture, we find our solution becoming itself a problem. No single posture is uncritically celebrated, none is unequivocally condemned. Each is both scrutinized and, within the limits thus established, accepted. We do indeed enter Paradise along with Satan. We must pass interpretively as he must pass physically through an "undergrowth / Of shrubs and tangling bushes" that "perplexed / All path of man or beast that passed that way" (175–77). As we read, we experience not the vicarious antinomian consummation we might have been expecting, but rather the Arminian cognitive exertions that are required in order to be able to value right the good before us. Just when we are most likely to suppose that struggle might be remitted, at least for the time being, we are forced to face the fact that struggle is the one certain constant in the uncertain equation of our affairs.[13]

Perhaps the extent of my disagreement with the view that Milton was primarily an uncritical spokesman for "the saintly elite of a reforming middle class" has by now been made sufficiently clear. Far from celebrating one group of invulnerably regenerate creatures and disparaging the rest of us, *Paradise Lost* projects a universe that simultaneously invites and challenges everyone to participation and fulfillment. Repeatedly it presents moral and spiritual experience and moral and spiritual choice as the prerogative not of those who have been particularly and peculiarly elected, but rather of anonymous, "ordinary" Everyman: of "the pilot of some small night-foundered skiff" (I, 204), of a "belated peasant" (I, 783), a "careful ploughman" (IV, 983), or most simply and eloquently of all, of a laborer "homeward returning" from a day's laboring (XII, 631–32). In Milton's greatest poem, the Protestant extremes of antinomianism, which held that God had breathed his spirit into all peoples, and Arminianism, which insisted that God had made fundamental opportunities available to and imposed fundamental obligations upon all peoples, are enabled to meet and merge.

---

[13]Thus, I could not disagree more strongly with Jackie DiSalvo's view that Milton's Paradise is one of childish gratification, divorced from "the more strenuous joys of creativity"; see *War of Titans*, pp. 172–73, 299–300, 346. Joan Webber, *Milton and His Epic Tradition* (Seattle: University of Washington Press, 1979), p. 50, points out that all epics include a vision of paradisal bliss and also struggle with the tension between that vision and the epic hero's strenuous quest.

In relation to preponderant cultural trends, the Miltonic synthesis of antinomianism and Arminianism is a highly paradoxical one, for in both Puritan commonwealths, both New England and revolutionary old England, antinomian spiritism and spontaneity and Arminian will and works defined themselves in great part by negation of each other. Antinomians tended to stress that spiritual and ecclesiastical life had to be eruptive and disruptive, that in order to be authentic, it had to entail sudden rebirth and radical separation from the traditional, settled, and sinful world. And such encouragements to comprehensive dissent were precisely what Arminians, and quasi-Arminians, were most concerned to disavow and contain, as they emphasized the gradualness of spiritual experience and the stability and continuity of ecclesiastical institutions. They demanded preparation for and participation and acquiescence in precisely that settled, established world that was anathema to their spiritistic opposite numbers.[14]

Several advantages derive from the fact that in *Paradise Lost* Milton brings together and integrates, in the ways we have just seen, those patterns of Puritan belief and impulse which elsewhere confronted and opposed each other. Because he both shares in and takes the measure of both the antinomian and Arminian structures of feeling, both the longing for liberation and the requirement of discipline and control, he can, as we shall see in the next chapter, portray the characters who embody and enact each structure—in the antinomian case Eve, in the Arminian Adam—with a scrupulous evenhandedness. Because he had wrested this vision from his experience of the revolutionary years, and because he had seen how fragile and mutable all intellectual constructs had been in such tumultuous conditions, he can, as we shall see two chapters hence, imagine in Satan an enormous parody of his own vitalist and activist ideals. And above all, because Milton both deeply engaged himself with the substance of Puritan historical reality and stood apart from that reality by reshaping its components to suit his own purposes, he is able, as we shall see confirmed in Parts Two and Three, to grasp the long-term fragmentations and deformations that modern Anglo-American history would unfold with an impassive negative capability that has yet to be surpassed.

---

[14]My sense of this opposition is drawn from many sources, but most immediately from the contrast between John Bunyan and Richard Baxter in David D. Hall, *The Faithful Shepherd: A History of the New England Ministry in the Seventeenth Century* (Chapel Hill: University of North Carolina Press, 1972), p. 64.

Chapter 2

Adam and Eve

In Book V of *Paradise Lost,* the archangel Raphael descends from Heaven to the home of Adam and Eve in Paradise, having been commissioned by God to warn the human pair of the fact that Satan is planning and plotting to bring about their fall. Adam has the good fortune to witness Raphael's arrival on Earth, and he proceeds to communicate this experience to his spouse in the following manner:

> Haste hither Eve, and worth thy sight behold
> Eastward among those trees, what glorious shape
> Comes this way moving; seems another morn
> Risen on mid-noon; some great behest from heaven
> To us perhaps he brings, and will vouchsafe
> This day to be our guest. But go with speed,
> And what thy stores contain, bring forth and pour
> Abundance, fit to honour and receive
> Our heavenly stranger; well we may afford
> Our givers their own gifts, and large bestow
> From large bestowed, where nature multiplies
> Her fertile growth, and by disburdening grows
> More fruitful, which instructs us not to spare.
>
> (308–20)

The most striking feature of this speech is the ambivalent sexual politics it intimates. For the first five and a half lines ("Haste hither Eve . . . This day to be our guest") Adam speaks as helpmeet to helpmeet, manifesting that spontaneous impulse to communicate what one has seen to one's peers and comrades, which always seems to accompany what Milton elsewhere in the poem calls the opportunity "to descry new lands" (I, 290). But in the remainder of the passage, Adam turns from the sharing of discoveries to commanding ("But go with speed") and then to lecturing, dispensing a few *sententiae* on generosity, abundance, and gratitude from what is made to seem an amply stocked storehouse of received wisdom. Adam thus appears on the one hand to be regarding Eve as his partner in the full range of challenges and fulfillments made available in the unfallen universe. Yet on the other hand he seems to be eyeing her with a highly developed sense of her inferiority to him, as someone who is ignorant of the most elementary facts and proprieties and would probably mismanage the situation were it not for his elaborate and detailed guidance.

Eve's reply suggests a corresponding ambivalence on her part:

> Adam, earth's hallowed mould,
> Of God inspired, small store will serve, where store,
> All seasons, ripe for use hangs on the stalk;
> Save what by frugal storing firmness gains
> To nourish, and superfluous moist consumes:
> But I will haste and from each bough and brake,
> Each plant and juiciest gourd will pluck such choice
> To entertain our angel guest, as he
> Beholding shall confess that here on earth
> God hath dispensed his bounties as in heaven.
>
> (321–30)

To the extent that the prelapsarian little commonwealth is structured not as a hierarchy but rather as an egalitarian diversity—as a variety of gifts emanating from the one spirit—Eve is responding here as though Adam has just encroached, even if ever so slightly, upon her own special territory of the domestic arts. Not only does she firmly correct him on the question of "store," preserved as opposed to fresh food, she also proceeds to answer him in kind, lecturing in her turn about the principles underlying a field of endeavor in which she, not he (so she insinuates), is the expert. Further confirming this hint that she is a bit nettled by Adam's somewhat overbearing manner, she responds to his directive to go and fix lunch by resolving to turn in an absolutely first-class performance. With more than a trace of bombast, she declares that the meal she will prepare will be (almost literally) out of this world, such a meal as Raphael "beholding shall confess that here on earth / God hath dispensed his bounties as in heaven." It is precisely the response that might be expected from someone who has just been both respectfully loved and anxiously, hoveringly required to prove herself.

What are the social and cultural realities of which these undercurrents of psychic friction amount to an imaginative reconstruction? In *Tetrachordon*, the last of his divorce tracts, Milton wrote that although in most marriages the man should definitely be the one who is in charge, "neverthelesse man is not to hold [woman] as a servant, but receives her into a part of that empire which God proclaims him to, though not equally, yet largely, as his own image and glory: for it is no small glory to him, that a creature so like him, should be made subject to him." Moreover, Milton allows for the possibility that in some cases the superiority of the man may have to be set aside: "Not but that particular exceptions may have place, if she exceed her husband in prudence and dexterity, and he contentedly yeeld: for then a superior and more naturall law comes in, that the wiser should govern the lesse wise, whether male or female" (*CPW*, II, 589). Nor was Milton the only Puritan to affirm that the politics of the domestic little commonwealth should somehow be both hierarchical and not hierarchical, that in some mysterious way women should be treated both as not equal to men and as not unequal to them. Puritan husbands were repeatedly exhorted to "spare not to bee inamored with" their wives, and to "rather have too high an opinion of [them], then too meane." When the perhaps female author of a pamphlet titled *The Women's Sharp Revenge* emphasized in 1640 that Eve was created from Adam's side, as a "fellow feeler" and not "out of his foote to be trod upon," she was only echoing Thomas Carter, the most impeccably orthodox of Puritan marriage counselors, who had stated in 1627 that Eve was created "not from the head of man . . . lest she should claim to rule . . . nor of the foot, lest she should be disdained and despised . . . but from the very body," in token that she and Adam were in some sense equals.[1] It seems likely that a situation in which both parties were expected to maintain relations that would, simultaneously, be both equal and unequal would be fraught with precisely the kinds of undercurrents and tensions we have sensed flowing be-

---

[1] David Leverenz, *The Language of Puritan Feeling: An Exploration in Literature, Psychology, and Social History* (New Brunswick, N.J.: Rutgers University Press, 1980), p. 70; Jackie DiSalvo, *War of Titans: Blake's Critique of Milton and the Politics of Religion* (Pittsburgh, Pa.: University of Pittsburgh Press, 1983), p. 332; Boyd M. Berry, *Process of Speech: Puritan Religious Writing and* Paradise Lost (Baltimore, Md.: Johns Hopkins University Press, 1976), pp. 239–40.

tween Adam and Eve in their respective responses to the arrival of Raphael.[2]

The relationship of Adam and Eve is a representation of Puritan domestic doctrine and practice, but as such, it is also a representation of a much broader phenomenon. For the domestic little commonwealth of Puritanism was a true microcosm, in that the unresolved, convoluted quality of the relationships within it was also to be found in the relationships obtaining within the Puritan church and the Puritan state. Like Adam, Puritan ministers and political leaders desired, on the one hand, that their followers should remain under their influence and control. On the other hand, contradicting themselves, they also encouraged those same followers not to think of themselves as followers at all but rather as autonomous fellow seekers and laborers on behalf of the kingdom of God. And the result was that Puritan authority was always precarious and unstable, as was revealed most dramatically when the mid-seventeenth-century revolution broke up into what Christopher Hill has called "two revolutions": even before the first revolution made the Cromwellian grandees and their Independent clerical allies the supreme authorities in church and state, their followers in the radical sects and the rank and file of the New Model Army began to turn against them and articulate such key points on the agenda of the second revolution as "a far wider democracy in political and legal institutions" and ecclesiastical disestablishment.[3]

But there is an important sense in which it is misleading to speak of two revolutions. As Hill's overall analysis makes clear, both revolutions emerged within a single overarching Protestant framework,

---

[2]The women's movement of the 1970s provoked a debate among Miltonists concerning the relationship of Adam and Eve and what it indicates about Milton's attitudes in the realm of sexual politics. For arguments that Milton's views are aggressively patriarchal, see Marcia Landy, "Kinship and the Role of Women in *Paradise Lost*," *Milton Studies* 4 (1972):3–18; Sandra M. Gilbert, "Patriarchal Poetry and Women Readers: Reflections on Milton's Bogey," *PMLA* 93 (1978):368–82; and DiSalvo, *War of Titans*, pp. 317–32. Writers who have argued that Milton is, on the contrary, a proto-feminist include Joan Webber, "The Politics of Poetry: Feminism and *Paradise Lost*," *Milton Studies* 14 (1980):3–24; Marilyn R. Farwell, "Eve, the Separation Scene, and the Renaissance Idea of Androgyny," *Milton Studies* 16 (1982):3–20; and Diane Kelsey McColley, *Milton's Eve* (Urbana: University of Illinois Press, 1983). My sympathies are with the proto-feminist group, but like its opponents, it does not sufficiently emphasize this key element of sociopolitical ambivalence and ambiguity and accompanying psychic strain. For sexual politics and "feminism" during the revolutionary era, see Keith Thomas, "Women and the Civil War Sects," in *Crisis in Europe,* ed. Trevor Aston (New York: Anchor Books, 1967; orig. 1965), pp. 332–57.

[3]Christopher Hill, *The World Turned Upside Down: Radical Ideas during the English Revolution* (New York: Viking, 1972), p. 12.

which stressed the power and the obligation of believers to discuss "all aspects of theology and politics in the light of the Bible" and to act upon the results of those discussions. The process of Protestant inquiry and disputation led Calvinists, limiting salvation, regeneration, and liberation from external restraint to a narrow, predestined elite, to radically different conclusions than it led Quakers, who envisioned the possibility that a saving, regenerating inner light might shine even in the heathen. The democratic communism of the Diggers was anathema to the wealthy Independent oligarchs of whom Oliver Cromwell was the most conspicuous and efficacious representative. Yet all these divergent and conflicting perspectives and persuasions arose within the same universe of discourse. Calvinists, Quakers, proto-capitalists, and proto-communists were all speaking the same language. So intimate were the connections and interactions among them that many of the different options on the spectrum of belief could, at any one time, be discerned among members of the same family. After George Fox converted James Lancaster to Quakerism, Lancaster's Presbyterian or Independent former brethren attacked Fox "with staves, clubs, and fishing poles." The Quaker missionary was briefly knocked unconscious by the blows, and when he came to he "saw James Lancaster's wife throwing stones at my face and James Lancaster her husband was lying over my shoulders to save the blows and stones."[4]

This confrontation between husband and wife over the body of George Fox is a highly dramatic indication that the diversities and disagreements engendered within a Puritan culture that was common to all parties frequently manifested the particular intensity and complexity that marks family interaction and conflict. After several generations of existence together as a separated "peculiar people," the Puritan community had come to be a closely knit one, and no Puritan relationships were more intimate and substantial than those between clergy and laity. It had been by the Puritan clergy that the Puritan laity had been nurtured, guided, awakened, and empowered. And during the revolution, when empowered lay thought and behavior moved in distinctly heretical directions, it was by the clergy that the laity were to be controlled and disciplined. A situation of profound relational connection and the emergence of profound difference, exactly the situation that often obtains between parents and children or husbands and wives, was bound to produce such encounters as the one that took place in 1646 when some Presbyterian ministers sought

---

[4] Ibid., p. 130; Berry, *Process of Speech*, p. 268.

to admonish members of the New Model Army and "the multitude of soldiers in a violent manner called upon us to prove our calling . . . whether those that are called ministers had any more authority to preach in public than private Christians which were gifted." The very violence of the soldiers' manner suggests that the revolution-within-the-revolution was a matter not of straightforward destruction of old relationships but rather, as in twentieth-century adolescence, of painful redefinition of them.

Two additional incidents further illustrate the texture of Puritan revolutionary experience. When a Mrs. Springett gave birth to a daughter in 1644, she refused to have the child baptized, having become convinced of the illegitimacy of infant baptism: "Such as were esteemed able ministers (and I formerly delighted to hear) were sent to persuade me; but I could not consent and be clear." Similarly, three years later Colonel Hutchinson of the New Model Army had undertaken at the behest of some Presbyterian ministers to put an end to deviant speculations among his men, but had instead himself come to agree with them that infant baptism lacked scriptural warrant. Since his wife (who had also come to anabaptist conclusions) was about to give birth, Hutchinson, "that he might, if possible, give the religious party no offence, . . . invited all the ministers to dinner, and propounded his doubts, and the ground thereof to them." As with Mrs. Springett, Hutchinson "could not consent and be clear," and the new child remained unbaptized.[5]

What is most striking about these situations is not only that the disagreements could not be resolved, but also that the relationships could not easily be broken. In the one case at clerical initiative, in the other at lay, the parties persisted with each other, making distinct efforts to restore a former situation of delighted teaching and learning. The efforts were not successful, and when we imagine the multitude of similar situations in which such efforts were repeatedly made and repeatedly failed, with this frustrating sequence virtually guaranteeing that sooner or later the interactions would begin to proceed in a violent manner, we begin to have an idea of the relational realities of Puritan life, especially after 1641. These realities are what are given the fullest possible embodiment in the story of Adam and Eve in *Paradise Lost*. They are also what would be "actively lived and felt" on through the eighteenth century in the more exclusively Puritan environment of Colonial New England.

[5] Hill, *World Turned Upside Down*, p. 82; Geoffrey F. Nuttall, *The Holy Spirit in Puritan Faith and Experience* (Oxford: Basil Blackwell, 1947), pp. 18–19.

The most immediate source of the faint stirrings of discontent between Adam and Eve which we have sensed in their respective responses to the arrival of Raphael may be what had taken place between them when they had awakened that morning. At the end of Book IV, the night before in the poem's narrative scheme, Satan is found "squat like a toad, close at the ear of Eve, / Assaying by his devilish art to ... / raise / At least distempered, discontented thoughts, / Vain hopes, vain aims, inordinate desires / Blown up by high conceits engendering pride" (800–801, 806–9). Despite being discovered and taken into custody by the guardian angels whom God has stationed in Paradise, Satan does succeed in inducing in Eve a seductive dream of boundless gratification. As something entirely new and unexpected, this experience distresses Eve a great deal. In the morning, Adam is surprised to find her "with tresses discomposed, and glowing cheek, / As through unquiet rest" (V, 10–11). After he awakens her and she, glad that she "waked / To find this but a dream" (92–93), tells him about what has happened, he says:

> The trouble of thy thoughts this night in sleep
> Affects me equally; nor can I like
> This uncouth dream, of evil sprung I fear;
> Yet evil whence? In thee can harbour none,
> Created pure. But know that in the soul
> Are many lesser faculties that serve
> Reason as chief; among these fancy next
> Her office holds; of all external things,
> Which the five watchful senses represent,
> She forms imaginations, airy shapes,
> Which reason joining or disjoining, frames
> All what we affirm or what deny, and call
> Our knowledge or opinion; then retires
> Into her private cell when nature rests.
> Oft in her absence mimic fancy wakes
> To imitate her; but misjoining shapes,
> Wild work produces oft, and most in dreams,
> Ill matching words and deeds long past or late.
> Some such resemblance methinks I find
> Of our last evening's talk, in this thy dream,
> But with addition strange.   (96–116)

Although Adam is clearly moved here by a genuine love and concern for his mate, he is not being entirely accurate when he claims that he has been affected as much as she has by "the trouble of thy thoughts this night in sleep." For he engages in only the briefest effort at probing, exploratory questioning before proceeding to locate Eve's dream within an impressive structure of general truths. It would be incorrect to say that he is being simplistic or overbearing in his explanation of those doctrines of faculty psychology which Perry Miller has shown to be an essential component of the hegemonic New England mind. Nor should we fail to acknowledge the probability that Eve is to a considerable degree consoled and calmed by his thus knowledgeably putting this unsettling occurrence in some sort of context. But Adam's comfortable discourse comes across, nevertheless, as received wisdom, marshaled against the new and the different. Even though the truths of Puritan scholasticism must presumably still be recent and exciting discoveries, as far as Adam himself is concerned, he nevertheless sounds more like a manager of experience than a participant in it.[6]

Such an impression of complacency is strengthened when Adam goes on to speak and act as if the travail and difficulty had not affected him at all. At bottom, he feels that the satanic dream is Eve's problem, not his, for he, so he seems to believe, remains settled and invulnerable in his divinely ordained superior position:

> yet be not sad.
> Evil into the mind of god or man
> May come and go, so unapproved, and leave
> No spot or blame behind: which gives me hope
> That what in sleep thou didst abhor to dream,
> Waking thou never wilt consent to do . . .
> So cheered he his fair spouse, and she was cheered,
> But silently a gentle tear let fall
> From either eye, and wiped them with her hair;
> Two other precious drops that ready stood,
> Each in their crystal sluice, he ere they fell
> Kissed as the gracious signs of sweet remorse
> And pious awe, that feared to have offended.
>
> (116–21, 129–35)

That Eve should so immediately and starkly qualify the narrator's declaration that "she was cheered" by beginning to cry is striking enough. But the anomalous impression made by her tears is only deepened when we recognize that the first set of them constitute an

---

[6]For faculty psychology in hegemonic New England ideology, see Perry Miller, *The New England Mind: The Seventeenth Century* (New York: Macmillan, 1939), pp. 258–59.

allusion to Luke 7:38, in which a sinful and penitent woman washed Jesus' feet with her tears "and did wipe them with the hairs of her head" (AV). Eve's situation seems to differ from that of the woman in the gospel story at least as much as it resembles it. For unlike that woman, Eve has just been told by Adam that she is not a sinner at all: "Evil into the mind of god or man / May come and go, so unapproved, and leave / No spot or blame behind." Adam nevertheless continues to worry that Eve might become a sinner: "which *gives me hope* / That what in sleep thou didst abhor to dream, / Waking thou never wilt consent to do" (italics mine). The woman in the gospel story, in contrast, is openly acknowledged as a sinner and freely forgiven by Jesus, so that her tears fall plentifully and creatively. In the detail to which Milton alludes, the objective "them" is beautifully ambiguous. Did the woman wipe her own tears or Jesus' feet with "the hairs of her head"? The answer of course is that she wiped both of "them" at once—her wiping away of her own tears was an aspect of her washing of Jesus' feet. Having been accepted in full, just as she is, she becomes an active participant in and shaper of the situation. Eve, on the other hand, weeps not in a mingled fullness of grief and gratitude, but rather in frustration and vexation at the complacency about himself and hovering anxiety about her conveyed by Adam's tone and manner, both of which contradict the reassuring content of his words. Adam acts as though Eve is *by definition* more of a potential sinner than he is, and that she therefore needs to be carefully watched and supervised. The character in the gospel story whom Adam here resembles at least as much as he resembles Jesus is the Pharisee at whose house Jesus is dining, and who continues to regard the woman at Jesus' feet as a sinner, no matter how creatively repentant she is. Thus, Adam's gesture of kissing the "two other precious drops . . . ere they fell," though it is full of love and tenderness, amounts to a method of keeping Eve hemmed in, of preventing the release of that same psychic substance that Jesus, on the contrary, encourages to flow fully and freely. Those prior tears of Eve's which are allowed to fall have nowhere to go in the world, no way of making an impact. Eve cannot wash anyone's feet with them; she can only wipe them away, turn them back in upon herself. Troubled and troublesome but also potentially salutary stirrings can only achieve the most inchoate of manifestations before they are summarily contained and controlled.[7]

---

[7]The allusion to Luke is also discussed in McColley, *Milton's Eve*, p. 103. She sees its primary function as a validation of Eve, not as a means of highlighting the problematic aspects of Adam's and Eve's relationship at this point.

Although they do not cause it or foreshadow it as inevitable, Eve's dream, and the complex and convoluted responses to it on the part of both her husband and herself, are obviously portentious occurrences in relation to the Fall. So also is the following discourse of Adam's of the night before:

> the timely dew of sleep
> Now falling with soft slumbrous weight inclines
> Our eyelids; other creatures all day long
> Rove idle unemployed, and less need rest;
> Man hath his daily work of body or mind
> Appointed, which declares his dignity,
> And the regard of heaven on all his ways;
> While other animals unactive range,
> And of their doings God takes no account.
>
> (IV, 614–22)

The impression of Adam we have gained from these incidents in Book V is evidently not a mistaken one. From the time of his entrance into the poem, he is portrayed as being a bit sententious, needing to construct a topheavy edifice of justification for the least little gesture, such as going to bed. It is as though he is striving to fence in every conceivable wayward impulse both in himself and in his subordinates. Then, by circling back and appending a repetition of the contrast between humans and animals, he testifies to his worry that this endeavor has not been entirely successful, that the carefully sorted and ranked orderliness of things has not been satisfactorily conveyed.

The hints of unease that are to be discerned in this subtle stiffness of manner are confirmed when Adam appends yet another reason for turning in for the night. They have a lot of work to do in the morning:

> To morrow ere fresh morning streak the east
> With first approach of light, we must be risen,
> And at our pleasant labour, to reform
> Yon flowery arbours, yonder alleys green,
> Our walk at noon, with branches overgrown,
> That mock our scant manuring, and require
> More hands than ours to lop their wanton growth:
> These blossoms also, and those dropping gums,
> That lie bestrewn unsightly and unsmooth,
> Ask riddance, if we mean to tread with ease;
> Mean while, as nature wills, night bids us rest.
>
> (623–33)

I cannot agree with Joseph Summers's view that "there is no anxiety here."[8] Before sunup, they "must be risen"—early to bed in order to be early to rise, in response to the necessities imposed by the nature of their tasks. Perhaps this is not anxiety, but it is certainly far from a relaxed or a delighted savoring of the joys of Paradise. As Adam surveys the paradisal landscape, he discerns on every hand pleasures degenerating into problems: arbors and alleys in need of "reform," "unsightly" natural refuse awaiting disposal. Indeed, the difficulties confronting the two of them are made to seem to border on the overwhelming when Adam declares that the "branches overgrown . . . require / More hands than ours to lop their wanton growth."

Adam's lecture in justification of going to bed does not achieve its interactional consummation until five books later, when Eve makes a proposal indicating that she has been reflecting very carefully on what her husband and teacher has had to say:

> Adam, well may we labour still to dress
> This garden, still to tend plant, herb and flower,
> Our pleasant task enjoined, but till more hands
> Aid us, the work under our labour grows,
> Luxurious by restraint; what we by day
> Lop overgrown, or prune, or prop, or bind,
> One night or two with wanton growth derides
> Tending to wild. Thou therefore now advise
> Or hear what to my mind first thoughts present,
> Let us divide our labours, thou where choice
> Leads thee, or where most needs, whether to wind
> The woodbine round this arbour, or direct
> The clasping ivy where to climb, while I
> In yonder spring of roses intermixed
> With myrtle, find what to redress till noon:
> For while so near each other thus all day
> Our task we choose, what wonder if so near
> Looks intervene and smiles, or object new
> Casual discourse draw on, which intermits
> Our day's work brought to little, though begun
> Early, and the hour of supper comes unearned.
>   (IX, 205–25)

---

[8]Joseph Summers, *The Muse's Method: An Introduction to* Paradise Lost (New York: Norton, 1968; orig. 1962), p. 169.

This is not Eve's first autonomous gesture by any means. As Marilyn Farwell insists, and as my own brief analyses have indicated, Eve has been learning all along how to make her own informed choices, and this moment in Book IX is therefore a logical development, not an unexpected departure.[9] But this is nevertheless the first time that Eve's independent functioning is such that Adam would be required to adjust his own behavior in response to it, and this is why the tensions inherent in the thoroughly Puritan relationship of our first parents are here brought right to the surface, whereas Eve's previous exercises in self-assertion had allowed those tensions to remain latent. Eve has chosen to extend autonomy in a way that challenges subordination. As the Puritan laity sooner or later always did, she is laying claim to a share in the government of the little commonwealth. And once she makes such a claim, she sets in motion a process that will enact for us those intractable contradictions that determined the structure of Puritan society and the rhythms of Puritan psychology.[10]

We should begin by appreciating both the thoughtfulness of Eve's initiative and the depth of the reorientation it implies. She accepts the problem exactly as Adam has defined it, complete with verbal echoes. Adam had talked of "branches overgrown," which "mock" them in their efforts "to lop their wanton growth." Eve refers to how "wanton growth derides" whatever they "lop overgrown." Adam had looked forward to the time when there would be "more hands than ours" to help with the work, and so Eve presents her idea as a provisional solution "till more hands / Aid us." In the absence of these additional

---

[9]Farwell, "Eve," p. 14.

[10]Interpretations of the separation disagreement are as varied as are the interpretations of every other aspect of *Paradise Lost*. Joseph Summers, Joan Bennett, and Dennis Danielson argue that Adam should have persisted until Eve had been brought around to acceptance of his superior understanding of the situation; see *Muse's Method*, pp. 170–74; "'Go': Milton's Antinomianism and the Separation Scene in *Paradise Lost*, Book IX," *PMLA* 98 (1983):398–401; and *Milton's Good God: A Study in Literary Theodicy* (Cambridge: Cambridge University Press, 1982), pp. 127–28, 145–47. For additional discussion of Danielson's view, see below, n. 18. Diane McColley (*Milton's Eve*, pp. 140–81) and Marilyn Farwell ("Eve," pp. 15–17) tend to stress the substantiality of the case Eve puts forward and to see the disagreement as an expressing and working through of tension that is on the whole successful. I agree with McColley and Farwell on the even-handedness of Milton's presentation, but disagree with their idea that the underlying tensions have been mostly resolved by the time our first parents part company. The general idea that in the separation scene Adam is in the position of the Protestant authority figure and Eve in that of the Protestant layperson (and thus in that of the Protestant radical or incipient radical) is acknowledged in Bennett, "'Go,'" pp. 400–401; McColley, *Milton's Eve*, p. 174; and Georgia Christopher, *Milton and the Science of the Saints* (Princeton, N.J.: Princeton University Press, 1982), p. 156.

hands, there seem to be few options available other than the one she brings forward. But beyond this, there are two particular ways in which her suggestion of a division of labor is a highly creative one. One of these has to do with the stated and thoroughly dramatized features of Eve's relations with Adam, the other with the historical referents of those relations. Adam had unburdened himself to Raphael in the previous book (VIII, 521–33) about his tendency to regard Eve as an alluring siren, a provocation to passion rather than a partner in upright labor. As Eve now argues, to work separately will be to inhibit this tendency in a practical way. But to make such a serious, thoughtful proposal about the organization of labor at all, as Eve is doing, is to engage the issue even more fundamentally, for it is to challenge the reductive definition of her that has caused Adam's overly fond behavior in the first place. "I am not the vehicle of your rapture which you seem to think I primarily am" is a large part of what Eve is saying to Adam at this point in the poem. Similarly, in the history of New England, John Winthrop had anticipated in his "Modell of Christian Charitie," the lay sermon he had preached to the first settlers of Massachusetts Bay while they were still sailing across the Atlantic, that the new Puritan commonwealth would be characterized by a tightly unified communal lovingkindness. Everyone would be "knitt together in this work as one man." But before long this was experienced by many New Englanders as confining, if not cloying. And they, like Eve, responded by demanding separation, moving away into their own new communities and, very often, opting for a version of Eve's division of labor, enclosed and individualized farms, rather than open-field and communal ones.[11]

The essence of the encounter Eve has initiated will be that a profound uncertainty about the boundary between autonomy and subordination will force each party to concentrate on consolidating his or her own position, rather than on listening to the other party, and as this mutual incomprehension develops, the original uncertainty will become more and more of an irritant. Adam's first response to Eve's suggestion is to attempt to assimilate and incorporate it: "Well hast thou motioned, well thy thoughts employed / How we might best fulfil the work which here / God hath assigned us, nor of me shalt pass / Unpraised: for nothing lovelier can be found / In woman, than to study household good, / And good works in her husband to pro-

[11]For this general pattern, see below, chap. 4, n. 38. For its manifestation in the area of New England we shall be examining with particular care, see below, chap. 5, n. 1. McColley, *Milton's Eve*, p. 146, also remarks on Eve's opening propositions here as a creative response to Adam's tendency to be smotheringly passionate.

mote" (229–34). Adam both applauds Eve's entirely proper display of intellectual and social autonomy and immediately sets about to contain it within a framework of dogmatized establishmentarian theology and domestic doctrine, and he continues operating in this same mode of unfolding settled general principles as he turns to take up the points he finds problematic: "Yet not so strictly hath our Lord imposed / Labour, as to debar us when we need / Refreshment, whether food, or talk between, / Food of the mind, or this sweet intercourse / Of looks and smiles, for smiles from reason flow, / To brute denied, and are of love the food, / Love not the lowest end of human life" (235–41). It may well be that this already feels a trifle annoying to Eve, since it may seem in its comfortable abstraction to amount to avoidance of the specific emotional distortions within their relationship which probably have in part prompted her request to function at a greater distance. In any event, there is no doubt that she is annoyed when Adam, betraying his tendency to elaborate his defenses ad infinitum, proceeds to a more concrete objection:

> But other doubt possesses me, lest harm
> Befall thee severed from me; for thou know'st
> What hath been warned us, what malicious foe
> Envying our happiness, and of his own
> Despairing, seeks to work us woe and shame
> By sly assault; and somewhere nigh at hand
> Watches no doubt, with greedy hope to find
> His wish and best advantage, us asunder,
> Hopeless to circumvent us joined, where each
> To other speedy aid might lend at need.
> (251–60)

It is prudent and wise of Adam to be concerned about Satan and shrewd of him to grasp that in union there would be greater strength against him, but in the accumulating social and psychological circumstances of the moment, his sagacity is worse than useless. It now seems as though all of his previous generalized discourse was but rationalization of what was really bothering him all along: he doesn't trust Eve—the subordinate, the weaker vessel, the weak link. True, he speaks in terms of mutual vulnerability in the final two lines, but by this time it is probably too late. His sincere effort to proceed delicately and diplomatically, arising from a genuine respect for Eve as an autonomous being, now comes across, as a result of his equally genuine sense of her as a subordinate being, as not having been sincere at all, as having merely been a way of insinuating, rather than openly avowing, his desire to keep her in her place. The egalitarian pole of Adam's version of contradictory Puritan sociology seems for the moment to have been rendered inauthentic by the hierarchical one.

Eve is made a little touchy by the implication that of the two of them, she is the one who is peculiarly vulnerable, but she retains a "sweet austere composure" (272) as she defends the moral and spiritual dignity that, it seems to her, Adam has unaccountably called into question:

> That such an enemy we have, who seeks
> Our ruin, both by thee informed I learn,
> And from the parting angel overheard
> As in a shady nook I stood behind,
> Just then returned at shut of evening flowers.
> But that thou shouldst my firmness therefore doubt
> To God or thee, because we have a foe
> May tempt it, I expected not to hear.
> His violence thou fear'st not, being such,
> As we, not capable of death or pain,
> Can either not receive, or can repel.
> His fraud is then they fear, which plain infers
> Thy equal fear that my firm faith and love
> Can by his fraud be shaken or seduced.
>
> (274–87)

Despite her composure, Eve's sense of grievance leads her, in the first part of the passage, into distortion of the truth. She implies that Adam has only just now chosen to inform her of the existence of Satan, as though he had deliberately withheld this information until he could use it to his own advantage. Moreover, she alleges, nobody had ever bothered to communicate directly with her; apart from what Adam has now sprung on her, she had only been able to find out about Satan by eavesdropping. But in fact, at the time to which Eve must be referring, at the end of Book VIII, when Raphael was about to depart and Eve was of her own volition away working in her nursery, Raphael had said nothing at all about Satan. There had been nothing for Eve to overhear. And at the time Raphael had indeed issued his clearest warning about Satan being a threat to the human race, at the end of Book VI, Eve had been present along with Adam. When it came to being instructed on such a crucial point, she and Adam had been placed on a level. But now, feeling pressured by Adam's unexpected insistence upon her subordination, Eve contrives to justify herself, clear some psychic room to maneuver, by portraying the order in which she has been living as more monolithic and repressive, less kindly and supportive, than it has actually been.

Eve is beginning to become conscious of a deep-seated sense of grievance, but she lacks the intellectual tools to bring this dawning awareness into clear definition and focus and therefore can cope with her resentment only by the distorted means of mounting a sniping counterattack. Certainly what is brought out in the second half of the passage is Eve's lack of intellectual maturity. One can almost picture her taking a deep breath before speaking, straining to hold herself together and gather the courage to talk back to an authority that has suddenly turned strangely unbenevolent. Beginning with "but that thou shouldst," there is discernible in Eve's words a trace of bombast, much more than a trace of overconfidence in drawing inferences, and a mounting sense of determined outrage. She seems to be heading toward that bristling estrangement in which the New Model Army soldiers who in 1646 attacked the Presbyterian ministers "in a violent manner" were trapped. But she now proceeds to struggle against the developing logic of the situation, appealing to Adam for assistance in stepping aside from the ill feeling that is beginning to build: "Thoughts, which how found they harbour in thy breast / Adam, misthought of her to thee so dear?" (288–89). The breakdown of syntactical coherence is beautifully expressive of Eve's confused desire that her quest for a fuller autonomy entail not the destruction but the strengthening of her relationship with her husband.

Unfortunately, Adam's initial reaction to Eve's plea is far from satisfactory:

> Daughter of God and man, immortal Eve,
> For such thou art, from sin and blame entire:
> Not diffident of thee do I dissuade
> Thy absence from my sight, but to avoid
> The attempt it self, intended by our foe.
> For he who tempts, though in vain, at least asperses
> The tempted with dishonour foul, supposed
> Not incorruptible of faith, not proof
> Against temptation: thou thy self with scorn
> And anger wouldst resent the offered wrong,
> Though ineffectual found.   (291–301)

Eve's defensive sense of having been belittled elicits from Adam a defensive denial that there is any reason at all for Eve to be upset.

Adam then enunciates another generalizing precept: "For he who tempts, though in vain, at least asperses / The tempted with dishonour foul." In this continued manifestation of the mental habits of a spokesman for the established order, Adam seems to be stubbornly settling, in recoil from Eve's now slightly prickly self-assertion, into an outlook more rigid than the one he has espoused up to now. For this maxim contradicts the assurance we have heard him give Eve after her dream, that "evil into the mind of god or man / May come and go, so unapproved, and leave / No spot or blame behind" (V, 117–19). Thus, as Eve feels pushed by Adam toward an angry radicalism, so Adam in his turn gravitates toward exactly that more conservative definition of the status quo Eve has just now unfairly imputed to him.

Adam does an about-face at this point and manages to bring some more truly "healing words" (290) to bear upon the situation:

> I from the influence of thy looks receive
> Access in every virtue, in thy sight
> More wise, more watchful, stronger, if need were
> Of outward strength; while shame, thou looking on,
> Shame to be overcome or over-reached
> Would utmost vigour raise, and raised unite.
> Why shouldst not thou like sense within thee feel
> When I am present, and thy trial choose
> With me, best witness of thy virtue tried.
>
> (309–17)

Here for the first time since the discussion began is a full and unmistakable affirmation of conjugal mutuality and solidarity. It is Adam's equivalent of the awkward beseeching with which Eve has just concluded her own speech. And just as Adam had at first not heard Eve's gesture of conciliation, so Eve now fails to attend to Adam's corresponding gesture:

> If this be our condition, thus to dwell
> In narrow circuit straitened by a foe,
> Subtle or violent, we not endued
> Single with like defence, wherever met,
> How are we happy, still in fear of harm?
> But harm precedes not sin: only our foe
> Tempting affronts us with his foul esteem
> Of our integrity: his foul esteem
> Sticks no dishonour on our front, but turns
> Foul on himself; then wherefore shunned or feared

> By us? Who rather double honour gain
> From his surmise proved false, find peace within,
> Favour from heaven, our witness from the event.
> And what is faith, love, virtue unassayed
> Alone, without exterior help sustained?
> Let us not then suspect our happy state
> Left so imperfect by the maker wise,
> As not secure to single or combined;
> Frail is our happiness, if this be so,
> And Eden were no Eden thus exposed.
>
> (322–41)

This is in many ways a magnificent speech. As Diane McColley notes, Milton puts into Eve's mouth his own most fully developed and eloquent presentation of radical Protestant ideology, that of *Areopagitica*.[12] But ideological coherence, and Eve's emergence into intellectual maturity, are pretty much beside the point by this time. Or rather, they are the point, but only in a decidedly negative way. Adam's and Eve's twinned failures to take heed of their twinned efforts to make peace are the two key moments in the entire interaction, the points at which it is transformed from a dialogue, however strained, into a quarrel. After these moments, the momentum of ideological polarization becomes irreversible. Thus, although its content is in great part substantial and valid, in its context Eve's speech is highly contentious, a counterposing of a dubiously romanticized picture of moral experience over against Adam's overwrought argument for a static, untempted purity.

The separation scene comes to fruition as a full-scale confrontation between Puritan enthusiasm and Puritan order when Adam replies to Eve's articulation of Miltonic radicalism with an exposition of that structure of Miltonic restraint apart from which any radicalism, including his own, seemed to Milton irresponsible:

> O woman, best are all things as the will
> Of God ordained them, his creating hand
> Nothing imperfect or deficient left
> Of all that he created, much less man,
> Or aught that might his happy state secure,
> Secure from outward force; within himself
> The danger lies, yet lies within his power:
> Against his will he can receive no harm.

---

[12]McColley, *Milton's Eve*, p. 172.

But God left free the will, for what obeys
Reason, is free, and reason he made right,
But bid her still beware, and still erect,
Lest by some fair appearing good surprised
She dictate false, and misinform the will
To do what God expressly hath forbid.
Not then mistrust, but tender love enjoins,
That I should mind thee oft, and mind thou me.
Firm we subsist, yet possible to swerve,
Since reason not impossibly may meet
Some specious object by the foe suborned,
And fall into deception unaware,
Not keeping strictest watch, as she was warned.
Seek not temptation then, which to avoid
Were better, and most likely if from me
Thou sever not: trial will come unsought.
Wouldst thou approve thy constancy, approve
First thy obedience; the other who can know,
Not seeing thee attempted, who attest?

(343–69)

Even more than those of Eve which precede them, these words of Adam are doctrinally unassailable. But their tone ("O woman") reflects what is by now their quite thoroughly disputatious relational environment. Just as Eve had been attempting somewhat vindictively to pick holes in what Adam had been saying, so Adam, exasperated, now seeks to bend this wayward woman into submission to the more adequate definition of their mutual situation which he and he alone is authorized to lay down. Thus, what was previously an experientially based, open-palmed plea ("I from the influence of thy looks receive / Access in every virtue") is now a tight-fisted, dogmatic conclusion: "Not then mistrust, but tender love enjoins, / That I should mind thee oft, and mind thou me." Thus, Adam develops what one might have supposed would be a sufficiently conclusive account of the freedom but also the vulnerability to deception of the will ("But God left free . . . expressly hath forbid"); and then, instead of bringing his speech to an end and confidently awaiting Eve's acquiescence in his rational certitude, proceeds to repeat himself ("Firm we subsist . . . as she was warned"). And thus, Adam maintains the argumentative pressure to the very end of the passage, posing what he hopes will finally be a decisive, unanswerable rhetorical question: "Not seeing thee attempted, who attest?" He is putting pressure on himself as well as on Eve, beginning to sound like a desperate man, compelled not merely to refute objections, but to overwhelm an unexpectedly, mysteriously intractable resistance.

It is at this point that Adam leaves off and says: "But if thou think, trial unsought may find / Us both securer than thus warned thou seem'st, / Go; for thy stay, not free, absents thee more; / Go in thy native innocence, rely / On what thou hast of virtue, summon all, / For God towards thee hath done his part, do thine" (370–75). Adam would like to keep Eve under his influence and control, but like all Puritan authorities, he is unwilling to resort to simple coercion. He grants permission to go, but only grudgingly, within his cognitive frame of the vulnerability of her virtue, certainly not within hers of a redrawing of the boundary line between subordination and autonomy that might prove mutually beneficial. Even as he acquiesces reluctantly in Eve's autonomy, that is, Adam continues to hedge a potential troublemaker about with cautions and warnings and to express by repetition and redundancy an uneasy feeling that all such endeavors to contain and disarm irregularity will in the end prove unavailing. With Adam thus giving no ground at all, Eve continues to affirm the disturbingly brash and rash radical consciousness that has been engendered in her in the course of this troubled interchange: "With thy permission then, and thus forewarned / Chiefly by what thy own last reasoning words / Touched only, that our trial, when least sought, / May find us both perhaps far less prepared, / The willinger I go, nor much expect / A foe so proud will first the weaker seek; / So bent, the more shall shame him his repulse. / Thus saying, from her husband's hand her hand / Soft she withdrew" (378–86). The quarrel has not been resolved, only suspended. Both Adam and Eve are left languishing in a subtle, chafing frustration and unhappiness, and Eve's departure, withdrawing her hand, therefore conveys a suggestion that separation amounts to communal fragmentation, which is indeed what it would most often amount to in Puritan New England.

The usual Puritan explanation for the sorts of difficulties Adam and Eve have begun to experience was the one Ebenezer Parkman was prepared to offer during both of the major controversies in which he and his Westborough congregation became embroiled, that "our *grand Adversary*, envious at our Peace, & full of Malice to destroy us, has stirrd up this strife."[13] The "grand Adversary," Satan, certainly

[13]PFP, Box 2, Folder 1 (Notes on Church Meetings and Issues), "Concerning the Petition of the 11 Brethren, Nov. 18, 1774."

plays a key role in Book IX of *Paradise Lost*. Yet it is important to stress that by placing Satan's machinations within a frame constituted by the prelapsarian argument we have just examined and the fully rancorous postlapsarian quarrel we shall examine shortly, Milton crucially alters the standard interpretation of such situations. The grand adversary does not stir up the strife between Adam and Eve; he works with the strife that has already begun to develop simply in the course of Adam's and Eve's ambiguous, Puritanically contradictory dealings with each other. The Fall is not caused by an externalized enemy. Rather, it unfolds from deep within the essential Puritan social configuration.[14] Satan's function is to concentrate and distill those psychosocial and ideological tensions that have always been present in Adam's and Eve's relationship and that, to this point, have been controlled (ever more shakily) but have never been resolved.

The most obvious respect in which this is true is that Satan, now "imbruted" in the serpent, first accosts Eve with flattery: "Wonder not, sovereign mistress, if perhaps / Thou canst, who art sole wonder ... / Fairest resemblance of thy maker fair, / Thee all things living gaze on" (532–33, 538–39). Satan presents himself, that is, as someone who is prepared to grant unreservedly the respect and admiration Adam has just now appeared to withhold in what seems to Eve his "mistrust" of her. He seems to offer autonomy liberated entirely from subordination. That Satan's pretense of awed worship amounts to a redaction of the romanticizing passion to which Adam had confessed to Raphael in Book VIII, and against which Eve had reacted by coming forward at the start of Book IX as a sober, thoughtful steward of the garden, only enhances its psychological plausibility. For Eve's effort to break beyond the impositions of passion and adoration has just been thoroughly squelched, and one of the likely responses to such an experience is to seize with a certain defiance upon the self-image one has been told, so it seems, one must perforce retain.

On the other hand, Eve does not, of course, readily acquiesce in

[14]The old debate about whether the Fall was inevitable or not, and therefore whether Adam and Eve or God are to be held responsible for it, begins to seem based on a superficial and mechanistic notion of causation, once Milton's story is seen as expressive of the organic necessity of real historical experience and development. Herman Rapaport, *Milton and the Postmodern* (Lincoln: University of Nebraska Press, 1983), pp. 73–80, deduces from the fact that the Fall is a process rather than an identifiable event or point in time that Milton is concerned to depict that ontological "undecidable space" that is such a crucial principle in poststructuralist theorizing. Within its own terms, the debate about responsibility for the Fall is effectively resolved in Stanley Eugene Fish, *Surprised by Sin: The Reader in* Paradise Lost (Berkeley: University of California Press, 1971; orig. 1967), chap. 5.

Satan's invitation to think of herself as a "goddess among gods" (547). Her development is much more gradual and subtle than that. What Satan primarily plays upon throughout the ensuing temptation is not the courtly love of the Middle Ages and Renaissance, but rather the potentially radical Protestant spirituality of the Reformation, which has just been more distinctly engendered in Eve in the course of her disagreement with Adam. Eve, echoing *Areopagitica,* had criticized the apparently fugitive and cloistered virtue of Adam's point of view and had gone on to imply that it was virtually impossible for a truly upright person to fall into sin: "If this be our condition, thus to dwell / In narrow circuit straitened by a foe . . . / his foul esteem / Sticks no dishonour on our front, but turns / Foul on himself; then wherefore shunned or feared / By us?" In the serpent's mouth, this position modulates into the more extreme Ranter doctrine that for the regenerate there is no such thing as sin at all, that what the preachers "roared up for Sinne in their pulpitts" was really a great awakening into new life and new light, a necessary and fully desirable extension of regeneracy. The serpent/Satan testifies that after he had partaken of the fruit of the tree of the knowledge of good and evil, "ere long I might perceive / Strange alteration in me, to degree / Of reason in my inward powers, and speech / Wanted not long, though to this shape retained. / Thenceforth to speculations high or deep / I turned my thoughts, and with capacious mind / Considered all things visible in heaven, / Or earth, or middle, all things fair and good" (598–605). And this is the gambit that ultimately proves successful, for Satan's climactic, concentrated rhetorical assault on Eve is a tissue of these Ranter notions and reasonings: "Queen of this universe, do not believe / Those rigid threats of death; ye shall not die: / How should ye? By the fruit? It gives you life / To knowledge" (684–87). Eve is persuaded to regard herself as a "goddess among gods" in the specific antinomian sense of expecting after eating the forbidden fruit to be "*godded* with GOD."[15]

Yet even at this point, Eve does not become an out-and-out Protestant radical, secure in an alternative and oppositional point of view. Her last words before succumbing indicate that far from being liberated from the pressures of her ambiguous subordination, she is at the moment feeling those pressures with a particular acuteness and is ready to seize upon the handiest means of alleviating them: "What fear I then, rather what know to fear / Under this ignorance of good

---

[15]The Ranter element in the temptation of Eve is discussed in Christopher Hill, *Milton and the English Revolution* (New York: Viking, 1978), pp. 345, 397. For "*godded* with GOD," see below chap. 4, n. 29. The phrase about roaring up "for Sinne" is George Fox's; see Nuttall, *Holy Spirit,* p. 157.

and evil, / Of God or death, of law or penalty? / Here grows the cure of all, this fruit divine, / Fair to the eye, inviting to the taste, / Of virtue to make wise: what hinders then / To reach, and feed at once both body and mind?" (773–79). What the Fall brings most fully to the fore is not radical consciousness so much as a condition of being possessed and driven by a resentment that one is unable to render rationally coherent. "Greedily she engorged without restraint" (791). Eve's legitimate urge toward Protestant self-validation has literally become a consuming passion. Her mere entrapment in an intensifying longing for liberation from Puritan hierarchy, instead of her attainment of it, is poignantly conveyed in her first postlapsarian utterance. First she worships a succession of new deities—the tree of whose fruit she has just eaten, a personified "Experience . . . Best guide" (807–8). Then she speaks in a way that reveals she is now locked into relations with the established authorities which are far more cramping and confining than they have hitherto been. God she imagines to be an absolute and repressive monarch, "our great forbidder" (815). But more pertinent to our present purposes is her new attitude toward Adam:

> But to Adam in what sort
> Shall I appear? Shall I to him make known
> As yet my change, and give him to partake
> Full happiness with me, or rather not,
> But keep the odds of knowledge in my power
> Without copartner? So to add what wants
> In female sex, the more to draw his love,
> And render me more equal, and perhaps,
> A thing not undesirable, sometime
> Superior; for inferior who is free?
> This may be well: but what if God have seen,
> And death ensue? Then I shall be no more,
> And Adam wedded to another Eve,
> Still live with her enjoying, I extinct;
> A death to think. Confirmed then I resolve,
> Adam shall share with me in bliss or woe:
> So dear I love him, that with him all deaths
> I could endure, without him live no life.
>
> (816–33)

Here the danger that always lurked in Puritan "contention"–that it would engulf all morality and spirituality in a deadlocked, unalloyed struggle for place and precedence–is made quite explicit. But Eve cannot remain the cunning schemer she momentarily makes herself out to be. If she is calculating, she is also obsessive-compulsive, one moment wanting to push Adam and his authority away and the next seeking the protection and security he and it have always provided.

Adam's eating of the forbidden fruit does not stem from conversion to the Ranter ideology that Eve, parroting her new mentor, offers as a rationale for it: "I / Have also tasted, and have also found / The effects to correspond, opener mine eyes, / Dim erst, dilated spirits, ampler heart, / And growing up to godhead" (873–77). Instead, feeling guilty about the extent to which his resistance to Eve's proposal for a division of labor had indeed been based upon mistrust of her, Adam reverts to the impassioned, worshipful mode of apprehending his mate he had discussed with Raphael in Book VIII:

> O fairest of creation, last and best
> Of all God's works, creature in whom excelled
> Whatever can to sight or thought be formed,
> Holy, divine, good, amiable or sweet!
> How art thou lost, how on a sudden lost,
> Defaced, deflowered, and now to death devote?
> Rather how hast thou yielded to transgress
> The strict forbiddance, how to violate
> The sacred fruit forbidden! Some cursed fraud
> Of enemy hath beguiled thee, yet unknown,
> And me with thee hath ruined, for with thee
> Certain my resolution is to die;
> How can I live without thee, how forgo
> Thy sweet converse and love so dearly joined,
> To live again in these wild woods forlorn?
> Should God create another Eve, and I
> Another rib afford, yet loss of thee
> Would never from my heart; no no, I feel
> The link of nature draw me: flesh of flesh,
> Bone of my bone thou art, and from thy state
> Mine never shall be parted, bliss or woe.
>
> (896–916)

Adam's decision, following the dictates of his heart instead of tamely obeying a stern (and apparently heartless) father, has won its share of admirers over the years, the most notable one recently being Christopher Hill.[16] But in relation to the dialectics of Puritan culture,

---

[16]Hill, *Milton*, pp. 128–29, 376.

what seems most striking about this choice is that it meshes so nicely with Adam's established psychic processes. His tendency to place Eve on a pedestal proceeds here in tandem with that settled dogmatism of his which has sometimes been complacent and sometimes stubborn, depending on the situation, but which has never not been a prominent part of his presentation of himself. A priori reasoning of this sort is very often a defense against thought rather than an engaging in it. It is rational only in a formal sense. Eve urges Adam that he "also taste, that equal lot / May join us, equal joy, as equal love; / Lest thou not tasting, different degree / Disjoin us, and I then too late renounce / Deity for thee, when fate will not permit" (881–85). If Adam had known how to be truly rational, which is to say thoughtful, at this moment of crisis, he would have sought for ways to transform crisis into opportunity. He might have disentangled this plea for a more equal and mutual relationship from the issue of tasting with which Eve conflates it, and he might have also gone on to question the literalistic fatalism of Eve's interpretation of the prohibition against tasting, might have recalled all that he has both experienced at first hand and learned from Raphael about how he lives in a universe of openness and possibility, of invitations "to descry new lands," not one of mechanistic necessity. But such exploratory rationality is precisely what is devastatingly absent when Adam comes immediately to the conclusion, at once emotionally troubled and intellectually untroubled, that Eve is "now to death devote." The sense of the indispensability of restraint he had been led to emphasize in his argument with Eve, in opposition to her emerging sense of adventurous liberation, now becomes the projection of a rigid status quo that is nothing but restraint: "The sacred forbiddance . . . The sacred fruit forbidden!" Since its context is thus basically a thoughtless one, one of unexamined dogma, the outpouring of natural affection by which Adam goes on to express his decision to join Eve in disobedience is deformed, I find, by an undercurrent of sentimentality. At the moment of his fall, the essential conservatism of Adam's mode of rationality and the pristine nonrationality of his emotional condition make him into an all-too-perfect exemplification of Perry Miller's mistaken idea that the essential contradiction in Puritanism was one between a purely rational hegemonic order and a purely emotional radical pietism.[17]

---

[17]See below, chap. 4, n. 3. For a related argument that the faith manifested by the unfallen angels during the war in Heaven might, at this moment of crisis and choice, have been exemplary for Adam, seeing that he has been told of it, see Stella Perce Revard, *The War in Heaven: Paradise Lost and the Tradition of Satan's Rebellion* (Ithaca, N.Y.: Cornell University Press, 1980), pp. 281–87. With the arrival of the Son on the

Paradise Lost's representation, in its central story, of Puritan relational dynamics is brought to a climax in the unrestrained quarrel
between Adam and Eve which erupts after they awaken from their
postlapsarian sexual extravaganza. Adam is the first to break forth in
a voice full of "high passions, anger, hate, / Mistrust, suspicion, discord" (1123–24): "Would thou hadst hearkened to my words, and
stayed / With me, as I besought thee, when that strange / Desire of
wandering this unhappy morn, / I know not whence possessed thee;
we had then / Remained still happy, not as now, despoiled / Of all our
good, shamed, naked, miserable. / Let none henceforth seek needless
cause to approve / The faith they owe; when earnestly they seek /
Such proof, conclude, they then begin to fail" (1134–42). This obviously is a further hardening of the psychosocial posture, that of the
superior party, which, as we have seen, Adam has never truly aban-
doned. He wraps himself in a mantle of self-righteous retrospection
and iron-clad dogmatic pronouncement.

Adam's haughtiness simply drives Eve into that violent manner of
the Puritan radical from which she has until now held back: "What
words have passed thy lips, Adam severe, / Imput'st thou that to my
default, or will / Of wandering, as thou call'st it, which who knows /
But might as ill have happened thou being by, / Or to thy self perhaps . . . / Was I to have never parted from thy side? / As good have
grown there still a lifeless rib" (1144–48, 1153–54). Throughout this
speech, but particularly in the whiplash scorn of the final two lines,
Eve plays subordinate fire to Adam's superordinate ice, repelling censure with the accusation frequently made by Puritan enthusiasts that
those who were censuring them were merely rationalizing their own
lack of spiritual authenticity and vitality. Eve also goes on to display,
in a manner now entirely petulant and infuriating, the same push-
and-pull ambivalence she had manifested just after her fall: "Being as
I am, why didst not thou the head / Command me absolutely not to
go, / Going into such danger as thou saidst? / Too facile then thou

---

third day of the war, the landscape of Heaven had been restored to its former beauty
and perfection, after it had been devastated by the mountain-throwing battle of the day
before. Adam might have inferred from this sequence the possibility of Eve's comparable restoration. Before he actually partakes of the fruit, Adam shores up his having
been "fondly overcome" with speculations that the basic state of affairs probably will
not be disturbed by their disobedience after all: "Nor can I think that God, creator wise,
/ Though threatening, will in earnest so destroy / Us his prime creatures, dignified so
high, / Set over all his works, which in our fall, / For us created, needs with us must fail,
/ Dependent made" (938–43). In a way, Adam remembers here what I am saying he
forgets, God's creative goodness. But of course the spirit of his words is the opposite of
that exploratory posture on whose absence I am insisting.

didst not much gainsay, / Nay didst permit, approve, and fair dismiss. / Hadst thou been firm and fixed in thy dissent, / Neither had I transgressed, nor thou with me" (1155–61). One can certainly sympathize with Adam's feeling that he is damned if he does and damned if he doesn't, confronted as he clearly is with an absolute psychic instability that one moment bursts out in spiteful disdain of his authority and the next betrays an inability to do without the security and legitimacy it is his role, in its positive aspect, to guarantee.[18]

But while Adam's response is perfectly natural, it is also perfectly unhelpful. He deals with flagrant provocation not by recognizing it as such but by seeking to win an argument with it:

> Is this the love, is this the recompense
> Of mine to thee, ingrateful Eve, expressed
> Immutable when thou wert lost, not I,
> Who might have lived and joyed immortal bliss,
> Yet willingly chose rather death with thee:
> And am I now upbraided, as the cause
> Of thy transgressing? Not enough severe,
> It seems, in thy restraint: what could I more?
> I warned thee, I admonished thee, foretold
> The danger, and the lurking enemy
> That lay in wait; beyond this had been force,
> And force upon free will hath here no place.
>
> (1163–74)

He is totally, overbearingly, crushingly in the right, having based his conduct on known and settled principles, having refused to encroach upon Eve's subordinate rights and privileges, and even having transcended this impeccable rectitude in the magnanimity of his decision to unite with her in sin and death. Always the Puritan, Adam makes use of only a modicum of icy sarcasm ("Not enough severe, / It seems, in

---

[18]Dennis Danielson insists (see above, n. 10) that Eve is correct when she tells Adam he ought to have forbade her absolutely to separate from him. Despite the claims made by Adam to this effect in his reply, such a command would have been no more coercive than God's absolute prohibition of the tree of knowledge had been all along. In both cases, the creature or person who is the recipient of such an edict retains the freedom to obey or not. This is the point at which Danielson's theological explications reach the limit of their usefulness. His argument is plausible on the level of doctrinal logic (what Raymond Williams calls "formally held and systematic beliefs"). But on the level of relational experience which I am seeking to elucidate (Williams's level on which "meanings and values . . . are actively lived and felt"), such "freedom" of subordinates to disobey the absolute commands of their social superiors is surely an empty and irrelevant technicality.

thy restraint"), relying primarily on earnest lecturing to bring Eve to heel. As he has done just a moment before, he rounds his presentation off with a pompous, sententious generalization: "Thus it shall befall / Him who to worth in woman overtrusting / Lets her will rule; restraint she will not brook, / And left to her self, if evil thence ensue, / She first his weak indulgence will accuse" (1182–86). The utter futility of such an attempt to impose peace by main intellectual force, exerted from on high, is as evident in the poem as it was in the actual historical arena of Puritan culture. Having revealed the way in which Adam and Eve have locked themselves into dialectical exacerbation of each other, Milton brings his account to an end in the only truly appropriate manner, by acknowledging the dragged-on and dragged-out endlessness of the situation: "Thus they in mutual accusation spent / The fruitless hours, but neither self-condemning, / And of their vain contest appeared no end" (1187–89). The situation is reminiscent of the way in which the mid-century revolution degenerated, in 1659 and 1660, into futile squabbling among those Puritan factions that had not already opted for a Restoration. It is also, and more so, prophetic of the contentiousness that, as we shall see, would be the fate of a great many Puritan communities in Colonial New England.[19]

[19]There is of course a crucial additional chapter to the story of Adam and Eve; for an analysis of those further developments, see below, Conclusion, nn. 3–9.

Chapter 3

Satan

In turning from Adam and Eve to Satan, we turn to the aspect of *Paradise Lost* which dominated discussion of the poem from the 1930s to the 1970s. Although there is no need for us to review here the particulars of the often rancorous debate that took place, it is germane to emphasize that those who participated in it were in full agreement in one crucial respect: they all joined together to enforce a conspiracy of silence about the specific seventeenth-century context from which *Paradise Lost* had emerged. Such satanists as F. R. Leavis and A. J. A. Waldock came no closer to acknowledging the connections between satanic cosmic rebellion and seventeenth-century sociopolitical rebellion than did such antisatanists as C. S. Lewis and Douglas Bush to realizing that their Milton, constantly harping on ceremony and obedience, would have been, most implausibly, entirely acceptable to the Anglican apologist Richard Hooker or even to the archprelatist William Laud.[1]

[1] Essentially, the satanists were elaborating on points made by Blake and Shelley. The key satanist texts are F. R. Leavis, *Revaluation: Tradition and Development in English Poetry* (New York: Norton, 1963; orig. 1936), pp. 42–67; T. S. Eliot, "A Note on the Verse of John Milton," *Essays and Studies* 21 (1936):32–40; *Milton* (Oxford: Oxford University Press, 1947); both Eliot essays reprinted in *On Poetry and Poets* (London: Faber and Faber, 1957), pp. 156–83; A. J. A. Waldock, Paradise Lost *and Its Critics* (Cambridge: Cambridge University Press, 1947); and William Empson, *Milton's God* (Norfolk, Conn.: New Directions, 1961). Major spokesmen for the antisatanists included C. S. Lewis, *A Preface to* Paradise Lost (New York: Oxford University Press, 1961; orig. 1942); Douglas Bush, Paradise Lost *in Our Time* (Ithaca, N.Y.: Cornell University Press, 1945); and more recently and ingeniously, Stanley Eugene Fish, *Surprised by Sin: The Reader in* Paradise Lost (Berkeley: University of California Press, 1971; orig. 1967). Within its own ahistorical terms, the dispute was brought to a highly satisfying resolution in William G. Riggs, *The Christian Poet in* Paradise Lost (Berkeley: University of California Press, 1972), chap. 1.

The writer who has most strongly insisted on the relevance of Milton's sociopolitical experiences and commitments to his literary choices and productions is Christopher Hill, who sees Satan reflecting both the heroism of the English Revolution and also its degeneration into "self-interest, jealousy, ambition."[2] Among the many advantages of Hill's reading is that it helps us make sense of the obvious complexity and ambivalence of the portrayal of Satan, rather than forcing us to choose between the false alternatives of a one-dimensional heroism or a one-dimensional villainy. However, to relate the significance of Satan exclusively to the events and immediate issues of the English Revolution may be to limit it more than necessary. As already noted, Hill himself has taught us the extent to which the revolutionary decades were decisive in insuring England's long-term capitalist future: in the countryside, the vestiges of feudal patterns of land ownership were eliminated, and the trends toward market-oriented agricultural production and "the disappearance of the small cultivator working on his own land" were accelerated; in manufacturing, various impediments to the free circulation of goods and services were removed, while at the workplace "monopolies and government interference were ended: craftsmen were left at the mercy of employers"; in foreign policy, the Cromwellian regime passed the Navigation Acts of 1650 and 1651 and built up a naval force that was "deliberately used to win commercial advantages," in effect establishing "a monopoly area of privilege for British merchants," extending the nascent capitalist order far beyond the confining coasts of a North Atlantic island and thus laying the foundations of the British Empire.[3] So it may be that in his representation of Satan, Milton is responding not so much to the outward failure of the English Revolution as to its inward and momentous socioeconomic success. Satan may embody both the sweep and grandeur of the emergent capitalist revolution and also the license it would for generations and centuries give to diverse forms of self-interest, jealousy, and ambition.

Before we can turn to the direct exploration of this possibility, however, we must consider that broader sociocultural process of which the developments in revolutionary England constituted one crucial phase and which has come to be known by the name given to the most influential interpretation of it. In Max Weber's classic account of "the Protestant ethic and the spirit of capitalism," the differences between the Protestant approach to questions of faith and

[2]Christopher Hill, *Milton and the English Revolution* (New York: Viking, 1978), pp. 366–67.
[3]See above, Introduction, n. 9, first three works cited.

works and that of medieval Catholicism pertain both to "justification" (what justifies a person in the eyes of God, makes him or her eligible for salvation) and "sanctification" (how the justified person is obliged to conduct him or herself in this life).[4] The Reformers' initial endeavor, argued Weber, was to eradicate the complacent sense of human merit that arose from the Roman Catholic doctrine of justification by works, which held that one might, in a straightforward, one-to-one moral accounting, atone for one's particular sins by the performance of particular good works. Both Luther and Calvin denied that works could be a means of justification, that human exertions and (by human standards) human deserts were causally related to ultimate human destiny. Justification was "by faith alone," not by works, and faith was itself a state of mind and spiritual condition that was brought about not by one's own choice and effort, but solely as a result of God's predetermined decree and gratuitous gift.

But having thus debarred works from any entrance whatsoever by the front door, the Reformers immediately turned around and hustled them in by the back. Although works were not a *means* of justification, they insisted, they might well be a *sign* that one was indeed justified. Calvinism in particular affirmed that, in Weber's words, "the religious believer can make himself sure of his state of grace . . . in that he feels himself to be . . . the tool of the divine will." Far from conducing, through its predestinarian mode of justification, to passivity, Calvinism enjoined its adherents to an activism the purpose of which was to glorify God and sanctify the world, and the advantage of which for those adherents was that it provided a circular proof of their own salvation. Such activism was far more strenuous and systematic than what had been required by medieval Catholicism. While Catholicism had outwardly and explicitly legitimized works, inwardly it had allowed them to remain haphazard, "a succession of individual acts." Protestantism, and especially Calvinism, changed this randomness into "a life of good works combined into a unified system." As the English theologian John Downame put it, "We are called to be Gods labourers; and therefore we must intend our business, that it may prosper in our hand, and not undoe in one day, that which we have done in another." Moreover, Protestantism widened the environment of divinely "called" endeavor. A life of "ascetic action," which in Catholicism had been the peculiar province of "the spiritual

---

[4]In my reflections on the Protestant ethic and the Weber thesis, I have been aided considerably by the discussion in Michael McKeon, *The Origins of the English Novel, 1600–1740* (Baltimore, Md.: Johns Hopkins University Press, 1987), pp. 189–200.

aristocracy of monks outside of and above the world," became in Calvinist Protestantism the prerogative of "the predestined saints of God within the world." And the definition of action "within the world" that came very quickly to be emphasized was action in the realm of economic enterprise. As Richard Baxter declared in the seventeenth century, "You may labour to be rich for God."[5]

Such were the doctrines promulgated in the Protestant Reformation, and particularly influential in the Protestant Reformation in England, which led Max Weber to posit a historically decisive connection between Protestantism and capitalism. Upon material economic pursuits that earlier forms of Christianity had regarded as fraught with moral and spiritual peril, as inviting to covetousness, greed, luxury, and a multitude of other sins, Protestant Christianity now conferred, Weber maintained, an ultimate moral and spiritual legitimacy. Subsequent analysts, beginning with R. H. Tawney, have stressed more than did Weber the extent to which Protestantism, even as it redefined economic activity as sanctified, sanctifying, and significant of justification, also retained the traditional suspicion of it. As Michael McKeon summarizes the scholarship on this point, "Both Luther and Calvin reaffirmed as moral law the medieval church's strict prohibitions against individualistic economic enterprise, and . . . mainstream Puritan writings before 1640 generally and explicitly express opposition to social mobility, usury, monopolies, and unrestrained profit-seeking." This can be stated even more forcefully. When Richard Baxter, speaking after 1640, affirmed that "you may labour to be rich for God," he still took care to add, "though not for the flesh and sin." Protestantism not only retained but intensified the traditional abhorrence of worldly self-seeking. To the extent that it reconceived economic enterprise as spiritually exalting, when undertaken for truly

[5]Max Weber, *The Protestant Ethic and the Spirit of Capitalism*, trans. Talcott Parsons (New York: Scribner's, 1930), pp. 112–21, 162; Stephen Foster, *Their Solitary Way: The Puritan Social Ethic in the First Century of Settlement in New England* (New Haven, Conn.: Yale University Press, 1971), pp. 104–5. Anthony Low, *The Georgic Revolution* (Princeton, N.J.: Princeton University Press, 1985), pp. 5–6, 155, seems to wish to call into question the historical significance of the Protestant ethic in the development of the modern world's positive evaluation of labor. But to emphasize the fact that Protestantism was not the first movement in the history of Christianity to hold hard work in high esteem, as Low does by his account (pp. 167–78) of medieval monastic ideals, or that there were other forces in the seventeenth century making for what Low calls a "georgic" attitude, such as Baconianism (pp. 117–54), does not seem to require such minimizing of the role played by the Protestant Reformers and their adherents. Low's skepticism is based on an anachronistic view of English literature as an autonomous field (p. 155) and an erroneous interpretation of the impact of Calvinist predestinarianism upon attitudes toward work (p. 214).

pious motives, precisely to that extent did it look upon such enterprise as most heinously debased and degraded, when pursued as an end in itself.[6]

What primarily interests us is not the specific arguments regarding justification and sanctification which were propounded by the Reformers and which commanded the allegiance of their followers, but rather the psychic consequences of those arguments, the structure of feeling they engendered which was "actively lived and felt" long after they themselves came to be viewed as outdated. Part of that structure of feeling is brought out by Stephen Foster when he remarks: "Precisely *because* men labored for God and *not* for gold (or status or honor), they had to continue working in their callings constantly: material needs or even the desire for riches might be satisfied at some finite point, God never." Here is one source of the strong undercurrent of agitation in John Cotton's depiction of a supreme exemplar of the Protestant ethic, a man who would *"rise early, and goe to bed late, and eate the bread of carefullnesse*, not a sinful, but a provident care, and . . . avoid idleness, cannot indure to spend any idle time, takes all opportunities to be doing something, early and late and looseth no opportunity, go anyway and bestir himselfe for profit, this will he doe most diligently in his calling: And yet bee a man deadhearted to the world." After the Restoration, John Collinges exhorted those to whom he addressed his *Weavers Pocket-Book* not to content themselves with "a least [degree] of good works which may evidence grace," but rather to "strive that all active grace may abound in us, that we be rich in good works." It was the infinitude of the end of works, that their purpose was to bring the world into fuller conformity with God's will, which necessitated that vocational labor be heroically strenuous. But once strenuosity had been thoroughly inculcated and idleness cast out as the unpardonable sin, there then arose the prospect of strenuosity becoming detached from the piety that had stimulated it in the first place and persisting as a determination to impose upon the world not the divine, but rather one's own merely human will. When this happened, as it did in numerous cases, an energy that originally had been mobilized by faith was transformed into a compulsion to control and domineer.[7]

[6]McKeon, *Origins of the English Novel*, p. 190 and chap. 5, n. 25; Weber, *Protestant Ethic*, p. 162.

[7]Foster, *Their Solitary Way*, pp. 105, 121; J. C., *The Weavers Pocket-Book: or Weaving Spiritualized* . . . (1675), pp. 29, 133 (I owe this reference to Michael McKeon); Christopher Hill, *The World Turned Upside Down: Radical Ideas during the English Revolution* (New York: Viking, 1972), pp. 261–62.

This was perhaps the primary way in which the activist, reforming, sanctifying dimension of the Protestant ethic eventually became secularized as that competitiveness, that Darwinian-like struggle for existence and mastery, that is so obvious a feature of the society and culture of the Anglo-American nineteenth century. But a consequence of the Protestant ethic which, though less often stressed, is perhaps of even greater long-range significance relates less to sanctification than to justification, less to action than to thought and speech. Briefly and baldly stated, this is that the Protestant ethic both maximized the need to justify oneself and minimized the need to ground such justification in external reality. The imperative need of justification arose from the infinity of the bar before which one was pleading and also (again as in the quotation from John Cotton) from the similarity, approaching to all appearances identity, between sanctified entrepreneurial endeavor and covetousness, "the mother sin." The liberation of justification from external constraints derived from the same sources. Because God was an infinite judge, one could not be justified by the standards of a finite rationality. The demonstration of intelligible links between causes and effects, means and ends, would be to no avail. One could be justified only symbolically, as one came to understand the pattern of one's existence as a sign that God's otherwise inscrutable will was indeed being fulfilled.

But as all literary critics are aware, the reading of signs is a notoriously fluid and open intellectual enterprise, inviting to fertility of imagination and invention and in and of itself requiring little in the way of mental obedience to the sheer givenness of things. This inherent subjectivity of hermeneutic intellection was in Protestantism made only marginally to submit to an independently existing external order by the requirement that one's "reading" of oneself be confirmed by one's congregational fellows. The way Calvinist soteriology thus encouraged those who subscribed to it to engage themselves with the external world only insofar as that world could be subsumed within its circular hermeneutic system was aggravated by the fact that the only plausible criterion by which to distinguish between covetous and saintly enterprise the Protestant ethic ever devised was the purely internal one of motive. The "provident care" of John Cotton's pious tradesman might in the ultimate scale of values differ as night from day from the "sinful care" of his grasping alter ego. But that scale of values was located only in the inner world of the heart and the upper world of the great taskmaster's eye. It was most definitely not located in the outer world of observable behavior and measurable results, except insofar as the community was obliged to judge the credibility of one's testimony that one's actions were being undertaken in a saintly rather than in a sinful spirit.

For the most part, therefore, the outer world did not provide reliable ways of distinguishing regenerate saint from damnable sinner. By offering such inducements to float free of externality altogether, the Protestant ethic made itself vulnerable to a logic of secularization in the intellectual sphere comparable to that which we have just now noted in the material sphere. Just as working strenuously as a tool of the divine will might mask or become a strenuous determination to work one's own will, so elaborately justifying one's labor as purposeful and providential might turn, once the already tenuous rational discipline to which such hermeneutic and casuistical cogitation was subject was further eroded by the death of the God of Christian tradition, and the consequent attenuation of congregational discipline and fellowship, into justifying it by a subjectivity now altogether divorced from distinct external realities. Such an unbounded subjectivity would be free to fabricate universes of moral and spiritual purpose which would be accountable to no processes of verification and validation whatsoever.[8]

The transformation of the Protestant ethic into the spirit of capitalism may, over the long term, have ushered in a world of competition, aggression, and subjectivity. But is there any reason to believe that Milton came to view capitalist development and ideology from a perspective that was sufficiently critical to enable him to represent these larger historical consequences in *Paradise Lost*? The evidence bearing directly on this question is fragmentary and tentative, and much of it, it must be conceded, points in the direction of Milton having uncritically reflected capitalist values rather than having critically reflected upon them. In his *Defence of the People of England* (1651), he articulated what remained a commonplace on into the nineteenth century, that the "middle class" produced "the greatest number of men of good sense and knowledge of affairs," as opposed to the upper and lower classes, the former being disqualified for true liberty "by excessive wealth and luxury" and the latter "by want and poverty" (*CPW*, IV, 471). Christopher Hill compiles, mostly from *Christian Doctrine*, a long list of "the bourgeois aspects of Milton's thinking ... frugality or thrift, industry, selective rather than indiscriminate alms-giving, refusal to make provision for those who are idle," and so on. "Milton seems to

---

[8]This discussion of justification is based in part on the analysis of Protestant "inner conviction" and spiritualization of economic process in Christopher Hill, *Change and Continuity in Seventeenth-Century England* (Cambridge, Mass.: Harvard University Press, 1975), pp. 96–99. For covetousness as the "mother sin," see Foster, *Their Solitary Way*, p. 121.

aim at an aristocracy of merit, an opportunity state," Hill concludes. As we have seen, in this respect at least, Hill is in essential agreement with such other recent expounders of Milton's sociopolitical attitudes as Andrew Milner and Jackie DiSalvo, both of whom argue that Milton did not question but rather contributed in a major way to the triumphant legitimation of capitalism by Protestantism.[9]

Yet there are a number of indications that this view of Milton may be somewhat distorted, that he may, at least on occasion, have regarded the emergence of the spirit of capitalism with a distinctly jaundiced eye. He was certainly no Digger, no vanguard communist. Yet the version of the Protestant ethic he heard articulated in his childhood by his family's parish minister, Richard Stock, included denunciations of "usurers whose ostentatious charity restored only a fraction of their ill-gotten gains" and of "the landlord or employer who oppressed his inferiors, confident that 'there is no civil law against him, or if there be, either his greatness or purse will carry it out well enough.'" Such objections to "unrestrained profit-seeking" were quite as commonplace in Puritan culture as were essays in self-congratulation, and evidently these particular objections were not lost on the young moneylender's son. Indeed, in his sociopolitical maturity, Milton chose to come forth with his own anticovetous utterances just at the most dramatic moments of his service to the revolutionary cause. As Hill notes, the conclusion of Milton's two prose defenses of the revolution is not a defense and celebration at all, but rather a warning to "the people of England" that "unless you repel avarice, ambition and luxury from your minds . . . you will find at home and within that tyrant who, you believed, was to be sought abroad and in the field" (*CPW*, IV, 680).

Six years later, in 1660, it had become agonizingly clear to Milton that his "warning voice" had not been heard and heeded. As he brought the quixotically courageous second edition of *The Readie and Easie Way to Establish a Free Commonwealth* to its termination, spitting directly into the ill wind of an inevitable Restoration that was only days away, he devoted most of his final paragraph to excoriating the people's betrayal of the revolution for filthy lucre's sake:

> But if the people be so affected, as to prostitute religion and libertie to the vain and groundless apprehension, that nothing but kingship can restore trade . . . if trade be grown so craving and importunate through the profuse living of tradesmen, that nothing can support it, but the

[9]Hill, *Milton*, pp. 263–65; for Milner and DiSalvo, see above, chap. 1, n. 1.

luxurious expences of a nation upon trifles or superfluities, so as if the
people generally should betake themselves to frugalitie, it might prove a
dangerous matter, least tradesmen should mutinie for want of trading,
and that therefor we must foregoe & set to sale religion, libertie, honor,
safetie, all concernments Divine or human to keep up trading, if lastly,
after all this light among us, the same reason should pass for current to
put our necks again under kingship, as was made use of by the *Jews* to
returne back to *Egypt* and to the worship of thir idol queen, because they
falsly imagind that they then livd in more plentie and prosperitie, our
condition is not sound but rotten, both in religion and all civil prudence;
and will bring us soon, the way we are marching, to those calamities
which attend alwaies and unavoidably on luxurie. (*CPW*, VII, 461–62)

The passion and bitterness of these words, the way they broaden and
intensify the indictment of trade and luxury each time they circle back
around to it, suggest that Milton is here doing what Christopher Hill
says he will do in *Paradise Lost*. He is brooding in public on the failure
of the revolution, and he is attributing that failure not merely to a
generalized "self-interest, jealousy, [and] ambition," but to a specific
conflict between that structure of Protestant ethics and spirituality
("religion and libertie") which he had supposed it was the purpose of
the revolution to install in power, and that appetitive spirit of capitalism which, as Hill shows, the revolution had in sober fact brought
much closer to dominance.

Hill has called our attention to those such as the Ranter Abiezer
Coppe and the extreme Quaker James Nayler who spoke out as early
as the 1650s against the tendency to turn the Protestant ethic into a
rationalization of the spirit of capitalism. Nayler sarcastically placed
the direct command of God—"Thou shalt not covet"—over against
what he saw as the canting self-deceptions of the capitalistically Protestant Antichrist: "Thou must live by the wits that God hath given
thee, and this is not covetousness but a provident care; and he that
will not provide for his family is worse than an infidel, and if thou
stand to wait upon God and do not help thyself by thy wits, both thou
and thine may be poor enough." Milton should be seen as standing
ultimately with Coppe and Nayler, rather than with those whose values these radicals so effectively satirized. The man who brought his
two decades of political activism to a close by fixing responsibility for
the demise of his revolutionary hopes and dreams upon those who
were prepared to "set to sale religion, libertie, honor, safetie, all concernments Divine or human to keep up trading" was a man who was,
in his own way, dissenting as sharply as were Coppe and Nayler from
the emergent alliance of Protestantism and capitalism. At those moments when his imagination is fully engaged, Milton seems like

Coppe, Nayler, and others who experienced the revolutionary years to have passed so "tumultuously through the secularization process that would take [his] culture several centuries to experience, [that he] bypassed the stage of capitalist ideology altogether." And so the Protestant epic poet was able to dramatize in the Satan of *Paradise Lost* a Protestant ethic gone so utterly awry that "all concernments Divine or human" are degraded. Satan is a figure of sufficient magnitude to anticipate and encompass, in the areas of both sanctification and justification, those many centuries of the secularization process from which Milton and other English revolutionaries had, in advance, critically disengaged themselves.[10]

The event that propels Satan on his course of rebellion is the elevation and exaltation of the Son of God over the angels in Book V. We must first take note of the care with which Milton sets the scene for God's announcement of this new dispensation:

> on such day
> As heaven's great year brings forth, the empyreal host
> Of angels by imperial summons called,
> Innumerable before the almighty's throne
> Forthwith from all the ends of heaven appeared
> Under their hierarchs in orders bright
> Ten thousand thousand ensigns high advanced,
> Standards, and gonfalons twixt van and rear
> Stream in the air, and for distinction serve
> Of hierarchies, of orders, and degrees;
> Or in their glittering tissues bear imblazed
> Holy memorials, acts of zeal and love
> Recorded eminent.   (V, 582–94)

[10]Hill, *Milton*, pp. 25, 194–95; *World Turned Upside Down*, pp. 268–70; McKeon, *Origins of the English Novel*, p. 198. Milton seems to have become disillusioned with the revolution, on the grounds that its leaders "fell to huckster the Commonwealth," by the late 1640s; see "The Character of the Long Parliament," in *The History of Britain, CPW*, V, 443–45. Evidence that many other Puritan radicals were unhappy in the 1650s with the materialistic course the revolutionary leaders seemed to be pursuing is presented in Christopher Hill, *The Experience of Defeat: Milton and Some Contemporaries* (New York: Viking, 1984), pp. 56–57, 93–94, 107. And from pp. 281–82, we learn that Milton's language in the *Second Defence*, "avarice, ambition and luxury," became a virtually formulaic explanation for the failure of the revolution. A century and a half later, John Adams was still availing himself of it, exclaiming in 1788, à propos of Milton's recommendation in *The Readie and Easie Way* of a perpetual governing council: "What! Cromwell, Ireton, Lambert, Ludlow, Waller, and five hundred others, of all sects and parties, one quarter of them mad with enthusiasm, another with ambition, a third with avarice, and a fourth of them honest men, a perpetual council, to govern such a country!" See George F. Sensabaugh, *Milton in Early America* (Princeton, N.J.: Princeton University Press, 1964), p. 133.

Those ensigns, standards, and gonfalons that "for distinction serve / Of hierarchies, of orders, and degrees" are the sort of thing that led C. S. Lewis and others of like mind to suppose that *Paradise Lost* teaches Obedience and Order. But the flags and banners also constitute a record book of "acts of zeal and love." At least in part, the legions of unfallen angels are the disciplined hosts of activist Puritan saints, laboring for God, as ever in their great taskmaster's eye. And precisely because they are so eager and so resolute in the performance of acts of zeal and love, they must live as ever with the temptation to be proud of themselves. The possibility of pride, of breaking the ranks of godly discipline, lurks in the very joy and exaltation of discipline and service, in the "glittering tissues" of the standards and gonfalons, and in the emblazoning and recording eminent of such vigorously pious deeds. In its insistence on what looks like a neofeudal conservatism of hierarchies, orders, and degrees, the passage seems to recognize how potentially disruptive were the energies and forces awakened by Protestant zeal and faith.[11]

In other words, just as the Fall in Book IX reveals Milton's insight into the ambiguities of Protestant and Puritan hierarchy, so the fall of Satan here in Book V shows Milton's recognition of the deeply ambiguous nature of Protestant and Puritan activism. Even as the angelic saints are empowered to the performance of acts of zeal and love, they evidently must also be held strictly in check. Clearly it is a sense of this latter necessity which suffuses the Father's ensuing announcement of the exaltation of the Son:

> This day I have begot whom I declare
> My only Son, and on this holy hill
> Him have anointed, whom ye now behold
> At my right hand; your head I him appoint;
> And by my self have sworn to him shall bow
> All knees in heaven, and shall confess him Lord:
> Under his great viceregent reign abide
> United as one individual soul
> For ever happy: him who disobeys
> Me disobeys, breaks union, and that day
> Cast out from God and blessed vision, falls
> Into utter darkness, deep engulfed, his place

---

[11]The fact that the angelic flags "can record acts of virtue as well as insignia of rank" is mentioned in David Aers, Bob Hodge, and Gunther Kress, *Literature, Language and Society in England, 1580–1680* (Totowa, N.J.: Barnes and Noble, 1981), p. 192, but the authors do not integrate this point into their subsequent interpretation of Satan.

Ordained without redemption, without end.

(603–15)

A. J. A. Waldock's observation that this speech has "a distinctly curt and challenging air" is surely a valid one. But perhaps there is ample historical reason for this. Milton's God is the God who must cope with the Protestant ethic. He must preside over a universe of abundant and vigorous and always potentially wayward willpower, and as a result, his Divine Will sounds here like one will striving among many. God appears to be a tense, vigilant being forced to remain as ever on the lookout for the first signs of rebellion in the ranks, as ludicrously entangled in the perplexities of discipline and fulfillment as the drill sergeant who orders his men to sign up for the company softball team with the absurd command "You will enjoy it" ("abide / United as one individual soul / For ever happy"). Whatever the theological technicalities pertinent to it, the emotional basis for the begetting and elevation of the Son is God's uneasy perception that the Protestant energies that can be poured into faithful actions are also capable of being poured into gestures of disobedience and pride. The Son himself will shortly inform us that "all regal power" was "given me to quell their pride" (739–40). What we have here is the spectacle of Milton—the poet who was the product of a culture that tended not to stress the Son as all-important, the proto-Unitarian denier of the Son's divinity who repeatedly emphasized the sonship of all believers—suddenly thrusting the Son as far forward as possible, presenting him as a King Jesus who is less an internal, energizing source of antinomian empowerment than an external ruler, a setter of limits. Milton the Arminian makes his God puritanically discipline Milton's own Arminian, activist Puritanism, clamping aggressively down on its tendency to become a law unto itself.[12]

There are two responses to the Father's announcement, one expressive of Milton's Puritan ideals, the other of his recognition of emerging Puritan realities. The former response is that of the angels who remain "well pleased" (617), spending the rest of the day in heavenly delight: "In song and dance about the sacred hill, / Mystical dance, which yonder starry sphere / Of planets and of fixed in all her wheels / Resembles nearest, mazes intricate, / Eccentric, intervolved,

---

[12]Waldock, Paradise Lost *and Its Critics*, p. 72. At least one other recent study agrees with Waldock; see Robert Thomas Fallon, *Captain or Colonel: The Soldier in Milton's Life and Art* (Columbia: University of Missouri Press, 1984), p. 217. For the minimizing of the Son in Puritanism, see Boyd M. Berry, *Process of Speech: Puritan Religious Writing and Paradise Lost* (Baltimore, Md.: Johns Hopkins University Press, 1976), pp. 24–60.

yet regular / Then most, when most irregular they seem. . . / Forthwith from dance to sweet repast they turn / Desirous . . . / They eat, they drink, and in communion sweet / Quaff immortality and joy" (619–24, 630–31, 637–38). Depending on one's point of view, this reaction to the Father's grim and restrictive edict is either sublimely or ludicrously incongruous. The Father has just laid down a law of even stricter regimentation upon an angelic army that is already strictly ranked and ordered, yet Milton would have us believe that the effect of his words is to transform rigidity into extravagant motion and uninhibited feasting. The poet longs for a world in which the Protestant ethic has been transcended and faith as work has become faith as play. But himself a supreme child of the Protestant ethic, his only imaginative recourse is a naked, willful conjuration of such a condition of transcendence. Like his God, he seeks to work his will by sheer imposition.

Unlike his God, however, Milton was quite well aware that such a course must be self-defeating. The willful suppression of willpower might engender spiritual bliss in some pious souls, but in others it was certain to provoke an answering willfulness. Intending by the elevation of the Son "to quell their pride," God succeeds in doing just the opposite, for Satan is immediately "fraught / With envy against the Son of God" and "could not bear / Through pride that sight, and thought himself impaired" (661–62, 664–65): Where does this envy and pride come from? The poem does not directly answer this question, but it does provide some relevant hints. Since Satan has to this point been "of the first, / If not the first archangel, great in power, / In favour and pre-eminence" (659–61), we must suppose that he has been first in acts of zeal and love that have been emblazed and recorded eminent. He has been one of those who post o'er land and ocean without rest, at God's bidding and in his behalf, someone who, in Max Weber's words, "[has made] himself sure of his state of grace . . . in that he [has felt] himself to be . . . the tool of the divine will." That Satan's preeminence has been earned in a world governed by the dictates of the Protestant ethic is further suggested by the nature of the pretext he finds it politic to invent in order to mobilize an army of followers for himself. Those who have functioned thus far under his leadership are to be told that "by [God's] command, ere yet dim night / Her shadowy cloud withdraws, I am to haste, / And all who under me their banners wave, / Homeward with flying march where we possess / The quarters of the north, there to prepare / Fit entertainment to receive our king / The great Messiah, and his new commands, / Who speedily through all the hierarchies / Intends to pass triumphant, and give laws" (685–93). In a manner to which they have doubtless become accustomed, the satanic hosts will be exhorted to be up and doing, hastening about their Father's business, functioning as tools of the Divine Will by preparing "fit entertainment to receive our king / The great Messiah."[13]

Satan's reaction to the exaltation of the Son is, then, that of the most thoroughly Protestant of God's many Protestantly angelic tools and servants. He views the bestowing of a crucial role upon the Son as a belittling of his own supremely empowered and enfranchised self, and as he does so, we cannot but be reminded of a fact to which we have already alluded, that in *Christian Doctrine* Milton himself denied the divinity of the Son. In acknowledging that an apprehension of the Son comparable to his own might well proceed from envy and pride, might be one appalling but logical end point of a process that began when Calvin, as characterized by a Roman Catholic commentator, "wickedly and unlearnedly denie[d] Christ himself to have deserved or merited anything for himself," Milton is acknowledging the considerable degree of truth there was in conservative assessments of Protestantism. There was no way to arrest the logic of Protestant liberation, declared Catholics disputing with Protestants and Anglicans with Puritans. "No bishop, no king," said James I at the turn of the seventeenth century, and he might have added, "in the long run no Son, no Father, and no God." That long run is what is contracted into an instant in Satan's decision to regard the enforcement of discipline and humility as the institution of a reign of tyranny and servility similar to the medieval ecclesiastical order from which Protestants had struggled to emerge. "New laws thou seest imposed; / New laws from him who reigns, new minds may raise / In us who serve, new counsels, to debate / What doubtful may ensue" (679–82), he complains to Beelzebub. Here is the Protestantism and Puritanism that provoked Charles I's chief secular adviser, the Earl of Strafford, to complain to his sacred counterpart, Archbishop Laud: "The very genius of that nation of people leads them always to oppose . . . all that ever authority ordains for them." Satan is Strafford's remark taken quite literally. In telescoping a century and a half of Protestant development into three lines—the new laws of the sixteenth-century papacy raising new minds in Luther and others, leading to the counseling and debating so prevalent in the years immediately preceding *Paradise Lost* in the

---

[13]Weber, *Protestant Ethic*, pp. 113–14. Overlooking the fact that Satan thinks it needful to disseminate this thoroughly Protestant rationale to them, Aers, Hodge, and Kress state (*Literature, Language and Society*, p. 193) that Satan's followers "are motivated by respect for traditional values, by unthinking allegiance to status."

English Revolution—the falling archangel imparts an automatic, knee-jerk quality to the essential Protestant impulse of resistance and the essential Protestant principle of rational accountability.[14]

In the two speeches he delivers to his followers after they have returned to their northern realm, Satan espouses his unyielding Protestantism more fully. He appeals to the Protestant sense of elected sainthood when he demands of his auditors that they know themselves as "natives and sons of heaven possessed before / By none" (790–91). Sons of Heaven all, as opposed to the Son abruptly and arbitrarily set over them. When Satan employs such language, when he goes on to insist that the angels have until now all been "free, / Equally free" (791–92), and when he adds that there was no reason for God to "introduce / Law and edict on us, who without law / Err not, much less for this to be our lord" (797–99), readers familiar with Milton's pamphlets will hear a distinct echo of the magnificent arguments from Christian liberty in the *Treatise of Civil Power* (1659):

> Hence it planely appeers, that if we be not free we are not sons, but still servants unadopted. . . . Ill was our condition chang'd from legal to evangelical, and small advantage gotten by the gospel, if for the spirit of adoption to freedom, promisd us, we receive again the spirit of bondage to fear; if our fear which was then servile towards God only, must be now servile in religion towards men: strange also and preposterous fear, if when and wherin it hath attain by the redemption of our Saviour to be filial only towards God, it must be now servile towards the magistrate. Who by subordinating us to his punishment in these things . . . in effect abolishes the gospel by establishing again the law to a far worse yoke of servitude upon us then before. It will therfore not misbecome the meanest Christian to put in minde Christian magistrates . . . that they meddle not rashly with Christian libertie, the birthright and outward testimonie of our adoption. (*CPW,* VII, 265)

Satan sees the threat to Christian liberty and Protestant awakening arising not, as Milton does, from an overbearing magistrate, but rather from an overbearing God. In the poem, it is God who has imposed "a far worse yoke of servitude on us then before." Moreover, Satan misconstrues as oppression exactly what Milton identifies as a source of empowerment, the role played by the Son in sacred history. But what must be stressed is not the obvious fact that Satan's rhetoric constitutes an abuse of Miltonic Protestantism, but rather the far more interesting fact that through the medium of Satan Milton recog-

---

[14]Berry, *Process of Speech,* p. 25; Hill, *Change and Continuity,* p. 91.

nizes so clearly just how vulnerable his own Protestantism is to abuses of exactly this sort. In a contradictory Puritan world in which the God who had seemed to be an old priest had been slain by the aroused saints, only to be reinstated by some of those same saints as a harsh new presbyter, the progression no bishop, no king, and no civil magistrate could and did lead many of the remaining saints on—both during the English Revolution and long after—to no authorities and values of any kind, save those improvised by self-aggrandizing individualism.

And indeed, that fuller secularizing movement already occurs during these initial counsels and debates. Abdiel, the only one among Satan's legions to speak up for God after Satan's designs have been revealed, insists upon the infinite gulf between divine creators and angelic creatures. It was by the instrumentality of that very "begotten Son" against whom Satan is fraught with envy, declares Abdiel, "as by his Word [that] the mighty Father made / All things, even thee, and all the spirits of heaven" (836–37). But Satan is only made, like many another stiff-necked Puritan, "more haughty" (852) by Abdiel's rebukes: "That we were formed then say'st thou? And the work / Of secondary hands, by task transferred / From Father to his Son? Strange point and new! / Doctrine which we would know whence learned: who saw / When this creation was?" (853–57). Into these lines are poured generations of Protestant disdain for the Roman Catholic conception of tradition as coequal with the gospel ("Strange point and new"). The posture adopted here by the archrebel is very close to the posture to be adopted by Milton himself when, in *Of True Religion* (1673), he will ridicule such "Scholastic Notions" as "Trinity, Triniunity, Coessentiality, Tripersonality, and the like" (*CPW*, VIII, 424–25). The theology of the Son as creative Word is viewed by Satan, as the arguments for the Trinity were viewed by Milton, as an obscuring of the sonship of all creatures by popish superstition. That the world could very well do without a God who invites such unintelligible conceptions of himself was the conclusion drawn by many of those formed by Anglo-American Protestant culture, and it is the conclusion now drawn by Satan. He proceeds to espouse views that became widespread and approached dominance only in the nineteenth century: positivist empiricism, an optimistic evolutionary sense of history, and a Protestant ethic that has dispensed entirely with the requirement that one's laboring must be for God alone:

> We know no time when we were not as now;
> Know none before us, self-begot, self-raised

> By our own quickening power, when fatal course
> Had circled his full orb, the birth mature
> Of this our native heaven, ethereal sons.
> Our puissance is our own, our own right hand
> Shall teach us highest deeds, by proof to try
> Who is our equal.   (859–66)

From acts of zeal and love performed in a spirit of piety and service, to highest deeds accomplished by a creature who believes himself to be the quintessential self-made man: in the second half of Book V Satan makes the journey made by Anglo-American culture as it moved from the sixteenth to the late nineteenth century. He transforms himself from heroic, disciplined Protestant saint to heroic, enterprising secularized sinner. He becomes the figure we have already seen, admired and lamented in Books I and II.

From Dryden onward, those who have been impressed by Satan's heroism in the first two books of *Paradise Lost* have tended to associate him with the protagonists of Greek and Roman epic or with the figure of the undaunted medieval or Renaissance warrior aristocrat. One recent account states that he "stands for much that is best in the old patrician class. . . . He is the doomed champion of the old order." There can be no doubt that Milton encourages such perceptions. He tells us, for instance, that Satan far surpassed in his heroism all those either "that fought at Thebes and Ilium" or "who since, baptized or infidel" have engaged in chivalric warfare (I, 578, 582). Clearly the Satan of the opening books is in part to be viewed in what we might, intent upon our present concerns, call these non-Protestant contexts. Yet at one of the turning points of the narrative—the demonic debate has been brought to a conclusion when Satan heroically volunteers to undertake the hazardous mission to Earth—Milton chooses to interpose the comment that "neither do the spirits damned / Lose all their virtue; lest bad men should boast / Their specious deeds on earth, which glory excites, / Or close ambition varnished o'er with zeal" (II, 482–85). The phrase "which glory excites" indeed links Satan with the traditions of classical and aristocratic warrior heroism, but the next line, "Or close ambition varnished o'er with zeal," alternatively identifies satanic heroism with precisely that Puritan type—outwardly pious, inwardly grasping and conniving—which such Puritan radicals as Abiezer Coppe and James Nayler so scathingly portrayed.

So if Satan is a classical and aristocratic hero in this portion of *Paradise Lost* in which he is most manifestly heroic, he is evidently a Puritan and Protestant hero as well, and Milton's identification of him as such begins to seem quite pointed once the passage's allusion to Paul's letter to the Ephesians is recognized: "For by grace are ye saved through faith; and that not of yourselves: it is the gift of God: Not of works, lest any man should boast" (Eph. 2:8–9; AV). By referring us to this scriptural analysis of the complex dialectics of faith, works, and pride, Milton informs us that Satan is to be understood in great part as a heroic exemplar of the Protestant ethic and its extreme vulnerability to that secularizing process in which works, and the rationalizations of works, float free of faith and take on a prideful life of their own. Books I and II both acknowledge the magnificent achievements of such a secularized work ethic and assess its obvious moral and spiritual limitations.[15]

As Max Weber argues, the distinguishing characteristics of the practitioner of the Protestant ethic were the continuousness and the intensity of his labor. John Cotton's saintly entrepreneur "cannot indure to spend any idle time, takes all opportunities to be doing something." Such unremitting strenuosity is precisely what is required of Satan in the first two books and precisely what he provides. He shows what A. J. A. Waldock calls "fortitude in adversity, enormous endurance" from the time he first opens his eyes upon his "dismal situation waste and wild" (I, 60) to the moment near the end of his journey to the created universe when he "with difficulty and labour hard / Moved on" through Chaos (II, 1021–22).[16] A sense of satanic striving and struggling pervades both the most minute and intimate syntactic and also the largest and most encompassing narrative realities of this part of the poem, and one sequence in Book I will serve to illustrate both levels of heroic manifestation.

"If thou beest he," Satan begins his opening address to Beelzebub. But he is unable to move on to the anticipated "then" clause. The sight of his comrade immediately becomes itself an adverse circumstance, disrupting his train of thought and forcing it down a different path: "If thou beest he; but O how fallen! how changed / From him, who in the happy realms of light / Clothed with transcendent brightness didst outshine / Myriads though bright" (I, 84–87). Striving to collect one's thoughts is thus overwhelmed for a second by the overwhelming fact of defeat, but Satan persists nevertheless with the task he has set for

---

[15]Aers, Hodge, and Kress, *Literature, Language and Society*, pp. 192–97; see also Stella Perce Revard, *The War in Heaven: Paradise Lost and the Tradition of Satan's Rebellion* (Ithaca, N.Y.: Cornell University Press, 1980), pp. 198–234. For Dryden's remark that "the Devil" is the hero of *Paradise Lost*, see *Of Dramatic Poesy and Other Critical Essays*, ed. George Watson, 2 vols. (London: Everyman's Library, 1962), 2:233.

[16]Waldock, Paradise Lost *and Its Critics*, p. 77.

himself. He renews his interrupted syntactic foray, proceeding to mobilize his recollections of glory and comradeship in order to give to his words a desperately needed rhythm of emotional ascent: "If he whom mutual league, / United thoughts and counsels, equal hope / And hazard in the glorious enterprise, / Joined with me once, now misery hath joined / In equal ruin" (87–91). But the "then . . . now" pattern suggested by "joined with me once" at this point threatens to break free of the larger "if . . . then" structure built upon "if he whom": "In equal ruin: into what pit thou seest / From what highth fallen, so much the stronger proved / He with his thunder: and till then who knew / The force of those dire arms?" (91–94).

It is as though Satan's own words are turning into so many obstacles in his path, blocking the way forward from defeat and immobilization. Forming a distinct predication is beginning to seem quite impossible. But this only means that once a distinct predication is finally consummated, it will seem like a tremendous achievement indeed:

> and till then who knew
> The force of those dire arms? Yet not for those,
> Nor what the potent victor in his rage
> Can else inflict, do I repent or change,
> Though changed in outward lustre, that fixed mind
> And high disdain, from sense of injured merit,
> That with the mightiest raised me to contend.
>
> (93–99)

The overall pattern of this surmounting of the avalanche of conditionality and ascending to indicative proclamation is entirely illogical: "If you are Beelzebub, nevertheless I do not repent or change." But of course what matters is the irrefutable emotional logic of this fractured and reconstituted rhetorical structure. Satan has wrested victory from defeat. He has improvised what feels like a highly satisfying resolution, when all the syntactical circumstances are pressuring him toward incompletion and anticlimax. To take any heed at all of this first satanic utterance is to have an experience that is almost visceral of the structures of thought and speech being bent and molded to the service of what Satan will soon call his "unconquerable will" (106).

But as befits this lapsed Protestant who "cannot indure to spend any idle time," momentary resolution and success only open onto the next challenge and the next task. No sooner has Satan managed to reestablish his own will and resolve than he must deal with his companion's wavering and uncertainty: "O prince, O chief of many

throned powers, / That . . . / endangered heaven's perpetual king; /
And put to proof his high supremacy . . . / Too well I see and rue the
dire event, / That with sad overthrow and foul defeat / Hath lost us
heaven, and all this mighty host / In horrible destruction laid thus
low, / As far as heavenly essences / Can perish: for the mind and spirit
remains / Invincible, and vigour soon returns, / Though all our glory
extinct, and happy state / Here swallowed up in endless misery" (128–
29, 131–32, 134–42). Beelzebub's syntax follows a course the reverse
of Satan's. Where Satan's falls at first and then in consequence rises all
the more heroically, Beelzebub's attempts feebly to rise, only to fall all
the more dispiritingly. Remembering the glory of the past merely
produces a discouraged assessment of the present. Assent to Satan's
inspiring insistence that "the mind and spirit remains / Invincible"
trails weakly off ("though") into exactly that listless anticlimax Satan
had transcended. Having demonstrated that his will, unlike Satan's, is
eminently conquerable, Beelzebub is at least being consistent when he
proceeds to project an entirely necessaritarian universe, in which
grudging belief in an almighty God is accompanied by works that are
coerced from automatons rather than elicited from willing and striving servants: "But what if he our conqueror, (whom I now / Of force
believe almighty, since no less / Than such could have o'erpowered
such force as ours) / Have left us this our spirit and strength entire
/ . . . [To] do him mightier service as his thralls / By right of war"
(143–46, 149–50).

But Satan's own energies are immediately called into action at the
spectacle of Beelzebub's complete lack of energy. He replies "with
speedy words," transforming a future of tame submission into one of
unceasing resistance:

> of this be sure,
> To aught good will never be our task,
> But ever to do ill our sole delight,
> As being the contrary to his high will
> Whom we resist. If then his providence
> Out of our evil seek to bring forth good,
> Our labour must be to pervert that end,
> And out of good still to find means of evil.
>
> (158–65)

As he rejects Beelzebub's letter of Protestant acceptance of the sovereignty of God, Satan resolves that the devil's party will guide itself
by the spirit of the Protestant ethic. Where the saints are enjoined to

vocations of militant good works, Satan pledges himself and his fellow sinners, with all the vehemence of a Puritan divine, to a calling of malignity. And by the end of Book II, after he has awakened and encouraged his troops, mobilized them to the building of Pandaemonium, maneuvered them into a purposeful course of action, and himself struggled with and mastered the many obstacles placed in his path to the created universe, we are invited to affirm that Satan's laboring for sin has been exemplary in its diligence:

> But now at last the sacred influence
> Of light appears, and from the walls of heaven
> Shoots far into the bosom of dim Night
> A glimmering dawn; here nature first begins
> Her farthest verge, and Chaos to retire
> As from her outmost works a broken foe
> With tumult less and with less hostile din,
> That Satan with less toil, and now with ease
> Wafts on the calmer wave by dubious light
> And like a weather-beaten vessel holds
> Gladly the port, though shrouds and tackle torn.
>
> (II, 1034–44)

Satan, having arisen from Hell and outwitted Sin and Death, and wafting now with ease under the sacred influence of light, has won his way through to what feels for a moment like salvation, exemplifying that sense of meritorious works which the Protestant ethic both existed to humble and secretly encouraged.

This passage's concluding image of "a weather-beaten vessel" making for port, "though shrouds and tackle torn," may call to mind those industrious and adventurous seagoing Protestant British merchants who were at the time of Milton's writing being greatly assisted in their laboring to be rich for God by the maritime policies of the great Protestant and Puritan Lord Protector.[17] And this may help us begin to recognize that Books I and II take the measure of the Protestant ethic not only as a set of character traits, but also as a social phenomenon and force. At the conclusion of Satan's stirring exhortations to his troops to "awake, arise, or be for ever fallen" (I, 330), the troops do not have to be told what is the most readily available vocational path to tread. "A numerous brigade" (I, 675) hastens forthwith to a spot on the hellish landscape beneath which it is evident that "metallic ore" (673) is to be found. The group is headed by Mammon, who

[17]See above, Introduction, n. 9, first and third works cited.

even in Heaven had always kept "his looks and thoughts / . . . down-ward bent, admiring more / The riches of heaven's pavement, trod-den gold, / Than aught divine or holy else enjoyed / In vision beatific" (680–84). Laboring still to find means of evil, laboring for sin, turns quite naturally into laboring to be rich for sin, under the leadership of a once saintly, now secularized entrepreneur.

Milton's denunciations of such crudely covetous behavior are both unambiguous and highly traditional ("Let none admire / That riches grow in hell; that soil may best / Deserve the precious bane" [690–92]), but they do not interfere in the least with his appreciation of the devils' technical ingenuity:

> Nigh on the plain in many cells prepared,
> That underneath had veins of liquid fire
> Sluiced from the lake, a second multitude
> With wondrous art founded the massy ore,
> Severing each kind, and scummed the bullion dross:
> A third as soon had formed within the ground
> A various mould, and from the boiling cells
> By strange conveyance filled each hollow nook,
> As in an organ from one blast of wind
> To many a row of pipes the sound-board breathes.
> Anon out of the earth a fabric huge
> Rose like an exhalation, with the sound
> Of dulcet symphonies and voices sweet,
> Built like a temple.   (700–713)

It is a panorama of expansive civilization building that resembles in many respects the nineteenth century in both England and the United States. This appears to be an economy that has reached the stage that has been called "takeoff" by economists of development. Just as, many historians have argued, the reason the great transfor-mations wrought in the nineteenth century by the Industrial Revolu-tion went forward in relatively straightforward, unimpeded fashion was that the agricultural and ideological contexts for them had been laboriously building for the previous two or three centuries, so there is an ease and freedom about the devils' technological and archi-tectural exploits here that is attributable to the fact that they are the beneficiaries of Satan's far more strenuous laborings of every sort through Book I to this point.

The concluding lines—"Anon out of the earth a fabric huge / Rose like an exhalation, with the sound / Of dulcet symphonies and voices sweet, / Built like a temple"—are perhaps best appreciated when considered in conjunction with such a typical dulcet symphony of the nineteenth century as this 1845 celebration of the interior of a Lowell textile mill:

> The ponderous wheel that communicates life and activity to the whole establishment; the multitude of bands and cogs, which connect the machinery, story above story; the carding machines, which seem like things of life, toiling with steadfast energy; the whirring cylinders, the twirling spindles, the clanking looms—the whole spectacle seeming to present a magic scene in which wood and iron are endowed with the dexterity of the human hand—and where complicated machinery seems to be gifted with intelligence—is surely one of the marvels of the world.

In a poem that makes frequent use of wind as a metaphor for the presence of the Holy Spirit, and of temples as figures for genuine sanctification, the sardonically reverential exhalation of this demonic temple constitutes a remarkably accurate premonition of the nineteenth century's many cloying bestowals of an odor of sanctity upon the march of industrial progress.[18]

The first use of the devils' magnificent secular temple is to serve as the setting for their deliberations about what to do next. The course and conclusion of these deliberations, and with them the overall narrative structure of the first two books, seem to incorporate a reference to the expansive inner logic of capitalism. The first speaker, Moloch, urges impulsive action, the equivalent, perhaps, in a universe of bad works of the less strenuous and less systematic good works that sufficed in medieval Catholicism. Next, Belial recommends what Milton explicitly derides as "peaceful sloth" (II, 227). Mammon then proposes that the devils should "work ease out of pain / Through labour and endurance" (261–62). This solution, to continue along the lines indicated by the construction of Pandaemonium and build up an imitation heaven in Hell, amounts to a cautious, stabilized capitalism, an ethic of working diligently and thriving moderately within a strictly circumscribed domain. Significantly, Mammon's idea is the first one that gains any particular support: "Such applause was heard / As Mammon ended, and his sentence pleased, / Advising peace" (290–

---

[18]Perry Miller, *The Life of the Mind in America: From the Revolution to the Civil War* (New York: Harcourt, Brace and World, 1965), p. 300. The most convenient introduction to the agrarian foundations of the Industrial Revolution is to be found in the relevant portions of the works of Christopher Hill cited in the Introduction, n. 9. For the early stages in the long process of constructing capitalist ideology, see his *Society and Puritanism in Pre-Revolutionary England*, 2d ed. (New York: Schocken, 1967); and Michael Walzer, *The Revolution of the Saints: A Study in the Origins of Radical Politics* (New York: Atheneum, 1973; orig. 1965).

92). Perhaps this is because it is the first of the proffered alternatives that could in the late seventeenth century be felt to have any historical viability, referring, as it evidently does, to the post-Restoration Nonconformist and Quaker attempt to combine political quietism with industrious commercial endeavor.

But in the long run, the debate seems to imply, capitalism would not remain so soberly and prudently retired. The energies poured into the construction of Pandaemonium are too vigorous to confine themselves indefinitely in the backwater of Hell, just as English and New English merchants were not content to trade only in coastal waters but were sailing the world over, and just as New Englanders would eventually break through geographical and ideological constraints and colonize and exploit the entire vast North American continent. The decision to attempt the conquest of the newly created Earth is, in short, a decision to embark on a course of imperialism:

> this place may lie exposed
> The utmost border of his kingdom, left
> To their defence who hold it: here perhaps
> Some advantageous act may be achieved
> By sudden onset, either with hell fire
> To waste his whole creation, or possess
> All as our own, and drive as we were driven,
> The puny inhabitants, or if not drive,
> Seduce them to our party.   (360–68)

This passage, particularly the final lines, should be understood in the context of such far-left critiques of the emergent British Empire as those voiced in the 1649 Digger pamphlet *Tyranipocrit Discovered:* "Although their dealing concerning the Indians' goods be bad, yet they deal worser with their persons; for they either kill them, which is bad, or make them slaves, which is worse. I know not what to say concerning such impious proceedings with them poor innocent people."[19]

---

[19] Hill, *World Turned Upside Down*, p. 272. Jackie DiSalvo, *War of Titans: Blake's Critique of Milton and the Politics of Religion* (Pittsburgh, Pa.: University of Pittsburgh Press, 1983), p. 283, notes that "Satan's colleagues in demonic council bear strong resemblances to enemies within the bourgeois revolution, and one of them, fittingly, is Mammon." Fallon, *Captain or Colonel*, p. 140, places the satanic designs upon Earth in the context of Milton's own experience of diplomacy and power-political maneuvering. Low, *Georgic Revolution*, pp. 314–16, argues in a manner that is entirely compatible with the present account that Satan constitutes an admonition against the "false pursuit of imperial georgic. For Satan is a laborer as well as a warrior, who understands full well that an empire cannot be built without sweat and toil." Low instances the inverted work ethic of I, 162–64, the building of Pandaemonium, Mammon's arguments in the de-

To perceive in the maneuvers of the devils' party a commentary on the emergence of modern imperialism is to begin to describe *Paradise Lost*'s representation of the deformations wrought by Protestant sanctification in its secularized forms. We can gain a more comprehensive view of what the poem has to tell us about such deformations by considering more carefully the particular form of the Protestant ethic that is most obviously pertinent to Satan. Boyd Berry helps us to see how the warrior ethic and the Protestant ethic could be exemplified by one and the same character when he calls our attention to the onward Christian soldiers *topos* in the ideology and rhetoric of seventeenth-century English Puritans. "Above all creatures, [God] loves soldiers," declared Thomas Sutton in 1624. This was because, as Berry explains, "soldiering both required the expenditure of a great deal of energy and could express an inner, spiritual state of faithfulness and almost realism." Furthermore, "military drilling particularly attracted Puritans because it provided such an excellent way to keep busy and thereby foil the Devil." Indeed, the labor of godly soldiering called for exactly that ceaselessness of endeavor which Max Weber identified as the hallmark of Protestant vocation. "We are all soldiers as we are Christians," insisted Thomas Adams. "Now to this war every *Christian* is a professed *soldier*, not only for a spurt, for sport, as young gentlemen use for a time to see the fashion of the wars, but our vow runs thus in Baptism: that every man undertakes to fight manfully under Christ's banner against sin, the world, and the devil, and to continue his faithful soldier and servant to his life's end."[20]

Obviously Satan is not a Puritan soldier. Nevertheless, he is best understood not as representing an alternative to Puritan military values and styles—as an undisciplined Cavalier fighting "for a spurt, for sport"—but rather as exemplifying those Puritan values and styles in reverse. When he proclaims at the end of his first heroic utterance in Book I that he intends "to wage by force or guile eternal war / Irreconcilable to [his] grand foe" of God (I, 121–22), he is allowing us to see that his identity as a warrior is the mirror image of that of the Puritan soldier who undertakes to fight manfully to his life's end against his grand foes of sin, the world, and the devil. Similarly, Satan's army, once awakened and arisen in response to his call,

monic debate, and the laboriousness of Satan's travels through Chaos. As far as I can tell, this is the only (oblique) acknowledgment in Low's entire book that the actual historical result of his "georgic revolution" was not an egalitarian commonwealth in which Adam delved and Eve span and no one was then the gentleman, but rather the wholly unequal, alienated world of imperial capitalism.

[20]Berry, *Process of Speech*, pp. 177–78. See also Revard, *War in Heaven*, pp. 108–15.

organizes itself in a manner that does not differ from, but rather parodies, gathered Puritan militance and steadiness. This is evident from the views Milton provides of the unfallen and fallen armies on the march. The unfallen is "in mighty quadrate joined," moving into battle "to the sound / Of instrumental harmony that breathed / Heroic ardour to adventurous deeds" (VI, 62, 64–66). The fallen army likewise proceeds "in perfect phalanx to the Dorian mood / . . . such as raised / To highth of noblest temper heroes old / . . . and in stead of rage / Deliberate valour breathed, firm and unmoved" (I, 550, 551–52, 552–53).[21]

The clear resemblances between satanic and godly soldiering, and the fact that soldiering was apprehended by many Puritans as the most appropriate of all symbols of the Protestant ethic, suggest that Milton is using Satan and his followers to explore the possibility that those living by the Protestant ethic might suffer a fall into sheer bellicosity, an approach to war that could "but endless war still breed" ("On the Lord General Fairfax" [10]). Such a fall would occur at the point at which the person formed by Protestant culture would no longer be proceeding with the guidance of a vision of a fully sanctified world, would no longer imagine an ultimate resting point beyond labor and battle, but would continue nevertheless to maintain the warfaring posture dictated by the Protestant ethic—the posture in which life is understood to consist of an endless series of contests with all manner of resistant obstacles. This is the point to which Satan has already come at the beginning of *Paradise Lost,* when he places at the center of his world view not a bountiful creator, not even an all-powerful unmoved mover, but rather an opponent, someone or something to be struggled with and overcome, "the potent victor in his rage" (I, 95). Possessed of an unconquerable will, Satan had set out to conquer a world that existed, as far as he was concerned, only to be conquered. Defeated (in Book VI), he immediately seeks out (in Books I and II) new worlds to conquer, new worlds that—again in his view—exist primarily and precisely to be conquered. Such determinedly militarized perceptions are seen in Satan's more particular thoughts and utterances, as well as in his overarching schemes of struggle and conquest. He evidently believes that his own followers are restrained from attacking him only by contorted calculations to the effect that "where there is then no good / For which to strive, no strife can grow up there / From faction" (II, 30–32). And his mouthpiece Beelzebub imagines, on no ground other than general

---

[21]This similarity is also noted in Revard, *War in Heaven,* p. 172.

satanic principle, that the creatures of the new world are forever poised for battle: "This place may lie exposed / The utmost border of his kingdom, left / To their defence who hold it" (360–62).[22]

Satan's indiscriminate construing of all and sundry as obstacle and enemy is on display throughout *Paradise Lost,* but its dismal significance is exposed most fully in the narrative of the war in Heaven in Book VI. In Book V, as we have seen, Satan revolts against a vision of the sanctified community (enacted, however incongruously, immediately after the elevation of the Son) and falls immediately into a posture of struggle and combat on behalf of liberation from tyranny. In Book VI, however, Satan rallies his troops after the first day of battle by proclaiming that his professed ideals of liberty have been superseded by naked ambition, and that he relishes the prospect of war breeding endless war:

> O now in danger tried, now known in arms
> Not to be overpowered, companions dear,
> Found worthy not of liberty alone,
> Too mean pretence, but what we more affect,
> Honour, dominion, glory, and renown,
> Who have sustained one day in doubtful fight
> (And if one day, why not eternal days?)
> What heaven's lord had powerfulest to send
> Against us from about his throne.
>
> (VI, 418–26)

The archrebel's progression from Book V to Book VI seems, in short, to be almost perfectly described in the famous lines from one of Milton's sonnets about those who "still revolt when truth would set them free. / Licence they mean when they cry liberty" ("On the Detraction which followed upon my writing Certain Treatises" [10–11]).

The license Milton has in mind in the sonnet is, at least in part, the degeneration of Puritan soldiering into sheer, purposeless aggression and violence, for in the final line he blames licentious Puritan libertarians "for all [the] waste of wealth and loss of blood" of the Civil War. And what immediately follows the speech from *Paradise Lost* just quoted is the starkest possible revelation of exactly this form of Puritan license. One of Satan's soldiers, Nisroc, begins to complain about the setbacks and sufferings he has experienced in the course of the day's engagements: "Pain is perfect misery, the worst / Of evils, and

---

[22]Fallon, *Captain or Colonel,* p. 140, also notes that Satan perceives Earth solely in terms of struggle and conquest.

excessive, overturns / All patience" (462–64). Nisroc sounds not like a disciplined Puritan, but rather like one of Thomas Adams's dilettantish aristocrats who believes that war is to be conducted "for a spurt, for sport." But the role of Nisroc's commander in this episode is precisely to talk him out of this mistaken point of view. Outwardly at least, pain has not overturned all Satan's patience. This first setback in his career of still revolting when truth would set him free and of meaning license when he cries liberty does not dislodge Satan from his posture of stable Puritan determination. It simply pushes him farther down the road of secularization, along which his unconquerable will ("to strength and counsel joined / Think nothing hard" [494–95]) is conjoined with that nimble resourcefulness that would come to be known as Yankee ingenuity and know-how:

> Which of us who beholds the bright surface
> Of this ethereous mould whereon we stand,
> This continent of spacious heaven, adorned
> With plant, fruit, flower ambrosial, gems and gold,
> Whose eye so superficially surveys
> These things, as not to mind from whence they grow
> Deep under ground, materials dark and crude,
> Of spiritous and fiery spume, till touched
> With heaven's ray, and tempered they shoot forth
> So beauteous, opening to the ambient light.
> These in their dark nativity the deep
> Shall yield us pregnant with infernal flame,
> Which into hollow engines long and round
> Thick-rammed, at the other bore with touch of fire
> Dilated and infuriate shall send forth
> From far with thundering noise among our foes
> Such implements of mischief as shall dash
> To pieces, and o'erwhelm whatever stands
> Adverse, that they shall fear we have disarmed
> The thunderer of his only dreaded bolt.
>
> (472–91)

Without the least glimmer of recognition that he has done so, Satan achieves one of the poem's loveliest, most lilting evocations of divine immanence and antinomian creativity: "Whence they grow / Deep under ground, materials dark and crude, / Of spiritous and fiery spume, till touched / With heaven's ray, and tempered they shoot forth / So beauteous, opening to the ambient light." The lines evoke the multitude of blessings dispensed by all forms of light throughout

Paradise Lost—not only the "holy Light" of grace invoked at the start of Book III, but also the "all-cheering" natural light of the "radiant sun" (III, 581; II, 492)—conveying precisely that truth, in the universe Satan inhabits, which would set him and his followers free.

But vision and truth are conjured up here only to reveal the full, revolting meaning of still revolting in their presence. The imagery of violation in the ensuing lines is entirely appropriate—the impregnating of the womb of nature so that it gives birth to crudely phallic "hollow engines long and round / Thick-rammed," which will ejaculate "with touch of fire / Dilated and infuriate"—for what Satan is proposing and planning is a rape, the rape of vision by the unconquerable will. And the violation is to be experienced in the structural and sound effects of the verse, as well as in its images: clusters of grunting monosyllables ("long and round / Thick-rammed"), and a syntax that enacts Satan's hubristic feeling of irresistible power on the march ("shall send forth / From far . . . / Such implements of mischief as shall dash / To pieces . . . / . . . that they shall fear"). This is Satan's way of demonstrating that "we can preserve / Unhurt our minds" in the midst of combat (443–44), his remedy for Nisroc's complaint that pain "overturns / All patience." It is to evince a mind so deeply hurt, a mind in which, at bottom, patience has been so utterly overthrown, a mind so bent on battle that it wages total war, "wasting the earth, each other to destroy" (II, 502), even during a moment of respite from war.[23]

———————————

The satanist critique of *Paradise Lost* was essentially that in the later books the poem arbitrarily denies what in the earlier books it had magnificently affirmed: the heroism of Satan. In the words of A. J. A. Waldock, "the alleged 'degeneration' of Satan" is really no such thing, for "the changes do not generate themselves from within: they are imposed from without. Satan . . . does not degenerate: he is *degraded*."[24] But anyone contemplating the broad outlines of Anglo-American development during the past three centuries must see not willful literary manipulation but rather profound historical understanding in the degradation of Satan from a rebel against authoritarianism and an indomitable laborer and builder in the wilderness to an imperialist policy maker and insatiably combative tech-

[23]Joan Webber's comment, in *Milton and His Epic Tradition* (Seattle: University of Washington Press, 1979), p. 214, that Satan is "an alienated technocrat who has made the modern world into a desert of external things" thus applies to the Satan of *Paradise Lost* as well as to the Satan of *Paradise Regained.*
[24]Waldock, Paradise Lost *and Its Critics*, p. 83.

nocrat. Milton's devil anticipates to a very considerable extent what would result from the secularization of the Puritan commitment to sanctification. What remains to be demonstrated is that a similar historical acumen informs the other major aspects of Satan's degradation, those pertaining not to his actions, but to his patterns of thought and speech, to the secularization not of sanctification but rather of justification.

Boyd Berry states that "the essence of the Puritan style is a quest for a permanent, fixed, static, even rigid order," adding that such a tendency on the Puritans' part is "not surprising when we reflect how many changes were occurring in the world about them." It is even less surprising when we reflect how many of those changes were brought about by the Puritans themselves. If, as Berry contends, the Puritans "increased the distance between God and man . . . [and] emphasized his stability and permanence . . . in order to keep God clear of all the mess they saw about them," there was a particular and peculiar intensity in their manner of doing so which was in direct proportion to their uneasy sense of their own responsibility for that mess.

But what if, secularizing themselves, the Puritans made God so remote that he disappeared over the horizon altogether, and what if, at the same time, they continued to make a mess about them, creating a world of ever-accelerating change? In such circumstances, it seems quite likely that the impulse to project a transcendent fixity would be retained, but it would find itself compelled to improvise, to conjure up substitutes for the God who had departed but whose stabilizing presence was still devoutly desired. Faced with such a challenge, the secularized Puritan might well lean heavily on one of his old habits. He might have recourse to what Berry calls a style "redolent of such terms as 'justification,' 'sanctification,' 'salvation,' and 'damnation,'" a style that establishes fixity and transcendence by turning "potentially transitive acts" and potentially lived processes "into solid, manageable" and abstract nouns. Such abstracted substantives might begin to constitute a quasi-Platonic realm, subsisting in relation to the terrestrial flux that had given birth to it in the first place not as overruling and stabilizing power, but rather as an alternative that, in its stability, would be irresistibly alluring. The Puritan taste for transcendence might then begin to betoken a compulsion not to control, but rather to escape.[25]

Such intellectual and rhetorical consequences of secularization are depicted in Book I of *Paradise Lost*. Let us return to Satan's first

[25]Berry, *Process of Speech*, pp. 8–9.

speech, which has already been analyzed from the point of view of sanctification: "If he whom mutual league, / United thoughts and counsels, equal hope / And hazard in the glorious enterprise, / Joined with me once" (I, 87–90). With our present interest in justification, it is important to notice the way Satan takes actions, events, and processes and projects them outward and upward as fixed objects: mutual league, united thoughts and counsels, equal hope and hazard. It almost seems as though the very naming of such entities endows them with a creative potency, as though "the glorious enterprise" is bound to spring forth from the dense clustering of the previous grandiose substantives. But the impression that Satan is enclosing himself in a world separate from the poem's real world of God, angels, devils, and humans arises most distinctly from the syntax. Beelzebub, who presumably was one of the joint creators of the situation now being characterized as one of mutual league and united thoughts and counsels, is here the grammatical object, "he whom," while that which Beelzebub had helped to create is the grammatical subject: mutual league and its fellows evidently joined Beelzebub with Satan once. Nor is this a mere matter of Satan's subordinating someone else (in this case Beelzebub) to such mental constructions, for a few lines later he places himself in similar thrall to them: "that fixed mind / And high disdain, from sense of injured merit, / That with the mightiest raised me to contend" (97–99). Such high-flying discourse as Satan evidently prefers constitutes an almost picture-perfect exemplification of Karl Marx's definition of reification as an intellectual proceeding in which "productions of the human brain appear as independent beings endowed with life, and entering into relations both with one another and the human race."[26]

Satan's tendency to involve himself in reification and fantasy is perhaps brought out most clearly of all in his second speech, in the lines to which I have already called attention as an inversion of the Protestant ethic: "If then his providence / Out of our evil seek to bring forth good, / Our labour must be to pervert that end, / And out of good still to find means of evil" (162–65). Here the very language of action, becoming, and process is being forced to undermine itself. Beneath Satan's rhetoric is, we can discern, a world in which good and evil begin to be words made flesh as they begin to be associated with a subterranean image of a woman laboring in childbirth. But in the satanic rhetorical overlay, good and evil are wrenched free of specific forms of becoming, drained of semantic value and referential capaci-

---

[26]Quoted in DiSalvo, *War of Titans*, p. 61.

ty, and transformed into phantasmagorical combatants in an endless, static perpetuation of the glorious enterprise of rebellion. As C. S. Lewis justly remarked, "What we see in Satan is the horrible co-existence of a subtle and incessant intellectual activity with an incapacity to understand anything." Like the secularized Puritan rhetoricians of nineteenth-century New England we shall be getting to know, who were also excessively fond of the high style, Satan remains incapable of understanding anything to the extent that he refuses to bring his incessant intellectual activity into contact with anything that diverges from his a priori framework—into contact, that is, with anything real.[27]

So while Satan's initial rhetoric is truly magnificent, suited to the grandeur of his struggle with unrelieved adversity, it is also militantly superficial at best, and at worst escapist, forbidding, in its addiction to syllogistic abstraction, any genuine weighing of alternatives. Satan has always been what he is identified as being in the course of his voyage to Earth, someone who "stayed not to inquire" (III, 571). Therefore, the intellectual and rhetorical changes to be discerned in him in the later parts of the poem are changes not of essential procedure but only of tone. By Book IV, his escapism comes to be expressed in a style not of soaring vision but rather of glib deceit and self-deceit.

Here for example is a bit of the "incessant intellectual activity" induced by Satan by his first view of Adam and Eve:

> O hell! What do mine eyes with grief behold,
> Into our room of bliss thus high advanced
> Creatures of other mould, earth-born perhaps,
> Not spirits, yet to heavenly spirits bright
> Little inferior; whom my thoughts pursue
> With wonder, and could love, so lively shines
> In them divine resemblance, and such grace
> The hand that formed them on their shape hath poured.
>
> (IV, 358–65)

Satan's words, "so lively shines / In them divine resemblance," echo the narrator's own introductory view of Adam and Eve: "For in their

[27]Lewis, *Preface to* Paradise Lost, p. 99. I am arguing, in effect, that in *Paradise Lost* Milton bestowed on Satan those habits of mind of his own which, I have elsewhere argued, brought it about that "in his political prose, concepts and visions do not emerge from a human context. They substitute for it." See Keith W. Stavely, *The Politics of Milton's Prose Style* (New Haven, Conn.: Yale University Press. 1975), p. 113. For another discussion of the high incidence of reification in Milton's prose, see Aers, Hodge, and Kress, *Literature, Language and Society,* chap. 7.

looks divine / The image of their glorious maker shone" (291–92). It appears for just a second that Satan might break free of his envy and his chain-of-being prejudices and appreciate reality as it has been created and given. But what is for the narrator the starting point of inquiry is for Satan a perceptual terminus. He proceeds to reconstrue and reshape "the good before him" so that it accords with his intentions and schemes:

> Ah gentle pair, ye little think how nigh
> Your change approaches, when all these delights
> Will vanish and deliver ye to woe,
> More woe, the more your taste is now of joy;
> Happy, but for so happy ill secured
> Long to continue, and this high seat your heaven
> Ill fenced for heaven to keep out such a foe
> As now is entered.   (366–73)

Now you see the creatures of divine resemblance, and now you don't. Creatures of satanic convenience—entirely vulnerable and pathetic— swim into view and are installed in their place, creatures who answer to the tired pastoral cliché of "harmless innocence" (388).

Moreover, once Satan has embarked on a course of deft cognitive fabrication, there is nothing to prevent him from pouring himself into it, exploiting the good before him with an absolute exuberance and abandon:

> league with you I seek,
> And mutual amity so strait, so close,
> That I with you must dwell, or you with me
> Henceforth; my dwelling haply may not please
> Like this fair Paradise, your sense, yet such
> Accept your maker's work; he gave it me,
> Which I as freely give; hell shall unfold,
> To entertain you two, her widest gates,
> And send forth all her kings; there will be room,
> Not like these narrow limits, to receive
> Your numerous offspring.   (375–85)

First, in the previous passage, the genuine complexity of what it might mean to live securely in bliss without the externalized security of being fenced in is obscured by a reductive prediction of purely innocent joy turning inevitably to utterly fallen woe. Then in this passage, the complex reality that has been made to disappear is replaced by the bogus complexity of conceptual games and wordplay. The contours and colors of reality are effaced in order to make reality seem to be in need of the garish rhetorical improvements Satan stands ready to provide. There is really no conflict between such an interpretation of Satan's mental functioning at this point and the view of William Empson and A. J. A. Waldock that the lines "hell shall unfold, / To entertain you two, her widest gates, / And send forth all her kings" have the ring of sincerity, for Satan has become as adept at smooth deception of himself as he is at deception of others.[28]

As an intellectual and rhetorician, the only difference between the early and the late Satan is that the early Satan involves himself in a subjectivity that is strenuous and sonorous, whereas the later Satan is content to be merely breezy. As in the sphere of action and sanctification, such a development suggests not an author's illegitimate impositions on his material, but rather his prophetic insight into historical tendencies and trends. We shall see that the early Satan finds any number of analogues among practitioners of the floridly subjective rhetoric of the early and middle years of the nineteenth century in New England. And by the late nineteenth century, floridity has evolved into that fluency and facility that continues to be capitalism's preferred mode of expression even today. Thus, the sequence of representations through which Satan embodies the development of capitalist style over the past century and a half comes to an appropriate climax in his two temptations of Eve, which would measure up well in competition against more recent specimens of energetic fantasizing in the service of commodity fetishism. When Satan urges Eve, in the dream he induces in her in Book V, to "taste this, and be henceforth among the gods / Thy self a goddess, not to earth confined, / But sometimes in the air, as we, sometimes / Ascend to heaven, by merit thine, and see / What life the gods live there, and such live thou" (77–81), his words have the exact tone and timbre of that American Dream of freedom, spaciousness, and ease obtained by way of consumption which is the underlying and overarching pretense of all late capitalist huckstering. When he assaults Eve in Book IX with an avalanche of fast-talking speciousness ("God therefore cannot hurt ye, and be just; / Not just, not God; not feared then, nor obeyed: / Your fear it self of death removes the fear" [700–702]), he sounds like someone who might function comfortably in our modern world, awash as it is in sophisticated discourse—in the media, the univer-

---

[28]William Empson, *Some Versions of Pastoral* (London: Chatto & Windus, 1935), p. 168; *Milton's God*, p. 67; Waldock, Paradise Lost *and Its Critics*, p. 88.

sities, and bureaucracies—which is not required to be grounded in any particular experience or vision, or devoted to any particular purpose, save self-interest and self-promotion.[29]

In the temptation scenes, Milton is of course drawing on a whole host of rhetorical traditions, most directly on the conventional figure of the oily-tongued mountebank, which had in Milton's own childhood been memorably portrayed in Ben Jonson's *Volpone*. But Satan is a unified character, and his participation in such traditions and conventions is consistent with other aspects of his temperament and behavior which they do not encompass. He has propelled himself in the direction of becoming a peddler of shabby dreams and glib points of view by the intensity of his need to spiritualize the course of self-aggrandizement upon which he has embarked. That he is being moved along by some deep inner logic he cannot control continues to be suggested as his career comes to an end. Consider his strange determination to make a show out of his return to Pandaemonium after the successful completion of his mission:

> he through the midst unmarked,
> In show plebeian angel militant
> Of lowest order, passed; and from the door
> Of that Plutonian hall, invisible
> Ascended his high throne, which under state
> Of richest texture spread, at the upper end
> Was placed in regal lustre. Down a while
> He sat, and round about him saw unseen:
> At last as from a cloud his fulgent head
> And shape star bright appeared, or brighter, clad
> With what permissive glory since his fall
> Was left him, or false glitter: all amazed
> At that so sudden blaze the Stygian throng
> Bent their aspect.   (X, 441–54)

Living as we do in a culture constituted by fantasy and spectacle and false glitter, but which originated in the heroic dreams of the Protestant ethic, we should not find it the least bit forced or manipulative that Satan, who also began in the heroic dreams of the Protestant ethic, should degrade himself as he prepares to take his leave of us by indulging in a bit of gratuitous theatricality.

---

[29]In 1658 Milton's friend Isaac Penington declared that "the forbidden fruit in the Garden of Eden had been 'knowledge without life . . . beware of the imagining, conceiving mind'"; see Hill, *Experience of Defeat*, p. 124.

Satan's situation, sailing on a vast sea of aggressively facile mediations, engaged in perpetual and pointless war irreconcilable, is our situation under the hegemonic dispensation of capitalism fully matured. So also is Adam's and Eve's situation at the end of Book IX still our situation. In our schools and workplaces, we remain entangled in a vain contest that appears to have no end between an ambiguous and uncertain autonomy and an equally ambiguous and uncertain authority. By this time, nothing could be more obvious than that the Puritan flight to what Cotton Mather called, in the opening sentence of his *Magnalia,* "the *American Strand*" was in fact not so much an escape from "the Depravations of *Europe*" as a journey into specifically Puritan forms and modes of depravation. In the remainder of this book, we will see just how remarkably accurate and abidingly useful is Milton's prophetic tracing of our protracted and continuing fall.

PART TWO

Uneasy Within: The Nature

of Puritan Hierarchy

And if it should happen that a Brother should speak contrary to the Motion made [by the minister at a church meeting] silence is required and the poor Slave shuts up his Mouth and down he sits, uneasy within.

Ebenezer Frothingham, The Key to Unlock the Door (1767)

Among unequals what society
Can sort, what harmony or true delight?
Which must be mutual, in proportion due
Given and received; but in disparity
The one intense, the other still remiss
Cannot well suit with either, but soon prove
Tedious alike.

Paradise Lost, VIII, 383–89

Chapter 4

Order and Enthusiasm
in New England, 1630–1780

The great pioneer of twentieth-century New England studies, Perry Miller, acknowledged in a general way the existence of those same Puritan polarities—elitism and egalitarianism, restraint and liberation, order and enthusiasm—which Christopher Hill has seen at work in the mid-seventeenth-century English Revolution and which I have shown are both analyzed and synthesized in *Paradise Lost*:

> There was in Puritanism a piety, a religious passion, the sense of an inward communication and of the divine symbolism of nature. . . . But in Puritanism there was also another side, an ideal of social conformity, of law and order, of regulation and control. At the core of the theology there was an indestructible element that was mystical, and a feeling for the universe which was almost pantheistic; but there was also a social code demanding obedience to external law, a code to which good people voluntarily conformed and to which bad people should be made to conform. It aimed at propriety and decency, the virtues of middle-class respectability, self-control, thrift, and dignity, at a discipline of the emotions.[1]

Miller seemed to grasp the contradictory nature of Puritanism, yet such an understanding played a curiously minor part in his examination of the Puritanism that actually took root in New England. He justified the rhetorical structure of his major work with the claim that "the first three generations in New England paid almost unbroken

---

[1]Perry Miller, *Errand into the Wilderness* (Cambridge, Mass.: Harvard University Press, 1956), p. 192.

allegiance to a unified body of thought . . . individual differences among particular writers or theorists were merely minor variations within a general frame." If early New England manifested no intellectual change or development, then in effect it had no intellectual history. Therefore, the first volume of *The New England Mind* does not tell a story. Instead, it proceeds topically, analyzing a group of established doctrines, commonplaces, and themes. It takes us on a guided tour of an intellectual stately home, describing and displaying the design and furnishings of the various chambers that together make up that unified body of thought to which, Miller believed, the first three generations in New England paid almost unbroken allegiance. Miller's work thus proceeds from a gesture of masterly circularity, as axiomatic assumption of static intellectual order generates a well-ordered—indeed a majestic—rhetorical structure, which in turn, by its very air of authoritative stability, validates the assumption of authoritative stability upon which it is itself based. The massive, unitary New England mind sits stable and secure through one dense and lengthy volume and stirs into a motion that might best be called glacial through a second volume that is just as dense and just as lengthy. As it spans and dominates an entire century and survives the transition from colony to province with minimal perturbation, the New England mind is made to seem even more august and imposing by Miller's decision to consign the rhetorical minutiae attendant upon historical documentation to the oblivion of the Harvard College Library.[2]

Miller's retreat from his own awareness of Puritan contradictions is substantive as well as rhetorical. In the quotation above, it is an opposition between reason itself and emotion itself that he discerns in Puritanism, not one between two sets of ideas, each of which devised its own methods of adjudicating the relations between reason and emotion. Nor is this a mere quirk of this particular passage. Miller's entire first volume is based on the premise that the Founding Fathers of New England were the seventeenth-century spokesmen for rational control and order, as against the unchecked Augustinian piety that led the enthusiasts of the Civil War era into "an attack upon all human reason and secular learning." Each of the key elements in New England scholasticism—faculty psychology, Ramist logic and rhetoric, the Federal theology—stood as a rational bulwark against the threat of an irrational pietism. In Miller's account, all rationality, and therefore all possibility of a coherent view of the world, is preempted

---

[2]Perry Miller, *The New England Mind: The Seventeenth Century* (New York: Macmillan, 1939), pp. vii, ix.

by the ruling elite, who would thus not have been displeased by such an acceptance of their own universalized presentation of themselves. Dissenters are deemed to be committed not to alternative Puritan ideas, but only to Puritan emotions, which, being inherently unstable and transitory, must fight against overwhelming odds in any struggle with a thought-out, fully articulated world view. Miller's conclusion that "the colonists thenceforward were progressively more swayed by factors in the intellectual heritage than by the hunger of the spirit" follows ineluctably not from the historical evidence, but rather from the antienthusiastic prejudices he uncritically absorbs from the hegemonic spokesmen he is writing about. Since the changes undergone by the intellectual heritage could not have been the result of the initiatives of especially pietistic Puritans—who were by definition devoid of ideas—those changes amounted not to an unfolding of Puritanism in all its dialectical complexity, but rather to the gradual ebbing away of Puritanism altogether and its replacement by such things as a nascent spirit of capitalism, a general adaptation to the environment of the New World, and a slow stealing in of the Augustan Age of Reason. We shall return to the question of whether Puritan enthusiasm and radicalism constituted a coherent ideology, comprised of "rational" or intellectual components, as well as emotional ones.[3]

Edmund S. Morgan, probably Miller's single most distinguished student, sometimes echoed his teacher in speaking of Puritanism as though such terms as "order," "uniformity," "hierarchy," and "subordination" could adequately communicate its sum and substance: "Sin was a violation of order, grace a restoration of order. All the main tenets of Christian religion could be stated in terms of this concept, and the Puritans so stated them again and again. . . . Subordination was indeed the very soul of order, and the Almighty as a God of order formed his earthly kingdom in a pattern of subordination. . . . The Puritans were no levelers. Social classes and the various offices, orders, and positions of social rank existed for them as part of a divinely ordered plan." Having committed himself to such a one-sided view of Puritanism as a system of traditional social dogmas, Morgan had little choice but to echo Miller in his sense that all social change and devel-

[3]Ibid., pp. 73–84, 286, 295, 302–3, 351, 367, 396; Perry Miller, *The New England Mind: From Colony to Province* (Cambridge, Mass.: Harvard University Press, 1953), pp. 50, 110–13, 269–70, 273, 278–86, 397, 428–29, 435–36, 460. For related criticisms of Miller's assumptions concerning intellectual consensus in Colonial New England, see Philip F. Gura, *A Glimpse of Sion's Glory: Puritan Radicalism in New England, 1620–1660* (Middletown, Conn.: Wesleyan University Press, 1984), pp. 5–6.

opment in New England was development away from Puritanism and into something entirely new. When New Englanders grew "prosperous and comfortable," above all when they allowed environmental contingencies to divert them into "tribalism," then "Puritanism no longer deserved its name."[4]

The study from which these quotations are drawn was one of the first systematic attempts to relate New England ideology to New England institutions and customs. Another influential practitioner of New England social history is Darrett B. Rutman. In his early work, Rutman seemed to challenge the idea of a one-dimensional Puritan orthodoxy, stating that his investigation of Boston during the first two decades of its existence showed that the town was "made up of ordinary people, neither wholeheartedly humanistic nor frigidly glacial, neither entirely emotional nor entirely rational." He even went so far as to hint at the total dissolution of Puritanism as a historical category: "Indeed, the adjective 'Puritan,' together with arguments surrounding it, have seemed inapplicable to Boston in any meaningful way, the total community being fragmented from almost the very beginning." But Rutman's repudiation of the term "Puritan" has no particular effect upon his actual argument, the main lines of which are essentially the same as those of Miller and Morgan. John Winthrop's founding ideal of unity in stratification, as spelled out in "A Modell of Christian Charitie," is shown to have been immediately and steadily eroded by the abundant economic opportunities of the New World. By the time Winthrop died in 1649, the society of loving hierarchy he had sought to establish had become a world of "individualism and materialism, a Franklinesque morality, a clear distinction between the sacral and secular affairs of men" and associational pluralism—in short, a world of modernism in embryo. The dominant Puritan ideology is thus conceived to have been undermined not by an alternative ideology proceeding from the same premises as itself, but rather by forces that were fundamentally alien to Puritanism and were as yet ideologically ill-defined.[5]

Others who wrote in the 1960s and 1970s about early New England society basically agreed with Rutman, who, as we have seen, was himself in essential agreement with Perry Miller. Historians differed only in their estimates of exactly when it was that monolithic, conservative

---

[4]Edmund S. Morgan, *The Puritan Family: Religion and Domestic Relations in Seventeenth-Century New England* (New York: Harper Torchbooks, 1966; orig. 1944), pp. 15, 17–18, 186.

[5]Darrett B. Rutman, *Winthrop's Boston: Portrait of a Puritan Town* (Chapel Hill: University of North Carolina Press, 1965), pp. viii–ix, 9–10, 21, 278.

Puritanism began to be subverted by modernism. Richard L. Bushman found that the Puritan social order existing in Connecticut in 1690 was one of surveillance and control, hierarchy and subordination. This society changed "from Puritan to Yankee" in the course of the eighteenth century as a result of economic, geographic, and psychological factors external to Puritan ideology. John Demos sketched the institutions and values that made for authority, discipline, and repression in seventeenth-century Plymouth, and the almost immediate beginnings of the processes of economic exploitation and geographic dispersion "whereby the community left behind the ideals of the first settlers." Philip J. Greven, Jr., inferred from his study of the probate records of one village, Andover, that unlike Boston, "with its commerce and its fairly disparate population, the small rural agricultural towns like Andover probably proved to be excellent places in which to realize the goals of order, hierarchy, and the closely-knit community." It was not until the mid-eighteenth century that conservative ideals and realities began to be significantly displaced in such towns by economic and geographic mobility. Kenneth A. Lockridge came to similar conclusions about another such town, Dedham. Dedham established itself as "a holy covenanted corporation mixing mutuality with hierarchy and Christian love with exclusiveness." But by the early eighteenth century, this Puritan utopia had come to be beset by individualistic farming, geographic attenuation, and sectional disputes, all of which were bringing New England "out of the Puritan matrix" and into modern pluralism. Finally, Timothy H. Breen and Stephen Foster argued that "the Puritans' greatest achievement" was the social cohesion they maintained in New England through most of the seventeenth century. The society remained basically unified under a Puritan ideology from which egalitarian elements had been removed once the rule of king and bishops had also been removed. This Puritan consensus lasted until the uprisings against the Andros regime in the 1680s, after which time covenant ideals gave way to a tendency to define "the common good in narrow, personal terms."[6]

[6]Richard L. Bushman, *From Puritan to Yankee: Character and the Social Order in Connecticut, 1690–1765* (Cambridge, Mass.: Harvard University Press, 1967), pp. 3–22, 53–61, 108–17, 135–42, 160–61; John Demos, *A Little Commonwealth: Family Life in Plymouth Colony* (New York: Oxford University Press, 1970), pp. 6–12; Philip J. Greven, Jr., *Four Generations: Population, Land, and Family in Colonial Andover, Massachusetts* (Ithaca, N.Y.: Cornell University Press, 1970), pp. 270–71, 277–82; Kenneth A. Lockridge, *A New England Town—the First Hundred Years: Dedham, Massachusetts, 1636–1736* (New York: Norton, 1970), pp. 18, 80–83, 100, 117–18, 170–71; Timothy H. Breen and Stephen Foster, "The Puritans' Greatest Achievement: A Study of Social Cohesion in Seventeenth-Century Massachusetts," *Journal of American History* 60 (1973):10–13, 17–20.

Among the first to cast doubt on the view that New England was throughout the seventeenth and eighteenth centuries a land of conservative ideological consensus was David D. Hall, writing in 1972. In presenting the English background to the role played by the clergy in seventeenth-century New England, Hall recognized that enthusiasm and radicalism were constant possibilities and presences within the Puritan movement itself. Thus, the radical Elizabethan Separatist Henry Barrow is important not for his own sake so much as for the way in which his views reveal "the strains that threatened every Puritan's allegiance" to a moderate Calvinist position on matters of ecclesiology. Similarly, when John Smith, one of the leaders of those Separatists who took refuge in the Netherlands in the early seventeenth century, came to stress the rights of the laity to preach and to administer the sacraments, this "exposed certain tendencies to which every Puritan was subject." In Hall's view, the sixteenth-century Presbyterian spokesman Walter Travers was certainly not the last conservative Puritan to confront a fundamental Puritan dilemma: "Radical laymen like Barrow were already complaining that the presbyterians did not go far enough in giving power to the people, and it was such pressure from the left, fueled by the rhetoric of the presbyterians themselves . . . that Travers was forced to recognize."[7]

During the past ten years, other historians have joined Hall in his realization that the Puritan ideology that established itself as predominant in New England contained within itself the seeds of sharp ideological conflict. Paul R. Lucas has found that seventeenth-century Connecticut was not the society of rigidly enforced uniformity Richard L. Bushman had discerned. Throughout the colony, churches and communities were embroiled in power struggles between clergy and laity almost continuously from the 1630s to the 1720s. In two recent articles, Stephen Foster has shown that "religious controversy in early New England . . . was the consequence of ambiguities in the Puritan movement in England on the eve of the Great Migration of the 1630s." The deeply rooted traditions of lay spiritual initiative—"private . . . conferences for scriptural exegeses and the resolution of personal doubts, private fasts for public misfortunes"—survived the passage across the Atlantic and before long generated confrontations with other Puritan traditions that were just as deeply rooted, those that emphasized the need for "a standing ministerial order" and "a

[7]David D. Hall, *The Faithful Shepherd: A History of the New England Ministry in the Seventeenth Century* (Chapel Hill: University of North Carolina Press, 1972), pp. 6, 28, 32, 39–41.

religious establishment charged with an evangelical and civilizing mission." Philip F. Gura has presented a similar view of Puritanism internally divided, stating that the "Puritan radicalism" he finds played a prominent part in New England between 1620 and 1660 was a manifestation of "the radical potential *within* the established body of Puritan dogma."[8]

Both Foster and Gura stress that the primary and most effective response made by the Puritan order of New England to the disruptive presence of Puritan enthusiasm within it was not to repress, but rather to incorporate and assimilate. By 1660, says Foster, the guardians of the "volatile synthesis of potentially contradictory impulses" which was New England Puritanism had learned how to keep their society and culture in "equilibrium . . . by regular shifts in the balance" between such contradictory impulses. Thereafter, the clergy and others in positions of authority would "rediscover the multiple ways to envelop the people of New England in a pervasive, irresistible set of values." That the hegemonic dispensation of New England was one that sought, for the most part successfully, to tame its enthusiasts and dissenters rather than to silence them altogether is a point I also shall argue. But any regime that relies on "repressive tolerance," as opposed to outright repression, must always run the risk that the strains of dissidence it is tolerating and incorporating will retain a measure of their original viability. For example, an antinomian spiritism could be, as it was, institutionalized and routinized, confined within the ecclesiastical formulas of visible sainthood; but this might also mean, as it did, that at any point it would be possible to adopt a spiritistic posture of leveling skepticism with respect to outward ordinances and authorities and to reappropriate in something like its emergent vigor the conceptual and rhetorical apparatus that spiritism had developed for the articulation of such a posture. What I argue in this chapter is that throughout the Colonial era, a coherent ideology of Puritan radicalism did persist in just such a semiincorporated state. From its planting in 1630 until the American Revolution, New England was inhabited by both Adam and Eve. Adam sought to rule in a manner that would be indulgent and adaptive as well as firm, and Eve

[8]Paul R. Lucas, *Valley of Discord: Church and Society along the Connecticut River, 1636–1725* (Hanover, N.H.: University Press of New England, 1976), passim; Stephen Foster, "New England and the Challenge of Heresy, 1630–1660: The Puritan Crisis in Transatlantic Perspective," *William and Mary Quarterly*, 3d ser., 38 (1981):626–28; "English Puritanism and the Progress of New England Institutions, 1630–1660," in *Saints and Revolutionaries: Essays on Early American History*, ed. David D. Hall, John M. Murrin, and Thad W. Tate (New York: Norton, 1984), pp. 7–8, 9–11; Gura, *Glimpse of Sion's Glory*, p. 58.

sought to acquiesce and obey without surrendering her ultimate birthright of autonomy. And the result was that Adam and Eve fell to wrangling.[9]

That Puritan radicalism should prove to be particularly durable in New England is hardly a startling proposition, for the entire enterprise of planting New England was essentially a radical, idealistic one. In the sixteenth and early seventeenth centuries, writes David Hall, the English Puritan clergy was "more prophetic than pastoral, more spiritistic than sacramental . . . the starting point for New England history became that portion of the [Puritan clergy] that valued purity the most." In our terms, this was the portion that was most unlikely simply to be horrified by enthusiasm and radicalism. Two of the most prominent emigré ministers, Thomas Hooker and John Cotton, had affirmed the potentially antinomian proposition that a poor and ignorant person might be spiritually more advanced than a learned and eminent one. Hooker had been castigated by the Presbyterian John Paget for his willingness to hold communion with Separatists and for his belief "that Private men might preach and expound the Scriptures at set times and places where the members of sundry families met together." Hooker was endorsing, although not without a certain degree of apprehension, that tradition of semi-Separatist private meeting or "conventicling" which had become "deeply ingrained in the religious life of the Puritan laity" during the seventy years or so prior to the settlement of New England, and which immediately took root in the new plantation, being within the first decade protected by law in both Massachusetts and Connecticut.[10]

During the first thirty years in Massachusetts, there occurred the two confrontations between Puritan order and Puritan enthusiasm of which anyone with even a casual acquaintance with New England history is aware: the Antinomian Controversy of the late 1630s and the repression of the Quakers in the late 1650s. It is clear from the work of Foster and Gura that neither of these were crises arising suddenly and unexpectedly from a situation otherwise marked by harmony and obedience to those in authority. The Antinomian Con-

[9]Foster, "New England and the Challenge of Heresy," pp. 654–55, 660; "English Puritanism," p. 37; Gura, *Glimpse of Sion's Glory*, pp. 14, 162–68. With the phrase "repressive tolerance," I am of course referring to Herbert Marcuse, "Repressive Tolerance," in Robert Paul Wolff, Barrington Moore, Jr., and Herbert Marcuse, *A Critique of Pure Tolerance* (Boston: Beacon Press, 1969; orig. 1965), pp. 81–123.

[10]Hall, *Faithful Shepherd*, pp. 36, 55, 71; Miller, *Errand into the Wilderness*, p. 46; *Orthodoxy in Massachusetts, 1630–1650: A Genetic Study* (Cambridge, Mass.: Harvard University Press, 1933), p. 110; Foster, "English Puritanism," pp. 7–8, 9.

troversy was only the most dramatic manifestation of an intense, enthusiastic piety that was, in Darrett Rutman's words, "running rampant" through Massachusetts in the 1630s, partly as a result of the fact that as the decade proceeded, those who were arriving from England tended increasingly to be those whom the repressive policies of Archbishop Laud had merely hardened in "their sense of autonomy from clerical control and their already well-developed conceit of themselves as the saving remnant in a wicked and persecuting world."

In the Boston church, the general coming together in New England of a pietistic clergy with an emboldened laity took the specific form of a coming together of the Reverend John Cotton's homiletic emphasis on the special powers and prerogatives of the regenerate with the vigorous lay conventicling organized and led by Anne Hutchinson, who had been Cotton's parishioner back in Boston, Lincolnshire, as well as now in Boston, Massachusetts. No doubt to Cotton's extreme chagrin, the Hutchinsonians claimed only to be practicing what Cotton had preached when their antinomian scorn for outward regulation and restraint led them to refuse to behave with deference and restraint in the presence of Boston's social and intellectual leaders, such as John Winthrop and Cotton's clerical colleague John Wilson. As one minister later recalled, "After our Sermons were ended at our publike lectures, you might have seen halfe a dozen Pistols discharged at the face of the Preacher, (I meane) so many objections made by the opinionists [i.e., the Hutchinsonians] in the open Assembly against our doctrine delivered, if it suited not their fancies." One opinionist was heard to aver that Hutchinson herself "preaches better Gospell then any of your black-coates that have been at the Ninniversity. For my part . . . I had rather hear such a one that speakes from the meere motion of the spirit, without any study at all, then any of your learned Scollers, although they may be fuller of Scripture." The Antinomian Controversy offers an almost perfect illustration of what would become the perpetual New England ideological situation: a learned and eloquent clergyman, John Cotton, who in the next decade would become one of the chief systematizers of New England orthodoxy on every level, from densely argued treatises down to catechisms, was in the meantime in great part responsible for this first sharp intrusion into New England of that form of popular intellection which those whom it threatened always called heresy and which was invariably accompanied by a determined anticlericalism.[11]

---

[11]Rutman, *Winthrop's Boston*, pp. 114, 119–20; Foster, "English Puritanism," pp. 8, 14; Emery Battis, *Saints and Sectaries: Anne Hutchinson and the Antinomian Controversy in*

The Antinomian Controversy, which had seemed to throw the church and town of Boston into a condition approaching anarchy, combined with the accusations made by the English Presbyterian clergy during the 1640s that the "New England way" had given far too much encouragement to the insubordination and heresy of English revolutionary Independents and sectarians, led those in authority in Massachusetts to see the necessity of developing more effective forms of ecclesiastical and social discipline. In 1644 and again in 1646, the General Court decreed the banishment of Baptists, and a series of ecclesiastical synods culminated in the promulgation in 1648 of the Cambridge Platform. This was a document designed to increase the power of the clergy and of translocal structures of authority as against the obstreperous laity and particular churches, by such provisions as granting to the minister an ultimate veto power over the decisions of the congregation, and insisting that it was "an ordinance of God" for each church to be subjected, in however ill-defined a way, to just such synods as the one that had debated and composed the platform.[12]

Such measures did not result, however, in the cessation of excessively assertive and wayward lay thought and action. If Thomas Painter, a laborer from the town of Hingham, refused in 1644, prior to the enactment of legislation against anabaptism, to relinquish under punishment his opinion that infant baptism was "antichristian," William Witter of Swampscott was equally adamant in 1645 and 1646, after such legislation was in force. Witter was summoned before a grand jury in Salem after he had declared "that they who stayed whiles a child is baptized do worship the divell . . . take the name of the Father, Sonne, & Holy Gost in vayne, [and] breake the Sabaoth." He remained obstinate in the face of all attempts to reclaim him. To the grand jury he "justifyed the former speech," and subsequently he declined to confess and change his views before either the Lynn church, to which he belonged, or the General Court. Witter's tenacious adherence to the conclusion he had reached that infant baptism lacked scriptural validation was revealed again in 1651, when he opened his home to the itinerant Baptist exhorters John Clarke, Obadiah Holmes, and John Crandall.[13]

the Massachusetts Bay Colony (Chapel Hill: University of North Carolina Press, 1962), pp. 102–3; Gura, Glimpse of Sion's Glory, pp. 69, 176–77.

[12]Foster, "English Puritanism," pp. 27–29; Records of the Governor and Company of the Massachusetts Bay in New England, ed. Nathaniel B. Shurtleff, 5 vols. (Boston, 1853–54), 2:85, 149 (hereafter Mass. Recs.); Rutman, Winthrop's Boston, p. 267.

[13]Winthrop's Journal "History of New England," 1630–1649, ed. James Kendall Hosmer, 2 vols. (New York: Scribner's, 1908), 2:177; Mass. Recs., 3:67–68; William G. McLoughlin, New England Dissent, 1630–1833: The Baptists and the Separation of Church and State, 2 vols. (Cambridge, Mass.: Harvard University Press, 1971), pp. 19–21.

Meanwhile, some who were more highly placed in embryonic New England society had also come to heterodox theological and ecclesiastical conclusions. In 1644 the wife of Theophilus Eaton, the governor of New Haven Colony, "fell under Baptist influence and doubted the validity of her own infant Baptism," as a result of which she suffered "humiliation at the hands of the New Haven church." Mrs. Eaton's daughter was married to Edward Hopkins, the sometime governor of Connecticut Colony, and the daughter proved to be even more susceptible than the mother to the deviance that seemed always to lurk in the vicinity of Protestant reasoning. She was, Winthrop tells us, "a godly young woman, and of special parts," but as of 1645 she had "fallen into a sad infirmity, the loss of her understanding and reason, which had been growing upon her divers years, by occasion of her giving herself wholly to reading and writing, and had written many books." Mrs. Hopkins was brought by her husband to Boston and left with her merchant brother, David Yale, "to try what means might be had here for her. But no help could be had." Winthrop does not reveal what Yale did to aid his sister in her affliction, but we may doubt that he looked upon it, as Winthrop did, as a simple case of a woman's meddling "in such things as are proper to men, whose minds are stronger, etc." Yale took a relatively broad-minded view of the results of a person giving herself wholly to reading and writing. He adhered to that faction in the Boston mercantile community which had petitioned for the abolition of the anti-Baptist law of 1644 and generally believed that Massachusetts ought to implement the ideas of its Independent brethren in England and set "all opinion free."[14]

The Cambridge Platform was no more effectual a device than the anti-Baptist laws in establishing orthodoxy on a more secure foundation. In such far from negligible quarters as the Boston church (persisting in its Hutchinsonian tradition of lay autonomy and assertiveness) and the lower house of the General Court, objections were raised that the entire enterprise of calling a synod and having it draw up an authoritative codification of doctrine and discipline amounted to a crypto-presbyterian infringement on congregational liberty. When the platform was submitted to the Boston church for ratification in 1649, some of the brethren sarcastically asked whether ministers would ever exercise the veto power the platform would grant to them so as to "consent to their own casting out." And two years later,

[14]Robert Emmet Wall, Jr., *Massachusetts Bay: The Crucial Decade, 1640–1650* (New Haven, Conn.: Yale University Press, 1972), p. 238; *Winthrop's Journal*, 2:225; Rutman, *Winthrop's Boston*, pp. 253–55. David Yale and his sister were the uncle and aunt of Elihu Yale, through whom the family name was in the next century bestowed on Yale College.

fourteen of the forty deputies in the lower house refused to vote in favor of endorsing the platform. According to David Hall, they were continuing to articulate "suspicions of the ministry among the population at large." Edward Johnson set about a few years later to admonish the various opponents of the Cambridge Platform, but he only succeeded in testifying to the stubborn persistence in New England of a fundamental Protestant populism:

> Some sorts of persons have been much opposite to this Synod, first those that are so inured with the broad beaten path of liberty, that they fear to be confined in the straight and narrow path of truth; the second are such as have their wills wedded to some singular rare conceited opinion, for which they have been admired of many, and now they fear their gain will be gone, if this spirit be cast out; the third and last sort are more honest then the two former, and only scared with their big words, who tell them of the Popish and Prelatical Synods, what a deal of trash and cannon Laws they have brought in, and that if they will fall to receiving books once, they shall have more and more thrust upon them: As also if any shall say its only to declare the doctrine and discipline the churches in N. E. hold, its enough, quoth they, that our faith concerning these things is contained in the Bible, and this is all the accompt we need to give to any.

Here is reluctant contemporary confirmation of Stephen Foster's judgment that the Cambridge Platform basically articulated a stalemate between the imposition of order from above and the refusal from below to allow local and lay dignities to be eroded. The laxity of tolerationists and the singularity of cranks and crackpots both were evidently gaining a hearing among the "more honest" Protestant folk, by the rhetorical means of an antiauthoritarian biblicism to which such folk would find it virtually impossible not to subscribe, and to which the promulgators of the platform had themselves subscribed during the first years of plantation.[15]

As Foster notes, the attack on the Quakers in the late 1650s was only the most stringent and vehement of the responses to dissent the Massachusetts authorities felt called upon to make during that decade. Fear of the seemingly limitless proliferation of heresy under the Crom-

---

[15]Rutman, *Winthrop's Boston*, pp. 263–64; Hall, *Faithful Shepherd*, pp. 116, 129; *Mass. Recs.*, 3:240; *Johnson's Wonder-Working Providence, 1628–1651*, ed. J. Franklin Jameson (New York: Scribner's, 1910), p. 243; Foster, "English Puritanism," pp. 29–30. Foster argues that the opposition to the platform was primarily a manifestation of localism, rather than of anticlericalism. But it is doubtful that this is a particularly meaningful distinction, since in practice it would be the clergy who under the platform would be the primary enforcers of supralocal authority.

wellian regime in England prompted such actions as, in 1652, the General Court's tightening up of a 1646 statute against denying the Scripture to be the revealed Word of God; in 1654, its urging the Harvard overseers and all town selectmen "not to admitt or suffer any such to be contynued in the . . . colledge or schooles [as teachers] that have manifested themselves unsound in the fayth, or scandelous in their lives"; and in the same year, its prohibiting anyone from sitting as one of its own members who was "unsound in judgment concerninge the mayne poynts of Christian religion as they have bin held forth & acknowledged by the generallitie of the Protestant orthodox writers."[16]

The resolution concerning schoolmasters and Harvard tutors was occasioned by the falling into anabaptism of the president of Harvard himself, Henry Dunster. Dunster articulated those tendencies in Protestantism which contained great potential for social disruption when he argued in a 1654 public debate that a parent could never serve as an acceptable guarantor of the converted state of a baptized infant. "There is no further person but Christ for us to stand in," Dunster insisted. The source of a person's legitimacy was thus, in Dunster's view, not the orderly processes of natural birth and generational succession, but rather the enthusiastic ones of spiritual rebirth and drastic reorientation. A man who had come to such conclusions was hardly fit to preside over an institution whose very essence and mission was precisely that of the orderly transmission of values from generation to generation. Dunster was forced to resign, but his successor, Charles Chauncy, was also widely believed to be a "crypto-Baptist" and was hired only on condition that he maintain silence on all questions relating to baptismal practices.

Dunster and Chauncy were not the only clerical figures of the 1650s whose orthodoxy was precarious. Marmaduke Matthews, the candidate whom the church of Malden wished to call and ordain as its minister at the beginning of the decade, maintained the essentials of antinomianism: that "the gospel of grace and the sacred scriptures are a false foundation of faith to build our justification upon," and that "for my part I do reprove no sin in persons under the gospel, but unbelief, because all sins are included in unbelief." The opposite sort of deviance, the semi-Arminian sort, was set forth in 1650 by a prominent layman, Springfield fur merchant William Pynchon, in a book titled *The Meritorious Price of our Redemption*. This work was considered

---

[16]Foster, "English Puritanism," pp. 30–32, 35; *Mass. Recs.*, 2:176–80; 3:259–60, 343–44, 357.

sufficiently "false, eronyous, & hereticall" to prompt the General Court to order that it be "burned in the market place, at Boston," to call Pynchon in for examination, and to commission the Reverend John Norton of Ipswich to write a treatise in refutation. However, the deputies of the lower house did not concur in these measures against Pynchon, just as many of them dissented from the disciplining of Marmaduke Matthews and the Malden church, and just as many of them also refused, as we have seen, to approve the Cambridge Platform. Even when we consider only those in positions of authority and trust in New England at this time, we find ideological differentiation and conflict, rather than homogeneity.[17]

The early part of the 1650s yields evidence of the persistence of such differentiation and conflict on a more popular level as well. When the General Court sought in 1653 to regulate lay preaching, "a well-established Puritan practice," widespread objections forced it to repeal the law later in the year. A closely related and equally well-established Puritan practice, that of "private meetinge and prophesying," was upheld that year by one John Baker in a manner that caused enough "hindrance & disturbance of publicke assembling" to require censure and punishment by the court. Baker had uttered "abusiue & opprobrious speeches . . . against the minister & ministery," but a more colorful illustration of the way in which private meeting and prophesying might easily gravitate toward anticlericalism had been provided the year before, in 1652, by a Mrs. Holgrave. She had been presented at the Essex County Court for stating "that if it were not for the Law she would never come to the meeting, the Teacher was soe dead." Having the courage of her convictions, Mrs. Holgrave "persuaded Gudwife Vincent to come to her house on the Sabbath daye and reade good bookes, affirming that the Teacher was fitter to be a Ladye's chamberman than to be in the pulpit." David Hall states that there were numerous cases of such lack of respect for the clergy and others in authority during these years.[18]

The extreme measures taken against the Quakers in the late 1650s should therefore be understood as an outburst of frustration at this history of continuous failure to achieve ideological stability. Everything that had proved to be troublesome for three decades seemed to be gathered together into the claim of this "cursed sect . . . to be im-

---

[17]McLoughlin, *New England Dissent*, p. 21; Gura, *Glimpse of Sion's Glory*, pp. 67, 84, 121; Samuel Eliot Morison, *Harvard College in the Seventeenth Century*, 2 vols. (Cambridge, Mass.: Harvard University Press, 1936), pp. 322–23; *Mass. Recs.*, 3:215–16; 4, pt. 1:42–43; Hall, *Faithful Shepherd*, p. 129n.

[18]Foster, "English Puritanism," p. 35; *Mass. Recs.*, 3:317, 334; Gura, *Glimpse of Sion's Glory*, p. 70; Hall, *Faithful Shepherd*, p. 132.

ediatlie sent of God, & infallibly assisted by the Spiritt of God to speake & write blasphemous opinions, despising government & the order of God in the churches & common wealth, speakinge evill of dignities, reproaching & revileing magistrates & ministers." The General Court evidently believed that "diverse of our inhabitants have binn infected & seduced" by this message of comprehensive subversion. Such, at least, was its rationale for repeatedly increasing the severity of its penalties against both the Quakers and those who gave ear to them, from fines in 1656, to whipping, mutilation, and scourging in 1657, and to death in 1658.

The punishment of the Quakers was quite unpopular, which is why it was brought to an end by 1661. The absence of a secure basis of support for it had been revealed even as it had been enacted. It was the lower house of the General Court that once again resisted the imposition of ideological uniformity. The 1658 law stipulating that stubborn adherents to Quakerism be put to death was approved by the deputies by only one vote, and they insisted upon amending the law to provide for trial by jury. Those outside the General Court who were repelled by official rigor no doubt included Boston merchants and others moving toward theological and ecclesiastical indifferentism, but they certainly also included a fair number of people like John Warren. Warren had a long history of intellectual self-determination. He had been prosecuted in England in 1629 for refusing to kneel during the eucharistic ritual. After crossing over to Massachusetts in 1630 and becoming both a major landholder and a selectman in Watertown, he proved to be no less inclined in the New World than he had been in the old to go his own way and get into trouble. Having turned Baptist, he was convicted in 1651 of violating the anti-Baptist law of 1644. But evidently he was as stubborn as most such lay seekers, for in 1653 and again in 1654 he was fined for his frequent absences from public worship. In 1659 he was warned once again about this. By this time, he had begun to fall under suspicion of aiding and abetting the Quakers, and in May 1661 his house was ordered searched for evidence of their offensive presence. It seems that the more the authorities sought to keep the commonwealth free of heresy, the more determined became John Warren and others like him to stand by their essential Protestant and Puritan hostility to what they regarded as an overbearing and infringing upon "the libertie of the countrey, both ecclesiasticall and civill."[19]

---

[19]*Mass Recs.*, 3:415–16; 4, pt. 1:156–57, 308–9, 321, 345–46, 385–90; Foster, "English Puritanism," p. 34; Hall, *Faithful Shepherd*, p. 229; John Putnam Demos, *Entertaining Satan: Witchcraft and the Culture of Early New England* (New York: Oxford University Press, 1982), pp. 113, 439, nn. 88–89.

Those scholars who have recently insisted on the significance of radicalism and heresy for the period prior to 1660 have also declared that it was after 1660 that American Puritanism "entered at last into [an] austere golden age" in which it skillfully disabled dissent by assimilating it.[20] In the respect that the group was moderate and well behaved, not posing any real challenge to the ecclesiastical and social establishment, the founding and survival of a Baptist church in Boston in 1665 constitutes an early instance of such successful assimilation. And we may well view the effective prevention of draconian proceedings against this mildly dissenting church by a coalition of deputies and other prominent citizens as an important component of the apparatus of co-optation. Yet we should also recognize that these defenders of the right of the Baptists to exist were, in part, simply expressing their own ideological affinity with them. A Baptist such as Henry Dunster held that a legitimate church could not be based on ancestral inheritance, that it must instead be a gathering of adults maturely committed to Christ. There was precious little difference between this outlook and what lay behind the fierce opposition to the Halfway Covenant of such people as John Davenport, the founding minister of New Haven, and Anne Hutchinson's son Edward. In their view, the Halfway Covenant amounted to a serious compromising of the spiritistic requirement of visible sainthood for church membership, conferring as it did a certain legitimacy on the children and grandchildren of church members simply by virtue of their being possessed of such regenerate ancestors. There is an elegant ideological consistency in the fact that it was around the same time that Edward Hutchinson both "stood up and turned his back to the congregation" of his Boston First Church, in order to signify his displeasure over the Halfway Covenant, and signed a petition in defense of the Boston Baptists. Nor was this consistency lost on the supporters of the Halfway Covenant, for they accused their opponents of using Baptist arguments.[21]

The peaceable demeanor of the Boston Baptist church did not prevent it from insisting on such fundamental tenets of Protestant radicalism as the denial that "the spirit of God is locked up within the

[20]See above, n. 9.
[21]McLoughlin, *New England Dissent*, pp. 45–46, 50, 71–73; Hall, *Faithful Shepherd*, pp. 230, 236; E. Brooks Holifield, *The Covenant Sealed: The Development of Puritan Sacramental Theology in Old and New England, 1570–1720* (New Haven, Conn.: Yale University Press, 1974), pp. 179, 182. For the Halfway Covenant, see Miller, *From Colony to Province*, pp. 89–104; Edmund S. Morgan, *Visible Saints: The History of a Puritan Idea* (New York: New York University Press, 1963), pp. 125–36; and Robert G. Pope, *The Halfway Covenant: Church Membership in Puritan New England* (Princeton, N.J.: Princeton University Press, 1969).

narrow limits of Colledge-Learning." Similarly, the partial toleration the Quakers managed to win in Plymouth Colony did not make them forgetful of such a perennial radical theme, sounded in a 1678 petition demanding relief from religious taxation, as that "ministers should get their living as other men." When they felt they were being imposed upon, these less flamboyant dissenters were just as prepared as their predecessors before 1660 had been to make use of the utterly traditional radical argument that a Protestant establishment was virtually a contradiction in terms. John Pierce of Woburn became convinced that his infant baptism had been invalid, and he therefore proceeded to have himself rebaptized. After being told by a council of ministers that he would be punished by being allowed to attend neither the Woburn parish church nor the Boston Baptist church, Pierce referred the General Court in a 1679 petition to Matthew 28:18, where the apostles are commissioned to teach all nations in the name of Christ, to whom "all power is given . . . both in heaven & on Earth . . . therefore not as the pope says, all power is in my hands and such as I appoint goe and preach and such as will not hear you lett fire & fagott be there [their] portion."[22]

Most New Englanders were not Baptists or Quakers, of course.[23] Yet the late seventeenth century was perceived by many contemporaries as a time of "contention," and a large proportion of the quarrels of the period arose from that chronic mistrust between clergy and laity which seemed unavoidable within a militantly Protestant culture. Paul Lucas found evidence of ecclesiastical power struggles between 1650 and 1675 in nine out of ten Connecticut towns, and also in many towns in both the territory of the former New Haven Colony and the portion of the Connecticut River Valley that was in Massachusetts. David Hall noted similar disputes in Salem and Newbury in eastern Massachusetts. The most protracted and bitter of these struggles took place in Hartford, where the very formula drawn up to effect a compromise reveals the intractability of the contradiction between the orderly imperative of clerical authority and the enthusiastic one of lay intellectual autonomy: "Proposition: The Church of Christ at Hartford doe bynde themselves in the presence of God to Samuel Stone their teacher, to submit to every doctrine which he shall propound to them, grounded upon the sacred Scriptures, and confirmed by such reasons from the word of God, that noe man is able to gainsay. And Samuel

---

[22]McLoughlin, *New England Dissent*, pp. 84–89, 167.
[23]Ibid., p. 121, estimates that in 1735 probably no more than 4 percent of the population of New England dissented from the Standing Order.

Stone byndes himself to attend any reason which shall be presented to him by any brother of the church or any man who shall offer himselfe to dispute with him, and thearby bring any of his doctrine in publique tryall."

But some man was always able to gainsay the doctrines and reasons propounded to him by his minister, both in Hartford (the controversy there was not settled by this attempted compromise) and elsewhere. John Woodbridge wrote to Richard Baxter that in the 1660s New England congregations were filled with people not in the least prepared to submit to their intellectual superiors, who were, indeed, "grown so rude, Insolent, and Coltish (Independency has so fatted them) that the Ministers that have most Authority have not enough to stamp a Judgment and sentence of good metal to make it current with them." In 1684 Daniel Denison, a layman sympathetic to the clerical point of view, reported as being widely entertained among his lay brethren the propositions that a majority vote of the congregation "makes a Church act though the Elders consent not," and that "except in Preaching and Administration of the Sacraments, calling of and Moderating in Church Meetings," ministers "have no more authority, than any particular Brother." Like Woodbridge, Denison pointed to the tradition of Puritan radicalism such views were perpetuating when he summed them up under the name "Independency."[24]

The jeremiads that the clergy of the second and third generations grew so fond of delivering are thus to be understood within this context of ecclesiastical contention and unyielding Independency. When the ministers preached again and again that New England had gone into near irrevocable decline because of the worldliness of its people, they were attempting to moralize and universalize their own position and perspective and banish the "rude, Insolent, and Coltish" laity to the margins of social legitimacy. But although this was indeed an attempt on the part of the clergy "to envelop the people of New England in a pervasive . . . set of values," it was nevertheless a strategy that was less than "irresistible." The tradition of Independency continued to be capable of setting forth a well-defined alternative explanation for declension, and it was once again the deputies of the lower house of the Massachusetts General Court who functioned as the spokesmen for this more radical point of view. Drawn into the controversy surrounding the formation of the Boston Third Church—

---

[24]Lucas, *Valley of Discord*, pp. 46–47, 227 (chap. 2, n. 1); Hall, *Faithful Shepherd*, pp. 208, 212–14. In his quotation from the Hartford Controversy document, Lucas misprints the phrase "from the word of God" as "from the work of God."

which was itself a consequence of the debate over the Halfway Covenant—the deputies issued a report in 1670 blaming declension on a clerical "invasion of the rights, liberties, and privileges of churches; an usurpation of an lordly, prelatical power over God's heritage; a subversion of gospel order . . . these are the leaven, the corrupting gangrene . . . which hath provoked the divine wrath, and doth further threaten destruction."[25]

The first quarter of the eighteenth century is probably the period that comes closest to conforming to the consensual account of Colonial New England. Yet a good deal of evidence suggests that even at this time Protestant radicalism had not been entirely absorbed into a "glacial age" of hegemonic concord. Efforts to establish a system of translocal discipline and control that would be more effective than the Cambridge Platform were successfully resisted in Massachusetts by such vindicators of traditional congregational autonomy as the Reverend John Wise of Ipswich. Such a system, the Saybrook Platform, was adopted in Connecticut in 1708, but most Connecticut churches did not participate in it. The new minister at Canterbury was informed by one of his flock in 1723 that if he was ever misled by the platform into deviating from a respect for lay prerogatives and congregational autonomy, he would immediately stand exposed as a "Papish Jesuit." The pastor in East Windsor, Timothy Edwards (father of Jonathan), was one of the architects of the Saybrook Platform, but his own church nevertheless refused to ratify it. In the course of another dispute between Edwards and his congregation, Roger Wolcott, a leading lay spokesman and eventually the governor of the colony, wrote a manuscript treatise in which he echoed the Massachusetts deputies of sixty years before in alleging that the clericalism enshrined in the platform was what was responsible for a declension in Connecticut, "that so awfully Threaten[s] the Subversion of our church and Reducing us back into bondage." Samuel Johnson, later the first president of King's College (i.e., Columbia), certainly believed that Protestant radicalism had remained all too viable in Connecticut during the early eighteenth-century years when he was coming to maturity. He reports in his autobiography that what drove him

[25]Miller, *From Colony to Province*, pp. 105–13; Lucas, *Valley of Discord*, pp. 87–103; Foster, "English Puritanism," p. 37; Hall, *Faithful Shepherd*, p. 235. Divine retribution for sin was also a rhetorical staple in England at this time and was stood on its head by opponents of the Restoration ecclesiastical settlement just as it was by the Massachusetts deputies; see *CPW*, VIII, 439, and n. 91. According to its historian, New England's "sacramental renaissance" of the late seventeenth and early eighteenth centuries was also, like the jeremiad, a form of clerical resistance to lay pietism; see Holifield, *Covenant Sealed*, pp. 194, 226.

into the Church of England was the predominance in the circles in which he moved of "enthusiasm . . . the extemporary way" of praying and prophesying, and "the independent or congregational form of church government, in which every brother has a hand."[26]

This is not the place to enter into a detailed account of that revival of spiritism and enthusiasm known as the Great Awakening, which began in the 1720s and 1730s, emerged most fully in the 1740s, and eventually played, some historians have maintained, a significant part in the American Revolution. The major portion of the next two chapters is devoted to the psychosocial ramifications of the Great Awakening in one church and community. But it is necessary to stress at this point that since the ideology of congregational liberty and, to a lesser extent, of "extemporary" spirituality did endure between 1660 and 1730, the Great Awakening should not, any more than should the Antinomian Controversy or the 1650s furor over the Quakers, be viewed as an abrupt and surprising departure from years of deference and ideological concord. The sorts of radical emphases that in the mid-seventeenth century in old England had been associated with revolution, and at the same time in New England had caused considerable commotion, had never been driven so far underground as not to be readily available as ideological and cultural options. Naturally, therefore, people recalled the earlier days of more distinct spiritual enthusiasm and ecclesiastical insurgency when they saw what was happening all around them in the 1740s and after. A major rhetorical strategy of those such as Charles Chauncy who were hostile to the Awakening was to liken its New Light proponents to seventeenth-century Quakers and Hutchinsonians. Jonathan Edwards, the most illustrious of those proponents, certainly did not imagine that Quakerism and Hutchinsonian antinomianism constituted his own spiritual and ideological heritage, yet he was definitely linking the Awakening to the overall revolutionary context in which such enthusiasms had flourished when he declared that George Whitefield, whose evangelizing had been the catalyst of the revival, was possessed of the same "*zeal and resolution*" as had brought about the "great things that *Oliver Cromwell* did."[27]

[26]Miller, *From Colony to Province*, p. 291; Lucas, *Valley of Discord*, pp. 191–93; Bushman, *From Puritan to Yankee*, pp. 152, 153–55; *Samuel Johnson, President of King's College: His Career and Writings*, ed. Herbert and Carol Schneider, 4 vols. (New York: Columbia University Press, 1929), 1:10–11, 11–12.

[27]Edwin Scott Gaustad, *The Great Awakening in New England* (New York: Harper, 1957), p. 93; Alan Heimert, *Religion and the American Mind from the Great Awakening to the Revolution* (Cambridge, Mass.: Harvard University Press, 1966), p. 58. For the relations between the Great Awakening and the American Revolution, see Heimert, passim; Bushman, *From Puritan to Yankee*, pp. 235–88; and Philip J. Greven, Jr., *The Protestant*

Neither Chauncy nor Edwards was mistaken about the affinities between the Great Awakening and the transatlantic "Oliverian days" of the mid-seventeenth century. In both periods the basic Protestant principle of "the natural right of every Man to enquire and judge for himself in matters of Religion & that without Check or Control from any Man" was urged with sufficient insistence and intensity to cause a great deal of ecclesiastical and social disruption. A group in Newbury, Massachusetts, formulated the principle in these words in 1746, in the course of expressing its dissatisfaction with its pastor and petitioning to be allowed to separate from him and form a new church. As it had in the previous century, that is, the revival of "the natural right of every Man to enquire and judge for himself in matters of Religion" led straight to the revival of various forms of gathered and Separatist ecclesiology, ranging from this demand of the Newbury brethren for the carving out of a new parish, to Jonathan Edwards's renewed insistence in Northampton upon visible sainthood (which led to his dismissal), to the emergence of groups willing to name themselves Separatists, to the strengthening of such long-established dissenting groups as the Baptists. During the Revolutionary War, as during the English Civil Wars, there was an even greater proliferation of separatism and sectarianism. Just as Independency had proved, to its annoyance, to be the mother of Ranterism, Quakerism, and Muggletonianism, so separating Congregationalism and Baptism now reluctantly gave birth to Free Will Baptism, Sandemanianism, Universalism, and Shakerism.[28]

Some of these New Light groups flirted with a sense of total assurance of salvation and consequent total liberation from sin that was reminiscent of both English Ranters and Boston Hutchinsonians. Ebenezer Frothingham, a Connecticut Separatist, was in 1750 convinced that "a Saint of God having Divine Light shining into the Understanding, and the Love of God (or pure Charity, which is the same) ruling in the Soul, is also to know certainly that such and such Persons are true Converts, or the Saints of God." Separatist groups in Windham County, Connecticut, confessed formally their belief "that Christ did live on Earth, die and rise again for us in particular . . . so

---

Temperament: Patterns of Child-Rearing, Religious Experience, and the Self in Early America (New York: Knopf, 1977), pp. 336–60; and for the survival of radicalism only as an "underground tradition," see Gura, *Glimpse of Sion's Glory*, pp. 323–28.

[28]Heimert, *Religion and the American Mind*, pp. 92, 510; Ola Elizabeth Winslow, *Meetinghouse Hill* (New York: Macmillan, 1952), pp. 238–39; McLoughlin, *New England Dissent*, pp. 709–10, 717–21. For a detailed analysis of the sectarianism engendered during the period of the Revolutionary War, see Stephen A. Marini, *Radical Sects of Revolutionary New England* (Cambridge, Mass.: Haward University Press, 1982).

humbling us by Gospel Grace has made us Partakers of the Divine Nature, which being added to Christ's taking the Humane Nature makes up the Union between Christ and our Souls." To the established ministers of the county, "this, if any thing, is little short of the Blasphemy of Jacob Bekman [Boehme], our being *godded* with GOD, and *christed* with Christ." It is also, as we have seen, the blasphemy with which Satan tempts Eve when he holds out to her the prospect of becoming "a goddess among gods." Perfectionist groups, claiming to be godded with God and christed with Christ, did spring up in Windham and a number of other New England locales. Their behavior lent some credence to the Old Light leader Charles Chauncy's articulation in 1742 of the traditional accusation that Protestant enthusiasm "has made strong attempts to destroy all property, to make all things common, wives as well as goods."

For an instance of such extreme "ranting practice" involving one of our central characters, we may contemplate the unhappy situation in Grafton, Massachusetts, a town not far from Westborough. Ebenezer Parkman's ministerial colleague in Grafton, Solomon Prentice, had given his wholehearted support to the Awakening, but he received little in the way of recompence for his zeal. In fact, he had to stand by and watch his wife condemn the church to which he, her own husband, ministered as "no Church of Christ." Mrs. Prentice proceeded to become a Separatist, and Parkman felt called upon to warn her in the spring of 1747, during one of his collegial visits, "against Defect in Relative Dutys in the House; and giving occasion to others to suspect criminal Freedoms with the other sex, under the splendid Guise of Spiritual Love and Friendship." Two years later, in 1749, Parkman was called to another neighboring town, Hopkinton, to try to reclaim Nathaniel Smith and his three siblings, "who had fallen into very gross, familistical Errors." Ezra Stiles later provided a description of the group with which Smith was involved. Its leader was one Shadrach Ireland, and according to Stiles, "Rev. Mr. Prentice's Wife of Grafton" was another besides Smith of the "dozen or 15 wild Enthusiasts" who were Ireland's disciples. "She used to lie with Ireland as her spiritual Husband." The group "declared themselves IMMORTALS. . . . Formerly they walked round Hopkinton Meetinghouse sounding with Ramshorns and denouncing its Downfall, in vain." Parkman's pastoral labors with Smith were no more effectual than those with Mrs. Prentice had been. On that day in 1749 he "had some Discourse" with him, "but to very little purpose." No wonder. Like James Nayler, the revolutionary Quaker of the previous century, Smith eventually pushed an antinomian sense of being godded with God about as far as it could possibly go, proceeding "to assume & declare himself to be the Most High God & wore a Cap with the word God inscribed on its front. His Great Chair was a Holy Chair & none but himself must sit in it. He had a number of Adorers and Worshippers, who continue to this day to believe he was the Great God."[29]

Eighteenth-century New England enthusiasts emulated their seventeenth-century predecessors in other ways that were less colorful but no less centrally radical. The Connecticut Separatist Elisha Paine pursued the logic of private judgment and inner inspiration to the same conclusion as did Milton and the seventeenth-century sectarians when he declared in 1769 "that all religion which was established by civil authority was false." In 1750 Ebenezer Frothingham argued that a state-supported religious establishment was figured forth in the second beast of the Book of Revelation. If an ecclesiastical establishment was in its essence illegitimate, then the customs and institutions propping it up were also illegitimate and equally to be done away with. This reasoning lay behind the hostility of both seventeenth- and eighteenth-century radicals to a formally educated clergy and the hearty welcome such radicals simultaneously gave to "mechanick preaching" as the most edifying form of ministry.

We have already been treated to an invidious Hutchinsonian comparison between "your black-coates that have been at the Ninniversity" and those who preach "from the meere motion of the spirit." A century later, in 1752, Solomon Paine, the brother of Elisha, spoke tartly of how, in Connecticut, anyone aspiring to the ministry "must have Money enough to purchase the Ministerial Gifts, viz. Accademical Degrees in Philosophy and School Divinity." A Separatist of Sturbridge, Massachusetts, Sarah Blanchard, believed "that thes unlarned men ware the foolish things that God had chose to confound the wisdom of the wise . . . godliness and the gospel was a mistry out of the reach of all human larning and natural understanding." And Jonathan Edwards, undoubtedly possessed of more human learning and natural understanding than anyone else New England had yet produced, pointedly reminded his Northampton congregation, as he took his homiletic leave of them in 1750, that when a minister possessed

---

29C. C. Goen, *Revivalism and Separatism in New England, 1740–1800: Strict Congregationalists and Separate Baptists in the Great Awakening* (New Haven, Conn.: Yale University Press, 1962), pp. 47, 151, 201; McLoughlin, *New England Dissent*, pp. 357–58; Gaustad, *Great Awakening in New England*, pp. 87–88; PD, May 18, 1747; June 29, 1749; *Extracts from the Itineraries . . . of Ezra Stiles*, ed. Franklin B. Dexter (New Haven, Conn.: Yale University Press, 1916), p. 418. For Satan, Eve, and antinomianism, see above, chap. 2, n. 15.

"human learning, great speculative knowledge, and the wisdom of this world, without a spiritual warmth and ardor in his heart, and a holy zeal in his ministrations, his light is like the light of an *ignis fatuus,* and some kinds of putrifying carcasses that shine in the dark, though they are of a stinking savour." Conversely, God was apt to be lavish "in pouring out of his Spirit chiefly on the common people, and bestowing his greatest and highest favors upon them, admitting them nearer to himself than the great, the honorable, the rich, and the learned."

Finally, the radicals and enthusiasts of the Great Awakening echoed Milton and their other seventeenth-century forebears in advocating the principle of progressive revelation. To Ebenezer Frothingham in 1750 it seemed as it had to Milton in *Areopagitica* that "the Bane of Reformations, or what has hindered their Progress from time to time, has been the first Reformers stopping in the Light that they was first brought into, and so not duly pressing forwards for further Attainments." The Baptist Isaac Backus argued in the Miltonic manner in 1778 for freedom of conscience and discourse as the surest route to truth: "Streams and rivers are of great use, and cause a constant flow of refreshment wherever they come . . . the command of heaven is, *Let them run down;* put no obstruction in their way. No, rather be in earnest to remove every thing that hinders their free course." The seeking for fresh streams and new light undertaken by the adherents to the Great Awakening was in fact a retrieval of what had always been the sources of refreshment and illumination in the radical Protestant tradition.[30]

Nevertheless, in New England radical Protestantism never constituted, even during the Great Awakening and American Revolution, as serious a revolutionary threat as it had in old England during "the Oliverian days." It never developed into a force that "might have established communal property, [and] a far wider democracy in political and legal institutions." And a large part of the reason for this no doubt was, as Stephen Foster and Philip Gura have argued, the willingness manifested by the New England establishment from the beginning to accommodate and assimilate radicalism rather than to seek to wipe it out. The clearest evidence for this tendency to ideological incorporation is the respect with which the principle of congregational autonomy was always treated in New England. When experience brought home, as it in short order did, the necessity of some ecclesiastical oversight of a form of church government "in which

---

[30]Goen, *Revivalism and Separatism,* pp. 123, 128–29; McLoughlin, *New England Dissent,* pp. 403–4; Winslow, *Meetinghouse Hill,* pp. 234–36; Heimert, *Religion and the American Mind,* pp. 193, 396; Perry Miller, *Jonathan Edwards* (New York: William Sloane, 1949), p. 325.

every brother has a hand," it was not a presbyterian system of overt controls, but rather an impressive array of indirect measures and informal procedures that was put in place. The ministerial negative voice, a key provision of the Cambridge Platform, was part of a larger effort to enhance the clerical ability to persuade the laity "freely to consent to their Guides preparing & directing every matter." As John Cotton explained, there was great power in setting the agenda and leading the discussion at church meetings, restraining "any mans speech, whilest another is speaking," and cutting off any other speech "that groweth impertinent or intemperate." To increased clerical authority within each church was added that emphasis on consultation between neighboring churches which was also written into the Cambridge Platform, in the clause bestowing legitimacy upon synods. It was Cotton who again discreetly explained that "mutual conference between Godly, ingenuous and selfe-denying Christians is a notable meanes sanctified of God for the instruction & edification one of another, till wee all come to be of one minde in the Lord." The Massachusetts General Court brought out, in its law of 1653 against unauthorized public preaching, the way in which mutual conference was made time and again to serve the cause of peace and order. The law was occasioned by the frequent planting of new towns and the shortage of reliable clerical leadership for them. As a countervailing move against "persons of bolder spiritts and erroneous principles," it was therefore decreed that any prospective public preacher in one of these frontier areas had to obtain the "approbation of the elders of the fower next neighbouring churches."[31]

These two practices—the negative voice and mutual conference— thus set a precedent at the very beginning of New England history for what was always to remain the preferred style of social control in America: manipulation rather than blunt bossing about, and an overarching public opinion as the medium within which wayward particular opinions and actions would be contained and dissolved. Subsequent developments simply amounted to refinements of this basic scheme—additional techniques of manipulation and buttressings of public opinion. The subsequent development that is most relevant to the course of the present argument was the formation, beginning in the 1690s, of regional associations of ministers. Ebenezer Parkman was a charter member of the Marlborough Association, founded in 1725, serving as its secretary until shortly before his death in 1782.

[31]Christopher Hill, *The World Turned Upside Down: Radical Ideas during the English Revolution* (New York: Viking, 1972), p. 12; above, n. 9; Miller, *Orthodoxy in Massachusetts*, pp. 174–84, 187–93; *Mass. Recs.*, 4, pt. 1, 122.

The Marlborough Association advised its members on doctrinal and disciplinary cases, defined minimum standards of clerical competence and measured candidates against them, and made recommendations about ecclesiastical controversies within its domain. Thus, although they had no legal or coercive power, proto-professional associations of this sort constituted a means of institutionalizing mutual conference, which through the seventeenth century had functioned in a looser, more ad hoc manner.

In 1749 the Marlborough Association issued a report that provides a clear view of an accommodative, assimilative ecclesiastical and social order at work. Essentially a response to the Great Awakening, the report was framed by the old question of declension: "What shall best be done in our several Flocks for the preventing the awfull, threatning Degeneracy and Backsliding in Religion in the present Day?" Members were of course urged to bear witness against "the dangerous Errors which many have run into; particularly the *Arminian* and *Neonomian* on the one Hand, and the *Antinomian* & *Enthusiastical* on the other." But there was much about the Awakening to which the association saw fit to attach its semiofficial imprimatur. Members should "be excited to look with a proper Attention & Concern to our own Experiences in the Divine Life," and they should in their homiletic labors "dwell much upon the Doctrine of Regeneration & Conversion." Indeed, the members ought to take particularly to heart the possibility that "we have . . . given Strength & Boldness to the Ungodly when we have been testifying against the Extravagancys and Excesses of the late Times." Having yielded to enthusiasm to this degree, the association proceeded to draw the line against any further undermining of authority. Members must "lay aside our Disgusts one with another & study Brotherly Love, that it may revive & Continue. We must endeavor to be as near as we can of one Mind & to go on unitedly, harmoniously. . . . We might do well to *engage*, as far as we may be able, *all Persons* of *Distinction* & *Influence to unite with us in this Work of Reformation. . . . Justices, Schoolmasters, Candidates for the Ministry—and especially to assist us by their Example.*" Thus did the Standing Order proceed in its work of maintaining itself in equilibrium, now selecting and incorporating from the renewed initiatives of radicalism, now recomposing itself into a structure of consensus and example. It was not only "until the Great Awakening," as Stephen Foster writes, but also in response to it, that "every creak coming from the machine was another sign that it was still working."[32]

---

[32]Hall, *Faithful Shepherd*, p. 220; *Marlborough Association Records* (American Antiquarian Association microfilm copy; orig. in Marlborough First Church), May 17, 1749;

So by a policy of combining firmness with flexibility, by a periodic willingness to adapt, Adam was able to remain securely in control in New England throughout the seventeenth and eighteenth centuries. Yet Adam's recognition of the wisdom of adapting also testifies to Eve's ability to make her presence continuously and significantly felt. The procedures of social control in New England—guided discussion within churches and mutual conference between them—were procedures of rational consultation and dialogue. In their containment of dissent, they thus simultaneously embodied that very process of Protestant inquiry—"the natural right of every Man to enquire and judge for himself in matters of Religion"—which had stimulated dissent in the first place. Colonial New England's intellectual life was not what Perry Miller portrayed, the propagation from above and the unquestioning acceptance from below of a static ideology. Rather, it was a process of adjustment among initiatives emanating from all levels of the cultural hierarchy. David Hall has argued that in the early modern period generally, printing and books were not associated exclusively with an elite culture that was putatively rational, as against a popular culture that was oral and traditional and putatively subrational. Popular culture was not merely oral in sixteenth- and seventeenth-century England and France. Rather, the world of printing and books included a flourishing popular or extra-rational component of ballads, romances, devotional manuals, and other forms with broad appeal. And in New England as well, a cultural and intellectual leader and grotesquely prolific writer such as Cotton Mather almost always wrote in a decidedly popular vein, regularly mixing morality with sensationalism. Hall's argument is attractive and persuasive, but it should be complemented by the suggestion that if the intellectual labors of a ruling figure such as Cotton Mather reached downward to embrace the traditionalism and emotionalism commonly associated with the populace, so also did the collective mentality of the New England populace include a readiness to climb upward into the realm of rational deliberation commonly associated with the elite. We shall conclude this chapter with an account of an episode that illustrates this socially intermingled quality of New England intellection.[33]

Foster, "New England and the Challenge of Heresy," p. 660. The reference to having testified against "the Extravagancys and Excesses of the late Times" has to do with a "testimony" against the evangelist George Whitefield which the association published, over the objections of Parkman and Solomon Prentice, in 1745; see *Association Records,* Jan. 22, 1745.

[33]David D. Hall, "The World of Print and Collective Mentality in Seventeenth-Century New England," in *New Directions in American Intellectual History,* ed. John Higham and Paul Conkin (Baltimore, Md.: Johns Hopkins University Press, 1979), pp. 166–76.

During the 1730s a furor arose over the installation of Robert Breck, Jr., as the minister of the church in Springfield, Massachusetts. Breck, the son of the Reverend Robert Breck of Marlborough, had begun ministerial work on a trial basis in Windham County, Connecticut, in 1733, shortly after completing his studies at Harvard. His more experienced colleague in the neighborhood had been Thomas Clap, the future president of Yale. But stories had begun circulating that Breck was an Arminian, perhaps even an Arian. Clap had heard him deny that the Satisfaction of Christ was essential to salvation and affirm the salvation of those heathen "that liv'd up to the light of Nature." In Breck's view, "the contrary was a harsh doctrine." There was no difference that he could see between a historical and a saving faith; all that mattered was whether or not faith was accompanied by good works. The way in which this Arminian minimizing of inner spiritual intensity tended to upset Clap and others who came into contact with Breck may be deduced from Breck's fondness for such analogies as this one: suppose "a Company of Men being in a House, and that some Person came in and told them that the House would fall in two Hours, and they should be killed if they did not go out of it. It would not be their believing would save their Lives, but their going out of the House."

Breck had moved on to Springfield in 1734, still a ministerial candidate and still shadowed by these rumors about his dubious orthodoxy. In early 1735 he was required to explain his views before the ministerial association of Hampshire County, one of the members of which was Jonathan Edwards. He was able to convince only a minority of his examiners that his various doctrinal affirmations were indeed harmless. The majority insisted that the Springfield church suspend its consideration of Breck and await the results of further inquiry. But the church nevertheless proceeded defiantly to issue a call to Breck to settle as its pastor. Breck thereupon busied himself with obtaining testimonies to his orthodoxy from the leading ministers of Boston, such as Benjamin Colman. A council of ministers sitting to pass judgment on a candidate was the form taken by mutual conference at ordination proceedings, and Breck managed to form such a council for his own ordination consisting partly of representatives of these Boston divines and partly of the minority of the Hampshire Association which had endorsed him. On the day of the ordination, just as the council was in the midst of taking further testimony on Breck's theological opinions, Breck was arrested and taken before the Springfield magistrate on the basis of a complaint made by the disgruntled clerical majority of the Hampshire Association and lay minority of the Springfield parish over which Breck was to be settled. He was found guilty of blasphemy and atheism and ordered extradited to Connecticut, where his offenses had been committed. Connecticut eventually allowed the matter to drop, but the Springfield church and the Boston ministers who had had their ordination proceedings disrupted by a civil arrest did not. They demanded that the Massachusetts General Court express formal disapproval of this encroachment of the state upon the church, and in due course the lower house did so. Breck was finally ordained without further incident in 1736.[34]

One of the most striking things about this affair is the readiness of all those who participated in it to move freely back and forth between the terms of the contradictions inherent in Puritan ecclesiology. Breck presented himself to Thomas Clap as one of the guardians of Puritan order, imposing his richer understanding upon the mean-minded laity: "Mr. *Breck* said, That he would preach People out of those false and stingy Notions which they have been taught in; that the common People out of Pride, and self-conceit, confin'd Salvation only to themselves; but I will have them to know, that the Heathen may be Saved as well as they can." But upon meeting with demurral and resistance from Clap, Breck immediately transformed himself into a proponent of the liberties of hierarchical inferiors: "Mr. *Breck* said, I suppose you wou'd have it here, as it is in *Scotland;* there the young Ministers cannot think freely for themselves; but they must think as the old Ministers do, or else they will not ordain them."

William Cooper, the Boston clergyman who presided over the abortive ordaining council, drew similarly on the range of ideological postures made available by Protestant tradition. He wrote to William Williams that he hoped "the happy Harmony which has hitherto subsisted among the Ministers and Churches in your County, by which the Interests of Religion have no doubt been greatly serv'd, should be continued, and no Breach made upon it," thereby endeavoring to reassure this uncle of Edwards and dean of the Hampshire County ministers that he and Breck's other supporters were fully cognizant of the supreme value of order. But Cooper's primary rhetorical posture was that of an ardent advocate for local and lay rights over against a domineering pseudo-presbyterianism. Even had the Hampshire Association been in unanimous agreement that Breck was heterodox, which it had not been, "this Body of Ministers" would not have had "the Right of Jurisdiction over the first Church in *Springfield.*" To

[34]John Langdon Sibley and Clifford K. Shipton, *Biographical Sketches of Those Who Attended Harvard College,* 17 vols. (Cambridge, Mass.: Charles William Sever, Harvard University Press, and Massachusetts Historical Society, 1873–1975), 8:663–73 (hereafter *Harvard Graduates*); *A Narrative of the Proceedings of Those Ministers of the County of Hampshire* . . . (Boston, 1736), pp. 5, 42.

claim that the Springfield or any other particular church was obliged not merely to ask but to accept the advice of neighboring churches and ministers was to deny all "private Judgment" and liberty. The Hampshire Association had, alas, been "playing the Bishop in their Diocess."[35]

For its part, the Hampshire Association primarily conceived of itself as a prudent conservator of ecclesiastical order. "If we should have an heterodox Minister settled amongst us," it warned, " . . . it would tend to destroy the Peace of the Ministry of the County, and the Comfort and Benefit of mutual Society, and to poison our Flocks, and to bring our religious State into Confusion." Jonathan Edwards, deputed to give the Hampshire ministers the last word, berated the Boston supporters of Breck in a similar vein: "We suppose we have been the freest by far of any part of the Land from unhappy Contentions in our ecclesiastical and religious Concerns, 'till you have overthrown our Peace, and put us into the utmost Confusion, by coming from abroad, and intermeddling in our Affairs."

But a subtle shift of emphasis could move Edwards and the other Hampshire ministers away from order and toward enthusiasm, could give them the pleasures that went with feeling they were more lorded over than lording it over, the victims not of outside agitation but of oppression at the hands of a superior external power. Thus, far from acting upon pure congregational principles, the Springfield church had compromised its liberties in the most serious fashion when it had allowed candidate Breck to choose his own Boston ordainers, rather than choosing them itself or at the very least voting on Breck's nominees. Thus, as the machinations of the Breck-Boston claque ground usurpingly on, the Hampshire ministers were driven in desperation to the extremely disorderly step of calling upon the local civil authority to intervene. And thus, Edwards was able without any sense of incongruity to conclude his individual contribution to the ensuing polemics by striking on behalf of the Hampshire Association the classic Protestant pose of the inspired believer standing alone with his God against all the hostile authorities of this world: "Our only Hope is that GOD himself, who has lately so wonderfully poured out his Spirit, and wrought in this County, will again appear for the upholding his own Interest among us, and that he has suffered our Hands to be thus weakened, to prepare the Way for the greater Glory to his Power, by carrying on his Work in our Weakness, by his own immediate Hand."[36]

[35]Ibid., p. 56; William Cooper, *An Examination of and Some Answer to a Pamphlet, Intitled a Narrative* . . . (Boston, 1736), pp. 26, 33, 50, 81–82.

[36]*Narrative*, p. 79; Jonathan Edwards, *A Letter to the Author of the Pamphlet Called an*

On the level on which we have thus far examined it, the Robert Breck affair already begins to reveal that the New England situation was not one in which order and enthusiasm, Adam and Eve, stood fixed in distinction from and opposition to each other. The facility with which Breck, Cooper, and Edwards all availed themselves of the rhetoric of Protestant antiauthoritarianism shows us that Adam was imbued to a considerable extent with Eve's values. Similarly, the affair gives us intriguing glimpses of Eve continuing to maintain aspects of what Adam had previously taught, in the face of Adam's own abandonment of them. But before this part of the story is told, it will be helpful to look more closely at all those forms of contention and flux which have been brought to the fore in the New England historiography of the past thirty years and interpreted to portend the slow decay of Puritanism.[37]

Social historians have described a complex process in which geography, economics, and psychology are seen to have been thoroughly intertwined. Having planted themselves on the edge of a vast new continent, New Englanders soon found that "the magnetic influence of empty land was . . . powerful, and people of every age and condition yielded to it." All sorts of people sought to appease their hunger for land, but in Connecticut and perhaps elsewhere the trend was for the poorer and less prestigious strata of the population to gravitate away from the town center, away from the authority and control of the meetinghouse, and toward the seemingly anarchic outlands. As Richard L. Bushman writes, "The persons most in need of the restraining influence of governing institutions were usually the first to leave." After the population in these more remote areas had increased to a certain critical point, complaints began to be heard about the great distances the outlanders had to travel to the meetinghouse or their children had to travel to school. Virtually every town was sooner or later embroiled in dissension over the location of the meetinghouse, the locus and symbol of order and legitimacy, and in a multitude of cases such conflicts could only be resolved by fission. One or the other faction would eventually petition successfully to have itself recognized as a new town and parish.[38]

Sectional controversies were usually conducted with extreme ran-

---

Answer to the Hampshire Narrative (Boston, 1737), pp. 19, 36, 83. Edwards was referring to the dramatic revival of piety that had recently taken place in his own Northampton church.

[37]See above, nn. 5–6.

[38]Demos, *Little Commonwealth*, p. 11; Bushman, *From Puritan to Yankee*, pp. 54–82; Winslow, *Meetinghouse Hill*, pp. 119–35; Lockridge, *New England Town*, pp. 93–124.

cor, a phenomenon that has been traced to the rigor of Puritan authority and discipline. Comprehensively restrained from the time he or she was born, the Colonial New Englander "felt the need to raise defenses against the fathers who constantly threatened judgment and rebuke." Repression begat an inner rage that was expressed as self-hatred, as a readiness to take one's neighbor to court at the least trespass, and most openly and fully in the bitterness of townwide contention. Out of this intricate process, which was thus at work everywhere—within individuals, in communities, and ultimately throughout the region—was emerging the modern world of "communal diversity and political activism." But the modern world was emerging willy-nilly, despite what New Englanders consciously imagined they were doing. In the battles between outlying districts and village centers, so the account runs, both sides espoused the traditional Puritan ideal of hierarchy and corporate unity. Kenneth Lockridge sums up the manner in which the modern world is thought to have shoved Puritanism aside: "Thus the future came to many towns, not because some men envisioned that future and set out to undermine the old order in the name of the new, but because changing conditions provoked contradictions in the old order which in turn tumbled men all inadvertently into new experiences."[39]

But it was not exactly so. The process of social change in New England was not one in which a thoroughly conscious, fully elaborated Puritan Great Chain of Being was subverted by modernist ideals of pluralism, individualism, and egalitarianism which had not yet learned how to articulate themselves. "Changing conditions" did not "provoke contradictions in the old order." Rather, the old order was from the beginning riven by contradictions, the terms of which New Englanders had always known how to formulate and manipulate. A group in Connecticut which had, in the late seventeenth century, subsisted long enough away from the village center to think of itself as a separate community did not have to grope haltingly in a merely instinctual unease. It had at hand a rhetoric with which to impart to its petition for a new parish an air of rational coherence. It was "inconsistent with the designs of our fathers who came into this wilderness that

---

[39]Bushman, *From Puritan to Yankee*, pp. 19–22; Greven, *Protestant Temperament*, pp. 109–13; Demos, *Little Commonwealth*, pp. 49–50; Lockridge, *New England Town*, pp. 172–75. The idea that Puritan child rearing was monolithically repressive is questioned in David Leverenz, *The Language of Puritan Feeling: An Exploration in Literature, Psychology, and Social History* (New Brunswick, N.J.: Rutgers University Press, 1980), pp. 70–104.

they might injoy the ordinances of God in peace without disturbance . . . that wee should be thereby deprived of the liberty of quietly enjoing god in his ordinances," the petitioners informed the Connecticut General Court. Their invocation of piety and congregationalist liberty was as fully sanctioned by the Puritan tradition as an appeal to hierarchy and corporate unity would have been.[40]

In no part of New England is the envelopment of social change in the intellectual richness of Puritan ideology and rhetoric more striking than in the area of eastern Connecticut in which Robert Breck, Jr., got himself into such trouble at the outset of his ministerial career in the 1730s. According to Richard L. Bushman, between 1690 and 1735 this region participated as fully as possible in the geographic expansion and dubious profiteering that were allegedly eroding the homogeneous Puritan social order of the seventeenth century. Twenty new towns were founded in eastern Connecticut during those years, as opposed to only five in the western portion of the colony. At the same time, the area's share of the colony's tax assessments more than doubled, partly because the population was growing, but also because this population was composed of people who seemed, as one observer noted of the inhabitants of the town of Norwich, "with fixed Eye to be Set upon Trade and Commerce."[41]

If Puritan ideology was monolithic, if those establishing new towns and engaging in new economic departures were really leaving Puritanism behind altogether and moving (without knowing it) into modern secularism, then we might expect that when a proto-skeptic and proto-materialist such as Robert Breck, Jr., came into an area of new towns and new economic departures, his dashingly modern views would win at least some converts and disciples to his side. This is evidently what the Hampshire Association was apprehensive about, for they professed to regard the ordinary folk of New England pretty much as twentieth-century social historians have regarded them, as conspicuously lacking in intellectual resources, "illiterate Men, that were utterly unskil'd in Controversies."

But what transpired after the arrival of Breck in eastern Connecticut was a lot more interesting than the seduction of a set of yokels by a smart young fellow fresh from Harvard. In the controversial interchanges with the local laity in which Breck became involved, the laity gave, intellectually, as good as it got. Peter Robinson, Jr., of

[40]Bushman, *From Puritan to Yankee*, p. 65.
[41]Ibid., pp. 83–123; quotation from p. 123.

Windham, troubled by what he had heard Breck say from the pulpit and elsewhere about the salvation of the heathen, went to have a talk with him. He told Breck that if his views were correct, "it was better to be born in a heathen Country than under the Light of the Gospel, inasmuch as it was easier to live up to the Duties of the Light of Nature only, than it was to live up to the Duties required in the Gospel." Robinson insisted over against Breck's Arminian good works upon the Calvinist (and antinomian) indispensability of saving grace: "I told him I thought that no Man was able to attain a true and saving Faith, meerly by his own Power, or Strength, and that it was the Work of the Spirit, for the Scripture saith, that Faith was the Gift of GOD." Another layman of whom it proved to be even less true that he was "utterly unskil'd in Controversies" was Isaac Lawrence of Norwich, that town where everyone seemed "with fixed Eye to be Set upon Trade and Commerce":

> [Lawrence] proposed to [Breck] this Similitude, and said, Sir, Here is a Box of vast Treasure set up, the Gentleman that owns it, will bestow it on one of us, he well knows which he will give it unto, and says to us, run, that we might obtain it; the Offer is made to us equally, will you run for it with me? I'll try to run, I know I cannot obtain it without; Will you run, Sir? [Breck] replied, No I will not, if it be certainly for me I shall have it whether I run or no; I will tye my Legs first before I will run: Then I replied, you will not obtain it.

Breck's Arminian reasonings were outwardly similar to those Milton had set forth in *Christian Doctrine*. Nevertheless, it was Calvinist and layman Isaac Lawrence and not Arminian and clergyman Robert Breck, Jr., who had grasped the essential Miltonic distinction between foreknowledge and predestination and the essential Miltonic spirit of cooperation between human exertions and divine purposes. I can think of no better explanation for this moment, in which an average New England layman responds in a magnificently unperturbed manner to a young minister's clever logic, than that it was the result of a culture that gave comprehensive and substantial encouragement to intellectual self-reliance. In just a few short years, the eastern portion of Connecticut where these exchanges were taking place would, far from tumbling inadvertently out of the Puritan framework, be the area of New England that would be the most deeply stirred by the Great Awakening, and the convoluted struggle toward full Puritan apprehension and eloquence would be everywhere to be seen.[42]

[42]*Narrative*, pp. 52, 62, 70; Bushman, *From Puritan to Yankee*, pp. 191, 258–59; Goen, *Revivalism and Separatism*, pp. 186–87.

The Breck affair reveals how thoroughly convinced of the value of intellectual autonomy Colonial New England was, for it shows intellectual autonomy being actively lived and felt even when the theology being espoused by the culturally inferior party remained entirely orthodox and even when his insubordinate ecclesiology remained only indirect and implicit. Nevertheless, intellectual autonomy was not upheld and maintained without great psychic cost. After Peter Robinson spoke up to Breck about the need for a saving, regenerating faith of the spirit, as opposed to a merely historical faith of the letter, Breck replied with another of his smart-aleck analogies: "If a Man have Faith it is no matter how he comes by it. And suppose you have two five Pound Bills, one that you purchased, and another that was given you, they are both five Pound Bills, and one is as good and of as much Service to you as the other." Robinson was shaken by such strange opinions coming from such a high place. It seemed to him and to others in the neighborhood that the entire structure of authoritative piety and dogma was beginning to crumble: "Some told me that Mr. *Breck* was a Man of Learning, and that such a Man as I ought not to pretend to dispute with him, but to believe what he said was right . . . a Man [said] that he believed Mr. *Clap* was of the same mind, for all the young Ministers of late, held just as Mr. *Breck* did."[43]

The argument of this chapter should not be taken to imply that ministers and others in authority in New England were not held in great esteem and respect, for they were. They did for the most part secure acquiescence by persuasion, example, and accommodation, rather than by coercion. To place oneself in opposition to authority was thus not only to struggle free of a restraining hand; it was also to lose the comfort of a sheltering wing. And something of the hesitation and anxiety induced by finding oneself in such a position can be sensed in Peter Robinson's testimony about his dealings with young Robert Breck. Conversely, for a minister less youthful and flippant than Breck, the experience of being resisted by the likes of Peter Robinson and Isaac Lawrence was equally fraught with emotional complexity and consequence. Such resistance meant that one had failed in one's central function of exemplary persuasion. Yet one's Puritan self-esteem forbade bringing the wayward into line by sheer force. As we have heard Adam conceding to Eve at a crucial moment in *Paradise Lost*, "Go; for thy stay, not free, absents thee more" (IX, 372). Thus, when disagreements between superiors and subordinates

---

[43]*Narrative*, p. 53.

did arise in Colonial New England, as we have seen they repeatedly did, the ensuing controversy was likely to be prolonged and emotionally intricate. We turn now to examine such emotional intricacies as they are revealed in the life of one eighteenth-century community.

Chapter 5

Ebenezer Parkman: Order and Enthusiasm in Westborough, Massachusetts, 1725–1763

The town of Westborough, Massachusetts, is located at the eastern edge of Worcester County, about ten miles east of Worcester and thirty miles west of Boston. It was founded in 1717 by separation from Marlborough, seven miles to the northeast, and behind this separation lay a tradition of contention that went back at least as far as the 1650s. In the 1640s settlers moving west from Watertown, one of the seven original towns of the Massachusetts Bay Colony, had established the new town of Sudbury on a site they hoped would yield the more satisfactory land holdings they were seeking. But during the next decade, the younger men of Sudbury began to voice objections, both to the inadequate amount of land they felt they were being allotted and to the town fathers' refusal to allow enclosed fields and more individualistic farming. As I have suggested, the situation and the impulses behind it seem broadly similar to the moment in Book IX of *Paradise Lost* when Eve insists on working separately from Adam. And it also thus arose from exactly the sort of geographic mobility and socioeconomic restlessness historians have identified as central to the development of Colonial New England. Moreover, it very quickly manifested that intertwining of material grievance with the contradictions inherent in Puritan ideology which I have attempted to describe at the end of the preceding chapter. When the Sudbury minister, Edmund Browne, sided openly against the dissatisfied younger men of the town, their sense of oppression began to be expressed as Protestant anticlericalism. Many of them stopped attending church, and their leader, John Ruddock, explained to Browne, "Setting aside your office, I regard you as no more than another man." Subsequently, mutual conference intervened, in the form of a council of neighboring churches and ministers, and attempted to shore up the authority of Browne and the other town elders by handing down a judgment favorable to them. But this only served to provoke further resentment, and the dissident group decided they had no recourse but to move farther west and set up their own new town of Marlborough.[1]

Unfortunately, however, the first twenty years of Marlborough's existence were marked by conflict as severe as that which had made life intolerable in Sudbury, and in their new home the settlers found that economic and ecclesiastical disputes continued to feed on each other just as they formerly had. In 1660 nine of the inhabitants, "being deeply sensible of the want of the ordinances . . . accordinge to the order of the gospel," began the process of "imbodinge our selves in a church way," but it took six years before the gathering of a church in Marlborough could be completed. Although the exact connections between economics and ecclesiology are left obscure in the available sources, that there were indeed such connections was felt and acknowledged by observers of the new town's turmoil. Sharp disagreements over land allotments led to sharp disagreements over taxes, including the taxes assessed to support the minister, and this caused, as a Massachusetts General Court committee of inquiry wrote in 1663, "great disturbance of [the town's] peace, & hinderance of theire proceedings in cases civill & ecclesiasticall." The disturbance was great enough, in fact, to make the prospective minister, William Brimsmead, depart for Plymouth Colony. By the summer of 1664 Brimsmead had returned, but not to a situation liberated from disturbance. A council of neighboring ministers, called together in August to help resolve the ecclesiastical aspects of Marlborough's difficulties, and including Reverend Browne of Sudbury, had to take notice of continuing contention and, it appears, of disaffection from Brimsmead. The council spoke in general terms of "so long a time of troublesome differences wherein there hath not wanted both sin and affliction on all hands," and it specifically alluded to an unhappiness with Brimsmead arising from "the present temptations and troubles." It urged upon all parties "a promise through the Grace of God for the future to embrace each other in the Lord." Nevertheless, the General Court was confronted two months later with the persistent image of a town unable to compose itself either

[1]Sumner Chilton Powell, *Puritan Village: The Formation of a New England Town* (Middletown, Conn.: Wesleyan University Press, 1963), pp. 119–31, 136–37. For Eve's "separatist" demands, see above, chap. 2, n. 11.

civilly or ecclesiastically. Petitions to the court from opposing factions referred both to land disputes so bitter that the legitimacy of the "town booke," in which land allotments were recorded, was being called into question, and to charges and countercharges about people "going about to root out our minister." It was not until two more years had passed, in September 1666, that the Marlborough church was finally gathered and Brimsmead ordained to minister to it.[2]

But a contentiousness at once economic and ecclesiastical and at least quasi-ideological had not yet done with Marlborough. Land disputes broke out again within four years and dragged on throughout the 1670s. It appears from a report issued in October 1679 by another General Court committee of inquiry that some of these land disputes involved the holdings of Reverend Brimsmead and that the amount of Brimsmead's stipend was a further bone of contention. The committee judged that "the allowance at present made to [Brimsmead] is much short of his deserts, and of what is needefull for an honnorable maintenance, and therefore doe seriously advise to an amendment of that matter." This latest of the General Court's many involvements in Marlborough's troubles coincided with the ecclesiastical synod of 1679, which adopted Increase Mather's idea that churches should atone for their sins by renewing their covenants. As a matter of fact, the Marlborough church's Brimsmead Covenant bears exactly the same date, October 15, 1679, as the court committee's report. The movement for covenant renewal was, along with the development of the homiletic form known as the jeremiad, part of the clergy's effort to bring the stubbornly resistant laity to heel. Since Marlborough's disputes of the 1670s had involved paying Brimsmead "much short of his deserts" and may well have engendered other forms of irreverent carriage toward him, we may be justified in discerning not merely a generalized Puritan piety, but also a pointed reference to the local manifestations of troubled Puritan ecclesiastical politics in covenant language that committed church members to "a careful Enspection over our own hearts so as to endeavor by vertue of the Death of Christ the mortification of all our Sinfull passions worldly frames & Disorderly affections whereby we may be drawn from the living God."[3]

---

[2]*Massachusetts Archives Photostats* (Massachusetts Historical Society), documents of 1660, 1664; *Mass Recs.,* 4, pt. 2, 92; Charles Hudson, *History of the Town of Marlborough, Middlesex County, Massachusetts* (Boston, 1862), p. 50; *Miscellaneous Bound Mss.* (Massachusetts Historical Society), Oct. 1664; Oct. 17, 1664; *Collections of the Massachusetts Historical Society* 27 (1838):297.

[3]*Mass. Recs.,* 5:253; *MT,* July 11, 1878. For the covenant renewal movement, see David D. Hall, *The Faithful Shepherd: A History of the New England Ministry in the Seventeenth Century* (Chapel Hill: University of North Carolina Press, 1972), p. 243.

In 1702 the inhabitants of "the westerly part" of Marlborough peti-tioned the General Court for the establishment of that area as a sepa-rate town and parish, continuing a movement they had begun in 1688 when they had passed a resolution in town meeting defining a parish boundary line, should they "see cause afterwards to build another meeting house, and . . . maintain a minister." Geographic expansion and dispersion were proceeding apace, but there is no evidence to suggest that the developments leading to the separation of West-borough from Marlborough were being accompanied by the sort of gravitating toward ecclesiastical contention we have seen in the sepa-ration of Marlborough from Sudbury and in the first twenty years of Marlborough's existence. When Westborough finally did separate from Marlborough in 1717, this was accomplished with no particular tumult. It may be that the relative peace existing in Marlborough in the late seventeenth and early eighteenth centuries was a sign of the community's acquiescence in the Brimsmead Covenant, its participa-tion in an order and consensus imposed from above.

Yet there was one major outburst of contention in Marlborough during those years, and the way it developed suggests that those ideo-logical impulses were still alive which could easily bring conflict into focus as a contest between the enthusiasm and Independency of the laity and the quest for authoritative dominance of the clergy. After Reverend Brimsmead died in 1700, the effort to choose his successor led to four years filled, as some of those involved in the controversy said, with "the devious one sowing fears among us; we have ben likly to bite and devour one another." Such rancorous disagreements al-most always arose in Colonial New England when it was necessary to select a new minister. Their intensity and prolongation suggest the depth of the populace's concern about the ministerial function, its desire for proper leadership, and its suspicion and fear about the possibility of having to live without such leadership, with someone who would be either dissolute, heterodox, tyrannical, or some com-bination thereof. Thus the Marlborough brethren informed one of the candidates proposed as a successor to Brimsmead, John Emerson of Salem, that "there have ben many hints and noyses or storys [about you] raging about which have caused a disquiet amongst us." Nor was this disquiet eased by the workings of the process of mutual con-ference. Despite testimonials to his piety and good character, con-firmed by a council of neighboring churches, the call that had been made to Emerson had to be withdrawn because of the persistent apprehensions about him. Marlborough's "long time of trouble" in choosing its second minister (agreement was eventually reached to call Robert Breck, the father of Robert Breck, Jr.) was not a direct expression of anticlericalism and Independency, but it did manifest the sort of emotional climate from which a more explicit Protestant radicalism could at any time emerge. It is this emotional climate and this constant pull toward hierarchical tension and conflict that we will find characterizing the new town and church of Westborough as they made their way through the eighteenth century.[4]

Gathering a church and choosing a minister proved to be as difficult for Westborough at the outset of its history as it had been for Marlborough in the 1660s and again at the turn of the century. Dissension arose after a call was issued to one Daniel Elmer in 1718, and it was not until 1724 that the new civil and ecclesiastical entity could agree on a candidate.[5] The man finally chosen was Ebenezer Parkman, a recent graduate of Harvard. In deciding on Parkman, Westborough had acquired for itself a clergyman who would be the perfect foil to its own highly ambivalent attitude toward being subordinate to the clergy. For throughout his tenure in Westborough, which would last until his death in 1782, Parkman would espouse and embody virtually to perfection those contradictions inherent in Puritan ideology which we have been examining. On the one hand, the pastor of the Church of Christ in Westborough seemed to affirm in the most forthright manner the basic Protestant right "of every Man to enquire and judge for himself in matters of Religion." In 1757 he insisted to a Roman Catholic refugee who had taken up residence in Westborough after the French and Indian Wars: "Every Body must see for Himself in matters of Religion. . . . I did not want any of my people should trust me in that; but examine all I said by the Bible."

Nor was this a mere Protestant platitude, which would recede into insignificance in the absence of the challenge of converting a papist. The sermons Parkman read from the Westborough pulpit did include a number of exhortations to intellectual and spiritual autonomy. He informed the church in 1724, around the time it issued its call to him, that "our Searches ought to reach . . . into the Nature, doctrines, Enemies & opposites" of fundamental Christianity: "We shall never know too much of the Love of God in Christ, the Mysteries of our Redemption, Gods Manifestation of himself in Creation, preser-

---

[4]Heman Packard DeForest, *The History of Westborough, Massachusetts: The Early History* (Westborough, 1891), pp. 29, 33–34, 42–45; Local History Documents (Marlborough, Mass., Public Library), Folder 8 (First Parish, 1700–1703).

[5]DeForest, *History of Westborough*, pp. 51–52.

vation and Providence." Such matters are not reserved "for the Great and Learned men of the world to dive into," for "every *Christian* ought . . . to be ready to give an account of the Foundation of his Faith to Silence Gaynsayers, and give proof of his Calling." Fifteen years later, Parkman again stressed that "if we with great Zeal set up a particular Religion above all others in the world, and cry it up as containing articles of the utmost weight and worth; and pretend that we freely & heartily Venture our souls & all our Eternity thereon we should be capable to render some answer concerning the Grounds & principal articles of it." Believers must search and inquire and prove all things in a spirit of total commitment: "Don't be satisfyd with a mere Cursory formal Reading [of Scripture] as if Grace would come to you *so*: and as if Salvation would be the reward of your gratifying your Curiosity. . . . Make *every Thing* turn to this account. Be ever more gaining & learning & treasuring &c. what ever you read, hear, or that occurs—bend all your *force* this way, all your Advantages. *With all thy getting, get understanding.*" Such was the depth of Parkman's Protestant commitment to religious knowledge that he could at times sound downright antinomian: "Knowledge is the bright sparkling Gem in our Crown, and gives us somewhat of the resemblance of the most High. Knowledge is one of the inestimable Features of His glorious Image, and makes us like God Himself discerning Good & Evil. Have we not the Ambition, the laudable aspiring to be like God, in his imitable Excellencys? And what Excellency or perfection in God Himself shines brighter or more admirably than His *Knowledge?*"[6]

Thus did the Reverend Parkman uphold those principles and values that, as entertained by many New Englanders, led straight to radicalism, enthusiasm, and dissent. Yet the very same sermons that thus urge to daily growth in grace and knowledge are also careful to point out the one and only route to genuine fullness of apprehension: pay attention to the minister. "Let us Desire the Sincere Knowledge of the Word, and Let us Endeavour *to grow* thereby," Parkman preached in that youthful discourse of 1724, but let us do so by making use of "the Best Means . . . attendance upon public Preaching." And in Parkman's view, implicit in such attendance was unreserved assent to orthodox doctrine and uncomplaining acceptance of a subordinate position in a hierarchical ecclesiastical structure: "We must receive [public preaching] with *Faith*, i.e. Approbation and Consent: and *Love*, with Candor &

[6]PD, Jan. 26, 1757; PFP, Box 1, Folder 2 (Sermons, 1724–29), Sermons 19 and 20, pp. 4–5; Folder 3 (Sermons, 1730–39), Sermon on Prov. 4:7 (Mar. 11, 1739), pp. 3, 9, 18; Folder 4 (Sermons, 1740–49), 2 Sermons on Hos. 6:3 (June 1745), p. 13.

Ingenuity, not Carping Cavilling and Canvassing, but with holy & sincere Aims and cordial Affection to it." The priesthood of all believers was thus compassed about, so it developed in almost all of Parkman's sermons, by a requirement of implicit faith in the special priesthood of the clergy.

Indeed, it is hard to imagine how there could have been a more dedicated representative of that heightened clericalism that came to be characteristic of the Standing Order in the early eighteenth century. In 1728 Parkman transformed an acknowledgment of the diversity of Christian gifts and callings into a celebration of the particularly significant responsibilities and correspondingly great capacities of ministers. Laypeople are expected to be "Fellow Labourers" in "propagating and carrying on the Kingdom," but as it turned out, this mostly meant praying for ministers—especially for one's own minister. It was the minister who had to be "the wisest, most prudent & skillful Pilot to steer the Church steady and safe" through "Dark, Stormy Times of Divisions or Error." It was the minister who, possessed of "bright & Excellent Endowments of Knowledge & Wisdom," along with "much Constancy, Patience, Tenderness and Affection," would "watch over the souls of Gods people as Fathers, as Shepherds, as Stewards do faithfully vigilantly & painfully extend their Care and Rule over those committed to them." The same note was sounded many years later, in 1761, when it fell to Parkman to deliver the sermon to the annual ministerial convention in Boston. In order for ministers to accomplish their appointed tasks, he insisted, "what superior Wisdom and Prudence, what Penetration and sound Judgment, what Justice and Impartiality, Steadiness, Patience, Courage and Resolution, are demanded." But such spiritual heroism would receive its appropriate reward. The true minister would sit higher in the heavenly hierarchy than would the ordinary Christian believer and seeker: "We are thereby brought to a greater *Nearness* to God than by any other Means. The Priests are those that *draw nigh* Him.—And it is by divine Appointment that the Elders are to be *distinguish'd* by *double Honor*."[7]

There were, then, ecclesiastical and angelic hierarchies, at the pinnacle of which could be found the many clerical shepherds who were standing faithful. But these were merely the noblest among the many

[7]PFP, Box 1, Folder 2, Sermons 19 and 20, pp. 12–13; Sermon 439–40 (Sept. 15, 1728), pp. 2–6; *The Love of Christ Constraining Us* . . . (Boston, 1761), pp. 15, 23. For early eighteenth-century clericalism in New England, see J. William T. Youngs, Jr., "Congregational Clericalism: New England Ordinations before the Great Awakening," *William and Mary Quarterly*, 3d ser., 31 (1974):481–90.

hierarchical arrangements by which God had seen fit to constitute his universe. The same preacher who on occasion held out to his congregation the prospect of a virtually unlimited spiritual mobility, the acquisition of quasi-divine knowledge, on other occasions portrayed a neofeudal universe in which one's position was absolutely and utterly fixed: "God having so orderd & disposd your Lot and Station in the world to be this, you ought to submit to the Supreme & wise Appointment of the Great Ruler of all Things, with whom it was to have made thy Case far worse had He so pleasd; nay might have appointed Thee to have been of a lower Class or Order of Creatures." Acceptance of one's lot, like searching into Christian truth and attending upon public preaching, must be wholehearted and entire: "Here may not be sufferd any Rebellious, levelling Humor; nor a Temper that is searching continually for all the imperfections, & prone to magnifie the Infirmitys of a Master. that has a grudging and despising Spirit that is full of hatred & Envy & Impatience. But a Spirit of meekness must be cherished." By a spirit of meekness, John Winthrop's founding aspiration that New England would be a place where people would be "knitt together in this worke as one man" could still be brought to fruition: *Be of an humble mind,* be tractable & teachable and ready to acknowledge a fault. . . . In Peace you are like to Enjoy Every Good; your outward and your inward welfare is promoted. . . . For we are not born merely for ourselves. We are formd for society and are members one of another."

The only alternative to such loving hierarchical unity, Parkman declared, was nothing else than the most thoroughgoing satanism: "If you should be dissatisfyed that the Sovereign God hath ordaind that thou shouldst be in this world a Servant that same Spirit would have been restless if you had been a Master, and have hankerd to have been a *Magistrate* neither would that have contented thee unless you could be a Superior Magistrate or a Prince—nay it would not have been Quiet with being a man, nor unless it could be an Angel, the highest Angel— at last Heaven itself could not hold thee." In the end the contention that had plagued New England and prevented it from fulfilling its mission as a City upon a Hill could be traced to the archfiend having taken possession of too many New Englanders:

For hence men grow self opinioned and think they are never made enough of: They conceit Every one above them to be exalted out of due place and they are ever ready to quarrell with Divine providence for keeping themselves down on a Level with other men that they Ought in their Judgements to be Superior to. This Affectation of Superiority makes men Esteem the Behaviour of all men both above and below them to be inferiour to their worth and Dignity. They are therefore always full of Jealousies & Suspicions that this or that action or speech did not carry in it deference and respect enough; and offence is often taken where none was given, because they will magnify things and dwell upon them a long time.

But such a conservative analysis of the sources of contention in New England was, in its partiality, itself a contentious utterance. Since Parkman's Protestantism did not permit him not to cherish those principles conducive to Puritan enthusiasm, we are not surprised to find that his maintenance of neofeudal Puritan order was far from untroubled. It was a rage for order that the Westborough minister manifested, not the secure habitation of it. Divided as he was, he, no less than those beneath him in the Westborough church, was prone to "magnify things and dwell upon them a long time." But in order fully to appreciate the psychic complexity of the interactions between Parkman and his parishioners, we must get to know him not only as he was from the pulpit, in his public role, but also as he was in the privacy of his introspections and meditations.[8]

In many ways Parkman stood at the center of the theological, spiritual, and cultural crosscurrents of eighteenth-century New England. His Harvard classmates included both Charles Chauncy, who would be the principal opponent of the Great Awakening, and Ebenezer Pemberton, who would be one of its leading proponents, and during the Awakening Parkman maintained his relations with both the Old and New Lights among his clerical brethren in the neighborhood. Before entering Harvard, he received his schooling from John Bernard, who later espoused Arminian, proto-Unitarian views during his tenure as the minister of Andover. This early exposure to the more urbane proclivities of the eighteenth century perhaps lies behind such things as Parkman's possession and use of a telescope and his lifelong interest in the literary trends of his day. In both youth and middle age he tried his hand at sacred pastorals, and in the 1750s he endeavored to compile an anthology of the standard works of Augustan poetry. Fielding, Richardson, Swift, Pope, Addison, Goldsmith, Thomson, and Thomas Gray are among the authors he mentions he is reading. In the case of Swift, he wished "we might have the Instruction and Entertainment without so great Expence of Decency," and even *Clar-*

[8]PFP, Box 1, Folder 1 (Undated Sermons and Fragments), Sermon "Of Servants," pp. 4–5; Sermon on Job 42:10–17, p. 12; Folder 2, Sermon 258–59 (Oct. 23, 1726), pp. 3, 7.

issa needed, he felt, to be read "under strict Guard, & Caution." Yet *Clarissa* was helpful in acquiring the polish the age seemed to require and from the want of which his own daughters might otherwise suffer: "Such as are bred in the Country, & cant be afforded to live at Boarding Schools, may by those Means come to some Taste of brilliant Sense, when they cant be polishd by Conversation."[9]

But these explorations into more relaxed and refined ways did not constitute, in Parkman's case, a significant compromising of the traditional intensities of Puritan piety. He might have been composing a self-portrait when he wrote of his friend Sarah Pierpont of New Haven that she was fully acquainted with "the Best & newest Fashions of the Age . . . the Most Graceful & Genteel Carriage . . . the most improvd Arts & Sciences of the Schools as Rhetoric, Music &c. But then her Mind being early Seasond with Grace & devoted to God, she esteemed these things (Comparatively) as Empty Shadows, Golden Dreames, vain Amusements & childish Toies." The first entry in Parkman's diary is a brief spiritual autobiography in the classic Puritan manner. The date is August 24, 1719, just a few days short of the young man's sixteenth birthday. After counting his many blessings, he begins meticulously to record the rousing motions and lamentable backslidings that constitute his inner life: "On April 19 [year unspecified] I had Some Strivings and Motions of the holy Spirit to turn and live, and on December 27 allso but they Soon vanished as the Morning Cloud and as the early Dew." They vanished so completely, in fact, that Parkman "neglected this work (the Collection of Mercys) to my great Shame and Sorrow till February 19, 1719/20." At that point, he writes, "I was awakened out of my Sleepy Security of Sin, I was roused out of my Sloth, and the awakenings of my Conscience . . . began afresh upon me."

As frequently happened in the great Puritan struggle for inner rebirth, conviction of sin brought the sinner close to despair: "The Divil and my own wicked and abominably Sinfull and polluted heart persuading me that there was no hopes of Salvation lest That the Door of Mercy was Shut and the Day of Grace over—and that No man had Bakslidden or apostatized as I had done." Fortunately, his friend and Harvard classmate Samuel Barrett—later the minister of Hopkinton, adjacent to Westborough—reminded him of some con-

---

[9]*Harvard Graduates*, 6:511–27; PFP, Box 2, Folder 4 (Writings, 1718–71), "A Pastoral on the Death of Mr. William Charnock of Harvard Colledge, Cambridge, Aug. 18, 1721"; *Memoir of Sarah Pierpont* (1753), "Epistle Dedicatory" and "To the Memory of Madam Pierpont"; *Commonplace Book* (Massachusetts Historical Society), p. 44; PD, May 30, 1751; May 15, 1754; Jan. 9, 1756; Jan. 23, 1758; Oct. 3, 1765.

soling and hopeful passages of Scripture, the contemplation of which
drew him kicking and screaming in the right direction: "Little encouraged, utterly ashamed of my self and hating my self I resolved I
would return, and that I would once more Seek to God by Prayer."
He did so, but his struggle was far from over, as indeed it never was
for a Puritan of the genuine stamp: "But [I] soon grew Lookewarm
Neither cold nor hot wherefore I might justly have been Spew'd out
And Yet, through the Abundant, the Infinite grace and unparallel'd
Mercy of the Eternal JEHOVAH I have such privileges Yet, the Lord
knows how long they may be continued for there Never was any in the
world So unworthy as I am." Along with countless others in England
and New England from the sixteenth on into the nineteenth century,
Parkman apprehended himself in accordance with those psychic pat-
terns given their most memorable expression in John Bunyan's *Grace
Abounding to the Chief of Sinners*.[10]

Parkman's diary is replete with all aspects of the traditional Puritan
sensibility—he was deeply impressed by the sovereignty and omnipo-
tence of God, for example[11]—but what we will primarily examine will
be his thoroughly conventional realization that while success in spiritual and moral struggle was utterly beyond his power, given that he
was a miserable offender, just such endless struggle was nevertheless
his absolute and paramount obligation. For Parkman, as for many
other Puritans, the more one became aware of how hard one was
indeed struggling, the more likely one was to have one's sense of
unworthiness transform itself into its opposite—a sense of self-righteousness. To live as ever in one's great taskmaster's eye—a posture
Parkman formulated in his youth as "Gods Eye is allwayes upon *you*.
Therefore let your's allwayes be upon *him*"—was to be as ever tempted by the feeling that one was striving heroically in a world constantly
arraying itself in resistance and hostility to one's exertions. And this
was a temptation to which a Puritan might succumb even in situations
that seemed devoid of moral significance.

There was ample provocation to a sense of injustice and oppres-
sion, for example, in the circumstances confronting Parkman one
September day in 1758. Like all eighteenth-century country parsons,
Parkman kept a farm, and this was the day set aside for harvesting the
hay. But so many in the neighborhood were sick, including two of
Parkman's own sons, that it seemed certain all would be lost for lack of

[10]PFP, Box 2, Folder 4, *Memoir,* Part I (punctuation added); PD, Aug. 24, 1719.
Parkman speaks of "February 19, 1719/20," because Jan. 1 (as opposed to Mar. 25) was
not established as the beginning of the new year until the 1740s.
[11]See PD, Aug. 11, 1746.

hands. On top of that, Parkman's clerical neighbor, John Martyn of Northborough, scheduled to deliver the lecture at the Westborough church that day, would probably let him down, as he had in the past, and fail to show up. But what was he to do? He had to get in his hay somehow: "I hastily went up the Street to get Mr. *Adonijah* Rice but he was gone from Home—I went to [illegible] *Newton* who had an Hand with him—but could not persuade him in any wise." The "et tu Brute" stroke was delivered by one of Parkman's own deacons:

> In this extreme hurry and Confusion, the young man (Nathan) whom I had obtained so difficultly last night, now waiting and no body to work with him, I saw Deacon Tainter at Mr. Bectons Shop, and hearing him say he had been at Grafton yesterday & heard fine preaching there, the thought of our great Difficultys in this place for want of Help to get in our Hay which was suffering, there being so many sick in the Neigh-bourhood; more especially my own being obligd to let great part of my Grass & some of the best of my meadow Grass, stand & die; and *that* I had with much trouble got cutt was in Danger of being lost, (the thought of these and many more urgent things) pressing upon me, I told the Dea-con he should learn what that meaneth, I will have mercy & not sacrifice. You mean says he Mercy to your Hay, don't you. I answered *Yes*—& pass'd down the Road: for I was in great Haste to find somebody that would go to work. But not succeeding at Mr. Newtons, as aforesaid I returned to Bectons Shop, and told the Deacon (in Mr. Bectons Hearing) that I would not leave what I had said without adding that I acknowledgd he had been so kind & ready to help me, that there was no man like minded—what I said had the Effect, that he came down after me & pol'd out a Load of my Hay with *Nathan.*

So the story had a happy ending after all. Additional hands eventually pitched in, Martyn did show up for the lecture, and Deacon Tainter had the two reverend gentlemen over for dinner: "Thus was I calmd after great Tumult & confusion. . . . May God forgive what was amiss in me, at such a Time of Tryal." But salvation from what had seemed to be certain disaster does not seem to have liberated Parkman from his anxieties. His recollections of the day were set down after all was well, yet they are nevertheless organized so as to reproduce a sense of near intolerable stress and strain. Sequence is rearranged so that Deacon Tainter's remark about the good preaching in Grafton appears as dramatically as possible, as the last straw. Above all, the pressures toward frantic haste are made to pile up in a repetitious and con-voluted structure of participial suspensions. It may be that Parkman is simply displaying considerable literary skill here. Inner turmoil inten-sifies until it is expressed. Once it is out in the open, it can be healed by the deacon's blunt and salty rejoinder, by Parkman's deft manipulation of him, and by a steadily more comprehensive joining together in sociability. Yet the entry for the next day indicates that Parkman was still regretting that the circumstances of his farming were less than perfect: "And so I have now done Haying, after this Fashion—there being no Hands to cutt the Rest." The overwrought style in which Parkman records the trials and tribulations of his haying betokens not emotion recollected in tranquility so much as a determination to keep harrowing emotions as vividly present as possible, a desire to nurse along at every opportunity a sense of martyrdom. Opting for this frame of mind guarantees constant tension and turmoil, but it also guarantees constant engagement in the seductively pleasurable task of proving that one is basically in the right. Parkman's state of mind in this situation seems similar, though much intensified, to that of Adam in Book IV of *Paradise Lost* when he stresses to Eve the magnitude and gravity of the problems posed for them by the "wanton growth" of Paradise.[12]

Another example of this tendency shows embattled rectitude infiltrating Parkman's performance of his ministerial duties. While supplying a neighboring pulpit one March Sabbath in 1737, Parkman had to cope with an acquaintance of his who brought his child in for baptism at the very last minute, just as the duly appointed baptizing of another child was being completed. The minister had to refuse this latecomer:

My Reasons are these. Besides that, when I am spent with the foregoing Services, it is too much to expect me to repeat over them again. Besides that, such a custom indulged would involve us in great irregularity and Difficulty, but this administration for my known Friends would have forced me to make it a custom, and besides the impatience of many of the Congregation to get away home, being they live 4, 5 or 6 miles off. Besides those Reasons, I would urge that it was so very sudden upon me that I could not judge which way I could vindicate it if I should proceed. Again, by the suddenness I was too much confused to have my Power at command to perform the Devotions; nor was I furnished therefor (Eccl. 5, 1, 2). So that it would have been nothing short of horrible Presumption for me to have done it.

Between the lapses into present tense ("My Reasons are these"), the recourse to stiffly argumentative turns of phrase ("I would urge"),

12PFP, Box 2, Folder 4, "Rules of Behavior" (1719); PD, Sept. 7–8, 1758. For Adam's agrarian worries, see above, chap. 2, n. 8.

and the impression given that the reasons could be spun out indefinitely ("Besides . . . Besides . . . Again"), it is clear that Parkman is as closely engaged in debate and justification at the moment of recollecting and writing as he had been at the moment of refusing this irregular request.[13]

Our representative Colonial New England authority figure, ever mindful of God's eye always upon him, seems to inhabit a world in which one's moral identity is at constant risk and in which one can therefore never make one's fortifications too massive. This suggests another function of his diary: not only keeping the emotional and moral temperature as high as possible, but also maintaining a copious file of evidence against the day when explicit pleading on one's own behalf might become necessary. Ebenezer Parkman was a creature of script, keeping the records of both his church and his ministerial association, besides recording his daily affairs in voluminous detail. It appears from his final diary entry, only four days before his death, that he yielded to his gathering infirmity and set his pen aside for the last time only with the utmost reluctance. He was constantly drawing up written statements and memoranda on the various incidents with which he had to cope during his long clerical career, generating document after document as occasion seemed ever to require. As we shall see in the next chapter, this became a source of grievance in the course of the most serious crisis he had to deal with. He was himself not unaware of the spiritual and psychic significance of such compulsive self-documentation, for he frequently symbolized the restoration of Christian fellowship, the transmutation of self-defense and counterattack into grace and charity, as the destruction of these legalistic pieces of paper: "N. B. I had offer'd him that if he would withdraw his Letter to me he might burn my Reply to him." But alas, a spirit of wary, self-protective calculation and plea bargaining contaminated such gestures even as they were made. Parkman remained a defending and prosecuting attorney to the end of his days, always prepared to provide evidence and testimony on his own behalf. In 1772, after he had succeeded in establishing one of his sons as a tradesman, one Mr. Bass presumed to move to Westborough and set up a competing shop: "He falls upon me for my not visiting him since he came to Town. I made my Defence . . . it was not fit to play the Hypocrite & go & congratulate him & bid him welcome, when his coming here to trade was so much to my Damage, as *it was* to *mine* if it was to my *Son*'s, inasmuch as I was obligd to provide for him, & could not do it any where else as I could here . . . and *Breck* had made a

13PD, Mar. 25, 1737.

Business of informing him of his own Designs, & entreated him not to come, and this was so seasonably as that it was before he brought any Goods here." Having thus presented such a full summation of his case, Parkman felt free to rise above the dispute, but as he did so, he took care to arm himself for its possible resumption: "But I did not want to have any Contest with him: & thought it best to let him alone.—Mr. Thomas Twitchel was present and heard what I said."[14]

Ebenezer Parkman was a man driven and hounded by Puritan moral anxiety, and we shall be looking at a number of incidents in which this trait clashed with destructive effect against the laity's manner of asserting itself. But at those times when the Puritan structure of feeling inhabited Parkman in a less troubled manner, he evinced a level of moral and spiritual commitment that made him stay with a situation until some satisfactory resolution had been achieved. In August 1749 he had to do something about the invasion of his parish by Josiah Lyon, one of Mrs. Solomon Prentice's Separatist comrades from Grafton. Several times Lyon had been invited to preach by the young women of Westborough, and on this summer day he had finally accepted. Conservative parishioners "thought it might be no good for such Men to be here" and insisted that Parkman make Lyon leave. "After looking up to God and Considering the Matter, I got on my Horse and rode after him," Parkman tells us. But he did not run Lyon summarily out of town: "After Talk a long Time in the Mist on the Road I return'd home and he with me—he came in, and he tarried till it began to be Darkish. He deny'd that he pretended to have authority to preach—he deny'd his being in any Antinomian Errors, but declar'd he denounc'd them—affirm'd himself to be desirous to be in the way of Shepherd Hooker etc." Here we see the New England ecclesiastical system functioning virtually to perfection. By the exemplary power of patient dialogue, a member of a Ranter-like sect is brought out of the mist of his errors, brought in from the treacherous open road of itinerancy, brought home to the good old New England way of the militantly unantinomian "legal preachers" Thomas Shepard and Thomas Hooker. What Parkman was wont to call "that necessary Peace & Order" is preserved on this occasion not by suppressing enthusiasm but by taming it.[15]

[14]PD, Apr. 10, 1745; Aug. 13, 1772; Dec. 5, 1782. Breck Parkman was named after his mother, Hannah Breck Parkman, the daughter of the Reverend Robert Breck of Marlborough (and sister of the Reverend Robert Breck, Jr., of Springfield).

[15]PD, Aug. 10, 1749; PFP, Box 3, Folder 2 (Correspondence, 1735–69), "Letter to Mr. Pain" (May 19, 1743). For Shepard and Hooker as the leading "legal preachers" of the first generation, see Hall, *Faithful Shepherd*, pp. 162–66.

Parkman persisted with Lyon until it seemed that he had succeeded in gathering him back into the fold, until the heretical theology and spirituality Lyon had been espousing had in effect been co-opted. But what he was usually called upon to assimilate and incorporate in his dealings with his own people was not theological opinions so much as ecclesiological emotions. One summer Sabbath in 1755 quite a few of the brethren had submitted, in proper written form, requests for special prayers of petition or thanksgiving. Unfortunately, the pastor forgot about two of these prayers during the portion of the service set aside for them, and one of those whose offerings were thus not read, Lieutenant Bruce, took it extremely ill. Bruce barged into Parkman's home after the service: "The Storm abroad was great, Thunder, Lightening, and Rain. Yet the Storm of Brother Bruce's Passions was more grievous; uttering many bitter and grievous Things; neither could I at all lay his Passionate Heat by anything I could Say. He went away talking and in a Rage, notwithstanding it was the Sabbath, and the Storm which Should have Struck Terror, into each of our Hearts."

Appalled and distressed, Parkman decided to return to the meetinghouse and clear away any misconceptions about what had happened that might be entertained by the brethren who were still lingering there. On the way, being unable to "suffer him to go away in Such a Frame," Parkman sought out Bruce and again strove to mollify him, urging him to come to the meetinghouse and attend to the public explanation of the incident. But Bruce refused, and Parkman had to go on without him. "When I got into the Meeting House I was Somewhat out of Breath by my running through the Rain," he states, and one suspects that he was also impelled into such haste by an acute anxiety over what he felt he had done amiss. More people were gathered together than Parkman had anticipated, attracted no doubt by word of Brother Bruce's psychic storm, and Parkman therefore "conceiv'd it best for the prevention of further Mischief to declare that it was thro my Infirmity and no otherwise that [Bruce's prayer] was Neglected." Parkman also described to the assembled company "the violent Anger" that Bruce was in, "and continued in, though I did all in my Power to Compose and Satisfie him." Bruce had "assur'd me he would never bring me any Papers (to desire Prayers) any more." On the way home, Parkman "labour'd to pacifie" Bruce yet again, "but all was in Vain."

The day's diary entry had to be concluded with an acknowledgment that Bruce's adamant attitude "was a just Chastizement from God upon me, for my own Sloth and Negligence! the Lord be mercifull to me a Sinner!" It was not until Parkman called upon him the next day that Bruce "receiv'd me civilly—no word of yesterday." But Parkman knew that the labor of Christian reconciliation was not yet complete: "When I parted while I had him by the Hand I told him I would not have any Difficulty between him and me, and he answer'd Smiling, 'with all my Heart.'" Minor sin of omission, major offense taken and threatening to spread, consequent inner turmoil, not avoiding the offended party but rather repeatedly placing oneself in his way, insisting that the unpleasantness be terminated in explicitness—a good day's pastoral and moral work for the Reverend Mr. Parkman.[16]

The Lieutenant Bruce incident shows Parkman putting his Puritan moral sense to work in the most patient and determined, the most judiciously and scrupulously humane manner. Yet its most intriguing features are the gross disproportion between the intensity of Brother Bruce's wrath and the occasion of it, and the fact that Parkman did not pause to inquire into this disproportion. Lieutenant Bruce's fierce and intractable anger looks very much the result of what modern psychology calls an "unresolved issue." It looks as if it is intruding itself into a situation with which it has nothing directly or rationally to do. From this point of view, Parkman's failure to read Bruce's prayer is not what Bruce is really upset about; this is merely the catalyst for some more fundamental sense of grievance which, precisely because it is so deep-lying, Bruce is unable to articulate in a more immediately intelligible manner.

Psychologists have tended to interpret the dynamics of unresolved issues as though they were primarily a function of individualized experiences, such as the oedipal traumas of early childhood. But the configurations of human life are clearly such that particularized family experiences are but one of many kinds of social factors contributing to the formation of the human psyche. An awareness of this elementary reality is what underlies the premodern and early modern convention of the family as a little commonwealth, a microcosm of the larger society. My inner life is as much the result of the fact that I am a child of the educated, professional middle classes of mid-twentieth-century America as it is of the fact that I am the child of my own specific parents. So even though we know very little about Ebenezer Parkman's fully individualized psychic history, and nothing at all about Lieutenant Bruce's, we may nevertheless still speculate with profit about the sources of their interactions in the summer of 1755. What are the overarching sociocultural factors that may help to account for "the Storm of Brother Bruce's passions" and Parkman's unwillingness to think about it?

The most convenient way to approach this question is to examine a

[16]PD, June 22–23, 1755.

few of the many other episodes in Parkman's ministerial career that are fraught with unresolved issues. In April 1727 the young Reverend Mr. Parkman was called to attend at the deathbed of Mrs. Samuel Forbush. In the prescribed manner, Parkman sympathized with Mrs. Forbush, asked about her spiritual condition, and upon being told that "she was under apprehension of the approach of Death and she could not but be under fears on So great an Occasion," set about systematically "to enquire into the grounds of her Fears telling withal that I should endeavour to remove them." It pleased Parkman to be able to note that "this process I managed in . . . an easy and familiar manner." Had the good woman fully repented of her sins? Yes. Had she been a faithful member of the church? Yes again. "Don't you find in you Such a Love to God as has made you both repent of Sin and Obey his Comands from a Desire of his Glory? etc. etc. . . . have you a pure love to the Godly; do you love the Disciples of Christ, those that you think bear the Image of God unfeignedly?" Mrs. Forbush's responses continued in the affirmative. All was proceeding with smooth regularity, redounding "much to her Comfort and benefit."

Unfortunately, one of the other people present, the dying woman's brother-in-law Thomas Forbush, had grown increasingly impatient as he listened to Parkman's catechistical exercise. Finally he could stand it no longer: "Sir, We are grown folks." Parkman was amazed at this interruption, but he was not dislodged from his composure and dignity: "I turned about in great Surprize and calmly looking upon him and then as calmly Speaking asked what he had said." Forbush's repetition elicited from the pastor a more imposing display of dignity, as he gave ear to his parishioner's explanation of his bizarre misconduct: "I asked him what then? (Now raising my Self up in my Chair) why then (says he) we understand these things already have read in the Bible and Some other Books, and ourselves know these things being grown folks and come into years."

Part of what is going on here is clearly a testing of the still relatively new, relatively inexperienced minister. The incongruity of a youth behaving with such easy condescension toward people whose experience of life was so much greater than his own is no doubt a large part of what makes Thomas Forbush's initial outburst so pithy: "Sir, We are grown folks." Such straight talk seems to be a long way from the opaque ferocity of "the Storm of Brother Bruce's passions." Yet Forbush's remark and Bruce's storm may nevertheless have arisen from similar sources, and what these are may be indicated by Forbush's amplification of what he barked out. He and the others present were "grown folks," in the sense that they understood "these things already have read in the Bible and Some other Books." That is to say, Forbush was an autonomous, intellectually empowered New England Protestant and Puritan layman, and therefore, even as he submitted to the orderliness of Parkman's deathbed ministrations, he chafed and squirmed under it. His response, with his sense of his own autonomy rudely elbowing its way into a situation that seemed to have become so guided and controlled, so *established,* as not to acknowledge its existence, expresses one side of the emotional equation engendered by New England ecclesiastical structures that were, like New England household structures, simultaneously and uneasily equal and unequal. Similarly, what may have enraged Brother Bruce so much in 1755 was that he had done exactly as Parkman always required. He had not intruded with a spontaneous, extemporary prayer. Rather, he had brought his "desires written," had prepared and submitted his petition in advance, accommodated his psychic and spiritual life to a structure of decency and propriety. Yet still he had been unable to make himself heard. Without being able to put it to himself or to Parkman this way, he had broken down in frustration over what seemed part of a process of limiting the exercise of his Protestant birthright.

Just as Thomas Forbush's interruption seems more coherent than Brother Bruce's outrage thirty years later, so Parkman's manner of dealing with Forbush here in his youth seems to indicate a greater interest in getting at the root of the matter than he subsequently showed in coping with Bruce. As Forbush continued to insist that "if I had been in your place I would not have asked Such Questions," Parkman "reply'd in defence of them." That is, he entered into discussion and debate, immediately validating Forbush's intuition that what his ecclesiastical superiors wanted from him was not childlike deference but grown-up, rational consent. Yet the ensuing dialogue could not be an equal, straightforward one between two rational Protestant "grown folks," for its real as opposed to its manifest content was too fundamental and enveloping to be precisely stated. Forbush had an uneasy awareness of having been in some way insulted, an inkling that there was something in the structure and tone of the situation that conflicted with his Puritan view of himself as a full-fledged adult, but since he could not define it, he could not rise to meet Parkman's entirely reasonable challenge: "I therewith pray'd him to Say which [questions] were improper and wherein. He appear'd not able to tell so much as what any one Question was that I had asked." He could only engage in a quite ineffectual sniping: "He Said Mr. Breck [Rev. Robert Breck, Sr., of Marlborough] would not ask Such. . . . You ask (Say'd he) whether she had not comfort in her having been at the Sacrament. How needless that question. What do you think She went to it for, Sir?"

Forbush's inability to specify his grievance makes him appear subrational, childish, only a step removed, after all, from Brother Bruce's sheer emotion. He has made it certain, therefore, that Parkman will appear to be overwhelmingly in the right: "I answer'd I was not now to enquire what Mr. Breck would ask, but I was able to affirm that the most Learned, the most pious and the most Judicious ministers would. . . . I admire at you Mr. Forbush. Your Sister's End was to testifie her Obedience to the Command of Christ, and to obtain of her Lord Divine Grace and Support under all Troubles and difficulties, to Engage Gods mercifull presence in a time of Extremity, especially when Death approaches. She has been I say, for these great and important things and now when She needs them most of all I ask whether she has got her Errand and how she is Sure She has these things and This is impertinent, etc., etc." From Parkman's unruffled manner, it is clear that the counterpart of lay petulance, which seems ungrounded only because it arises from the contradictions in which Puritan society was in fact ultimately grounded, is a complacent clerical rationality that sees no need to search beyond the terms and the agenda set by the status quo. And Parkman's openness to rational deliberation and dialogue thus turns out to be only a little less evasive than his striking failure to take note of Brother Bruce's vehemence.

In one of Forbush's cavils can be detected the seed of a more definitely spiritistic dissatisfaction with a church that had become so thoroughly established: "And You asked whether She lov'd the Godly? What a Question that is! I know what you mean whether She loves all that Appear professedly to be Christians. I havn't a Charity for everybody because they make a profession. There is some that I know of that I won't have a Charity for tho they have join'd to the Church." But if Forbush meant to register a criticism of hypocrites, and of a sense of charity and fellowship that had been reduced to a bland amiability, he was again unable to make such criticism rise to clear and distinct articulation, and the field was thus again left open for Parkman to expropriate all available mature understanding, all spiritual and moral generosity: "Mr. Forbush notwithstanding what you have last Said as to your Charity I'll tell you mine is So extensive that there is not a person in all Westboro but I would charitably hope he may be a subject for the Divine Grace to work upon. Well, he would not, etc."

Well, he would not. The two of them were stuck—stuck in their discussion and stuck with their complicated relationship: "Mr. Forbush ask'd I'd forgive him if he had said anything wrong but he thought he would not ask Such questions. So that I So far lost my labour with him." Neither Forbush nor Parkman could move beyond a root conviction that Forbush was the one who was to blame for what was happening, that it was up to the subordinate Forbush to petition for and to the superior Parkman to hand down the judgments and merciful dispensations that would define and govern the situation. But Forbush both was and was not a subordinate, just as he both was and was not a brother and a peer. Insofar as he was the latter, he could not relinquish his objections. But insofar as he was the former, he could not develop them. And since he was both, he could only repeat them: "I pray'd him to consider his sister. He was willing with all Saying that he knew not how soon he should need me on the Same account and therefore again desire[d] me to forgive his bluntness, but yet He could not desire me if ever I should to ask him such sort of Questions. Thus did he in a strange manner keep up the flame by throwing in oil when he pretended to cast in water to quench it." Whereupon Parkman threw in a little oil of his own by wrapping himself, in a manner he was later to perfect, in the mantle of the entirely conscientious fulfillment of his duties: "No, Mr. Forbush Said I with some earnestness, I'm afraid you would not care that I should deal feelingly with your soul. I now told him of my being oblig'd in Conscience to do my utmost for persons when as his Sister, etc. I shall take no further notice of the Strange reply he made me nor the long discourse he further occasion'd. I was griev'd heartily to See So much of his ignorance and passions."

This then was Reverend Parkman's special contribution to the convoluted emotional dynamic that was inherent in New England ecclesiology: as the strife dragged on and on, his complacent rationality was always being drawn toward a self-righteousness that was, in its way, just as stubbornly and aggressively defensive as was Forbush's inchoate clinging to his autonomy. Just so, in his dealings with Brother Bruce, Parkman was eventually moved to declare: "I had done and Said enough (and indeed it was too much) I would not trouble my Self any more." So long as Puritan culture would permit such people as Forbush and Bruce to be neither pulled up into full equality nor pushed down into unambiguous subordination, their controversies with those in authority such as Parkman could not be resolved (despite the appearance of resolution in the Bruce incident). Instead, all parties would feel compelled to "magnify things and dwell upon them a long time," until weariness would induce a temporary cessation of hostilities.[17]

---

[17]PD, Apr. 21, 1727; for "desires written," see PD, Apr. 12, 1747.

During the Great Awakening, Parkman attempted to steer a middle course, as indicated by the vote of the Westborough church in January 1743 to hold "a Day of Solemn Fasting & Prayer [in order to] obtain the Blessing & avoid the Snares [of] the present Times, which are full of Religious Commotions." What made the Awakening a blessing, as far as Parkman was concerned, was that it amounted to a widespread revival of piety. In December 1741 he informed Jonathan Edwards that "some observable reviving there is among our Youth particularly and no less than six Religious Societys (of all sorts) are sett up among us." He hoped "that Converts may be filled with . . . Joy in the holy Ghost & made meet for the Inheritance of the Saints in Light," and he asked Edwards to let him have "the Assistance of your fervent Prayers." In January 1743 he urged his son Ebenezer, Jr., to participate in the "peculiar awakenings" taking place in Grafton, while as for himself, his mind "wrought very much on my inward State and upon what God is doing among his people." It was no doubt owing to the influence of the Awakening that Parkman came "to fear that I have had too strong a Reliance and Dependence upon *Form*" and that he consequently did not observe his annual meditative "*Birthday Formalitys*" during 1741 and 1742.[18]

The snares that were laid during the Great Awakening arose, as far as Parkman was concerned, from its encouragement of unauthorized, itinerant preaching and evangelizing. In May 1743 Parkman's Westborough parish was invaded by one of the most forceful and able of these radical lay missionaries, Elisha Paine of Canterbury, Connecticut. Parkman wrote to Paine that he was "none of those who lord it over God's Heritage (as I humbly hope)." He was no mere clericalist, no foolish Old Light obscurantist, not the sort of defender of order who could see no value at all in enthusiasm. He had sought, on the contrary, to "encourage & promote whatever might tend by the Blessing of God to the reviving and Carrying on His Glorious work & Kingdom in this place." But it was nevertheless incumbent upon him to enforce "that necessary Peace & Order which the Great Lord & Head of the Church has requird all *his* to submitt to, for their Edification as well as Preservation." To Parkman's centrist, assimilationist way of thinking, enthusiasm was indeed to be expressed, but only to the extent that it could be integrated into the landscape enclosed by what he called, in his letter to those who invited Paine, the "Sacred

---

[18]*Records of the Church of Christ in Westboro* . . . (Westborough, Mass., Public Library; photocopy at American Antiquarian Society), Jan. 26, 1743; *Commonplace Book*, pp. 108–9; PD, Jan. 4–5, 1743; *Natalitia* (American Antiquarian Society), Sept. 5, 1743.

Fence" of the New England ecclesiastical establishment, just as his parishioners were to be allowed to present their prayers and petitions, but only in the proper, prepared form, not spontaneously or extemporaneously, but rather as "desires written."[19]

Parkman did succeed by and large in guiding his church through the Great Awakening in such a way as to "avoid the Snares" of explicit controversy in which the Grafton and other nearby churches became entangled. We have already observed the patient and skillful manner in which he dealt with the Grafton Separatist Josiah Lyon in 1749. His firm yet sympathetic way of both permitting and containing the enthusiasm expressed by a female member of the congregation one summer Sabbath in 1746 probably tells much about why Westborough remained relatively calm: "P. M. Mrs. Whitney cry'd out in the middst of the sermon. I pray'd her to be as compos'd as possible; and she was not long a Disturbance."[20] But if Parkman's ministerial career constitutes an illuminating case study in ecclesiastical co-optation, it is of even greater interest as a revelation of the costs of such co-optation. Two episodes of the 1740s show how during the Great Awakening hegemonic incorporation amounted, more clearly than at any other time during Parkman's nearly sixty years in his post, to a trivialization of the emergent, a turning aside from the invitation "to descry new lands."

The reason that Elisha Paine had come to preach and exhort in Westborough was that he had been asked to do so by a member of the Westborough church, Stephen Fay, the son of Deacon John Fay. Fay had not bothered to obtain Parkman's permission for this invitation. James Fay was Stephen's equally militant older brother. A few months before the difficulties over Paine, the Fays had taken to holding private meetings that bore the authentic stamp of revivalism: "A number of Children were suppos'd to be much fill'd with the Spirit and carry'd out in Spiritual Joy last Night at Mr. [James] Fays." At this point, Parkman was not opposed to what the Fays were doing. He had allowed his son Ebenezer, "under Special Charge," to go to this particular meeting. But relations became strained after the insubordination over Paine, and Parkman began to be confronted with disconcerting

---

[19]PFP, Box 3, Folder 2, "Letter to Mr. Pain"; "Letter to Deacon Fay." For Paine's prominence among Great Awakening radicals, see C. C. Goen, *Revivalism and Separatism in New England, 1740–1800: Strict Congregationalists and Separate Baptists in the Great Awakening* (New Haven, Conn.: Yale University Press, 1962), p. 115.

[20]PD, Aug. 24, 1746. For Grafton, see above, chap. 4, n. 29; and for other disrupted churches in the neighborhood, see PD, Jan. 19, 1744 (Shrewsbury); Feb. 1, 1744 (Upton, Hopkinton, and Leicester); Apr. 25, 1745 (Framingham); May 12, 1748 (Sutton); Feb. 7, 1749 (Concord and Sudbury).

tantrums of the same sort he had seen from Thomas Forbush and would see again from Lieutenant Bruce.

In May 1744, while paying a call at the house of Deacon Fay, he was accosted by Stephen Fay's wife, Ruth: "She desir'd to Speak alone with me, the Conversation the most unaccountable and intolerable that ever I met with Making Exceptions against the most inexceptionable parts of my Sermon today; and declaring her great Dissatisfaction to my preaching in general, and to my Ministration, and yet in plain Terms said she could not give any Reason why." It is the pattern of the Forbush and Bruce episodes: grievances too generalized and basic to attach themselves to a manageable reason why are expressed, with the aggrieved lay party both asserting herself over against her clerical overlord and manifesting her continuing umbilical attachment to her clerical nursing father: "Upon my reproving her for her unreasonableness, She freely Submitted to it, and when I ask'd her whether She thought these Things proceeded from the Spirit of God, She freely acknowledg'd that She did think they did not, but from the Contrary. But She desir'd I would not be angry, for She knew it was the Effect of prejudice reigning and prevailing in her against me, and She pray'd me to tell her what She Should do to get rid of it, or what I could do to help her?" In asking Parkman not to be angry, Ruth Fay was asking—it seems likely—that her inner strivings be taken seriously. She had been awakened, an experience that was troubling but also fascinating. A part of herself—the part that had not found a vocabulary, only a searching tone—wanted to wake up more completely, which would mean, as far as her relations with her minister were concerned, a passage from subordination, through obsession, to mutuality and authenticity.

Parkman, however, was not open to the possibility of mutual awakening to new relationship. As the official representative of things as they are, he endeavored to prevent, by his wonted method of complacent categorization, the emergence of potentially disruptive alterations: "I ask'd her whether She did not think She was under the influence of a Party Spirit. She said it was most likely. I told her the Apostle directed me to rebuke her Sharply that She might be Sound in the Faith and this therefore (I told her) I now did, for it was a great Sin and wickedness which She was guilty of herein, and I pray'd her to consider how dangerous it was to be So much under the Influence of the Adversary and bid her beware—with divers other Such Expressions—which She thank'd me for and we concluded." Parkman is successful in addressing the dutiful and conventionally pious side of Ruth Fay. The two of them conspire together to confine the quickenings of new spiritual life and potentially new ecclesiastical order within the reductive options provided by the dominant tradition: manifesting the "Spirit of God" as opposed to "a Party Spirit"; being "Sound in the Faith," as opposed to being "under the Influence of the Adversary."

Nevertheless, the symptoms of enthusiasm continued, in Westborough, to focus upon the Fay family. The women, including Ruth, were frequently moved to cry out during Sabbath services. The men began to object more cogently to Parkman's sermons, arguing about such things as his "allowing Recreations of any kind." James Fay took to deserting the Westborough meetinghouse in favor of the one in Grafton, where Solomon Prentice was endorsing the Awakening without any of Parkman's hesitations and reservations. Upon being interrogated by Parkman about this, James behaved in the same ambivalent manner as his sister-in-law, both denying and affirming that his relationship with his pastor had become problematic: "He told me that he had not been so disgusted as to leave us, but we were Crowded at our Meeting House, and he liv'd almost as near and handy to Grafton. . . . He, in the Course of the Talk told me my Conversation was but a little of Spiritual Things—that Mr. Prentices Sermons were lively, profitable and Excellent—that as for me I very much affected such ministers as were opposite—but especially I was Sett against those whom he could not bear to hear a word against: Such as . . . Mr. Prentice." Even as James Fay began to move away from Parkman, he testified to the ongoing presence and power of the hierarchical pole of New England ecclesiology, judging his minister not in direct relation to doctrine or piety or his own views, but rather by comparison with other ministers.

A sequence of entries in Parkman's diary for September 1745 show that the relationship between the Fays and Parkman had become thoroughly deadlocked. September 3: "[Stephen] last night in a great Flame, on the sudden, about [going to other meetings], but Came to me to Day to acknowledge his unguarded Passion and indecency at that time." September 4: "Visited Mr. James Fays family—much uncomfortable Complaint of me and my approving the Neibouring [Old Light] Ministers, Mr. Barrett Especially. [Parkman's Harvard classmate and the minister in Hopkinton] N. B. Stephen Fay came and return'd as far as his house with me; and just before parting flew into a dreadful passion with me that I did not Consent to his going away to other Towns on the Lords Day: and immoderately rak'd up my Strict Charge given him about Mr. Elisha Paine." September 5: "Stephen Fay here acknowledging his indecent Temper and Manner last Night, but stands to the Things that he Spoke. The Lord Shew him his Error!" This love-hate impasse was brought to a climax, of sorts, later in the month: "At Eve Stephen Fay here with his uneasiness Still, for my reproofs at the Time of Mr. Elisha Paine and for my saying at his Brother Fays that his wife had acknowledged to me that her dissatisfaction to Me and my ministrations was from a wrong Spirit which was true. See her talk with me, May 3, 1744."

Ruth Fay's struggle with new impulses of May 3, 1744, had been an integral part of the similar struggle of the entire family. That larger struggle had been obscured and deflected all along by Parkman's complacent and moralistic management of it, and as Parkman's objectification of his interchange with Ruth Fay into an evidentiary deposition foreshadows, it was now to be further reduced and impoverished into a legalistic wrangle:

> Messers. James and Stephen Fay and their wives here, and had a long Conference with me about their Uneasiness. They judg'd that Seeing Ruths Offence against me (May 3, 1744) was private, I ought not to have divulg'd it. I Reply'd that if She had not done it herself I Should not made [sic] the Reply that I did at James's that She confess'd to me that her Disaffection to me was from a wrong Spirit. They said she had not done it, for they never knew of what was done or said at the Time referr'd to; she had not told them. I return'd that by their telling me that she was dissatisfy'd with me, and expressing themselves as they did I could not but take it that She had, for that was the principal if not only Time wherein she had manifested dissatisfaction and disaffection to me. But I added that if she had not I misapprehended them, and I was Sorry that I said a word about it; and I desir'd James and his wife to take notice of it; but I hop'd they would not be so unwise as to Make any Noise about these Things, but prudently Conceal them. Lydia [James Fay's wife] Said I had pray'd them at their House not to mention what at that time I said of Ruth, and they did not intend to, but She drop'd something of it before she was aware. Stephen very much insisted and entreated I would humour him so much as to let him see what I had writ about his wifes Discourse with me. After some time refusing I gratify'd him (with her Consent) and putting the others into another Room, I read my Journal of that Time to them but she Seem'd not to Remember much about it.

The situation has come to be utterly suffused with reification, the transformation of processes into things. Ruth Fay's combined confrontation with Parkman and appeal to him of May 1744 might have formed part of a process of inner exploration and the altering and strengthening of relationships. Instead, it has been transfixed as a slightly melodramatic and somehow slightly shameful single event.

The Fays are now exhorted to join together with Parkman not in discovery and growth, but rather in keeping well out of sight the new lands that might have been descried. And the Fays do immediately begin to behave as Parkman wishes. Stephen Fay demands to be "humoured," and Parkman is only too happy to oblige, enhancing the "gratification" by tantalizing delay and secretive staging. It is a masterwork of co-optation, as the Fays' spiritual lives are reduced to prurient spectacle. Of course, Ruth Fay "seem'd not to Remember much about it." By this point there is nothing at all for her to remember.[21]

The Westborough blacksmith, Cornelius Cook, was more successful than the Fays in placing himself on a new footing with Parkman. Cook and his wife, Eunice, were in trouble from the beginning, being admitted to the church in 1727 only after confessing to fornication. In October 1741 the church found Cook guilty of "profane swearing," and for the next several years he struggled with his response to the loss of full ecclesiastical stature and privilege, now confessing that he had indeed been at fault, now seeming to call the entire apparatus of discipline into question. In September 1744, while Parkman and Cook were exploring the possibility of Cook's readmission, "without any Sign of Provocation that I know of . . . [Cook] bitterly told me that he had been more abus'd by me, and by my wife and Children than ever he had been abus'd in all his life." As with Thomas Forbush and Ruth Fay, the very abruptness of the outburst and the transparent lack of immediate justification for it testify to the probability that Cook's feelings of grievance were rooted not in this or that particular, but rather in the overarching structure and underlying tone of his entire relationship with his minister. And as we have seen in every instance examined, Parkman proceeded to cope with the problem by continuing to embody and enact it. He responded to Cook from too far overhead, meting out to him that combination of moralistic judgment and legalistic documentation which is probably what Cook had been referring to when he said he had been abused by Parkman: "After I had administered some Reproof and Reason'd with him and told him I should make a minute of this he left me." Cook therefore continued to play his assigned part of acted-out irrationality: "N. B. Cornelius Cook here and as violent as ever . . . remains very disorderly and under bitter prejudices."

[21]PD, Jan. 12, 1743; Jan. 13, 1743; May 3, 1744; May 28, 1744; June 3, 1744; July 1, 1744; July 9, 1744; Sept. 3–5, 1745; Sept. 25, 26, 1745. The Fays, both the James and Stephen branches, eventually moved away from Westborough and belonged to Separatist groups in Hardwick, Massachusetts, and Bennington, Vermont. Parkman was still maintaining contact with Stephen and Ruth Fay many years later; see PD, Mar. 4, 1777.

At some point during 1745 Cook's disaffection began to attach itself to the overt forms of enthusiasm which had emerged from the Awakening. When his next child was born in September, his wife had to bring it to the Westborough church for baptism by herself, Cook "being out of Frame & having gone for Some Time to other Meetings." Matters came to a head in January 1746, when an attempt was made to resolve the disagreement in the mediating presence of three members of the church. Not surprisingly, Cook refused to accept a reconciliation that was contingent upon his agreeing to "comply," which meant abandoning what his own experience was telling him and submitting entirely to Parkman's authority. But neither could he simply part in resigned alienation. What happened after the unsuccessful mediation came as close as anything in Parkman's entire career to spelling out for him the underlying causes and meanings of his repeated brushes with subenthusiasm:

When I was mounted on my Horse to return home, he came out and seem'd to express his desire of Forgiveness; and thereupon—giving him my Hand told him I was willing if he acknowledg'd, and was Sorry for his undutifull Conduct towards me in Time past, and would Carry it (by the Help of Grace) in a Suitable Manner becoming his Relation to me, for the future. This he seem'd once to Consent to, but afterwards drew back from it; and Seem'd to expect an acknowledgment from Me also with regard to my Carriage towards him—which I could see no ground for; and ask'd whether it could be expected when I admonish'd those under my Pastoral Care whom I found defective, if it came Close to them and they should frett at it if it was no more than was necessary for them, and my own indispensible Duty? I left him with the Brethren, hoping that if he was truely Sensible, and reform'd I Should soon know it; but any thing that was only Sudden and Strain, would (I conceiv'd) not last long. N. B. his unaccountable ways of Softening his Several harsh allegations against me, and heavy Complaints of me from Time to Time. Exceeding great his Explanation of his Saying "I had abus'd him more than any Man in the world—why," he said, "one word from me, from Mr. Parkman was worse than any body else could Speak." Again, when he told me that a main Thing he had against me was "That I was an Enemy of the Work of God." This he said he meant thus, that we all had naturally an Enmity against God and his work: and the ministers being at Variance one with another was a great Hindrance and discouragement, and that I had taken Such ways and methods as he could not judge were so prudent and fit to promote the Work of the late Times; and he likewise endeavor'd to enervate and interpret away his Strange Message by Noah How to me, "that he felt So towards me and Sometimes that he could Bite Me."

One can only stand in awe of the insight into his situation gained by this rough blacksmith, against all odds and in the teeth of all authoritative resistance. He recognized how deeply rooted the New England hierarchy was, how its very intelligence and benevolence had only enhanced its capacity for subtle and saturating domination. Yet he also realized, unlike more superficial radicals both before and since, that there could be no simple separation from or destruction of an authority and order that was thus psychically entrenched. Cook both acknowledged the depth and strength of his feelings about Parkman's all-pervasive influence and control, and affirmed the traditional Protestant right of judging his teacher. As best he could, he was inviting Parkman to join with him in a redefined relationship of mutual responsibility, intellectual partnership, and avowed psychosocial intimacy: in short, a relationship transformed from hierarchy into fraternity. Parkman's ensuing disregard of this man's laying himself at his feet and making him a present of his deepest experience is an extremely low point in the reverend gentleman's pastoral labors: "Nothing being effected, nor much prospect of it, and my wife being ill at Home, I came home." Thud. But Cook's self-assertion may have amounted to a giant step forward for him, if not for Parkman. Two years later, when Parkman again offered reconciliation on condition of eating humble pie, Cook was able to decline without rancor: "We parted this Time in peace." He is next seen having Parkman officiate at his son's wedding, and a year later we find him quietly helping with the raising of Parkman's new house. As so often in America, someone seeking renewed community had to settle for a purely individual autonomy.[22]

Cornelius Cook came closer than anyone else in eighteenth-century Westborough to transforming the impossible Puritan synthesis of hierarchy, equality, love, and a stubborn assertiveness all around into a genuine alternative vision. He played a role here in the winter of 1746 quite similar to the one we shall find Eve playing at a crucial postlapsarian moment in *Paradise Lost*. But unfortunately, the most significant respect in which Ebenezer Parkman differs from Adam is in his failure to open up to Cook's overture as Adam, eventually, does to

---

[22]*Church Records*, Dec. 31, 1727; Oct. 9, 1741; Jan. 26, 1743; July 1, 1744; Sept. 22, 1745; PD, Sept. 11, 1744; Oct. 23, 1744; Feb. 25, 1745; Jan. 15, 1746; June 17, 1748; Feb. 6, 1749; Jan. 17, 1750. Two of Cook's sons became notorious vagabonds and criminals, one of them, indeed, making himself into a colorful Robin Hood figure in the neighborhood, styling himself "the leveler." Like his father, the younger Cook chose to maintain his relations with Parkman in the midst of his deviant and rebellious behavior; see PD, Nov. 14, 1776; Aug. 27, 1779; July 4, 1781.

Eve's. More broadly, the pattern of interaction and response we have thus far seen between Parkman and his parishioners is in many ways the pattern of Adam's and Eve's descent into a vain contest that appeared to have no end. Thomas Forbush, Ruth, Stephen, and James Fay, Cornelius Cook, and Eve all speak distortedly and overheatedly about fundamental difficulties they do not know how to articulate more clearly, and they all evince an uneasiness that makes them now reject the person in authority and now cling to him. For their part, both persons in authority—Parkman and Adam—help ensure that these situations of psychosocial strain will remain deadlocked by stubbornly intensifying, rather than astutely modifying, that hegemonic mode of dogmatic, a priori reasoning characteristic of each of them. All that was needed in Westborough to make its ecclesiastical life conform completely to the model laid out in *Paradise Lost* was the development of a controversy into which the entire community would be drawn. And such a controversy did indeed arise in the tumultuous atmosphere of the era of the American Revolution.[23]

[23]For Eve after the Fall, see below, Conclusion, nn. 7–8.

Chapter 6

Of Their Vain Contest Appeared
No End: Westborough, 1763–1775

Just as Ebenezer Parkman was not simply an unreconstructed Old Light during the Great Awakening of the 1740s, so he was not simply a Tory during the revolutionary era of the 1760s and 1770s. Once again he sought to "obtain the Blessing & avoid the Snares" of a time of tumult by a strategy of containing popular agitation and enthusiasm within the established order. At the end of 1774, in a letter to a special town meeting called to consider the measures of resistance to British policy recommended by the Continental and Provincial congresses, he spoke out against the "dreadfull Slavery with which we are now threatned." He was, he declared, "a true Friend to Liberty in Church & State." But as far as Parkman was concerned, this was a conservative rather than a revolutionary stance, for what was occurring amounted, he believed, to a defense of "all the Rights & privileges this Province has been wont to enjoy, thro the Goodness of God to us, by our invaluable Charter & platform . . . that as we receivd them from our worthy renowned ancestors, [we] may deliver them inviolate to our posterity." Events that appeared to be innovative were thus in Parkman's view really the very opposite of that. Their purpose was to preserve the essential New England tradition, not to disrupt it.

Such was the assimilationist posture Parkman endeavored to maintain from the time of the resistance to the Stamp Act in 1765 to the outbreak of war in 1775. But this time the center would not hold. Popular radicalism was finally refusing to be absorbed. For example, not signing the Non-Importation Covenant, which was a choice Parkman made in the summer of 1774, did little to help the revolution remain moderate. It merely made the community suspect that their minister was, after all, little better than a Tory. Whatever he may have stated in public about his wholehearted support of a rational and orderly opposition to British imperialism, in private Parkman sensed that what the crisis really portended was sheer disorder, the advent of a rough beast whose hour had come round at last. The very next day after he told the special town meeting that the protection of tradition was what the struggle was all about, he set down in his diary a rather different summary of the events of 1774: "Mobs & Riots; *Whiggs* & *Torys*—as if our Happiness were nigh to an End! O God save us!"[1]

What lay behind this earnest supplication was not merely the chaotic spectacle presented by the Massachusetts civil landscape on the eve of the Revolutionary War. Parkman's sense of beleaguerment also arose from issues and events closer to home. By the end of 1774 the people of Westborough were suffering from twelve years of virtually continuous struggle among themselves. All that time they had been demonstrating anew that the New England tradition was not, despite Parkman's claims to the town meeting, one of untroubled consensual enjoyment of "Rights & privileges . . . by our invaluable Charter & platform," but rather one of perpetual uneasiness within, arising from the ambiguous nature of exactly those rights, privileges, and essential documents to which Parkman was referring. The community's internal difficulties had begun sometime in the early 1760s, probably in 1763, when a couple by the name of Andrews moved to Westborough from the Chebacco parish of Ipswich (the area now forming the town of Essex, on the North Shore between Ipswich and Gloucester) and set up shop as innkeepers. George and Eunice Andrews had been members of the church in Chebacco of which John Cleaveland was the pastor. Cleaveland had grown up in Canterbury, Connecticut, that nursery of pietistic enthusiasm which had also been the home of Elisha and Solomon Paine. He had been expelled from Yale in 1745 after refusing to disavow his participation in Separatist meetings in Canterbury, proceeding thereupon to become involved in 1746 with a group in Chebacco which was seceding from the established church there "on grounds similar to those which had caused a separation in the Canterbury church"—grounds, that is, of dissatisfaction with the Old Light, established minister. This group asked Cleaveland to minister to it once it was fully gathered together as a church. Cleaveland accepted

---

[1]United States Revolution Collection (American Antiquarian Society), statement from Parkman to Westborough Town Meeting, Dec. 30, 1774 (microfilm copy at Westborough Public Library); PD, July 4, 1774; July 7, 1774; July 18, 1774; Aug. 22, 1774; Aug. 29, 1774; Dec. 31, 1774.

the call, and in 1747 the dissident church was gathered and he was ordained.[2]

The new church began immediately to demonstrate its allegiance to the tradition of Puritan enthusiasm sketched in Chapter 4. People from neighboring parishes began to apply for admission to membership in it, which could be accomplished in accordance with the custom and rule of the Standing Order only if the churches to which they already belonged would grant them "dismissions." But this the standing churches would not do. What was at stake was explained by Reverend Benjamin Tappan of Manchester, four of whose parishioners had sought dismissions in order to join Cleaveland's church and been refused. In 1751, upon receiving a request from Cleaveland's church for a meeting to discuss the issue of dimission, Tappan wrote back that there was basically nothing to discuss. Anyone desiring membership in the Separatist Chebacco group could not be granted a dismission from his or her standing church, because this would amount to *"an Acknowledgment of your Society, as a regular Church."*

As usually happened in cases of this sort, such a withholding of legitimacy simply confirmed and hardened Cleaveland's church in its radical inclinations. It formally resolved that "a Member may lawfully remove from one Church to another, on the Principle of Edification," citing the unimpeachable early seventeenth-century divine William Ames as providing authority and warrant for this proposition and adding that when a believer's old church obstructed the quest for edification by refusing to grant a dismission, it was exercising "dominion over her Members Faith and Conscience" and making itself into "a Prison, contrary to the Gospel, and also our Platform." It was the clear Christian and Protestant duty of the church in which such a believer judged he or she would be more greatly edified to accept him or her as a new member. To hesitate because a dismission had not been granted by the old church would be to sell a seeker after light and truth into slavery to legalism.[3]

According to Cleaveland, his church had succeeded in gaining semiacceptance and respectability after these initial confrontations with the Standing Order, a claim perhaps substantiated by the fact that he was finally granted a degree by Yale in 1763. But in that very

[2]PD, Nov. 6, 1766; Franklin Bowditch Dexter, *Biographical Sketches of the Graduates of Yale College . . .* , 6 vols. (New York and New Haven: Henry Holt and Yale University Press, 1885–1912), 2:30–31.

[3]John Cleaveland, *A Short and Plain Narrative of the Late Work of God's Spirit at Chebacco . . .* (Boston, 1767), pp. 34–37.

same year the Great Awakening recurred in Chebacco. As had happened twenty years before in many parts of New England, the people of the town began to experience intense convictions of sin, followed by powerful stirrings of grace and rebirth. In the course of one particularly memorable Sabbath, reported Cleaveland, "it appeared to me, That the Kingdom of Heaven most evidently suffered Violence, and the Violent took it by Force; People pressed into it! Such a Day and Evening I never saw before, for the Display of God's powerful Grace!" And the experience of intensified spirituality brought with it this time, as it had in the 1740s and indeed had always in the history of Protestantism, the specter of disruptive ecclesiology. Cleaveland's church again took up the practice of admitting new members from neighboring churches "on the Principle of Edification," and those neighboring churches again objected strenuously to this on the grounds that it was subversive of their "necessary Peace and Order"—which it was.

In 1765, defending the Chebacco revival, Cleaveland reaffirmed that "old protestant Principle" that when pursued with single-minded consistency had always rendered Protestant order precarious and problematic: *The Right or Liberty of private Judgment in religious and spiritual Matters*. I think all my Parishioners have an equal Right, or Liberty to judge for themselves, as I have to judge for myself." The mutuality of this right meant that in a discussion between Cleaveland and a lay brother or sister, "I must tell him, that he must see for himself, or with his own Eyes, and not pin his Faith to my Sleeve. For a Person to act at Random, without any Judgment at all, whether the Thing appear to him to be right or wrong; and for him to act my Judgment, because it is mine, without exercising his own Judgment concerning mine, whether it is right or wrong, are equally absurd."[4]

Ebenezer Parkman had disposed of implicit faith with similar clarity and ease in his chat with a Roman Catholic refugee in 1757. But the removal of George and Eunice Andrews to Westborough confronted him more starkly than ever before with the contradiction between such principles of Puritan autonomy and the Puritan urge to establish a necessary peace and order. Mrs. Andrews wanted to become a member of the Westborough church, and she and her husband had been members of Cleaveland's radical, illegitimate church in Chebacco. There was an almost pristine, abstract beauty to the way the issue was being raised, for the Andrewses were not themselves personally associated with those features of the Chebacco church which made it unacceptable: they had not been affirming the enthusi-

---

[4]Ibid., pp. 5–11, 44; Dexter, *Yale Graduates*, 2:30.

astic "Principle of Edification" when they had joined the church, having been residents of Chebacco parish at that time; nor had they participated in the revival of 1763, having already removed to Westborough by the time it commenced. Nevertheless, whatever Mrs. Andrews's own principles were, to admit her into the Westborough church would be to accord legitimacy to Cleaveland's church, in all its uncompromising spiritism and defiance of ecclesiastical regularity.

We are well enough acquainted with Parkman by now to realize that this was something he could never bring himself to do. He was informed by his clerical colleagues Wigglesworth of Ipswich and Jaques of Gloucester that Cleaveland's church had been judged by an ecclesiastical council to be "*a Separate*" and that all the neighboring churches refused to commune with it. The New England order of "mutual conference" had spoken definitively, and that was good enough for Parkman. He wrote haughtily to Cleaveland: "Now Sir, why should there be any striving? This Church here, to which I am related, are so averse to Separations, that they would never countenance them, by holding Communion with them." Mrs. Andrews could be admitted only if she would renounce all association with illegitimate enthusiasm, however fortuitous: "If she no longer adheres to, but grieves for what was unhappily amiss among the People she came from, in those Times of Darkness and Temptation, which have passed over them, and will (by the Grace of God) walk agreeably to the Rules of the Gospel, I will endeavor to farther her Admission into this Church of Christ here." Cleaveland received this letter "in the very Height of the late remarkable divine Influences." The timing of the correspondence may have been what induced him, in his reply, to add the following to his denial that his church was a Separatist one in any significant sense: "But if what some have observed is true, viz. To be averse to all Separations, is to be averse to all Reformations; then what you say of your Church, will imply, That they are averse to all Reformations; and that, if so, it can be no great Privilege to have Communion with such a Church! but I hope better Things of your Church." It was probably as distinct a drawing of the battle lines between enthusiasm and order as had ever occurred in the history of New England.[5]

Just as the bare outlines of the Andrews situation brought home to Westborough the essential ideological polarities discussed in Chapter 4, so Parkman's actual relations with these newcomers, who were to him symbols of disorder, were permeated by intensified manifestations of those psychological intricacies examined in Chapter 5. The

[5]Cleaveland, *Short and Plain Narrative*, pp. 50–56.

diary for the period between May 1761 and July 1764 has not survived, so we do not know the specific sequence of events leading to the encounter of August 1, 1764, the first face-to-face meeting between Parkman and the Andrewses that remains available to us:

> p.m. I visited Mrs. Andrews—I find that she has strangely wrot her self over to say what never was . . . for she says [her husband] said to me, at the time of my proposing to write Letters, that I might write to *any Man in Connecticut* as well as to Mr. Wigglesworth. [Whereas Mr. Andrews used that expression at a later time.] When I told him it was with his Consent that I wrote to Mr. *Wigglesworth* he answered Do you think I would go to hinder? you might write to who you pleasd, to any gentleman in Connecticut if you would, I should not hinder it.

It is the same impasse we have already had ample occasion to observe. The lay party to the situation has " strangely wrot her self over" into an aggrieved and eerily concentrated focus on the clerical authority figure, a focus she is unable to understand or articulate and which therefore takes the distorted form of contesting details that are in themselves of little significance. The authority figure, for his part, joins all too eagerly with his lay antagonist in evading the real issues, succumbing to the temptation to win a pyrrhic victory in a diversionary debate. Indeed, this present incident constitutes a truly breathtaking example of the intractability of the dialectics of Puritan enthusiasm and Puritan order, given that the sources of the conflict are here relatively close to direct expression. George Andrews had all but drawn Parkman a picture of his resentment at the way the Standing Order was imputing spiritual uncleanness to him and his wife, and Parkman, a sensitive and intelligent man, had remembered and was able to reproduce in his diary the very accent and cadence of this resentment. Both the Andrewses and Parkman thus clearly seemed to be aware of what the real emotional content of the situation was. Yet just as clearly, they conspired together to make themselves less than fully conscious. Parkman recalls George Andrews's words not in order to ponder their seemingly obvious sarcasm and bitterness, but only for his own pedantic vindication in the sterile argument with Mrs. Andrews. What we see here is a mutual and multilayered avoidance, the function of which, in the psychic economy of New England Puritanism, is to ensure that the underlying deadlock will be perpetuated, even at a moment when the materials for its resolution seem manifestly to be at hand.[6]

[6]PD, Aug. 1, 1764.

Like the Fays and Cornelius Cook, the Andrewses found them-selves at the cutting edge of New England's central ideological contra-diction. On the one hand, they longed for the full acceptance into the community which only Parkman, the established authority figure, was in a position to bring about. It was precisely because Parkman was on the whole successful in making the Puritan order of Westborough seem a humane and benevolent one that the Andrewses were so upset by his quarantining of them. "How do you think we can desire any Favor of you, since you count us to have the Spirit and practice of Separates," Mrs. Andrews angrily asked when Parkman called on her and her husband later on in August 1764, a few days after she had given birth to a baby. Although separation—geographical, eccle-siastical, ideological, or an unstable compound of all three—was a recurrent and major phenomenon in Colonial New England, there were nevertheless never very many New Englanders who were pre-pared to embrace Separatism and dissidence as the foundation of identity. On the other hand, the continuing need of the Standing Order to define and legitimize itself by defining some people as being tainted by that which it was not—as "Separates"—meant that the people thus tainted were in effect always being pressured toward a less ambiguous, more open radicalism, toward becoming Separates after all.

Thus, some months later, in the course of trying to arrange some arbitration of the affair, Parkman insisted to George Andrews that it was he, Parkman, who was far more sinned against than sinning: "I had met with such Things from him & his Wife, as made me at a loss." Parkman went on to imply that the righteousness of his position was the righteousness of the entire New England system: "I would not have him think I was afraid to lay it before *proper Judges*—He asked who they were? I answered that the way of Church proceeding was &c. and if the Church did not settle it, there should be a *Council* & if the Affair was with *Ministers* then there should be *Ministers*." But this was precisely the structure of ecclesiastical propriety which had al-ready wounded and enraged the Andrewses by placing them beyond the pale. Under the guise of mediation, Parkman was, on behalf of the Standing Order, expropriating all available virtue and rationality. And the immediate consequence was simply to make George An-drews bristle and become more determined and articulate in his alien-ation: "He said he would never while he lived be out one 'rabin [?] *Penny* towards one—and were it not for his Family he would not set his Foot again into that House, pointing to the Meeting House."

This same molding of the fluidities of psychic tension into the distinctness of ideological polarization had occurred two months before, in January 1765. Parkman had sent the Andrewses a letter of reconciliation which was, in all probability, as unyielding as his discourse to George Andrews about *"proper Judges."* And the response had been that "Mr. Andrews & his wife are extremely Violent & charge me with many Untruths—She believes I have not a spark of Grace &c." Eunice Andrews had felt deeply wounded by being accounted "to have the Spirit and practice of Separates." Yet here she was coming forward with the very essence of the radical Protestant spirituality that informed most versions of Separatism. What seemed to be happening was that Parkman, not knowing how to search for a point of mutuality, could only engage in gestures that were perceived by the Andrewses as renewed denials of social legitimacy. And they in their turn, equally in the dark about what might constitute a meeting ground, found the powerful emotions surrounding social legitimacy propelling them into counterattack. Their scornful doubt about Parkman being possessed of even "a spark of Grace" amounted to an inversion of the established hierarchy. If Parkman was at the top and the Andrewses at the bottom in the order of society and nature, then the traditional framework and language of Protestant enthusiasm provided the Andrewses with a means of bolstering their self-esteem by reversing this situation: in the order of grace, it was the rigid and self-righteous minister who was inferior and illegitimate. The dynamics of this moment are quite familiar to those of us living in a world in which various forms of romanticized authenticity are constantly arraying themselves over against various forms of bureaucratized regularity and rationality.[7]

These direct dealings between Parkman and the Andrewses were no doubt troublesome and painful for all involved, but what turned the situation into a major crisis was, as Parkman recorded in his diary in December 1764, "that such a number of the Brethren of this Church are disquieted with me and will not be convincd of the Disorder & Irregularitys of the *Chebacco* Separates, nor of the ungrateful Behavior the very unchristian and abusive Conduct of these persons." Here is striking evidence of the strength and durability of the New

---

[7]PD, Aug. 22, 1764; Jan. 17, 1765; Mar. 6, 1765. For a discussion of the attitudes toward dissent which probably informed Eunice Andrews's sense of grievance over being labeled a "Separate," see Christine Leigh Heyrman, "Spectres of Subversion, Societies of Friends: Dissent and the Devil in Provincial Essex County, Massachusetts," in *Saints and Revolutionaries: Essays in Early American History,* ed. David D. Hall, John M. Murrin, and Thad W. Tate (New York: Norton, 1984), pp. 38–74. Mrs. Andrews's gibe about Parkman not being illumined within by any spark of grace may well have sent the sort of pang through him that would be instantly recognized by any liberal academic who lived through the "countercultural" years between 1965 and 1975.

England tradition of Protestant radicalism, this tolerance of enthusiasm, even attraction to it, in a church that had always been guided by an apostle of order who, for all his compulsions and anxieties, cannot be described as overbearing or repressive. After a century and a half of skillfull co-optation in New England as a whole, and four decades of it in Westborough, there were still to be found average New Englanders who were unwilling to perceive enthusiasm solely by way of the hegemonic distaste for "Disorder & Irregularitys." Moreover, among those sympathetic to the Andrewses and the "*Chebacco* Separates" were many of Westborough's most substantial citizens, including both of the deacons of the church and two of the largest property holders and most prosperous farmers in town.

In August and September 1766 there occurred particularly unpleasant meetings between Parkman and substantial delegations of these disquieted brethren. In each case, the possibility of mutual understanding and reconciliation was very quickly extinguished by a process of settling into confrontational postures. At the session in August, when Parkman attempted to provide "some narrative of the [Andrews] affair, that they might understand the first Beginning of Mrs. *Andrews's* Disquietment and might see how little Reason she had to be offended with me," the brethren "soon grew unwilling to hear." Thus had matters degenerated to the point that the very orderliness of Parkman's presentation, its overwhelmingly superior rationality, was felt to be partial and aggressive, a way of defining the terms of discussion so as, in effect, to forestall discussion and compel obedience. But the brethren lacked the intellectual tools required for the articulation of an alternative agenda, so their resistance could only take a form that appeared to be no more than a sullen petulance, a refusal to hear. And this posture, in its turn, provoked from Parkman an even more aggressive and domineering display of rationality, as he immediately resorted to a strategy of legalistic, vaguely menacing documentation: "Upon their manifesting such a Frame, and I fearing what advantage might be taken at what I said, upon my mentioning [Mrs. Andrews's] name, I turnd my self about to see who they all were, I observd to them that I should be carefull to minute down who I spoke to & what I said as had been my manner to do in this matter, that I might be able to defend my self, when occasion should arise to require it."

So neither side would listen to the other, and as with the dealings between Parkman and the Andrewses themselves, the primary effect of each side's manner of staking out its own position was to push the other side into a more extreme version of its position. Parkman would not budge from such a bedrock principle as that the Westborough church "never would have Communion with Separates." Correspondingly, the most forceful and determined of his lay opponents, Captain Jonas Brigham (the wealthiest man in town), did not manage to open the situation up to broader discussion and exploration. He did not offer a rationale for having "communion with Separates." Like Thomas Forbush many years before, he could only snipe at the dogma upon which Parkman was insisting, pointing out that the church did allow Stephen and Ruth Fay to participate in communion during their occasional visits to Westborough, despite their involvement in a Separatist group in Hardwick, Massachusetts. On some points, Parkman did seem to relent a bit and adopt a more inquiring and beseeching posture: "I earnestly askd the Brethren what I could possibly do more for her Recovery? I had already taken the utmost pains, & all was ill taken & in vain." But alas, the terms in which a helpful response to this question might have been formulated lay beyond the purview of Parkman's auditors no less than that of Parkman himself, requiring, as they would have, the raising of the possibility that New England's ecclesiastical and social structures might be in need of fundamental scrutiny and alteration. Parkman's incapacity to embark on such uncharted seas is indicated by his immediate recourse to a virtuous sense of already having taken "the utmost pains." Meanwhile the brethren, in the person of their principal spokesman, Captain Brigham, proceeded to come up with an answer that was so pathetically inadequate and utterly arbitrary that it merely confirmed their pastor in his frustrated feelings of benevolence unregarded and virtue unrewarded: "He did not see that my going to visit at their (Andrews's) House would do any good. . . . Thus I must be blam'd on both hands; for others are ready to complain that I let them alone so much, & don't go there to try what might be done." Parkman was at this moment suffering all the worst consequences of a semihierarchical, semiegalitarian world none of them knew how to see beyond. As a leader and fount of authority, he was the focus of everyone's deepest anxieties and aspirations. As a leader of empowered Puritans, he was also the focus of everyone's most stubborn perceptions. And in a situation that stirred up all such anxieties, aspirations, and perceptions, he was thus bound to be the target of free and irrational censure on every hand.[8]

[8]PD, July 18, 1764; Dec. 6, 1764; Aug. 5, 1766. The economic position of Jonas Brigham and many of the others sympathetic to the Andrewses can be gathered from *The Massachusetts Tax Valuation List of 1771*, ed. Bettye Hobbs Pruitt (Boston: G. K. Hall, 1978), pp. 362–66. Parkman might have appreciated the lament of John Bulkley fifty years before that anticlericalism was rampant in Connecticut not only "among the more

At the meeting a month later, in September 1766, the brethren crowded into Parkman's house late in the evening and turned a deaf ear to his pleas about "how unhappy it was to come at this Time; how unprepard I was for it—that I could not attend upon it—that it was unkind not to give me more seasonable Warning of their Designs." It is likely that Parkman's lack of preparation was precisely what encouraged the brethren to stay stubbornly on. They were contriving to minimize his habitual control of such situations, and they proceeded to indicate resistance to the entire apparatus of New England order: "Some of them especially were very zealous in Mrs. *Andrews* Behalf— rejecting what ever Defence I could make: especially making light of the Results of the Councils, Letters of Ministers, Informations which a Number of Ministers have given me, besides other persons, especially of late, of the great irregularitys among that people at *Chebacco*." Yet the categories that might enable the Westborough brethren to show what might lie beyond a concern with "great irregularitys" remained unavailable, and therefore the stalemate persisted, with Parkman continuing to be impressed by the benevolence and generosity of his own proceeding, within the established categories and structures, and the brethren able to express their sense of what those structures and categories excluded only with a mystifying, highly emotive generality: "Nor could any thing I could say, appease them who so warmly withstood me—nor did it signifie for me to endeavour to set them right in Things they had taken wrong. Yet vehemently urging & pressing that I *must* be reconcild—that I *must*—tho I assurd them that I had done many Things in order to it, and had informd them so, over & over— yet it was in vain."

A week later, at a gathering of Parkman, the Andrewses, and four brethren who had agreed to help mediate the dispute, development toward more conscious polarization was evident. Parkman had had the time denied him by the brethren the week before to "make Preparation," and he had availed himself of it to draw up a written "narrative (about 8 pages) of the very first visit I made them & what occurd afterwards that it might be seen how Mrs. Andrews had askd—& what kind of Denial I gave her: & whether I ever gave her the least Ground of Offence." He was adding his own document about the Andrewses to the structure of documented rectitude, reasonableness, and judgment—votes of ecclesiastical councils and ministerial associations, let-

---

Base and Vile . . . but even among such as would hold a place among those of Rank and Quality." See Richard L. Bushman, *From Puritan to Yankee: Character and the Social Order in Connecticut, 1690–1765* (Cambridge, Mass.: Harvard University Press, 1967), p. 155.

ters from ministerial colleagues—which had already demonstrated to its own satisfaction that the Chebacco church from which the Andrewses had come was entirely unacceptable. But the Andrewses and the mediators who were assisting them, Captain Jonas Brigham and Nathaniel Whitney, were able this time, in response to the efforts of the system of order to define and control them, to do a bit more than simply fly into a rage or engage in inarticulate naysaying. Brigham and Whitney urged Parkman, as Cornelius Cook had done, to consider the possibility that he himself had "been to blame" along with the Andrewses. When queried by Parkman as to how he had been in the wrong, "they answered In my calling them *Separates*." What to Parkman was the official, righteous verdict on the Chebacco church and the Andrewses ("it was what the Books that were printed about them frequently usd, & what they were calld in the Letters from the Ministers who had writ about them and what I had my self found 'em to be") begins here to be redefined by Brigham and Whitney as something rather less august and rather more blameworthy: "calling them *Separates*," calling names. The emotions expressed by Eunice Andrews two years before ("How do you think we can desire any Favor of you, since you count us to have the Spirit and practice of Separates") have thus been partially rationalized. And in the Andrewses and their supporters telling Parkman that "they wanted that my papers might be burnt," there is the germ of a detached, relativized view of quasi-official documents as devices of entrapment and oppression, rather than as expressions of universally valid reason and value.[9]

In view of such an increasingly distinct drawing of the battle lines, it is not surprising that "altho on each part we professd to be for Peace, yet we unhappily broke up without Reconcilement." The development or consolidation of the respective ideological postures was proceeding incompatibly alongside a sincere and mutual wish for rapprochement. But perhaps emboldened by the degree of support she seemed to be receiving, Eunice Andrews began at this point to behave as though self-affirmation over against her opponent was more important to her than peace and harmony. She made a formal request for a church meeting to consider "whether she may have transient Communion with us." Parkman's reaction, in preparation for the meeting, was to pile up and pile on the documentary rationales and judgments: more letters from ministers in the neighborhood of

---

[9]PD, Sept. 15, 1766; Sept. 23, 1766. Nathaniel Whitney was the grandfather of Eli Whitney, the inventor of the cotton gin. His son, also named Eli, was to play a part in Westborough's next visitation of ecclesiastical turmoil; see below, n. 22.

Chebacco testifying to the disorderliness of John Cleaveland's church; a resolution by the Marlborough Association stating that it would be inadvisable "for any of our Churches to admitt members of that Separate Society [of Chebacco] to Communion in special Ordinances" or to "admitt Mr. *Cleaveland* into our Pulpits"; and a draft of the remarks he planned to make at the meeting. In this draft, Parkman invoked not only the Winthropian doctrines of order, but also the Winthropian emotions of loving unity which had endowed those doctrines with such social presence and potency: "Can any one person desire and take Delight in seeing us, the Brethren of this Church, after living so many years in Peace, plungd into hot Contention & Divisions & torn all to pieces by horrible Discord, so as never to enjoy Communion in Gods holy Ordinances any more together? Surely we should not be Ignorant of Satan's Devices: Devices to destroy all that is good among us."

But if Parkman was conducting himself in a manner that was more and more aggressively unyielding, Mrs. Andrews likewise proceeded to displays of acted-out hostility that were as exasperating and hurtful as they were no doubt intended to be. She taunted Parkman by circulating the shrewd and "slanderous suggestion, that the Reason why the ministers were so much against Mr. Cleaveland, was, they could not bear to see that he so much out-shind & people esteemd him so much higher than them." She also failed to put in an appearance at the church meeting she had herself requested. When the meeting was, forbearingly, rescheduled, she and her husband made use of the intervening period to invite John Cleaveland to preach at their home, no doubt in an attempt to demonstrate just how much Cleaveland "out-shind" Ebenezer Parkman. Needless to say, they did not trouble themselves to obtain Parkman's permission to bring the very source of the Chebacco disorder right into Westborough itself. And when the rescheduled meeting finally took place, in November 1766, the contentious, vindictive spirit that was animating Mrs. Andrews revealed itself more openly. It turned out that she was "not only absent, but designedly, & gone a Journey as several members . . . testifyd." Moreover, "it was also testifyd that tho she had requested Communion with us, yet that she said she would not come if her request was voted by the Church &c."

The state of mind that probably propelled the Andrewses into these gestures bears comparison with Eve's scornfully implying, at the end of Book IX of *Paradise Lost,* that Adam's views and ways amount to turning her into "a lifeless rib," and also with her simultaneously rejecting Adam's authority and demanding that she be protected by it.

But Mrs. Andrews had obviously overplayed her hand. Even the brethren who had spoken up for her to their pastor's face were not going to conspire with her to humiliate him. There were only a few feeble objections to the overwhelming evidence against the Chebacco Separatists in general, and Mrs. Andrews in particular, which Parkman had made ready, and a motion to dismiss Mrs. Andrews's petition for transient communion was passed "by a pretty full majority. . . . Thus we went thro the Affair without much Heat," Parkman noted with relief. But just as Adam's superficial and momentarily triumphant rectitude merely perpetuates his "vain contest" with Eve at the nadir of the Fall, so Parkman did not feel particularly secure after he had effected the church's disapprobation of Mrs. Andrews. A few days before the meeting he had already revealed to the reader of his diary how the controversy was wearing away at him, having had "a most unusually troublesome & distressing Dream . . . which makes me full of apprehensions respecting new Afflictions & Tryals," and he continued after the meeting to sense that the conflict was far from resolved, praying with foreboding that "we be preservd from all further Disturbance about this Woman!"[10]

There was one additional document with which Parkman had taken care to arm himself prior to this triumphant church meeting of November 1766. He had had Rebecca Warrin, wife of Timothy Warrin, listen to him read out his transcription of her account of an evidently unpleasant altercation between himself and Mrs. Andrews back in August 1763 and confirm that this written-out version of her testimony was indeed accurate. Then just before the meeting, he had taken the additional precaution of having Mrs. Warrin present again while the Westborough schoolmaster, John Cushing, wrote down this same testimony. It is unclear whether Rebecca Warrin dictated her testimony anew to Cushing or simply sat by while Cushing copied out what Parkman had already written, but in any case the maneuver to have this particular bit of evidence against Mrs. Andrews available in some hand other than Parkman's own turned out to compound the minister's difficulties immeasurably over the next several months,

---

[10]PD, Oct. 3, 1766; Oct. 14, 1766; Oct. 17, 1766; Oct. 21, 1766; Oct. 30, 1766; Nov. 1, 1766; Nov. 6, 1766; *Church Records*, Oct. 5, 1766; Oct. 17, 1766; Nov. 6, 1766; *Marlborough Association Records*, Oct. 21, 1766; PFP, Box 2, Folder 1 (Notes on Church Meetings and Issues), "Church Meeting, Oct. 17, 1766: To Hear Mrs. Andrews's Letter & Request." For the climax of the contention between Adam and Eve, see above, chap. 2, nn. 18–19.

providing yet another point of focus for the volatile emotions surrounding the ambiguities of Puritan ideology and community.

In March 1767 Timothy Warrin demanded that Parkman hand over to him a copy of his wife's testimony on the Andrews matter. He "seem'd to be apprehensive of some Difficulty, I know not what, arising from some Quarter." The mystery deepened later that same day when Rebecca Warrin herself asked Parkman to come and see her. When Parkman complied with her request, "she said nothing of special note; her Husband was not returnd." Another church member, David Batherick, informed Parkman several days later that a number of the brethren had joined Mr. and Mrs. Warrin in their concern about Mrs. Warrin's testimony. Schoolmaster Cushing was also present, and Batherick shed some light on the nature of the difficulty by asking Cushing whether it had been at Mrs. Warrin's own request that he had made his transcription of her testimony on the day of the church meeting the previous November. Apparently, Mrs. Warrin had been led to believe that Parkman had somehow browbeaten or manipulated her into giving that testimony yet again, which was probably why she was reluctant to talk to Parkman in her husband's absence. He would use his mysterious cultural superiority to twist her words to his own advantage once again. To his credit, Parkman seems to have recognized that this half-formed accusation of tampering with the evidence was not completely groundless, for he immediately engaged in "much searching of Heart on Account of the Trouble, so stirring up, respecting Mrs. Warrin." If Mrs. Andrews had given way back in November to imprudent extremes of impertinence and scorn, perhaps Parkman had also overthrown himself by exploiting his hierarchical upper hand too flagrantly, pushing his superior capacity to bolster himself with documentary justification beyond the bounds of social acceptability, if not ethical propriety.

After two weeks of increasing uneasiness on this new issue among many church members, Parkman and the Warrins held a peace conference that appeared to produce a satisfactory result: "At length we came to an Agreement and I dind there. Master Cushing came in, & I read the Agreement to him. Mr. Warrin assures me I shall find him the same at Even—I may trust him if there be no writing." In their search for a solution, Parkman and Warrin here seem to tether themselves in labyrinthine fashion to the very same compulsions that had created the problem. Warrin having been brought by the legalistic use of writing and documentation to the point where he regards Parkman in the cautious manner usually reserved for slick lawyers, Parkman goes on to enshrine the transcendence of wariness and suspicion in yet another document, thus allaying and reviving that wariness and suspicion in one ingenious stroke. At a more formal conference in the evening, the same dynamic was reenacted:

> The agreement which was writ to Day at Mr. Warrins was read & I gave my consent to it. Mr. Warrin had some [illegible] & Questions—& wanted some alterations in some parts of it; but I put him in mind of its being our *Agreement*—I was not willing to depart from it. Captain Brigham, & his Brother & Mr. Tainter were not fully satisfyd with it—Mr. Daniel Forbes wanted the word *Wrong* should be put in along with *Mistake*—but I made no alteration—at length it was so far closd, that we gave up, & Each of the Papers, viz the Paper writ by Mr. Cushing, & the Copy I gave Mr. Warrin, were both of them burnt. So that (thro divine goodness) we parted amicably as I hope. Thus had I deliverance out of this snare. May God be praisd & his Name magnifyd! May I have Grace to be Cautious and Watchful at all Times henceforward!

The way the entire dispute kept coiling in upon itself is again nicely illustrated here. The Standing Order's insistence on legalistic definitions and documents was one of the primary sources of the trouble, starting with the legalistic quarantining of the Chebacco church and ending (for the moment) with Parkman's legalistic methods of justifying himself and condemning Eunice Andrews. The idea of making a ceremony of burning the documents causing so much anxiety and unhappiness indicates an awareness on the part of everyone involved of the limits and costs of such a managerial approach to human experience. Nevertheless, a new legalistic document arises phoenixlike even before the old ones have been consumed by fire, and the last-minute haggling over its specific provisions suggests that the managerial and contentious frame of mind was still very much alive in all parties. Parkman was still trying to minimize, and the brethren to maximize, the minor realignments of Puritan power politics implicit in Parkman's having seemed to overreach himself. And the conclusion of the passage therefore constitutes a sad abuse indeed of the language of Puritan piety. For it was not the divine goodness that brought people to grace through conviction of sin that presided in Parkman's heart at the end of this day. It was only an ever more knotted up, sidelong, profoundly uneasy management of self-interest.[11]

The futility of legalistically repairing the damage done by overbear-

[11]PD, Mar. 5, 1767; Mar. 11, 1767; Mar. 17, 1767.

ing legalism was amply demonstrated over the next several weeks, which amounted in many ways to the nadir of the entire controversy, from Parkman's point of view. The Warrins were so little reconciled as a result of the rigorously defined agreement between them and Parkman that they were, it developed, contemplating taking their minister to court. "The Storm seems to increase more & more," Parkman lamented. "It takes away my rest by night, & fills me with much Distress. The Lord look upon me in my sore Affliction." Much as we may wish to sympathize with Reverend Parkman in the deepening of his sore affliction, we must nevertheless observe his continuing failure to burn up his justificatory and judgmental documents in any meaningful sense. Preparing for a church meeting in late April 1767, called to secure the church's endorsement of the agreement between himself and the Warrins, the minister reaffirmed the legal and moral validity of the document, which in the promulgation of the agreement he had ritually committed himself to do without: "It follows that the Paper of [Rebecca Warrin's] Testimony (wherein it is allowed to stand good) is not to be complaind of, as doing Wrong. And yet if it *does,* who does it, (the Wrong?) but she that so testifies and not I?" Indeed, Parkman appears here to be following the example of the Andrewses and those of his parishioners who had been resisting him. He was laboring under the pressure of the Warrins' threat to haul him into court, just as his parishioners always labored under his power to confer or withhold full standing in the community. And just as they, unable to find alternative means of justifying themselves, were wont to pick away at any weakness in Parkman's case, so Parkman here seeks to save himself by taking a poke at the Warrins, blaming the illiterate or semiliterate woman he had himself enlisted in the cause of "that necessary Peace & Order" for any of the possibly inhumane repercussions that might arise in the course of imposing and maintaining such order. Parkman was normally the opposite of a cruel man, but on this as on a few other occasions, faced with the prospect of rewriting the Puritan equation in such a way that his own hierarchical superordination would be slightly diminished, he did alas resort to bullying.[12]

When the church met, it voted to accept the agreement between Parkman and the Warrins, and also Parkman's rather grudging confession that something had been minimally amiss in his handling of the Rebecca Warrin evidence. But this vote of confidence was not as meaningful as it might have been, for in the course of the meeting

---

[12]PD, Apr. 10, 1767; Apr. 14, 1767; PFP, Box 2, Folder 1, "Concerning Mrs. R. W.'s Evidence."

Timothy Warrin had become so enraged by something Parkman said—perhaps Parkman did utter the unpleasant remark about "the Wrong" in Mrs. Warrin's testimony being her responsibility and not his—that he and his wife had stalked out of the church. Subsequently, Warrin expressed his continued alienation by persisting in his threat to press charges against Parkman. Thus, despite all the distress, all the agreements, all the overtures toward reconciliation, and all the symbolic enactments of it, the situation remained essentially what it had always been: the party of clerical authority and ecclesiastical order, possessed of the resources to generate a massive, solidly documentary rationale for itself, remained trapped within that very rationale; meanwhile, the party of lay assertiveness and incipient enthusiasm was still confined in emotions and gestures rather than arguments and visions, was still unable to generate a clear critique of that which it was experiencing as oppressive.

So it continued at a peace conference between Parkman and the Andrewses a week after the church meeting. Unlike the conference of the previous September, this exercise in Puritan collective bargaining did produce a measure of agreement. Parkman relented on the question of his "taking minutes of Conversations" sufficiently to consign three of his "loose papers" to the flames. The Andrewses, for their part, were willing to set aside some of their lesser grievances. It was therefore possible for the evening to be concluded with a touching peace ceremony: "At length Mr. Andrews & his wife came one after the other and with joining Hands endeavored to join Hearts and mutually forgave—and it was written & signd by all three—and each party had one. Upon which we gave praise to God singing part of 133 Psalm." Yet unfortunately this ritual enactment of peace was also expressive of the perpetuation of war, which was fitting in view of the fact that neither Parkman nor the Andrewses had given way at all on the central issue of attitudes toward the church in Chebacco. To emphasize, as Parkman in his diary account did, the documentary nature of the new covenant and the distribution of copies of it to "each party" was to create the impression that further conflict would be prevented not by a wholehearted consensus on first principles, but only by an aura of legalistic coercion; that is, by precisely that in which the conflict had originated and by which it had in great part been fueled all along.

As though in confirmation of these limitations, Timothy Warrin continued to hold out in anger and opposition—perhaps because Parkman had indeed in the course of this arbitration insisted that "if there was harm to Mrs. Andrews by [Rebecca Warrin's testimony], it could not be laid to me but to Mrs. Warrin because: that which related to Mrs. Andrews in it, she retaind & it was still in its full strength." This flare-up over the documentation of Rebecca Warrin's testimony suggests an amendment of the points made at the end of Chapter 4 about the sociology of literacy in New England. Puritan culture seems to have encompassed situations of both intellectual continuity and wholeness of dialogue among "elite" and "popular" representatives (as in the debates between Robert Breck, Jr., and the laity of Windham County, Connecticut), and also (as here) contrasting situations in which the elite and the popular are sharply divided and opposed; and intellectual empowerment becomes not the medium in which everyone lives and moves, but rather a discrete, reified issue in itself. It may be more to the point to be alert to a range of possible configurations of the sociocultural consequences of literacy, rather than to seek to discover some one essential sociocultural structure that literacy will bring about in any and all circumstances.[13]

The agreement between Parkman and the Andrewses must have included a commitment by Parkman to allow the church to reconsider Mrs. Andrews's request for "transient Communion" with it, for Parkman gave such allowance before the peace conference broke up. A month later, in early June 1767, the church voted acceptance of the following resolution on the matter of Eunice Andrews's former membership in the Chebacco church and present ecclesiastical status:

That as many of those Disorders, so far as we can understand, were years before Mrs. Andrews joined to the Society, 'tis likely she was not fully knowing to them, and therefore she desires she may not be chargd with them. And as to any Disorders that have been complaind of since she came from them we hope if she has not countenanced them, she is not to be blamd for them—If this Church do therefore first bear their Testimony against the Disorders complaind of in that Society, & would not be understood to hold Communion with that Society, in any Point or Article wherein they may have departed from the Rule and Order of a Gospel Church, or from the Platform which this Church has submitted to as a Rule (under the Scriptures) for Church Discipline—that she, declaring before the Brethren that she does not abet such Disorders, but is willing & ready to bear Testimony against them & that she will by Grace from God walk agreeable to the Rules of the Gospel that then Mrs. *Andrews*, considering her Circumstances not being active in, or countenancing

[13]PD, Apr. 23, 1767; Apr. 29, 1767; Apr. 30, 1767; *Church Records*, Apr. 23, 1767; above chap. 4, n. 33.

those disorders, as by the Providence of God become an Inhabitant among us, & her walk & Conversation is regular—may be, in our Judgments admitted to transient Communion in this Church.

A committee that had been balanced between the pro- and anti-Andrews factions in the congregation had been officially charged with the drafting of this resolution, but it seems probable that Parkman himself had a decisive influence on the final result. His refusal to compromise the absolute value and validity of "the Rule and Order of a Gospel Church" is evident not only in the content of the resolution, but also and especially in its syntax, cadence, and tone. In the introductory clauses, Mrs. Andrews is all but cleared of any association with the Chebacco Separatists. Nevertheless, there is no feeling at all of having safely disposed of this issue. Both the Westborough church and the supposedly uncontaminated Mrs. Andrews are required further along in the resolution to "bear their Testimony against the Disorders complaind of" in Chebacco. Moreover, there is a feeling toward the end of the resolution, just before the suspended syntax customary in such formal declarations is resolved, of checking up on Mrs. Andrews again at the very last minute ("not being active in, or countenancing those disorders . . . & her walk & Conversation is regular"). To say the least, the resolution does not build toward its concluding words as toward a climactic gathering of Mrs. Andrews into the community. Rather, it delays and procrastinates, finally admitting Mrs. Andrews as though taking care of a disagreeable chore that can no longer be avoided. The resolution also conveys anxiety. The repetitious disavowals of the Chebacco irregularities serve not to contain and control them, but rather only to make them lurk and loom with ever more mischievous and menacing potency. Both the Westborough church and Mrs. Andrews are made to seem so locked into negation that it is hard to see how any energy or inclination could be left over for the positive labor of building Christian community.[14]

The controversy appeared to have been settled at long last, and on terms Parkman doubtless regarded as amounting to a victory for himself. In Westborough, enthusiasm had yet again been deftly coopted by order. Or so it seemed. The day before the next scheduled observance of the Lord's Supper, Parkman called on Mrs. Andrews, "supposing that she designd, by vertue of the late vote of the Church, to come to the Communion." But to his consternation, "when she

---

[14]*Church Records*, May 19, 1767; PD, June 2, 1767; PFP, Box 2, Folder 1, undated text of committee report.

came to understand what the Church had done about her by my Reading the Vote of the Church, &c. she would not accept of it; nor did she give any Reason to suppose she would come tomorrow. Copys of the Vote of the Church in appointing a Committee and of the Report of that Committee were given them [George Andrews was also present]. But she did not appear willing to come to Communion tomorrow notwithstanding all I did to mollifie & Compose her."

Thus commenced yet another scene in the same old play. Without being able to explain that this was what she was doing, Mrs. Andrews was resisting, with the reactions of an empowered Puritan layperson that seemed virtually instinctive, being admitted to the church as a second-class citizen. Whereupon Parkman proceeded as he had many times before to throw documents at the situation ("Copys of the Vote of the Church . . . and of the Report . . . were given them"), going on to reveal that this present visit amounted to a putting into practice of all that was offensive to Mrs. Andrews in the very document he was handing over: "I told her I was come to make her a Visit as a Pastor would to a Communicant before the Supper; & as I had told the Church that I would take a Time (if I could) to examine into her Knowledge & soundness in the Faith, so this was my present Errand, & would have her take it in good part." If Parkman made a regular practice of calling on communicants prior to the eucharistic ceremony, he made no mention of this in his otherwise minutely detailed diary. He was being disingenuous, probably with himself as well as Mrs. Andrews. His visit was the behavioral equivalent of the tone of the church's resolution; it was a gesture of distaste and apprehension, an attempt to fence in someone who, he continued to feel, remained a source of mischief. Parkman was sufficiently attuned to the psychic undercurrents he had always had to live with to realize, even as he began to gather the evidence he would need for the ongoing vindication of himself and the establishment he represented, that this was how his action would be interpreted: "This Conduct of theirs I fear will give me new Trouble, as I doubt not those who are prejudicd against me, and deeply engagd in their Defence, will lay even this also to me, as if I were the Cause of her not coming. But tis well I had some Body (Dr. *Hawes*) with me, to bear witness of what was said."[15]

Within two weeks of this pre-eucharistic visit, the Andrewses had indeed begun spreading it about that the purpose of the visit had been "opposite to the Church's proceedings," had been in fact "the prevention of her Coming to the Communion." And the story, which was only

[15]PD, June 13, 1767.

technically untrue, as Parkman on some level realized, was being widely believed. It was just at this point of Parkman's particular vulnerability that the meddlesome John Cleaveland issued his *Short and Plain Narrative*. Cleaveland's book, justifying the disorders he had succeeded in spreading to Westborough and other Massachusetts towns, was read eagerly by many in Westborough, doubtless including Captain Jonas Brigham, who soon accosted Parkman in a manner that was "full of wrath & hard Speeches." Perhaps taking his cue from Cleaveland's straightforward radicalism, Brigham declared that Parkman "had contrived the Vote for the Committee and . . . had assisted them in drawing up their Report." He did not shrink from calling Parkman "a *Wicked man*" and a liar, but he concluded the conversation by stating that, like Cornelius Cook, he was not prepared simply to sever relations with his pastor: "He told me he was come to deliver his mind to me & leave it with me; but because he could not prove things against me, he should come to his Duty—meaning I suppose to the Lords Supper." Brigham was closer than anyone since Cook had been to realizing that the troubles arose not from anything specific, limited, and provable, but rather from the fundamental structure of their common ecclesiastical life. But Brigham was behaving much more rancorously than had Cook, was not making himself at all imploring and vulnerable. He resembled the belligerent Eve of the end of Book IX of *Paradise Lost* more than the creatively penitent Eve of Book X. Parkman was therefore more adequately warranted here with Brigham than he had been with Cook in merely vindicating himself and dismissing Brigham's state of mind as a diseased one: "May the Lord pity this poor unhappy Brother & pardon him! for what a frame he is otherwise like to come to the Sacrament in!"[16]

On through the summer and into the fall of 1767, now fully four years into this seemingly endless wrangle, there continued to simmer and fester among many of the brethren a great deal of "anger & Wrath on account of Mrs. *Andrews*," even though those who were unhappy "could fasten on Nothing but what was easily answered." An inarticulate sense of grievance jostling against clerical answers that were all too easy had been the norm throughout the entire crisis, and it continued to govern its final stages. At the end of December there was a major confrontation, reminiscent of those of August and September of the previous year, between Parkman and a substantial delegation of church members. It was perhaps another sign of the influence of John Cleaveland's radical pamphlet that Captain Brigham and his comrades now spoke more explicitly and fully in vindication

[16]PD, June 24, 1767; July 21, 1767; July 23, 1767.

of how the enthusiastic Chebacco church had conducted itself, and that they engaged in "much Debate of inumerable Things relative to the *Platform* & members *breaking* order &c." But there remained a significant residue of a more searching, ill-defined disquiet that, in the atmosphere of complacent inflexibility emanating from Parkman, could only turn more bitter and shrill: "However, the Evening was spent without shewing what was their particular aim in having this Conference—but it seemd to be in general to Manifest uneasiness at what had been done; and their Desire that the Church would still do something or other. . . . This tarrying gave a new Opportunity for them to break forth anew, & insisted upon my consenting to another Church Meeting & to put the Vote whether the Woman shall have leave to Come or no?—I expostulated—. It did but enrage—I told 'em at length that I would consider of it. Thus was finished this troublesom conversation."

A few days later, Parkman consented to the demand for another church meeting. But more than four years of going around and around in a circle, more than four years of virtually preordained posturing on both sides, had taken their toll, and most of the participants were by now more interested in simply abandoning the contest than in continuing to struggle to resolve it. The standstill was so complete, however, that even a motion to this effect, "that since the Church has been so much worried with [the Andrews question], it might be dropd," could gain only a tie vote. When the meeting was reconvened after eight more days, a motion to admit Mrs. Andrews was taken up:

After much Debate & Dispute concerning the people of *Chebacco* & Mr. Cleaveland and for what Reasons to be held Communion with and for what Reasons they might not also the Conduct of Churches & Ministers with regard to them, the Pastor spake to this Purpose, viz 'I am truely willing this person should come to the Communion if it may be in any Orderly way in the world, & so as that we may be able to give a good account of it. We had better put an End to these fruitless controversies & Contests which we have so long been in about that Society whether it is one Thing or another and the other Churches Behavior towards them. Laying all this aside therefore, and without Regard to one Church or another, let us take the matter before us in general; thus, That Mrs. Andrews being a professing Christian, & her Lot being cast among us in this place If she will not countenance Disorders whether in the place she came from or otherwhere or whatever is contrary to the word of God & disallowd by the platform; and will endeavour to walk accorgding [*sic*] to Gospel Rule This Church also hereby testifying against Disorders whether in Chebacco or any where else are willing our Circumstances on each part being seriously considerd, to admitt her to Communion with this Church.

The tone is as grudging as that of the resolution of the previous June. Outwardly, the major amendment is the substitution of a merely generalized disavowal of disorder for the previous specific condemnation of the Chebacco church. But this alteration is subverted by the manner in which it is presented, and the result is the opposite of a more open-minded and generous declaration. By covertly insinuating the anathema upon Chebacco it has just overtly renounced ("If she will not countenance Disorders whether in the place she came from or otherwhere . . . testifying against Disorders whether in Chebacco or any where else"), this statement manages to add to the former general sense of foot dragging a sense of great reluctance on this specific point. The more genuine difference between this and the earlier resolution is in the open weariness of the preamble; the motion is a face-saving restatement of the one of a few days before, a more discreet method of allowing the controversy to "be dropd." It was passed by a large majority, and the church then demonstrated that it knew exactly what it was doing. It further voted that the two deacons should accompany Parkman when he read the result to Mrs. Andrews, and that no copy of the result be left with her. This delicate and precarious compromise was not going to be allowed to founder on Parkman's oft-demonstrated tendency to engage in expostulation that did but enrage, or Mrs. Andrews's well-developed capacity to smell out evidence that she had been insulted. Parkman took the hint, and the next day when the deacons arrived to bring him to the Andrews residence he insisted that they go on without him, pleading that "it was Cold & would bring me into Evening." A uniting of all in tactful avoidance of each other was what finally brought the long Andrews crisis to an end: "They returnd latish in the Evening & informd that it was accepted. for which we were much rejoicd.—The Praise be to God! May there be a right understanding and stedfastness!"[17]

The immediate crisis was over, but the fundamental ambiguities surrounding order and enthusiasm, hierarchy and equality, had not been cleared up. For months and even years, Parkman found it noteworthy that whenever he had anything to do with the Andrewses, "all the Behavior of that Family is benevolent." He was walking on egg-

[17]PD, Sept. 4, 1767; Dec. 29, 1767; Jan. 12, 1768; PFP, Box 2, Folder 1, "In Church Meeting, Jan. 11, 1768"; *Church Records*, Jan. 3, 1768; Jan. 11, 1768.

shells, checking to reassure himself that discord was not about to break out anew. Parkman also took special note for many years of the fact that his relations with Jonas Brigham appeared to be free of trouble, and perhaps he had even more reason to feel nervous about Brigham. It was Brigham who had been brought by the Andrews controversy the closest to a revolutionary ecclesiology, and it is therefore fitting that Brigham was the first member of the Westborough church to make "complaints respecting ministers—particularly in the *Bolton* Affair." The Bolton affair was a variation on the Chebacco affair, and it visited upon Westborough a replay of the Andrews affair. That the church and community were thus condemned to a repetition of the most painful aspects of their recent history constitutes the strongest possible evidence that they had been unable to resolve their contradictions.[18]

Unlike Chebacco, Bolton was located in the immediate vicinity of Westborough. The difficulties in the church there arose from the perception on the part of many in the congregation that their minister, Thomas Goss, drank too much. He had even been observed to be less than fully sober while conducting Sabbath services. Those who made these observations became determined to extract from Goss an unambiguous declaration of contrition. Goss, naturally, was equally determined to thwart all such efforts. The struggle over this issue eventually developed into a struggle over whether Goss should be allowed to continue in his post. After an ecclesiastical council of June 1771 refused to punish Goss by more than the mildest of verbal censure, the brethren who were opposed to him took the desperate step of calling a church meeting without him and declaring him not only dismissed but excommunicated on the technical ground that he had refused to hold a church meeting the brethren had legitimately requested, and on the more substantive ground that he "refuses to make Christian Satisfaction [for his public drunkenness] but Indeavours to justifie himself," despite his manifest guilt. The response of the ministers in the neighborhood to such an ecclesiastical coup was of course one of horror. The Marlborough Association passed two resolutions of strong disapprobation, the latter of which stipulated that any minister who would "either preach the Word, or dispense the Ordinances" to a people guilty of such gross disorder would thereby be "supporting scism." Thus were the battle lines between order and enthusiasm, clericalism and lay initiative, again sharply drawn.[19]

---

[18]PD, Nov. 2, 1770; June 20, 1771; Dec. 29, 1772.
[19]*Harvard Graduates*, 10:177–79; PFP, Box 2, Folder 3 (Notes on Proceedings of Ecclesiastical Councils), "Result of Council of June 11, 1771, on the Bolton Affair";

Parkman had been keenly interested in the Bolton dispute from the beginning and had of course been one of the prime movers of the Marlborough Association's condemnation of Reverend Goss's antagonists. But his involvement in the situation did not begin to assume major proportions until April 1773, when he was absolutely flabbergasted to learn that one of his colleagues, Reverend Elisha Fish of Upton, who had come to his assistance in the Andrews matter, had stated to Parkman's wife "that the best way to put an End to the Contention in *Bolton,* is to Settle a Minister there as fast as they can." This would amount to an endorsement of the rash steps taken against Goss and would to Parkman be "as if the true method of quenching a Flame was to throw Oyl upon it.—Unhappy people to be guided in this manner! So out of all Rule or Reason." On the same day, Parkman was confronted with the unpleasant fact that another of his parishioners (in addition to Jonas Brigham), Joseph Harrington, Jr., was showing signs of sympathy with the Bolton anticlericalists.

At the annual ministerial convention the next month in Boston, Parkman was appointed to a committee charged with the task of drafting a pamphlet in condemnation of the Bolton disorder. The other committee members included President Locke and Professor Wigglesworth of Harvard and such additional leading lights of the Massachusetts clergy as Charles Chauncy, Andrew Eliot, and Ebenezer Pemberton. A higher, province-wide level of mutual conference was being brought to bear on the situation, with those who had once been New Lights joining together with those who had been Old Lights against the threat from the laity and a few clerical renegades such as Fish. Meanwhile, Fish and the radical Bolton laity dramatized the breakdown of the apparatus of indirect, accommodative order by holding a council to ordain a new minister in Bolton, John Walley, on the same day in August 1773 that a council favorable to Goss (the members of which included Chauncy, Pemberton, and Eliot) was also convened. And just a month later the prediction Parkman had made to Fish, that "to drive on to a new Settlement immediately . . . must be unavoidably to the disturbing of all these Churches round them," began to come true. The malcontents in the Westborough church, gaining new adherents almost with each passing week, now had their own particular grievance on which to focus, the very same one that had stirred up such strife before: Susanna and Persis Baker of Bolton, the former of whom was engaged to be married to Joseph Harrington's

"Paper of the Aggrieved Brethren, Aug. 8, 1771"; transcripts of Marlborough Association statements of Aug. 20, 1771; Oct. 15, 1771.

brother Eli and both of whom were tainted with the radicalism of the Bolton congregation, were seeking admission to communion at the Westborough church.[20]

Many of those in Westborough who were most vocal and active in supporting the anticlericalism of their brethren in Bolton and thus in resisting Parkman also became active around the same time in the gathering movement for liberation from British tyranny, serving on the town's Committee of Correspondence. The convergence of the Bolton ecclesiastical contention with this civil turmoil doubtless had a great deal to do with the readiness of many to suspect Parkman of Tory sympathies.[21] The political crisis diverted attention from the ecclesiastical one until November 1774, when the disaffected church members demanded that a church meeting be held on the question of admitting to communion the former Susanna Baker of Bolton, now Susanna Harrington of Westborough. This engulfing of Westborough in the Bolton controversy made Parkman feel that he was "under the heavyest Troubles that I have (I think) at any time been in," perhaps forgetting for the moment the worst of the Andrews dispute. "[The] disquietness of my people with me . . . presses me sore & deprives me of sleep."

The venerable pastor did have good reason to be upset. More explicitly than they had done during the Andrews controversy, his troublesome people were calling into question the very foundations of the Standing Order. They showed disrespect for the tradition of mutual conference when, in their formal petition for a church meeting, they declared that their purpose was to have the Westborough church "bear Testimony against" what mutual conference had brought forth as regards the Bolton situation—against the pamphlet issued by the Massachusetts Ministerial Convention in May 1773, of which their own pastor was a coauthor; and against the statements issued by the Marlborough Association back in 1771, which they irreverently characterized as "private Combinations . . . Signing papers against a neighbouring Church." And represented by Joseph Harrington and Eli Whitney, they also involved themselves in "contesting & disputing" with Parkman about that other key feature of New England ecclesiology, whether "the Pastor had a *Negative* upon the Brethren." Parkman sought to appease Harrington and Whitney on this point by

---

[20]PD, Apr. 8, 1773; May 27, 1773; Aug. 5, 1773; Sept. 14, 1773; PFP, Box 3, Folder 1 (Undated Correspondence), "Letter to Rev. Mr. Fish." Joseph Harrington, Jr., had joined the church as the Andrews controversy was drawing to a close; see *Church Records,* Nov. 1, 1767.

[21]PD, June 17, 1774; above, n. 1.

noting that he "never had Occasion in all these Years to exercise that Power." He was pleading for continued acquiescence in an order based upon incorporation and co-optation, but these young hotheads were determined to raise the discussion to the level of abstract principle: "They said they should be offended with me if I held that a Minister had [such a veto power]. Upon which I shewd them Dr. *Cotton Mathers* Magnalia—the 30 Cases by 17 Ministers at College Library, Venerable *Higginson* and *Hubbards* Testimony; Mr. *Wise's* Book on Church Government &c. besides these the Platform. They acknowledged the old Books—for I handed down Mr. *Cotton* of the *Keyes,* Old Dr. *Mathers First Principles—Order of the Gospel.*" The "old Books" Parkman threw into the fray constituted a typical effort on his part to overwhelm opposition with a deluge of establishmentarian reasoning. But Harrington and Whitney were further along in their ideological development than anyone had been during the Andrews controversy. They dealt with all these authoritative documents with one simple question that showed they had learned the primary lesson the tradition of Puritan enthusiasm had to teach: "Maynt they Err?"[22]

When the church meeting that had been requested was finally held in February 1775, it dealt only with Susanna Harrington's petition for admission to communion. Parkman attempted to secure agreement to a formula similar to that used in the Andrews case, admitting Mrs. Harrington "as one that had joind with the Church of *Bolton* while it was in good Order, and on consideration that she had walkd soberly & Orderly (for ought we knew)." But this was decisively rejected, and the brethren went on to admit the applicant simply as she was, without qualification or special comment, as a member in good standing of what Parkman considered to be a schismatical group. Due to the outbreak of hostilities in Lexington and Concord, it was late May before the church could be reconvened to consider the broader issues raised in the petition of the previous November. The motion debated was an uncompromising one, comprehensively questioning those long-established customs and institutions constituting the New England Standing Order. Was it "the mind of this Church" that the 1773 Ministerial Convention pamphlet "be such in their opinion, as they are willing to receive as a rule to be governd by, when we do not know that this Church or any other Church, had any hand in Composing the Same"? Did this church consider it proper "to brake Communion

---

[22]PD, Nov. 7, 1774; Nov. 12, 1774; Dec. 1, 1774; Dec. 30, 1774. Eli Whitney was the son of the Andrews partisan Nathaniel Whitney (see above, n. 9) and the father of the inventor of the cotton gin. Like Harrington, he had joined the church just as the Andrews crisis was coming to an end; see *Church Records,* Dec. 6, 1767.

with any other Church, before admonition be given"? And was it of the opinion "that a Pastor of a Congregational Church, has a Legal Right and authority to negative and make Void, the Votes which such a Church Shall See Cause to pass"?

Having already pressed farther than in the Andrews affair and gained a complete victory on the immediate question of Susanna Harrington's ecclesiastical legitimacy, the dissident brethren were now, like true revolutionaries and for the first time in Westborough, demanding that matters of fundamental principle be voted up or down. Which was primary: order or enthusiasm, clericalism and hierarchy, or lay autonomy and equality? In the climate of May 1775, when as Parkman acknowledged "the present Torrent of Liberty is irresistible," there could not be much doubt about the outcome. In all three votes, the principles upon which the tradition of New England order had been erected were resoundingly denied. But nothing was affirmed in their place. The revolutionary church could only define itself in negative terms, and negativity was heaped upon negativity when Parkman declared that he *"did not Consent to the Vote,"* vetoing the brethren's vetoing of his veto power. One member gave expression to the bad feeling that inevitably accompanied such a thoroughgoing deadlock when he in turn moved that the votes be "recorded & read to the Church before they broke up." He did not trust Parkman not to exercise his negative voice by doctoring the church records. Fortunately, "several of the Church vindicated me, & resisted the motion as groundless & injurious." The meeting was then concluded. The votes stood as the declared and official negations of the church, while the manner in which the minister did choose to weigh in with answering negations was to obtain from subsequent candidates for admission to membership a tacit or stated consent to his own nonconsent to those same votes. They were all tied up in nots.[23]

Historians of the professionalism that emerged in the United States in the nineteenth century and developed into a major presence in American life in the twentieth have tended to draw a contrast between this new scientistic, competitive meritocracy and the tension-free world within which, they maintain, professional people had previously worked. According to one such historian, Daniel C. Calhoun,

---

[23]PD, Feb. 27, 1775; May 23, 1775; Aug. 28, 1775; Aug. 31, 1775; Sept. 21, 1775; *Church Records*, Feb. 27, 1775; May 23, 1775; PFP, Box 3, Folder 3 (Correspondence, 1770–79), "Petition of Brethren, May 23, 1775."

the Bolton controversy was seen by some of those caught up in it as a conflict between the "warm, textured, organic society" of tradition, and an embryonic new society of "cold calculation and mutual destruction." On through to the end of the eighteenth century, so runs the more general account provided by Mary O. Furner and Burton J. Bledstein, traditional professionals had been looked up to as "knowledgeable and reliable model citizens who could be trusted to manage affairs." Their professional lives consisted of a "series of good works or public projects, performed within a familiar and deferential society which heaped respectability on its first citizens."

But the present argument strongly suggests that this contrast is based on a highly sentimentalized understanding of pre-nineteenth-century society and culture, at least that of New England. Hierarchical relations in New England were marked not by deferential harmony, but rather by chronic ambivalence, uneasiness, and conflict. If this central reality is considered in conjunction with something else to be gathered from the work of the historians of professionalism, that modern professionalism was largely created by people of New England origin, then the contrast between the traditional and the modern is further eroded and begins, indeed, to be supplanted by a striking continuity. The prophets of professionalism in the nineteenth century may well have simply been carrying forward the work of their Puritan ancestors, adapting to new conditions a traditional yoking by violence together of hierarchical structures and egalitarian rhetoric. Anyone who has any experience at all with the educational system of modern America will recognize a profound similarity between the politics of the twentieth-century classroom and those of the eighteenth-century Church of Christ in Westborough. Modern students and the Westborough brethren, modern teachers and the Westborough minister—all have had the same intricate experiences of uneasiness within. And just as the power struggles that took place in Puritan New England led to an ignoring, and thereby a subverting, of the emotional and intellectual substance of the Puritan enterprise, so are the participants in contemporary American education always being pulled away from teaching and learning and pulled toward an obsessive focus on authority, control, and either alienated obedience or sullen, acted-out resistance. Our culture has never really broken free of one of the most unfortunate legacies of Puritanism, one that, as we have shown, Milton explores in *Paradise Lost* down to the last psychic vicissitude. In the Conclusion, we shall learn that not only does Milton foresee our uneasiness within and without, he also helps us to see and go beyond it. But before we can benefit from this portion of Adam's and Eve's experience, we must examine more systematically the affinities between satanic and capitalistic values and styles.[24]

[24]Daniel C. Calhoun, *Professional Lives in America: Structure and Aspiration, 1750–1850* (Cambridge, Mass.: Harvard University Press, 1965), p. 100; Mary O. Furner, *Advocacy and Objectivity: A Crisis in the Professionalization of American Social Science, 1865–1905* (Lexington, Ky.: University Press of Kentucky, 1975), pp. 5, 17–21, 37–38, 44–45, 49–51, 199 (quotation from p. 5); Burton J. Bledstein, *The Culture of Professionalism: The Middle Class and the Development of Higher Education in America* (New York: Norton, 1976), pp. 133, 173, 335–43 (quotation from p. 173). For a brief additional discussion, see below, chap. 7, n. 11.

PART THREE

Constant Progress Upward:

Puritanism and Capitalism

The New England elements are clearly dominant [in San Francisco] and through the whole Pacific Coast region; softened from their old Puritanic habits,—marrying themselves to the freer and more sensuous life of a new country with a cosmopolitan population, but still preserving their best qualities, of decency, of order, of justice, of constant progress upward in morality and virtue.

Samuel Bowles, letter home to the *Springfield Republican* (1865)

As he our darkness, cannot we his light
Imitate when we please? This desert soil
Wants not her hidden lustre, gems and gold;
Nor want we skill or art, from whence to raise
Magnificence; and what can heaven show more?

Paradise Lost, II, 269–73

Chapter 7

The Secularization of the Protestant Ethic in Nineteenth-Century New England

Christopher Hill has called attention to the inherent instability of Protestant ideology. As a Roman Catholic commentator noted triumphantly in 1668, "Unity in Doctrin (most known and remarkable in the Catholick Church) they have none, witnes those innumerable Sects which now swarm amongst them, and this new Faith hath produced of *Arminians, Zwinglians, Brownists, Independents* &c. And now our late *Quakers* are sprouted out of it, the last spring, perhaps, (though no body knows) of this Reformed Gospel." Hill has also stressed the way in which the Protestant ethic's emphasis on motive and "inner conviction" suited it to a society in which the indirect pressures of peer approval and public opinion would count for more than dogmas and institutions. What also might be affirmed is, first, that the Protestant ethic was thus the only feature of Protestantism that could in the long run be expected to countervail in the direction of equilibrium and consensus over against Protestantism's "anarchy of individual consciences," and second, that consensus around the Protestant ethic could only be fully enjoyed in a society such as Hill describes. And a society of that sort, one in which the church was finally disestablished and social control had therefore to be maintained even more exclusively than before by "invisible, refined, spiritual ties, bonds of the mind and heart," was exactly what nineteenth-century New England was. In the nineteenth century, the heirs of the Colonial opposition between order and enthusiasm buried the hatchet, for all practical purposes, and joined together in a secularized Protestant ethic that rationalized and spiritualized capitalist economic transformation, while also sometimes objecting to it with renewed espousals of the traditional "Puritan strictures against profiteering."[1]

Before we survey the forms of secular justification and sanctification developed in nineteenth-century New England, let us look briefly at a document that provides an unusually full view of the Protestant ethic's structure of feeling as it was during its seventeenth-century high noon and also confirms that the secularized patterns emerging so clearly later on were indeed implicit from the beginning. In 1653 the Boston merchant Robert Keayne composed the last of many versions of his "Last Will and Testament." Keayne had been given ample reason to make this document a final articulation of his impulses to sanctify (Last Will) and to justify (Last Testament). Even among the pious folk of first-generation Boston, Keayne was a notably pious man. It is to his taking of notes on sermons, lectures, and church meetings that we owe part of our knowledge of what transpired in the Boston church during the 1640s. He wrote out his own "exposition or Interpretation of the whole Bible," an accomplishment so cherished by him that, he declared in his will, "if I had 100^{lb} layd me downe for them, to deprive me of them, till my sight or life should be taken from me I should not part from them."

A man of such a temper was of course fully conversant with the Protestant formulas relating to faith and works. He assured all who cared to know that he did "desire from my heart to renownce all confidence or expectation of merritt or desert in any of the best duties or services that ever I have shall or can be able to performe acknowledging that all my righteousnes sanctification and close walking with God if it were or had bin a thousand times more exact than ever yet I attayned too, is all polluted and corrupt and falls short of commending me to God in point of my justification, or helping forward my redemption or salvation." Nevertheless, he went on, although he could not be justified by his works, "yet I beleive they may not be neglected by me without great Sinne, but are ordained of God for me to walk in them carefully in love to him in obedience to his Commandments, as well as for many other good ends and are good fruites &

---

[1]Christopher Hill, *Change and Continuity in Seventeenth-Century England* (Cambridge, Mass.: Harvard University Press, 1975), pp. 89, 93, 96–99; Edward Worsley, *Protestancy without Principles* (Antwerp, 1668), p. 99 (quoted in *CPW*, VIII, 436, n. 81); Daniel Walker Howe, *The Unitarian Conscience: Harvard Moral Philosophy, 1805–1861* (Cambridge, Mass.: Harvard University Press, 1970), p. 122 (quoting William Ellery Channing); Alan Dawley, *Class and Community: The Industrial Revolution in Lynn* (Cambridge, Mass.: Harvard University Press, 1976), p. 73. For a brief description of the Protestant ethic, and the forms of secularization to which it was particularly vulnerable, see above, chap. 3, nn. 4–8.

evidences of justification." As he surveyed his own life more specifically, Keayne found that it conformed in all essential respects to the prescriptions of the Protestant ethic. He had in his mercantile pursuits been "industrious & provident," and as a result he had been able over the course of forty years to "gett a 100^{lb} a yeare above his expences & a great deal more." Furthermore, he had done so "very honestly without hurting his owne conscience or wronging those that he [had dealt] with at all." He had not, that is, broken the Protestant rules against "unrestrained profit-seeking." Even when he had not been directly plying his trade, he had "not lived an idle lazie or dronish life," but had "endeavored to redeeme [his] time as a thing most deare & precyous to [him]" by his pious reading and writing. As he accumulated his fortune of 4,000 pounds, he was well aware that God's grace, not his own industry, was the real source of his prosperity and that he was therefore obliged, at his death if not before, to do whatever he could to insure that his private felicity redounded to the public benefit: "I have endeavored to honnor God with my substance & with the first fruites of all my increase & have endeavored to doe good with what God hath bestowed upon me, so farr as I might likewise provide for the necessities of my owne family, the care of carrying on my calling & other dealings in the world justly. . . . I have held it a great degree of unthankfullnes to God that when he hath bestowed many blessings & a larg or comfortable outward estate upon a man that he should . . . dispose none or very little of it to publique charitable or good workes such as may tend to [God's] glory & the good of others in way of a thankfull acknowledgment to him for so great favors."[2]

We may well imagine the reaction of a man like Keayne when he was accused, as he was in 1639, of precisely that unscrupulous profiteering he believed he had taken such care to guard against. A complaint was lodged against him of charging an excessive price for the hardware that was his stock in trade, and he was indeed eventually required by the resulting civil procedure to pay a fine and by the resulting eccle-

[2]Darrett B. Rutman, *American Puritanism: Faith and Practice* (New York: Lippincott, 1970), p. 10; *Winthrop's Boston: Portrait of a Puritan Town* (Chapel Hill: University of North Carolina Press, 1965), p. 131; Robert Keayne, "The Last Will and Testament of Me, Robert Keayne . . . ," in *A Report of the Record Commissioners of the City of Boston concerning Miscellaneous Papers*, vol. 10 of a series of these reports (Boston, 1886), pp. 1, 5, 15, 26–27, 42, 47. The abbreviations in Keayne's text have been spelled out. I have used this 1886 edition rather than *The Apologia of Robert Keayne*, ed. Bernard Bailyn (New York: Harper Torchbooks, 1965). Its lack of punctuation and paragraphing seems to me to convey Keayne's agitated state of mind more fully than does Bailyn's modernized version.

siastical one to submit to admonition and censure. Keayne paid his fine and outwardly submitted to the public definition of his conduct as covetous and oppressive of his neighbors, but inwardly he did not. "To be brought forth into an open Court as a publique malefactor" had been at the time "both a shame & an amazement to me. It was the greife of my soule," Keayne continued, "that any act of mine . . . should be an occasion of scandall to the Gospell & profession of the Lord Jesus, or that my selfe should be looked at as one that had brought any just dishonor to God." These words were written fourteen years after the fact, but their tenor and tone indicate that Keayne's amazement, shame, and grief had not abated with the passage of time. He is still determined to assert his innocence, that he "dare not subscribe to the justnes of that times proceeding against me, nor did my conscience to the best of my remembrance ever yet convince me that that censure was either equall or deserved by me."

But long before Keayne gets to this point of explicit justification, the intensity of his thirst for it shows itself in the way he repeatedly breaks in upon whatever his theme of the moment happens to be to discourse upon the absolute injustice of the accusation and verdict against him. Thus, after listing his two principal bequests, to his wife and son, he describes the various public benefactions it is his intention posthumously to make possible, commencing with an account of his plans for a gift of 300 pounds for the erection in the heart of Boston of a public building and a system of conduits for the prevention of fires. But before long he feels compelled to state that he has decided to bestow this gift despite "those unkinde & unneighborly discour-tesees that I have more latly & formerly mett with all, in this towne when time was (which I cannot easily forget though I desire to forgive & from many in the Church especially in those times of my troubles & more there [their] spirits & dispositions would have leade them too, had not the providence of God & the tendernes & wisedome of some others amongst us prevented there desires & endeavors, whose ac-tions & proceedings I could never take as a fruite of there love to my soule as much as a fruite of there prejudice against my person."

The aggressively digressive nature of this recollection, its detail and vividness, and the way in which it refuses to let go of its demonized protrayal of Keayne's accusers suggest that Keayne is still responding to this experience as to an utterly devastating assault on his core identity as an upright, faithful servant of God in his mercantile voca-tion. Moreover, what Keayne is digressing from here is not the direct description of his bequest, but an intermediate level of justificatory discussion, for upon completing the description of the bequest, he feels called upon to refute an imagined objection that his real reasons for wanting better security against fire and the construction of a public building on the particular site he had designated had to do not with public good but private gain, to protect his own property and increase his own trade. It is only after he refutes that accusation at great and wearisome length that he launches into the spontaneous and unyielding presentation of himself as entirely sinned against, when he had been accused of sinning. And the structure of this particular sequence is the structure of Keayne's apologia at large. Every legacy is defended against imagined censure, and over and over again the supreme crisis of Keayne's life is remembered as though it were happening anew, with his own uprightness and the absolute malevolence of those who brought the charges against him being maintained in the starkest terms and depicted in the greatest detail.

This document thus manifests both of the forms of probable secularization of the Protestant ethic described at the outset of Chapter 3. In its pages, a sanctifying activism is turned into willfulness and aggression, as Keayne defends himself by determined counterattack. Indeed, he reveals himself at one point to have been a skillful infighter. His principal antagonist had in the course of the dispute added to the charge of gouging the claim that Keayne had failed to pay back to him a debt of 200 pounds he alleged Keayne owed him. Fortunately, "by a singular providence of God," Keayne found a receipt proving that this debt had in fact been paid. But instead of rushing forward with this evidence, he kept it "private to my selfe," producing it only when it would maximize his own vindication and victory and his opponent's humiliation and defeat. But Keayne's last exercise of his will is even more clearly his last testament to his own probity, his last essay in justification. Drawing toward the close, he declares that his purpose has been "to give an account of my actions & endeavor to remove all jelousies as neare as I can, these being as it were my last words that will live to speake for me when I am dead & in my grave, and God may be pleased so farr to blesse something or other that I have had occasion to expresse in this will, that such which have taken libertie to load me with divers reproaches & long to lay me under a darke cloude may have cause to see that they have done amisse & now be sorry for it though they have not beene so before."

By sheer repetition and martyred vehemence—the latter exemplified here by a parting shot at his enemies even as he imagines their repentance for the wrongs they have done him—Keayne seeks to supersede the public view of his conduct, the view taken by the institutions making up the external world, with an opposing private view, which he in his heart and God in his heaven know to be the correct one. This overarching dimension of justification driven into fuller subjectivity is in short order conjoined with sanctification transposed into willfulness when Keayne declares that if his justification of himself in his will should itself "prove offencive" after it is made public, and if such disapprobation should then be "entertained or countenanced" by those in authority, then his "will is" that all but one of the public legacies he has stipulated and described "shall utterly cease & become voyd." Although Keayne's apology for himself could not be more deeply expressive of the piously Puritan culture of seventeenth-century New England, it is also, in its recoil from the prospect of sheer acquisitiveness, in the combativeness of its manner, and in the individuality of perspective that is inherent in its being a private correction of the public record, richly anticipatory of the secularized Puritan culture of nineteenth-century New England.[3]

In many of the most obvious respects, of course, the polarization between order and enthusiasm was sharpened rather than dulled in the nineteenth century, as Unitarianism emerged to espouse a more open and explicit theological and cultural liberalism and to take control of what was left of the Standing Order, and as Edwardsean Calvinism was thereby driven into alliance with the periodic revivalism that produced what have become known as the Second and Third Great Awakenings. But when it came to the central socioeconomic facts of the day, Unitarianism and evangelicalism, order and enthusiasm were of essentially the same mind. Both strove to convince themselves that economic change was leading to moral and spiritual betterment. If in 1841 William Ellery Channing saw a tendency of "the Present Age . . . to expansion, to diffusion, to universality," a tendency "directly opposed to the spirit of exclusiveness, restriction, narrowness, monopoly, which has prevailed in past ages," he was only adapting to the slower-paced rhythms of the Unitarian sensibility the same sentiment as had been expressed by a proponent of revivalism in 1830 when he had declared that "the spirit of the age is . . . a spirit of extraordinary enterprise . . . on a scale of noble daring and sublime extent, hitherto unknown on earth."[4]

[3]Bernard Bailyn, *The New England Merchants in the Seventeenth Century* (Cambridge, Mass.: Harvard University Press, 1955), pp. 41–43; Rutman, *Winthrop's Boston*, pp. 243–45; Keayne, "Last Will and Testament," pp. 9–10, 28, 32–34, 47, 49, 50. The fullest account of Keayne and his troubles is Bernard Bailyn, "The Apologia of Robert Keayne," *William and Mary Quarterly*, 3d ser., 7 (1950):568–87.

[4]Burton J. Bledstein, *The Culture of Professionalism: The Middle Class and the Develop-

But the Protestant ideological consensus of the nineteenth century is perhaps most fully represented by Henry Ward Beecher, that walking synthesis of evangelical enthusiasm and bland liberal order. As the son of Lyman Beecher, New England's leading revivalist and Calvinist of the 1820s and 1830s, Beecher had been reared in the culture of enthusiasm; but in the teachings of his maturity, he came to soften Calvinism into a Wordsworthian nature worship and sense of evolutionary progress that differed little from Unitarianism, while at the same time he presented these liberalized doctrines with something of the old-time evangelical fervor. Beecher's pronouncements on the capitalist triumphs of his day reveal all too clearly that those triumphs had only exacerbated what had always been the susceptibility of the Protestant ethic to degenerate into rationalization of the most arrant sort. As we have seen, Protestantism held that success in amassing material wealth might well be a sign of justification, that one had been vouchsafed a corresponding spiritual wealth. But in such comparisons, the material term might, in its presentness and palpability, tend to resist the intended metaphoric transformation into an absent and impalpable spirituality, and this possibility was apt to become a probability, if not a certainty, in societies such as nineteenth-century New England and the United States in which material wealth was being amassed on an unprecedented scale. In nineteenth-century evangelicalism, the traditional Protestant analogies between the material and the spiritual took the form of perceiving similarities between the energies that went into the creation of the new manufacturing enterprises and those that went into the creation of revivals. After the Panic of 1857, Henry Ward Beecher informed this particular similitude with vivid psychological detail:

> Let a hundred merchants and eminent mechanics—known and trusted men—gather in some vast hall in New York, and testify in regard to some new method of gaining wealth. Let them, one by one, declare the reality of the riches, exhibit his own winnings, declare the facility with which thousands more could acquire, and that joint testimony of a hundred honest men would strike a fever through a city in a day, and the veins and arteries of every occupation would throb with impatient desire. Such is the power given to a truth when many men, corroborating it, give it a blessed panic-power.

ment of Higher Education in America (New York: Norton, 1976), p. 181; Perry Miller, The Life of the Mind in America: From the Revolution to the Civil War (New York: Harcourt, Brace and World, 1965), p. 52. See chaps. 1–3 of Miller for an analysis of antebellum evangelicalism; for Unitarianism, see Howe, Unitarian Conscience, passim.

Here surely is a striking instance of the material sign overwhelming that spirituality it ostensibly signifies. Beecher inadvertently teaches us that the rituals developed by nineteenth-century revivalism (in this case, testimonies to "what God has done for me") constituted but a special instance of an overall climate of "impatient desire" engendered by the era's material pursuits and transformations. Theodore Parker was deliberately and sarcastically reenacting this same metaphoric reversal when he stated in 1857 that such revival "machinery" as Beecher was promoting was "as well known as McCormick's reaper."[5]

Yet it was when Beecher was espousing the semi-Unitarian liberalism that brought him closest to Parker that he managed to rationalize and spiritualize the new capitalist order with a disregard for the stubborn materiality of material wealth that was truly sublime. In *Norwood; Or, Village Life In New England* (1867), his attempt to beat his sister, Harriet Beecher Stowe, at her own game of writing novels, he elaborated in all sincerity on the blunt saying Daniel Defoe had put ironically into the mouth of the degenerate aristocrat in his *Compleat English Gentleman:* "Let the usurer lay up his money, 'tis my proper bussiness to spend it; 'tis my calling." One of the minor characters in *Norwood*, "an eccentric merchant and manufacturer, Mr. Brett by name," is not sure he ought to build a greenhouse as an annex to his residence. He is reluctant to "spend on myself while there is so much to be done with money,—so many poor; so many ignorant; so many tenements to be built and families to be regarded, and factory children to be educated; and besides, so much to be done for the world abroad." But Beecher's mouthpiece, Dr. Reuben Wentworth, assures Brett that he is troubling himself over nothing at all. It is a fine thing to give generously to "churches, schools and libraries, established public charities," but the man who would be both wealthy and scrupulous must remember that "the very way to feed the community is to feed the family. This is the point of contact for each man with the society in which he lives. Through the family, chiefly, we are to act upon society. Money contributed there is contributed to the whole." To Wentworth's (and Beecher's) way of thinking, there ought to be almost no limits whatsoever placed on the kind of charity that begins and ends (literally) at home:

---

[5]William G. McLoughlin, *The Meaning of Henry Ward Beecher: An Essay on the Shifting Values of Mid-Victorian America* (New York: Knopf, 1970), pp. 117–18; Miller, *Life of the Mind*, p. 92. McLoughlin's book is the source for the summary of Beecher's views at the outset of the paragraph.

Nothing is more remote from selfishness than generous expenditure in building up a home, and enriching it with all that shall make it beautiful without and lovely within. A man who builds up a noble house does it for the whole neighborhood, not for himself alone. He who surrounds his children with books, refines their thoughts by early familiarity with art, is training them for the State. In no other way could he spend so much money so usefully for the State. . . . Whatever expenditure refines the family and lifts it into a larger sphere of living is really spent upon the whole community as well. If no man lives better than the poorest man, there will be no leader in material things. A community needs examples to excite its ambition. A noble dwelling is, in part, the property of all who dwell near it. Fine grounds not only confer pleasure directly on all who visit or pass by, but they excite every man of any spirit to improve his own grounds. A family of children upon whom wealth has been employed judiciously, if they are at all worthy, represent in the community a higher type of life than can be found in poverty. Fine dress may be looked upon either as a matter of display or of worthy example. In the latter aspect, it is a duty as well as a pleasure.

Parson Buell, who has been listening to Wentworth along with Brett, seconds Wentworth's soothing words, chiming in with the observation that "it is certainly not selfish . . . to spend money on one's self, if thereby a higher influence is secured for society. It is upon that principle that one is justified in liberal expenditure for education, and even for travel, as an eminent means of liberal education." Brett is won over by these arguments, conceding at last that probably "there *are* faithful men" who own domestic greenhouses. Beecher's "talk about enjoying money" is one culmination and apotheosis of the Protestant ethic's teaching that moral and spiritual reality resided subjectively in the heart of the practitioner and the eye of the beholder rather than inhering objectively in those external things that were practiced upon and beheld. The most widely influential leader of Victorian Protestantism shows upwardly mobile readers who might still be caught up in the old Puritan fear of covetousness and luxury how to whisk away a world of consumerism and sentimental domesticity, a world of "display," and replace it with a world of systematic moral and spiritual fulfillment, a world of "worthy example."[6]

This aspect of what Eric Foner calls the "adaptation of [the Protestant] ethic to the dynamic, expansive, capitalist society" of the nine-

[6]Henry Ward Beecher, *Norwood; Or, Village Life in New England* (New York: Scribner's, 1868), pp. 209–19; Daniel Defoe, *The Compleat English Gentleman* (London, 1890; orig. 1728–29), p. 66. Beecher endorsed the capitalist order in more tangible ways also, lending his name to the sale of trusses, soaps, and Jay Cooke's Northern Pacific Railroad; see Bledstein, *Culture of Professionalism*, p. 52.

teenth-century North is the one most often noted. Protestantism is understood to have provided capitalism with ingenious and highly serviceable mechanisms of self-deception. Insofar as New England Puritanism means anything beyond sexual repression in popular historical consciousness, it thus conjures up the sequence John Winthrop–Benjamin Franklin–Lowell textile mills. But intellectual adaptation to socioeconomic transformation did not only proceed by such a straightforward route. Just as the dimension of Protestant and Puritan moralizing which lent itself to validation of material striving not only survived but flourished in the capitalized and secularized ambience of the nineteenth century, so also flourished that other dimension of Puritanism which was prepared to condemn any material striving that upon sober reflection could not be so validated. For every complacent Henry Ward Beecher, there was a descendant of John Cotton and Robert Keayne, appalled at the prospect of "unrestrained profit-seeking" and casting about for some means of bringing it under control. And in this mode no less than in that of direct justification of capitalism, the heirs of enthusiasm and the heirs of order came together in agreement and consensus. Both Unitarians and evangelicals saw the Panic of 1837 as a "judgment upon the commercial spirit," with its diverse forms of speculation. Speculation was to be as sharply distinguished as it always had been, insisted the Unitarians, from "honest industriousness in one's private calling." The worries that elicited from an evangelical orator in 1857 the pronouncement that "commerce cannot be entrusted with the moral interests of mankind. . . . She has no principle that can withstand a strong temptation to her insatiable cupidity"—these were the same worries that had prompted William Ellery Channing sixteen years before to include in his lecture "The Present Age" an indictment of that age's "feverish, insatiable cupidity, under which fraud, bankruptcy, distrust, and distress are fearfully multiplied."[7]

The views of the great Massachusetts educational reformer Horace Mann represent these more complex and ambivalent forms of the relationship in nineteenth-century New England between the Protestant ethic and the spirit of capitalism just as well as those of Henry Ward Beecher represent the simpler, untroubled forms of it. In Franklin, Massachusetts, where Mann grew up at the turn of the nineteenth century, the parish minister was Nathaniel Emmons,

---

[7]Eric Foner, *Free Soil, Free Labor, Free Men: The Ideology of the Republican Party before the Civil War* (New York: Oxford University Press, 1970), p. 13; Miller, *Life of the Mind*, pp. 53, 74; Howe, *Unitarian Conscience*, pp. 221–22, 232, 234.

Lyman Beecher's chief predecessor, along with Samuel Hopkins, as a promulgator of Edwardsean Calvinism. Periodically during Mann's childhood, the Franklin church was the scene of revival meetings. Mann was thus exposed directly to the patterns of thought and impulse characteristic of latter-day enthusiasm, but he reacted strongly against those patterns in the direction of a liberal rationalism, as is clear from his response to a sermon of Lyman Beecher's in 1822: "Dr. Beecher . . . published . . . a dolorous tale about the heathenish condition of the people of the U. States, six sevenths of whom were, according to him, sitting in the . . . shadow of death because . . . they had not *hopkinsian* . . . ministers to dispense the light of the Calvinist creed. . . . [This sermon] produced as great an effect upon my feelings as it would to have heard a great tragedy well performed at a theatre! *No more upon my belief;* for belief belongs to the understanding and should not be biased by hopes and fears." The sensibility manifested in this critique is fully consistent with the fact that when Mann became a member of the Massachusetts General Court and an active figure on the Boston scene in the 1830s, one of his friends and confidants was William Ellery Channing.[8]

During his New England childhood, Mann of course imbibed the Protestant work ethic: "Industry or diligence became my second nature . . . work has always been to me what water is to fish." And as might be expected, the rhetoric of the movement for public school reform of which Mann was the leader very often assumed, in the manner of Henry Ward Beecher, that it was virtually impossible that anyone who was truly working hard could actually be laboring to be rich for anything so despicable as the flesh and sin. Mann himself declared that public education could very easily be both "the most prolific parent of material riches" and also "a moral renovator." One of Mann's successors as secretary to the Massachusetts Board of Education, the Republican politician George Boutwell, insisted in 1857 that the reason the new system of public education was indispensable to the new system of factory labor was that such labor called for a maximum of intelligence and creativity: "The laborer is no longer servile, yielding to laws and necessities that he cannot comprehend, and therefore cannot respect, but he has been elevated to the regions of art and works by laws that he appreciates, and aspires to a perfection as real, at least, as that of the sculptor, or poet. . . . The laws of

[8]Jonathan Messerli, *Horace Mann: A Biography* (New York: Knopf, 1972), pp. 13–20, 171–85; Ann Douglas, *The Feminization of American Culture* (New York: Knopf, 1977), pp. 37–38.

labor are the laws that exist and are recognized in art, eloquence and science. The great law of these latter unquestionably is, that every student shall be at the same time an original thinker, investigator, designer and producer." In this particularly fanciful instance of the spiritualization of economic process, Boutwell takes the most obvious reality of industrialized labor—which was, as a Massachusetts legislative report had recognized twenty years before, that "that minute subdivision of labor, upon which the success of manufacturing industry depends, is not a circumstance favorable to intellectual development"—and airily transforms it into its opposite, just as Henry Ward Beecher blithely turns conspicuous consumption into "worthy example."9

But for the most part, Mann and the other educational reformers did not content themselves with such simple exercises in highly subjective imaginative alchemy. In his report of the very next year, Boutwell listed a few of the consequences of industrial capitalism that seemed the opposite of sanctified and justified: "the activity of business, by which fathers have been diverted from the custody and training of their children; the claims of fashion and society which have led to some neglect of family government on the part of mothers; the aggregation of large populations in towns and cities, always unfavorable to the physical and moral welfare of children; [and] the comparative neglect of agriculture and the consequent loss of moral strength in the people." But it had been Horace Mann himself who had already, in his annual report to the Massachusetts Board of Education of 1849, seen Massachusetts turning into a land of greed and the grinding of the face of the poor, a land characterized by the "domination of capital and the servility of labor," in which "some toil and earn," while "others . . . seize and enjoy." Animated by perceptions of this sort, Mann argued not that public education was designed merely to facilitate a process of sanctification which the process of capitalist development was already of its own accord carrying forward, but rather that such education was needed for the imposition of those moral and spiritual restraints that capitalism left to itself only knew how to erode and destroy. In 1840 and 1843 he had spoken of such a role for education in strictly prudential terms: "As population increases, & especially as artificial wants multiply, & temptations in-

9Messerli, *Mann*, p. 8; Michael Katz, *The Irony of Early School Reform: Educational Innovation in Mid-Nineteenth-Century Massachusetts* (Cambridge, Mass.: Harvard University Press, 1968), pp. 27–29; Carl J. Siracusa, *A Mechanical People: Perceptions of the Industrial Order in Massachusetts, 1815–1880* (Middletown, Conn.: Wesleyan University Press, 1979), p. 193.

crease, the guards and securities must increase also, or society will deteriorate. . . . Now I say the real insurance offices are the School Houses, provided you have a good *actuary* in each, and not a jackass."

But now in 1849 Mann discoursed upon the moral and spiritual function of public education with full visionary eloquence:

> [Education] knows no distinction of rich and poor, of bond and free, or between those who, in the imperfect light of this world, are seeking through different avenues, to reach the gate of heaven. Without money and without price, it throws open its doors, and spreads the table of its bounty, for all the children of the State. Like the sun, it shines, not only upon the good, but upon the evil, that they may become good; and like the rain, its blessings descend, not only upon the just, but upon the unjust, that their injustice may depart from them and be known no more.

Mann's words amount to a secular redaction of John Winthrop's great lay sermon "A Modell of Christian Charitie": "Wee must be knitt together in this work as one man, wee must entertaine each other in brotherly affeccion, wee must be willing to abridge our selves of superfluities, for the supply of others necessities, wee must uphold a familiar Commerce together in all meekeness, gentlenes, patience and liberallitie, we must delight in each other, make others Conditions our owne rejoyce together, mourne together, labour, and suffer together." As Darrett B. Rutman has argued, Winthrop was driven both to emigrate to New England and to formulate this utopian statement of the traditional "rule of charity" in reaction against an utterly "unrestrained profit-seeking" that seemed to him to be prevalent in the England of the 1620s. Two centuries later, after the acquisitive forces Winthrop had sought to restrain and transcend had evidently become fully dominant, Horace Mann's reliance on the secular gospel of education as a source of charitable human connection constituted his attempt to restore the City upon a Hill to that place of moral and spiritual eminence Winthrop had intended it to occupy.[10]

The rhetoric offered up by Winthrop and Mann in opposition to the glaring moral deficiencies of sheer material gain obviously deserves to be taken far more seriously than does Henry Ward Beecher's, or even John Cotton's, simply waving the magic wand of noble motive at a universe of such pursuits and enjoyments. Nevertheless, the very

---

[10]Katz, *Irony of Early School Reform*, p. 42; Messerli, *Mann*, pp. 340, 402–3, 492–93; Rutman, *Winthrop's Boston*, pp. 5–6, 10. For some of the evidence upon which Rutman bases his statements concerning Winthrop's antiprofiteering motives, see above, Introduction, n. 5.

intensity with which Winthrop and Mann recoil from unsanctified worldly endeavor imparts to their words much the same air of ungroundedness and unreality as is so manifest in Beecher's utterances. Both of these more agonized Puritan reformers have recourse to the summarizing global panorama, itself entirely dependent on metaphor, as their primary rhetorical device. Winthrop gathers the entire community together "as one man." His successor projects a universe in which all are traveling on spiritual avenues, all are dining at spiritual tables, all are abiding beneath moralized weather. Thus, if Beecher and Cotton present a recognizable external world and then go on to transform it, with extravagant implausibility, by arbitrary moral redefinition, Winthrop's and Mann's procedure is to remove the external world of material objects and appetites altogether from our view and invite us to refresh and renew ourselves in an alternate world composed of nothing but principle and spirit. Matter no longer needs to be metaphorically metamorphosed into spirit; the tension and risk inherent in that transaction have been eliminated with the elimination of matter from the discourse, and Mann's metaphors are then freed up to dissolve easily one into another. All this would be perfectly fine if our Puritan idealists would go on to offer some guidance as to how these vistas of sanctification are to be made solid rather than ethereal. But this alas is precisely what they do not do. They leave us suspended between the evidently incommensurable realms of a sordid material reality, on the one hand, and a splendid moral aspiration, on the other.

As Jonathan Messerli notes, the facts that Massachusetts embarked on drastic educational reforms in 1837, just four years after disestablishing the church in 1833, and that an influential politician such as Horace Mann was appointed chief administrator of the reorganized educational system, are extremely suggestive. The public school, a New England institution nearly as venerable as the church, was being looked to to replace the church as "the best means to maintain a set of common values and re-establish the older community of consensus on a newer urban and industrial foundation." The public school movement had deeper historical roots than the other forms of institution building engaged in by the latter-day Puritans. But those other initiatives—which included the public library movement and the creation during the latter part of the century of the modern university as the crucial and enabling institution of what has been called "the culture of professionalism"—were conceived just as definitely as was public school reform as attempts to impose new institutional forms of moral and spiritual restraint on the emergent capitalist order. And it was New

England and New Englanders that were in the forefront of all these efforts.[11]

Still another institutional component of the modern world which emerged in the nineteenth century and which until the end of the century also viewed itself, at least in New England, as a means of secular sanctification and salvation was the press. Taking note of the role of the press in the nineteenth century helps to remind us how thoroughly verbal and literary a culture nineteenth-century New England was. In 1826 Boston had 28 periodicals of various kinds; by 1848 the number had increased to 120, with a circulation of half a million. It seemed to an English traveler in 1853 that New Englanders "are a reading public: from the daily literature on the newsvender's counter, to the thoughtful volumes of the scholar's study, nothing escapes their attention; and to such a pitch is this determination to acquire knowledge carried, that the coachman who drives you to hear a lecture will pay his money to go in and attend its delivery.... In [New England] there is scarcely a village that has not some institute for the delivery of lectures, the formation of a library, and the study of various acquirements, while in all their cities and large towns there are at least two and sometimes three. (We have been told that there are upwards of three hundred in the six States.)" The lyceums, lectures, and libraries that so impressed this visitor were as popular and pervasive in what has been called the Yankee West as in New England itself, and this feature of New England civilization was sufficiently enticing, or overpowering, to command emulation by Irish immigrants, who established Catholic lyceums, literary societies, and newspapers very shortly after they arrived in the 1840s and 1850s.[12]

[11]Messerli, *Mann*, pp. 235–38, 241–42, 249, 253. For public libraries, see Jesse H. Shera, *Foundations of the Public Library: The Origins of the Public Library Movement in New England, 1629–1855* (Chicago: University of Chicago Press, 1949); and Sidney H. Ditzion, *Arsenals of a Democratic Culture: A Social History of the American Public Library Movement in New England and the Middle States from 1850 to 1900* (Chicago: American Library Association, 1947). In Dee Garrison's survey of the public library leadership of the 1880s, 64 percent of her sample was found to be of New England origin, 44 percent descended from prominent Colonial families; see *Apostles of Culture: The Public Librarian and American Society, 1876–1920* (New York: Free Press, 1979), p. 17. For the emergence of professionalism, see Bledstein, *Culture of Professionalism;* and Mary O. Furner, *Advocacy and Objectivity: A Crisis in the Professionalization of American Social Science, 1865–1905* (Lexington, Ky.: University Press of Kentucky, 1975). Eight of the nine college presidents Bledstein singles out as playing significant parts in the dissemination of the new professional ethos grew up either in New England or in New England–settled upstate New York; see *Culture of Professionalism*, pp. 335–43.

[12]Oscar Handlin, *Boston's Immigrants: A Study in Acculturation* (Cambridge, Mass.: Harvard University Press, 1979; orig. 1941), pp. 22, 170–75; Shera, *Foundations of the Public Library*, p. 119; Louis B. Wright, *Culture on the Moving Frontier* (Bloomington: Indiana University Press, 1955), pp. 230, 234.

So the old Puritan culture of the Word survived as a secular culture of multiple and diverse words. And this was true not only as a matter of social practice—that the means of communication were dramatically expanded in the first half of the nineteenth century, and that the people of the antebellum North did indeed avail themselves of these new intellectual opportunities—but also as a matter of ideology. In a Protestant society primarily held together, as we have already heard William Ellery Channing declare, not by laws, dogmas, and institutions, but rather by "invisible, refined, spiritual ties, bonds of the mind and the heart," literary and rhetorical communication was an indispensable means of social control. New institutional forms of social control were in fact developed in the nineteenth century, as we have just seen, but they were all of them either bookish and literary in their essence (public libraries, the press) or else educational and therefore heavily involved in verbal discourse (public schools, universities). Several decades before Matthew Arnold would do so, the Harvard Unitarians were affirming that the future of literature would, of necessity, be immense. It was thought that literature, by stirring up approved sentiments and emotions, might serve as a safeguard against excessive democracy and materialism, might prove generally invaluable in inculcating "invisible, refined, spiritual ties." As those urging the establishment of a public library in Beverly, Massachusetts, argued, "Nothing can be more true, than that the best means for destroying a taste for a lower pleasure, is by cultivating a taste for a higher." The Roman Catholic *Boston Pilot* was appealing to such a view of literature when in 1877 it criticized the educated members of the Irish community for failing to provide adequate leadership in this regard: "What reading rooms have they established to keep men from liquor stores and for their mental improvement? None whatever."[13]

It was Samuel Bowles, owner and editor of the *Springfield Republican,* who coined a phrase, "constant progress upward in morality and virtue," which aptly summarizes the theme under the umbrella of which economic process was most commonly spiritualized, whether in the untroubled Beecherian or the ambivalent Mannean modes, in the secular rhetoric that was thus institutionalized and ideologically dignified and that poured forth in such abundance from the pens, printing presses, and pulpits of nineteenth-century New England. Bowles would involve himself and his newspaper in virtually all of the politi-

[13]Howe, *Unitarian Conscience,* pp. 122, 137, 174–76, 182, 195, 222–23; Katz, *Irony of Early School Reform,* p. 121; Handlin, *Boston's Immigrants,* p. 222.

cal struggles of the mid-century for constant progress upward in morality and virtue, from the antislavery Republicanism of the 1850s to the anticorruption Liberal Republicanism of the 1870s. In 1856 he thought he had never seen "a political convention in which there was so much soul" as that which nominated John C. Fremont as the first Republican presidential candidate. "It was politics with a heart and a conscience in it." In 1871, in the midst of postwar venality, Bowles insisted that "every honest, God-fearing man must make the performance of even trivial public duties a question of conscience."

Like Horace Mann, Bowles was an extremely successful practitioner of the Protestant ethic in the sphere of culture, building a provincial weekly into a truly distinguished daily of national fame and influence. Perhaps it was a consciousness of the energies that would propel him into a future that would be both expansive and full of strenuous endeavors in sanctification that prompted Bowles in 1851, the year he took control of the *Republican,* to engage in the most grandiose rhetorical justification of his own journalistic calling:

> Nations and individuals now stand immediately responsible to the world's opinion, and the world, interesting itself in the grand events transpiring in its various parts, and among its various parties, has become, and is still becoming, liberalized in feeling; and being called away from its exclusive home-fields has forgotten, in its universal interests, the petty interests, feuds, gossips, and strifes of families and neighborhoods. This wonderful extension of the field of vision, this compression of the human race into one great family, must tend to identify its interests, sympathies, and motives. . . . The press is destined, more than any other agency, to melt and mold the jarring and contending nations of the world into that one great brotherhood which through long centuries has been the ideal of the Christian and the philanthropist. Its mission has but just commenced. A few years more and a great thought uttered within sight of the Atlantic will rise with the morrow's sun and shine upon millions of minds within sight of the Pacific. The murmur of Asia's multitudes will be heard at our doors; and, laden with the fruit of all human thought and action, the newspaper will be in every abode, the daily nourishment of every mind.

Bowles exploits to the utmost the device of which we have seen both John Winthrop and Horace Mann availing themselves, that of the global panorama. The Harvard Unitarians conceived of individual growth and development as endless movement toward "a higher realm," until constant progress upward in morality and virtue would finally lead one into a state of godlike perfection. Bowles's persona in the above passage is that of someone who is surveying from such a divine developmental apex the constant progress upward of the rest of the world. Diction rises suitably to accord with the vast perspective, both spatial and temporal, which is sustained from beginning to end: "the grand events . . . universal interests . . . wonderful extension . . . one great family . . . one great brotherhood . . . a great thought." Syntax is appropriately suspended, and speech is deliberate, measured, and seasoned with mellifluous assonance and alliteration: "the world, interesting itself . . . in its various parts, and among its various parties, has become, and is still becoming . . . and being called away . . . has forgotten . . . to melt and mold the jarring and contending nations." Ordinary human manifestations and expressions are made over into personified abstract entities that live and move and have their being in companionship with the majesty of the sun and the oceans: "a great thought uttered within sight of the Atlantic will rise with the morrow's sun and shine upon millions of minds within sight of the Pacific. The murmur of Asia's multitudes will be heard at our doors."

Bowles has provided a translation into social experience of Ralph Waldo Emerson's absolute spiritualization of natural experience: "Standing on the bare ground—my head bathed by the blithe air and uplifted into infinite space—all mean egotism vanishes. I become a transparent eyeball; I am nothing; I see all; the currents of the Universal Being circulate through me; I am part or parcel of God." By such fanatical floridity, the secularized Puritans of nineteenth-century New England sought to convey the experience of inhabiting a special and separate realm that was, like a Gothic cathedral, at once massively bounded and soaringly boundless. Their essays in justification were idealistic not only in the moral sense, but also and especially in the epistemological sense. Along with that emergence of literature as an institution and an ideology of which it was a central manifestation, the high and highly subjectivized style of latter-day Puritanism was doing its part to build the world in which we now live: one in which experience is comprehensively and continuously mediated and in which the very existence of an objective reality has therefore become problematic.[14]

[14]George S. Merriam, *The Life and Times of Samuel Bowles*, 2 vols. (New York, 1885), 1:59, 99, 151; 2:8–9, 137; Howe, *Unitarian Conscience*, pp. 114–15, 119–20; Ralph Waldo Emerson, "Nature," in *The Selected Writings of Ralph Waldo Emerson*, ed. Brooks Atkinson (New York: Modern Library, 1940), p. 6.

Perhaps we have put ourselves in position to gain a somewhat better understanding of the fact that the nineteenth century was the first great age of satanist readings of *Paradise Lost*. As we have seen, the Satan who addresses us in Book I of the poem, who in his first speech encloses himself in a universe of such sonorous abstractions as "transcendent brightness" (86) and "the glorious enterprise" (89), is a figure who bears a distinct resemblance as a rhetorician to Horace Mann, Samuel Bowles, and the other spokesmen for the age of constant progress upward in morality and virtue. Satan's spiritual ambitions, trusting "to have equalled the most high" (40), are those of Emersonian Transcendentalists and Harvard Unitarians alike. Moreover, like New England Puritanism in the nineteenth century, Satan has been disestablished, cast out as a result of his own secularizing impulses from his eminent and settled place in the traditional order. In Satan, Milton seems to have intuited both the circumstances of the idealistic reformers of nineteenth-century New England and their grandiloquently subjectivizing response to them. He seems to have predicted what the psychic and rhetorical results would be of people feeling a need to pull themselves up spiritually by their own bootstraps.

But if the Satan who is stiffly transcendental would have been at home in the culture of nineteenth-century New England, so also would the Satan who is both compulsively competitive and unable to avoid wallowing in cruder fantasies and illusions of the sort purveyed by Henry Ward Beecher. To see how this may be so, we explore in the next two chapters the relations between Puritanism and capitalism in the nineteenth century in a more intimate manner, observing how they worked themselves out in the life of one community.[15]

[15]For Satan's rhetoric in Book I, see above, chap. 3, nn. 16, 25–27.

Chapter 8

The Secularization of the Protestant Ethic
in Marlborough, Massachusetts, 1835–1890

As mentioned earlier, Marlborough, Massachusetts, is located seven miles northeast of Westborough, about twenty-five miles west of Boston, in western Middlesex County. So far as can be ascertained, it was a typical New England farming village from its establishment in 1660 until the 1830s. During that decade, however, the process commenced by which life in Marlborough was transformed from "the pastoral quiet of the village of 1836 into the manufacturing stir of the Highland City of 1890." The agent of this transformation was the shoe industry. In Lynn, long a shoemaking center, the industry was reorganized at this time by merchant entrepreneurs eager to produce the greatly increased numbers of shoes needed by the expanding nation. Marlborough was one of thirty-odd former Massachusetts agricultural communities that followed Lynn's lead in the 1830s and began converting its houses and barns into manufacturing units that the historian of the state's shoe industry has named "central shops": miniature proto-factories, characterized by "specialized work under supervision under one roof." Even before the advent of mechanization, this new system of production served the purpose for which it was designed spectacularly well. In 1837 Marlborough was making a hundred thousand pairs of shoes annually; by 1855, the total had jumped to two million.[1]

[1]*History of Middlesex County, Massachusetts . . .*, comp. D. Hamilton Hurd, 3 vols. (Philadelphia, 1890), 3:850 (all subsequent citations are to vol. 3); Alan Dawley, *Class and Community: The Industrial Revolution in Lynn* (Cambridge, Mass.: Harvard University Press, 1976), pp. 25–29, 47; Blanche Evans Hazard, *The Organization of the Boot and Shoe Industry in Massachusetts before 1875* (Cambridge, Mass.: Harvard University Press,

According to Daniel T. Rodgers, "The shoe industry was for most nineteenth-century Americans the preeminent example of the rate at which the new could obliterate the old." With the development of the central shop, which resulted in the extinction of the skilled, autonomous artisan shoemaker and the emergence of a labor structure of owners, supervisors, and unskilled employees, the new had already in effect obliterated the old, but it was not until machinery was introduced and central shops evolved into factories that the revolutionary nature of these changes became apparent for all to see. Full conversion of the boot and shoe industry to a mechanized factory system of production became possible after the introduction in 1862 of the McKay stitcher for the rapid mechanical sewing of the heavy leather of the bottoms of shoes. This machine made it possible to produce eighty pairs of shoes in the time it had previously taken to make one pair. By utilization of the McKay stitcher and the many other "labor-saving" devices following in its wake, Marlborough's production of shoes increased from the two million a year of 1855 to the nine million a year of 1889, making it at that point, according to some booster-ist claims, second only to Lynn among Massachusetts cities and towns in overall boot and shoe output.

Such thoroughgoing industrialization was accompanied, in Marlborough as elsewhere, by the various developments usually grouped together under the heading of urbanization. Population increased from two to six thousand between 1840 and 1860 and, despite the establishment in 1867 of one of Marlborough's neighborhoods as the separate town of Hudson, more than doubled again in the next three decades, reaching almost fourteen thousand by the time the town officially became a city in 1890. Population growth was of course accompanied by a great deal of residential and commercial construction and, during the 1880s, by such modernizing technological equivalents of the factory system in the sphere of urban daily life as streetcars, telephones, electric lights, and a municipal sewer system and waterworks.[2]

The capitalist transformation of Marlborough was not only a matter of global increase; as the town grew, the structure of its life was

---

1921), pp. 42–44, 86; Charles Hudson, *History of the Town of Marlborough, Middlesex County, Massachusetts* (Boston, 1862), pp. 261–63. For the founding and early history of Marlborough, see above, chap. 5, nn. 1–4.

[2]Daniel T. Rodgers, *The Work Ethic in Industrial America, 1850–1920* (Chicago: University of Chicago Press, 1978), p. 23; Dawley, *Class and Community*, pp. 92–93; *MT*, May 27, 1880; Mar. 2, 1882; Oct. 1, 1885; Oct. 18, 1888; May 23, 1889; Sept. 19, 1889; *History of Middlesex County*, p. 846.

also drastically altered. According to Jackson Turner Main, during the late eighteenth century the people of New England generally, and in particular of the east central Massachusetts area in which Marlborough was located, tended to cluster toward the middle range of income and wealth. Worcester County probate records for the 1760s and 1780s suggest that 70 percent of the county's population constituted a middle class of small property owners, a proportion that tax assessment records indicate also roughly obtained in the town of Harvard in 1771. This background of relatively stable egalitarianism probably did a great deal to stimulate expectations that the new era of capitalist enterprise would result in increased opportunity and prosperity for everyone, and such expectations were only heightened by the fact that until 1860 the shoe industry was one in which "low capital requirements . . . permitted petty entrepreneurs with nothing more than a horse and buggy and a little real estate to try their luck." As one former Marlborough manufacturer reminisced in 1889, "the boys . . . saw their chance to rise" in the 1830s and 1840s, founding as they did a multitude of small firms in such modest locales as "a part of John Holyoke's house on Pleasant Street" or "the C. L. Bliss barn."

But after 1860 a relatively open and equal local society became a relatively closed and stratified one. Considering for the moment only the ownership of shoe manufacturing resources, we find that of the fourteen entrepreneurs known to be in business in the early and mid-1860s in neighborhoods that remained part of Marlborough after the separation of Hudson in 1867, eleven were still producing shoes in 1891. Moreover, only one of the nine new firms that commenced operations during these years managed to survive. A stable and settled group of owners and bosses had evidently been created, composed of those who had prospered sufficiently during the days of low capital requirements to be able to maneuver successfully now that mechanization had brought about a situation of high capital requirements. And within this group, two companies had by the 1880s clearly emerged as the dominant ones, responsible in 1885 for nearly half of all the property taxes paid that year by Marlborough manufacturers.[3]

By definition, the existence of a wealthy and powerful elite entails the simultaneous existence of the much larger group of those who are less wealthy and less powerful. In the late nineteenth century the

[3]Jackson Turner Main, *The Social Structure of Revolutionary America* (Princeton, N.J.: Princeton University Press, 1965), pp. 20–23; Dawley, *Class and Community*, p. 37; *MT*, Mar. 28, 1889; *History of Middlesex County*, p. 838. Conclusions regarding stability and concentration of ownership after 1860 are based on ibid., pp. 837–40, and the property tax lists in *Marlborough Mirror*, Aug. 1, 1863; *Marlborough Mirror-Journal*, July 5, 1879; *MT*, Sept. 17, 1885; Dec. 24, 1891.

great majority of Marlborough's considerably enlarged population consisted not of small and middling property owners, but rather of workers and their families, dependent for their survival on the wages they were paid by their well-established, ever-expanding employers. To this socioeconomic stratification was added the cultural imbalances and inequalities that arose from the fact that by the 1870s and 1880s most of the people of Marborough were immigrants or the children of immigrants, whereas most of the owning and employing elite came from long-settled New England families—in the cases of the two most successful manufacturers mentioned above, from long-settled Marlborough families. By one reckoning made in 1890, the inhabitants of Marlborough consisted at that time of seventy-five hundred people of Irish, twenty-five hundred of French-Canadian, and four thousand of "Protestant" descent. That this estimate is probably a reliable one is suggested by analysis of the federal census returns for Marlborough for 1850, 1860, 1870, and 1880. Whereas in 1850 less than one-third of those working in the Marlborough shoe industry consisted of immigrants and their children, by 1870 more than two-thirds of the labor force was made up of this group, and by 1880 more than three-fourths. Although the Irish and French-Canadian people of Marlborough did find various ways to assert themselves, they remained nevertheless, as newcomers, culturally subordinate to the town's Protestant elite, in its secularized Puritan aspect, just as they were economically dependent on and controlled by that same elite, in its capitalistic aspect. The consequences of a cultural situation in which hegemonic values thus went relatively uncontested is the principal concern of this chapter.[4]

---

[4]*MT*, Aug. 14, 1890; Local History Documents (Marlborough, Mass., Public Library), Folder 7, transcript of manuscript returns for Marlborough of 7th U.S. Census (1850); manuscript returns for Marlborough of 8th U.S. Census (1860), 9th U.S. Census (1870), and 10th U.S. Census (1880), all examined at the Massachusetts State Archives, Boston. The foreign and children-of-foreign group was constituted by adding to those listed in the census as foreign-born all those with obviously Irish or French names. In 1850, 68 percent of those listed as "shoemakers" were Anglo-Saxon, while 32 percent were of foreign extraction. As the Anglo-Saxon percentage was dropping to 47, 31, and 24 percent in 1860, 1870, and 1880, the foreign and children-of-foreign group was correspondingly increasing, to 53, 69, and 76 percent. As between those of Irish and French-Canadian origin, the proportions were as follows: 1850—Irish, 37 percent, Canadian, 43 percent; 1860—Irish, 73 percent, Canadian, 25 percent; 1870—Irish, 64 percent, Canadian, 35 percent; 1880—Irish, 60 percent, Canadian, 38 percent. Census-taking terminology reflects the sociological ambiguities of the industrialization process. All involved in the shoe industry were called "shoemakers" in both 1850 and 1860. In the latter year, however, a new term, "manufacturer," began to appear informally in the returns. Some of those for whom this new language was clearly intended, the owners of the industry's capital resources, still preferred "shoemaker" in 1860, but by 1870 they no longer felt hesitant about their new identity.

As opposed, then, to 1780, when 70 percent of the people of Marlborough had been long-settled, middle-class, more or less independent owners and farmers, in 1880 roughly the same proportion were lately arrived, dependent wage workers. It was an entirely new society that had been created—new both in its structure and in the identity of its people. What kind of life was it that this new society offered to its new people? Although the evidence bearing upon this question is only fragmentary, enough is available to state categorically that the great expectations of the 1830s, when "the happy homes, the brighter times shone bright on every face," were not fulfilled. To begin with, the central fact of life for the worker in the mechanized shoe factory was regimentation. As Alan Dawley argues, the chief virtue of the factory system from the point of view of the manufacturers was that it gave them much greater control over the entire production process. No more farming out of parts of the operation to journeymen outworkers, who were "at liberty to break off work when they felt like it." No more interruptions for what a contemporary observer described as "some temporary enjoyment which was not always conducive to health and good morals." The rhythms of production were now determined not by the waywardness of artisans but rather by the invariability of machines and the commands of those who owned them: "Under the new industrial discipline, workers pursued their own momentary enjoyments at the risk of a head-on collision with the boss or his foreman and the loss of a job." Thus in the 1860s the Marlborough manufacturers promulgated such rules as "no shouting or other unnecessary noise will be allowed. No pedlars allowed in the rooms. . . . The bringing of Children and friends into the Shop is particularly forbidden." A new factory opening up in 1884 carried the imperatives of managerial control to their logical conclusion: "The main, or business, office will be on the second floor, where everything that goes on the elevator will be under the eyes of those in the office. . . . Every person coming into or going out of the shop, can be seen from the office."[5]

Besides routine and regulation, the factory laborer had to live with the possibility of suffering serious injury from the new machinery. Statistics on the incidence of industrial accidents in late nineteenth-century Marlborough are not available, but it is clear from even a casual perusal of the local papers that they occurred frequently enough to be a constant danger and worry. In February 1860 "Patrick

[5]Dawley, *Class and Community*, pp. 91–92; *Marlborough Mirror*, Oct. 6, 1860; Nov. 10, 1860; *MT*, Feb. 2, 1884; Mar. 28, 1889.

Fahey, a workman employed at Deacon Curtis's shop . . . had one of his hands badly jammed in a rolling machine." Twenty years later "Mr. Elliott Reed, a pegging machine operator at the T. A. Coolidge factory, had a portion of the fore-finger of his right hand cut off by the machine." In June 1877 Laura Goodwin, a child laborer at the John Frye factory, caught her left hand in the cogs of a heeling machine while she was cleaning it, with the result that all the fingers were cut off and the entire hand had to be amputated. During the holiday season of 1885 Timothy Hurley, an eighteen-year-old employee in the sole leather room of one of the Rice & Hutchins factories, caught the forefinger of his right hand in a sole moulding machine, "crushing it to a jelly and necessitating amputation." The most serious accident on record during this period occurred in 1891, at the main factory of S. H. Howe, who was by this time the leading manufacturer in town. Joseph Savoise, Jr., age sixteen, was trapped inside the belt of a pricking machine in the sole leather room. In the course of being whirled around by the machine, Savoise's left arm was torn from its socket and both of his legs were fractured. He subsequently died from his injuries.[6]

The conditions confronting the operative outside the factory and after working hours were equally discouraging. First, he or she might not even have a family or, having one, might not be able to live with it. This was because employment in the shoe industry was seasonally variable, with one-third to one-half of all workers being laid off in the summers and winters of most years. The consequence of this arrangement was that many were forced to become "floaters" or, as they were called when they were being stigmatized, "tramps." Moving about from town to town in the hope of finding work of some sort, such people were obviously in no position to lead a settled family existence. That there were a significant number of them moving in and out of the Marlborough work force is clear from the recurrent references in the local press to "our floating population," and from the fact that a great many of the residential structures erected in the 1870s and 1880s (mostly by the manufacturers themselves) were boardinghouses and tenements.[7]

Even the worker who did manage to establish a family life in one place suffered from the layoffs that were built into the shoe-industry production cycle, for his or her already minimal income was thereby

<hr/>

[6]*Marlborough Mirror*, Feb. 4, 1860; *MT*, June 21, 1877; July 12, 1877; Feb. 5, 1880; Dec. 31, 1885; Sept. 10, 1891.

[7]Dawley, *Class and Community*, pp. 53, 139–42; *MT*, June 13, 1878.

further reduced. In 1869 in New York, working in a shoe factory was the second lowest paid of the occupations surveyed that year by the *New York Times*. In Lynn and vicinity seven years later, the average annual income of a male shoe worker was $440. In the estimation of Alan Dawley, this was about $50 to $100 less than what was needed for a family to make ends meet, to fill its rented quarters with furniture (but not with china and silver) and to dine on meat on Sunday and perhaps one other day each week. It was definitely not enough to allow saving toward the purchase of a home. As Dawley sums up their situation, most of those working in Lynn's industrialized shoe industry remained "poised between the realms of poverty and meager subsistence [and] continued to be haunted by the specters of debt, disease, disability, and dependence."

Such evidence as has survived on the income and living conditions of Marlborough shoe workers is consistent with Dawley's findings for Lynn. In both 1875 and 1888 the wages of male shoe workers in Marlborough were about $12 a week, which would translate to an annual income in the same range as that of the Lynn workers in 1876, and which means that one of the books acquired by the Marlborough Public Library in 1888, *Family Living on $500 a Year*, should have had wide appeal. Some aspects of what family living on $500 a year or less really amounted to are revealed by an investigation of Marlborough's French-Canadian neighborhood made by the town Board of Health during a scarlet fever epidemic in 1881. In one building consisting of four dwelling units, "there was but one small privy for the four families and this in the most disgusting condition, while sink drains and pig pens with heaps of rotting garbage added to this Gehenna of filth." The only source of drinking water for all four families, a nearby well, sat next to "a large cesspool with several barrels of sewerage of the most filthy character." The building was typical of the entire street on which it was located, and the Board of Health ordered all the families in the neighborhood to make their surroundings cleaner and more healthful. It remained silent, however, about how this was to be accomplished.[8]

Grim as it is, our brief survey of the realities of working-class life in a late nineteenth-century shoe town has yet to take account of what may have been the most central reality of all: that the income of the typical worker, meager at best and already eroded by the seasonality

[8]David Montgomery, *Beyond Equality: Labor and the Radical Republicans, 1862–1872* (New York: Knopf, 1967), p. 41; Dawley, *Class and Community*, pp. 156, 159, 170; *MT*, Nov. 1, 1877; June 2, 1881; *An Historical Manual of the First Baptist Church of Marlboro, Mass., 1868–1888* (Marlborough, 1888), p. 49; *Annual Report of the Selectmen of Marlborough . . .* (1888), Library Report, p. 173.

of the industry, was further vulnerable to the unpredictable boom-and-bust fluctuations of the laissez-faire business cycle. In 1878, the most depressed of all the depressed years of the 1870s, the Marlborough manufacturers insisted on reducing the wages of their workers below a level that even a determined exponent of the manufacturers' point of view, the editor of the *Marlborough Times,* Charles F. Morse, conceded had been the minimum required if workers were "to see bread and butter, clothes and schooling for themselves and families." The workers were organized into a union, the Knights of St. Crispin, and over the next several months they responded to these wage cuts by going out on strike. Like most such actions during this era, the strike was not successful. Although the great majority of the striking workers did eventually recover their old jobs, they were hired back at rates of pay that were, again according to the refreshingly candid Editor Morse, 25 percent less than the already unacceptable rates that had compelled them to strike in the first place.

It was to this set of circumstances that Martha L. Ames, a former schoolteacher, was referring in August 1878 when she emphasized to readers of the *Times* that when "laborers in the vineyard" of the Marlborough shoe industry suffered a wage cut, "it means the loss of all luxuries, if, indeed, they ever had any; it means being obliged to live on the plainest food, and dressed in the plainest manner. It closes to those the doors of lecture and concert halls, even of the house of God itself, unless they would bear the taunt of 'stealing their preaching.' It means the crushing of all high aspirations, the merging of every noble thought, and feeling into the one great question, 'where is the next meal to come from?'" Ames was a conservative and a traditionalist. She disliked what she called "city fashions" and had no doubt that "the best brain and muscle of the country comes from the rural districts." She was no radical or labor reformer, but neither had she any particular reason to put herself forward as an apologist for capital. And so she was able to understand that the relationship between the institutions and dynamics of the capitalist economy of nineteenth-century New England and the aspiration to "constant progress upward in morality and virtue" of the secularized Puritan culture of nineteenth-century New England was far from an automatically harmonious one. As we shall see, Ames's firm grasp of reality is what was sublimely avoided by those who played the most prominent parts in industrial capitalist and secularized Puritan Marlborough.[9]

---

[9]Irwin Unger, *The Greenback Era: A Social and Political History of American Finance, 1865–1879* (Princeton, N.J.: Princeton University Press, 1964), p. 375; *MT*, Jan. 10, 1878; Aug. 8, 1878; Nov. 21, 1878.

Marlborough was a community that had during the Colonial era been fully exposed to the prescriptions of the Protestant ethic. In 1720, in a sermon that was clearly an articulation of the most commonplace assumptions and themes, the Reverend Robert Breck discoursed to the people of the new town of Shrewsbury, most of whom had formerly resided under his care in Marlborough, upon the need to practice "Labour, Diligence and Industry in [their] Callings" if they wished to manifest a proper consciousness of how they were "accountable to God" for their use of their time and also to "advance [their] Happiness and Prosperity." Breck simultaneously voiced a caution against "unrestrained profit-seeking," reminding his auditors that "ill gotten Goods . . . will not rest long in the Hands of an unjust Gainer, but will be in a constant motion till they revert to the lawful Owner."

In the nineteenth century, as Marlborough proceeded to experience its capitalist economic and social revolution, both of the principal methods of secularizing the Protestant ethic which the century developed could be heard from its pulpits. A former minister of the Congregationalist church was engaging in straightforward spiritualization and applauding of enterprise when, in 1858, reminiscing on the fiftieth anniversary of his ordination, he fell readily into the evangelical habit of lumping material and spiritual initiatives together as one sublimely edifying nineteenth-century spectacle: "Our country during this period has been unparalleled in its increase of wealth and numbers; in its progress in the arts and sciences; and in efforts to improve the condition of the race." The very year of these recollections had witnessed both the completion of the Atlantic telegraph, "the greatest enterprise of the age," and "the extensive Revival of Religion, which has pervaded our land. This has been most emphatically," the speaker concluded, "a year of the right hand of the Most High." Yet the present minister of this same Congregationalist church had, only the year before, taken a much more critical view of the emerging capitalist age, inveighing against such manifestations of unrestrained profit-seeking as "the great extravagance in the present style of living . . . a decreasing respect for honest labor" and a tendency on the part of "a host of adventurers and speculators . . . to commence and carry on business without capital; to enlarge and expand, where in fact there is nothing to expand."[10]

In addition to engaging in these direct evaluations of the capitalist

[10]Robert Breck, *The Surest Way to Advance a People's Happiness and Prosperity* (Boston, 1721), pp. 8, 9; Sylvester Bucklin, *A Sermon Preached . . . on the Fiftieth Anniversary of His Ordination . . .* (Worcester, 1859), pp. 36–38; Levi A. Field, *Crime—Its Causes and Remedy* (Marlborough, 1857), pp. 10, 11, 12, 13.

order, the cultural leaders of Marlborough participated in those institutional innovations of the nineteenth century which it was hoped would keep capitalism morally up to standard. The spokesmen for both the Marlborough Public Library and the Marlborough Public Schools were fully imbued with those expectations of constant progress upward which lay at the heart of the ideology of secularized Puritanism. The library trustees defined their purpose in 1878 as one of leading people toward "a higher plane of intellectual thought and moral culture." And the trustees recognized that such goals would require the library to involve itself in resisting and restraining some, at least, of the social consequences of emergent industrial capitalism. In 1884 they reported that the library's new periodical reading room was functioning, as intended, as an antidote to the temptations of urbanized street life: "Many boys have become interested in our periodicals, and though they may begin by turning over the leaves of illustrated papers they finally become interested to know what the pictures are all about. In this way, they become readers of a good class of literature, and they are thus kept out of the streets and away from evil associates, and put in the way of becoming better men."[11]

School officials spoke in even more fulsome terms of their institution as an agent of moral and intellectual betterment. "The pay [of a teacher] may be secular," declared the School Committee in 1865, "but the work is sacred." The committee of 1871 explained: "From the teacher must come the true light which is to illumine the morning haze of child life into the greater glories of the higher noon of true manhood and womanhood. To the teacher more than any other person, belongs the high office of developing the intellectual and moral natures, and bringing both to bear directly upon the character." With a view of its mission that was thus identical in its moral grandeur to that of the public library, the public schools developed a sense of the need to resist nineteenth-century social change comparable to that developed by the library. In a world filling up with "crime, pauperism, and want," adequate public education had become absolutely indispensable, insisted the committee of 1870: "None of the agencies for improving the condition of the poor, for defending society against crime, and for diminishing the number of the dependent, can exert any great and permanent effect until all classes are brought under the influence of a comprehensive system of education."[12]

[11]*Annual Report* (1878), Library Report, p. 37; *Annual Report* (1884), Library Report, p. 83.
[12]*Annual Report* (1865), School Report, p. 30; *Annual Report* (1870), School Report, p. 41; *Annual Report* (1871), School Report, p. 4.

Marlborough's culture of secularized Puritanism was in a general way aware that the new society of industrial capitalism was far from problem-free. But what did it have to say about the obvious and palpable problems industrial capitalism was creating right in its own backyard? A short but essentially accurate answer to this question was provided in 1880 by a display that a civic-minded group from Marlborough's neighbor and offspring, Hudson, contributed to a "trades procession" in Boston that September. One part of the exhibit was a diorama depicting how shoes had formerly been made. A family was shown going about its daily chores in its log cabin home, while an .itinerant cobbler sat at a table laboriously piecing together a pair of shoes. This scene was placed alongside a miniature version of "a modern shoe shop on wheels, in which [could be seen] all the machinery for the turning out of a shoe a minute, in perfect operation, the whole driven by a four-horse Baxter steam engine." This exhibit was thought to be so estimable that the Sunday after the parade a religious service was held in its honor. All the Protestant ministers of the town participated enthusiastically in the occasion, each in turn using "the machinery car for a pulpit." The most striking feature of this statement of the gospel of capitalist progress is that, in the portrayal of mechanized shoemaking, the human laborer has disappeared. The implicit claim is doubtless that technological innovations have liberated people from the drudgery imposed in the past on everyone, the shoemaker's clientele as well as the shoemaker himself. But in view of what we have seen of the actual working and living conditions engendered by the mechanized factory system in a shoe town like Marlborough, the more pertinent meaning of the omnipresence of human labor in the representation of the past and its complete absence in that of the present is probably that those who were benefiting from the new order were determined to avert their eyes from the experience of those who were not benefiting from it, those who were, indeed, being oppressed and exploited by it.[13]

That the predominant response to the unpleasant and the inconvenient should prove to be avoidance is of course hardly surprising. But the instances of avoidance that abound in the documentary remains of late nineteenth-century Marlborough are nevertheless worth examining in some detail. Since the town remained relatively small throughout this period, one might suppose that the trials and tribulations of the many would have forced themselves on the consciousness of the few who were well off, simply as those few went about their

[13]*MT*, Sept. 23, 1880.

daily business. The prospering native bourgeoisie lived almost literally next door to the struggling immigrant workers and their families. But the Marlborough bourgeoisie succeeded nevertheless in perceiving their immediate surroundings through a haze of sentimental fantasy, thereby offering striking testimony to the power of a hegemonic value system to shield itself from reality.

The flight from reality that took place in late nineteenth-century Marlborough was perhaps partly the result of the fact that its economic and cultural elites constituted, to an unusual degree, a single, integrated and cohesive ruling elite. In the 1870s and 1880s the people who had amassed the most economic resources and power were the same people who both exercised the greatest cultural influence and embodied, in their ancestries, the most substantial continuities with the Puritan past. The culture was thus not in a very good position to engage in critical analysis of the economy and society. Both of the leading manufacturers, Samuel Boyd and S. H. Howe, came from families that had settled in Marlborough in Colonial times; indeed Howe was descended, in both parental lines, from one of the founding seventeenth-century proprietors of the town. Similarly, the leading retail business, which had evolved from an old-fashioned general store to a modern department store as the town had grown and developed, was the property of the Bigelow family, which had come to the area at the turn of the eighteenth century. The firm was owned and operated during the years we are primarily analyzing by S. H. Howe's contemporary and friend E. L. Bigelow.[14]

The relationship between Howe and Bigelow now and then took the form of economic collaboration. When Howe invested in a California gold mine in 1881, Bigelow was one of his partners in the venture. But what was most significant about this alliance was the mutual dedication of the parties to the cause of constant progress upward in morality and virtue. Both Bigelow and Howe sought to be true to their Puritan ancestral credentials, participating energetically in the adaptation of the culture of their fathers to the new capitalist world. Both had graduated in the 1850s from Marlborough High School, where they had presumably imbibed from their high-minded teacher O. W. Albee the idea that "as a nation grows [wealthy], so does its capacity for doing good." This, the central teaching of a school of New England academic moralists widely influential in antebellum northern culture, had doubtless been imbibed by Albee while he was a

---

[14]Hudson, *History of the Town of Marlborough*, pp. 325, 331–32, 392–97; *MT*, Mar. 5, 1885.

student at Brown during the presidency of one of those moralists, Francis Wayland. In 1879 it was claimed of Albee that he "did more to mould and turn in the right direction the present generation of business men of the town than any one man."

Certainly two of the members of that generation of businessmen, E. L. Bigelow and S. H. Howe, behaved in their primes as though they had been molded by Albee in the direction of doing good with their wealth. Continuously from 1860 to 1890 they committed themselves to public service and cultural uplift, sitting, sometimes together and sometimes separately, on the Board of Selectmen, the School Committee, and in the General Court. Both were active in the Unitarian church, Howe being particularly prominent as Sunday school official and occasional lay preacher. Bigelow was the mainstay of the public library for forty years and more from its founding in 1871. Thus between them, Bigelow and Howe involved themselves centrally in most of the major institutions—Unitarian church, public library, public schools—of secularized Puritanism. In 1879 they added yet another such institution to the roster of their commitments to doing good when they both became stockholders in the *Marlborough Times,* a weekly newspaper founded two years earlier. Charles F. Morse, the editor of the *Times,* was a man of Bigelow's and Howe's generation, and like them he came from a long-established (dating from the early eighteenth century) Marlborough family. Morse was in fact a relative of both Bigelow and Howe, being Bigelow's brother-in-law and the first cousin of Howe's wife. Thus did the group that dominated Marlborough's economic, political, and cultural institutions come together as a single, unified entity.[15]

Editor Morse's contributions to secularized Puritanism in Marlborough are examined in Chapter 9. For now we are concerned with the ways in which his two colleagues contrived things so that their assiduous doing of good not only remained disengaged from the less beneficent realities of the new order over which they presided, but indeed served to hide those realities from view. As the moving and sustaining force behind the public library, Bigelow was obviously an agent of that institutionalization of literature and secular culture, and

[15]*MT,* July 10, 1879; Nov. 18, 1880; Sept. 1, 1881; Jan. 19, 1882; Apr. 26, 1883; Dec. 20, 1883; Apr. 14, 1887; Ella A. Bigelow, *Historical Reminiscences of the Early Times in Marlborough, Massachusetts and Prominent Events from 1860 to 1910* (Marlborough, 1910), pp. 169, 177, 212–13; D. H. Meyer, *The Instructed Conscience: The Shaping of the American National Ethic* (Philadelphia: University of Pennsylvania Press, 1972), pp. 13–15, 105–6; *Marlborough Mirror,* Sept. 22, 1860; *Pictorial Marlboro* (Nov. 17, 1879), p. 30; *History of Middlesex County,* pp. 845–46, 851; *Annual Reports,* School Reports (1881–83); Library Reports (1871ff.); Hudson, *History of the Town of Marlborough,* pp. 342, 416–19.

their promotion as a substitute religion, which has been briefly described in Chapter 7. In 1881 Bigelow's Unitarian pastor, R. A. Griffin, then serving alongside him as a library trustee, stated that Marlborough's library was "unusually rich" in elevating books "mainly due to the educated literary judgment as well as to the business enterprise and generous gifts of Mr. Bigelow." Nor did the E. L. Bigelow family confine its propagation of uplift to the library. Bigelow's wife sang in the Unitarian church choir and frequently directed the children of the parish, such as Charlotte Howe and "Faithie" Morse (daughters of S. H. Howe and Charles F. Morse), in "Little Old Folks Concerts." Mrs. Bigelow was also a painter. She gave drawing classes and twice a year turned her home into an art gallery, displaying her own work and that of her pupils in order "to encourage and foster a love of the beautiful in art." The featured painting at one such art exhibit in 1886 was Mrs. Bigelow's own three-quarter size portrait of her daughter Daisy, "dressed in the character of Madame Lafayette. . . . An Italian harpist furnished music while the exhibition was in progress." Literature and painting were deftly married by Mrs. Bigelow in 1879 when she donated portraits of Bryant, Longfellow, Lowell, and Whittier to the high school. The students wrote Mrs. Bigelow a thank-you note, indicating that they understood and appreciated the paintings (as Mrs. Bigelow had intended them to) as religious icons, as "an incentive to awaken and cultivate among the pupils of the school a love and taste for the high moral sentiment, and the beautiful literature with which these children of genius have adorned the English language."

Although these various activities were, in and of themselves, unexceptionable, it must be said that they were pursued in etherial disregard of their immediate material environment, which was, as we have heard Martha L. Ames remark, constituted for most of the inhabitants of Marlborough by circumstances that conspired to "the crushing of all high aspiration." The way the Bigelows' cultural activism encouraged escape from harsh realities, rather than the redeeming of them, perhaps conforms all too fully to the Hudson Unitarian minister's description of the Unitarian sensibility as one enamored of "that ideal world in which the noblest part of human activity finds a theatre—the world of thought and spiritual insight, of knowledge and duty, loftily elevated above that of sense and appetite."[16]

Functioning more centrally in Marlborough's socioeconomic order of industrial capitalism, S.H. Howe's contributions to the escapism of

[16]*MT*, Feb. 21, 1878; Apr. 4, 1878; June 13, 1878; Dec. 18, 1879; Feb. 3, 1881; May 15, 1884; Mar. 25, 1886; Apr. 1, 1886.

Marlborough's culture of secularized Puritanism were both more direct and more complex than those of Bigelow. An essential element in the mythology of the new order—expressed by such customs as factory baseball leagues and picnics in the summer and sleigh rides in the winter—was that factory life amounted to an extended family holiday. All the Marlborough manufacturers sought to create such an impression, but it was S. H. Howe who played the role of paterfamilias most effectively. In 1880, when he departed for California to look over his new gold mine, he remarked, "in his quiet, thoughtful way, 'I think I should like to be worth a million dollars. I should be glad to see all my help live in better houses.'" His friend Editor Morse claimed in 1883 that Howe's career had been a rags-to-riches story in a moral as well as a financial sense:

> He began his career as a poor boy in a small shop, not twenty rods from where he lives today, working in a 'team' making 'kacks' for Winslow Stevens, and he has worked right along, through every grade of the business, until he has reached the top . . . he gives his employees a share in the profits of the business which their skill and industry has helped to build up. Nowhere, in this town or any other, are the employees of any manufacturer better treated or better paid than by Mr. Howe, and a very large proportion of them own the houses they live in, and very good houses they are, too.

The sociology of Morse's biographical sketch is extremely doubtful. Howe was a high school graduate, as we have seen, and most high school graduates of the mid-nineteenth century were not poor boys. But whatever the fortunes of Howe's family may have been during his childhood (his father was a cooper, which suggests at the very worst a middling respectability), Morse's analysis of this entrepreneur's success gains its plausibility not from socioeconomic verisimilitude, but rather from the convergence of Howe's impressive New England lineage with the conventions and aspirations of the Protestant ethic. There is reason to believe that Howe was indeed a relatively benevolent employer. He was popular enough in this immigrant and working-class town to win its first mayoral election in 1890, running well ahead of other Republican candidates and carrying several wards that otherwise went Democratic and "ethnic." A spokesman for the union that organized a major strike in 1898 and 1899 stated that Howe and his superintendent treated him with much greater consideration and respect than did the other leading manufacturer. Thus, descended from a seventeenth-century Marlborough proprietor, the grandson of two of the pillars of the established church, Howe seemed to represent a putting of the Protestant ethic into practice that had been brilliantly successful in every way. He had engaged in the labor, diligence, and industry in his calling that Reverend Robert Breck had recommended in 1720, and he had managed to do so without succumbing to the many temptations to unrestrained profit-seeking held out by the expansive times in which he lived. In John Cotton's phrase, he had managed to remain to a noteworthy degree "deadhearted to the world." He had made himself into the genuinely Puritan capitalist depicted by his pastor R. A. Griffin in 1888, someone who preferred "a millionaire conscience to a millionaire fortune."[17]

But even if we accept at face value these depictions of S. H. Howe's character as an exemplary one, we must still conclude that his primary cultural function was to obscure the reality that for most factory workers, life was not a constant progress upward in morality and virtue, but rather a hand-to-mouth scramble merely to survive. During the strike of 1878 worker spokesmen said: "Our manufacturers ought to consider their moral obligations to the men they employ. They should be philanthropists as well as capitalists. They should remember that the less they pay the fewer will gain the advantages of education, the fewer houses will be built, and the more poorly the present houses will be furnished and adorned. . . . I would like the rest and leisure which would give me a chance to study, but have none save on Sunday." And for all his reputation as a manufacturer who did, preeminently, consider his moral obligations to the men he employed, who was sincerely seeking to help them make constant progress upward, S. H. Howe behaved at this moment of crisis exactly as did his brother capitalists. Pleading cut-throat competition in the industry, he required that his employees accept a pay cut, and when they refused and went out on strike, he installed new machinery and hired new workers. "I tell the men I must have my work done, and it is in the nature of things, if the manufacturer is struck upon he will introduce more and more machinery," he declared. "This is inevitable, and is a matter of business, not of sentiment." Once the strike was well under way, Howe stated that "he would never turn out" the strikebreaking new workers he had hired "until he was turned out himself."

Yet Howe also referred to "the kind relations that have subsisted

---

[17]*MT*, Jan. 22, 1880; Nov. 25, 1880; Nov. 1, 1883; Aug. 2, 1888; Nov. 1, 1888; Nov. 27, 1890; *History of Middlesex County*, pp. 845–46; *Hearings before the Joint Committee on Labor at Marlboro, Mass., . . . Feb. 28–March 1, 1899* (Massachusetts State Archives), pp. 16–17; Local History Documents (Marlborough, Mass., Public Library), Folder 12 (Second Parish, 1808–51), Warrant for Parish Meeting, Feb. 19, 1811.

between himself and his employees," and such was the strength of his reputation as a man who softened business with sentiment, so powerful were the Protestant ethical traditions he seemed to embody, that they were not particularly damaged by this instance of being overridden by the iron laws of capitalist economics. Worker rage during the strike was directed at those bosses who allowed themselves to be perceived as representing the antithesis of Howe, even though their actions were essentially the same as his. Two bosses in particular, relative newcomers to Marlborough, were so egregious as to snarl, in response to worker pleas that the wage cuts being demanded would mean starvation, that "any who were not satisfied with the price paid, could get out at once, and take their kit d___ quick," and to transport their strikebreaking new employees provocatively through the center of town. By providing such clear-cut instances of heroes and villains, paragons and scapegoats, the traditions of Protestant ethics served to divert attention from the ethical deficiencies of the system of industrial capitalism itself.[18]

The relationship between the Protestant ethic, in the fuller sense supposedly represented by S. H. Howe, and the spirit of capitalism, which Howe by his record of unbroken expansion and success also represented, was what was primarily on the mind of Howe's minister, R. A. Griffin, when he delivered a sermon on the Marlborough strike in early February 1878, while passions were still running high. Griffin was certainly thinking of Howe when he lamented the way in which "employers who have for years cared for their workers, whose brain and wealth have found them work," were being "exposed before the world, practically, in the same category as cruel oppressors or insensible task masters, their well-earned comforts the red flags to the dark passions of envy and rage. These tenderer ties which bind master and man are ruthlessly snapped," Griffin went on. Marlborough had succumbed to a "disease latent throughout the industrial world, which if unchecked, will grow worse and worse, and end in general collapse."

So Griffin evidently was prepared to engage in systemic analysis of the industrial capitalist order which had been installed in Marlborough. The framework within which he proceeded to do so was a modernized version of the traditional Puritan critique of unrestrained profit-seeking. The source of the disease that was latent throughout the industrial world and was threatening general collapse, said Griffin, was "combination," which he defined as a conspir-

___

[18]*Marlborough Advertiser*, Jan. 16, 1878; *MT*, Jan. 17, 1878; Jan. 24, 1878; Jan. 31, 1878.

acy to engage in profiteering above and beyond the price set by an unimpeded free market: "Now, combinations set an artificial price—a tax without representation—they insist people shall pay . . . according to the decree of the combination. So that if a coal ring pays its laborers below market price, they can make enormous dividends, benefitting neither the laborer nor the consumer. . . . If they have a right to tax you 10 per cent., they have a right to tax you 100 per cent.; by the same law [if] a laborer asks 5 per cent. above market price, he has a right to ask for all the earnings of the firm." In this account, the price set by the unregulated market, which in the seventeenth and eighteenth centuries had represented the abandonment of restraint, has in the fully capitalistic world of the nineteenth century become the source of restraint. It has become the just price, which is now, in its turn, being menaced and eroded by that monopolistic greed that was controlling the behavior of both capital and labor. Indeed, along with the just price, combination was destroying that other traditional prop of Puritan economic morality, the rule of charity:

> The master perhaps knows his men deserve more, earn more, and he can give more and wants to when in his best mood; but he is bound hand and foot—a thing neither divine, human nor diabolical—a thing which is inspired by mutual distrust and cupidity, composed merely of the secular part of man; and whose sole object is to secure advantage for one class at the expense of another; says, 'No you shall not be just or generous without our consent.' . . . So with labor leagues—men agree together in order to keep up an artificial rate of wages; as members of that organization they abandon the right of independent action as a matter of course. It may be a time will come when reason and conscience will tell them to work at lower rates. Affection for their employer, confident that he means right and is paying all he ought, or the memory of times when he found work for them out of simple good feeling may prevail with them, but they cannot act as generous men; they have laid their manhood at the feet of their interests.

Although Griffin seemed to be implying that capital and labor were equally at fault in their reliance upon conspiracies of selfishness, he had already declared with apparent forthrightness that in fact it was capital that bore the primary responsibility for compelling labor down the road to unrestrained profit-seeking:

> Labor combinations are the outgrowth of other combinations; they meet force with force. And as I view armies with abhorrence . . . yet I feel

sympathy for the weaker side, however mistaken, fighting against organized oppression. So I view labor and ask who can expect it to be the first to reform? The fact stares the workman in the face. If he works honestly at market price, his earnings are taxed by the vultures of combination, which pounce on his money in every conceivable form. . . . Not more do we need national government to protect us against thieves and invaders, than against the great corporations whose despotism assails the sacred, natural right of man to free contract and exchange. . . . The workmen fight against enormous odds; they meet army with army, illegitimate combinations with illegitimate combinations, do evil to check evil.

That was how the issue seemed to stand as Griffin surveyed the overall situation. This latter-day Puritan moralist seemed to recognize the central fact of the Marlborough worker's life, that such a worker was engaged in an unequal, losing struggle to make ends meet, and that it was the capitalist system within which the worker toiled that was keeping him confined at the edge of poverty. It was unfortunate, therefore, that when Griffin turned to consider what might be done by way of amendment and reform, he had nothing to offer but a merely metaphoric exhortation that both manufacturers and workers should somehow simply disengage themselves from all combinations: "Do as the pioneer amid the thick growths of the forest. He clears a little tract and lives there—it yields rather scant fare, but others will clear more, and bye and bye there will be smiling pastures. You stand amid forests of combination." As lame as this was, it was far worse that, from this point on, Griffin chose to speak as though the task of clearing out the forests of cupidity and creating smiling pastures of Puritan moral restraint and fellow feeling would devolve entirely upon the workers: "If I consent to work for [a manufacturer] I must live on what I get, just as if I worked on my own farm; I must be content with the living it yields." It would be too bad, of course, if that living should prove inadequate, but if it should, the morally rehabilitated worker must nevertheless remember that "poverty has no rights; it confers no patronage except pity. If a man cannot live on his wages, he must be ministered to; he must not exact."

Clearly Griffin was doing what he had insisted just a few moments before should not be done. He was asking labor to be the first to reform. In practical terms, as applied to the situation in Marlborough in February 1878, he was counseling the workers that the only morally laudable thing for them to do was to abandon their strike, even if they were indeed being coerced into working below the just market price: "As far as this town is concerned, there is but one remedy, that is for every order to disband, and each man to make his own contract.

If the offer is below the market price then each man can decline it."
Griffin did allow that if enough workers arrived independently, without any consultation among themselves, at the decision to decline the
proffered inadequate wage, then "they could honestly prolong the
strike indefinitely," perhaps surviving by forming a shoemaking co-
operative. But "if they refuse to work themselves, persuade and prevent others from working; if they stagnate the town industries," then
the consequences would be on their own heads: "the factory door is
locked by themselves, the town is permanently injured, and capitalists
are admonished to go abroad with their means, as so many have
done." The more Griffin thought about the way the working people
of Marlborough were behaving, the more indignant he became. We
may be sure that he was thinking once again of that mainstay of his
own church, S. H. Howe, an "employer who had for years cared for
his workers," when he rhetorically inquired: "Do men suppose their
employers are knaves to need a policeman in the shape of a trades
union to make them do their duty?"

Griffin's homily was a glaring instance of "uses" floating askew
from "doctrines." As an anonymous correspondent wrote to the *Marlborough Times* (which had featured the sermon on its front page) a few
weeks later: "If it is true that the employers combine to lower wages
simply because they have the power to do so, is it wholly pertinent to
ask workmen if they suppose their employers are to need a policeman
in the shape of a trades union to make them do their duty? According
to the gentleman's own showing I should think they did need just
that." This commentator touched on the sources of Griffin's curious
about-face when he went on to ask: "Is it true, as a general rule, that
employers combine to reduce wages simply because they have the
power? We used to know the Marlborough manufacturers, and have
continued to observe them, and are not quite ready to admit this of
them at least, even if of employers generally." Griffin was not quite
ready to admit this of them either, although his own portrayal of the
vultures of combination pouncing on the laborer's hard-earned money seemed to imply just such an admission.

Had the moral havoc caused by the capitalist scramble for profit
been wreaked among the manufacturers of "good old Marlborough,"
or had it not? This was the question that went resoundingly begging
as Griffin veered off to admonish the workers to surrender. He certainly could not bring himself to assent to the proposition that S. H.
Howe had behaved like a cruel oppressor or an insensible taskmaster.
But neither could Griffin muster a stout and explicit reaffirmation
that Howe, constantly expanding his operation as he stood amid for-

ests of immoral combination, had been undeviating in his practice of the true entrepreneur's restraint and honest dealing and the true master's justice and lovingkindness. Moral reality had become unavailable to secularized Puritan idealism. S. H. Howe's spiritual adviser had attempted to lift Marlborough out of the valley of the shadow of industrial despair and reestablish it as a City upon a Hill, a community "knitt together in this work as one man." But he was ultimately driven to resort to evasion and avoidance of the most creakingly awkward sort, thus revealing that the course of capitalist development had turned the New England moral tradition into the kind of thing S. H. Howe was wont to tell his Sunday school classes: "a pretty little story."[19]

Alan Dawley concludes of the shoemakers of Lynn that "their resistance to business domination was more persistent and pervasive, their control over community folkways more effective, and their militancy more notorious" than was that of the workers in most other New England factory towns. Despite numerous defeats, labor was able to maintain itself as a social and cultural power in the leading shoe town of Massachusetts because its "strong popular tradition of resistance to authority and defense of the Liberty Tree" had deep roots in the preindustrial era of household production. On through to the end of the nineteenth century Lynn's mostly Yankee factory workers remained the cultural children and grandchildren of those master workmen of the eighteenth and early nineteenth centuries who had been heads of households and had therefore exercised moral and spiritual as well as economic authority. It was in Lynn more than anywhere else in New England that Puritan enthusiasm was reincarnated, in the days of the central shop and antebellum reform, as that "radicalism [that] went with the smell of leather" recalled by Thomas Wentworth Higginson at the end of the century.[20]

In Marlborough this situation was precisely reversed. Marlborough had been a farming village, not a beehive of household industry. It had its share of Puritan traditions, but what it did not have was the specific Puritan tradition associated with the sturdy autonomy of the artisan. The only approximation of this social type who made his presence felt in industrial Marlborough was Editor Morse's brother Fred—who was descended from a Marlborough Colonial family; who

[19]*MT*, Feb. 7, 1878; Feb. 28, 1878; Apr. 1, 1880.
[20]Dawley, *Class and Community*, pp. 17–18, 225–26; Montgomery, *Beyond Equality*, p. 118.

240

liked to boast that in his youth he had hobnobbed with Thoreau, Emerson, and Hawthorne; and who was a leading spokesman for the labor cause in Marlborough in the 1860s and 1870s. But Fred Morse was an isolated figure. As Marlborough was changing itself from farming village to factory town, almost all of its Puritan cultural energies were being devoted not to the defense of the Liberty Tree, but rather to an expansive entrepreneurship that seemed to promise every kind of constant progress upward. With little recollection or experience of how Puritan enthusiasm could be applied to the socioeconomic realm, with a largely immigrant work force ruled and controlled by, as it seemed, a few fabulously successful embodiments of a happy harmony between the local Protestant ethic and the local spirit of capitalism, the town had few cultural resources with which to challenge the reigning mythology of benevolent capitalist paternalism. By the 1880s even Fred Morse was singing hosannas to the moral grandeur of S. H. Howe. Capitalist and secularized Puritan Marlborough was a community well insulated from reality; even in the crisis of 1878 it stuttered and stumbled only briefly in its articulation and enactment of the fantasies that were necessary to it.[21]

In Book II of *Paradise Lost,* as the fallen angels mull over their predicament, most of those who participate in the discussion seem to achieve a fairly firm grasp of the realities governing their situation. Belial recognizes that God is God and will remain God whatever strategy he and his friends choose to adopt: "He from heaven's highth / All these our motions vain, sees and derides; / Not more almighty to resist our might / Than wise to frustrate all our plots and wiles" (II, 190–93). Mammon, a proponent of the Protestant ethic, seems equally cognizant of the reality of divine power: "him to unthrone we then / May hope when everlasting fate shall yield / To fickle chance, and Chaos judge the strife" (231–33). And Beelzebub, speaking as Satan's mouthpiece, likewise realizes that God "in highth or depth, still first and last will reign / Sole king, and of his kingdom lose no part / By our revolt, but over hell extend / His empire, and with iron sceptre rule / Us here, as with his golden those in heaven" (324–28).

The devils have always seemed to me remarkably sober in their assessments of their situation, and therefore the way Milton forces these realists to retreat, each in his turn, into the most transparently soothing daydreams has always seemed correspondingly arbitrary. Belial reverses himself and fantasizes that a policy of inoffensiveness

[21]Bigelow, *Historical Reminiscences,* p. 172; *MT,* Nov. 15, 1883; July 23, 1885; Feb. 25, 1886; Mar. 22, 1888.

will eventually bring it to pass that "this horror will grow mild, this darkness light, / Besides what hope the never-ending flight / Of future days may bring, what chance, what change / Worth waiting" (220–23). Mammon imagines that "through labour and endurance . . . / Our torments . . . may in length of time / Become our elements, these piercing fires / As soft as now severe, our temper changed / Into their temper; which must needs remove / The sensible of pain" (262, 274–78). Beelzebub, finally, allows himself and his followers to hope that Satan's expedition to the earthly Paradise will bring not only sweet revenge, but possibly also the recovery of heavenly bliss. Maybe they will end up living

> Nearer our ancient seat; perhaps in view
> Of those bright confines, whence with neighbouring arms
> And opportune excursion we may chance
> Reenter heaven; or else in some mild zone
> Dwell not unvisited of heaven's fair light
> Secure, and at the brightening orient beam
> Purge off this gloom; the soft delicious air,
> To heal the scar of these corrosive fires
> Shall breathe her balm.   (394–402)

Belial, Mammon, and Beelzebub console themselves and their comrades with "pretty little stories," immediately after they have seemed to face up to the way things really are. This appears to be an instance of that moralistic interference with literary organicism and fair play of which A. J. A. Waldock and other satanist readers of *Paradise Lost* have judged Milton guilty. But now that we have delved into the cultural history of nineteenth-century Marlborough, Massachusetts, we can perhaps see more clearly that in this episode Milton is in fact demonstrating a great deal of insight into the dynamics of self-deception in the modern world of capitalist willpower. For as we have seen, that is the world depicted in the deliberations of the devil's party, a world of enterprise so energetic and expansive that it must sooner or later break forth as imperialism.[22] Each of the demonic entrepreneurs first faces unflinchingly up to the truth, or so it seems, then turns abruptly about and hopes vaguely and shimmeringly for a world of ease and bliss, just as R. A. Griffin first sees monopolostic birds of prey pouncing on vulnerable workers, then covers up this perception by invoking a wholly imaginary world of Winthropian charity and harmony. It would

[22]See above, chap. 3, n. 19.

have been just as inconvenient and painful for S. H. Howe to guide himself henceforth by a serious entertainment of the possibility that he might be turning himself into a vulture of combination as it would have been for Satan and his followers to abandon their rebellion and repent. For all concerned, it was far less disturbing and far more pleasant to gaze fondly at a hallucinatory "brightening orient beam" of sentimentalized salvation and brotherly love. What Milton has given us is an intuition of the determined superficiality on which the modern bourgeois world has needed increasingly to rely. However, if we are fully to appreciate Milton's insight into this aspect of capitalist culture, and also his realization of the close connection between sanctification and competition, we must become more closely acquainted with capitalist and secularized Puritan Marlborough's most interesting cultural figure and force.

Chapter 9

Charles F. Morse: The Secularized Puritan as Country Editor, 1877–1892

Nineteenth-century Marlborough offers an unusually clear view of what resulted from the convergence of New England genealogical continuity, Puritan cultural tradition, and capitalist economic and social revolution: a structure of secularized Puritan values—hard work, just dealings, education, communal solidarity under kindly and authoritative leadership, constant progress upward—which could not claim even a tenuous validity in relation to exploitative industrial capitalist realities. But of course there is no reason to expect that those community leaders whose acquaintance we have thus far made would have assessed the world they were so energetically remaking more realistically. E. L. Bigelow and S. H. Howe were businessmen, not intellectuals; sociocultural analysis was not their job. Although I have argued that the New England tradition made for widespread intellectual empowerment, I have also stressed that the intellectual autonomy of the average Colonial New Englander manifested itself within a society that was essentially stable and a culture whose complexities and contradictions were long established and well understood. The problem of gaining an adequate apprehension of revolutionary change did not arise for the lay thinkers of the Colonial era. So we should not be particularly surprised or troubled to find that when it did arise for such lay thinkers of the nineteenth century as E. L. Bigelow and S. H. Howe, it was hardly recognized as a problem.

But Marlborough did have during the 1870s and 1880s an influential citizen whose job it was to describe reality and articulate credible values. As was briefly mentioned in Chapter 8, in 1877, Charles F. Morse became the editor of a weekly newspaper, the *Marlborough*

Times. Morse announced in an early issue that the purpose of his paper would be to tell the truth—to "view . . . things with broad day light shining in on a cool head"—and to invest the telling of it with moral significance, to be "as a wise man in his family, praising and blaming, as the praiseworthy and blameworthy occur." Morse liked to think of himself as an Independent in politics and a determined opponent of received opinion on any number of social and cultural issues. Yet as we have seen, he was as fully involved in the local hegemony as were E. L. Bigelow and S. H. Howe, descended as he was from the Morses who had settled in Marlborough at the turn of the eighteenth century, brother-in-law of Bigelow, first cousin of Howe's wife, and after 1879, editor of a paper whose stockholders included Bigelow, Howe, and many other members of the elite. Endowed, and burdened, with such connections, Morse was ultimately not in a position to provide a more substantial perspective on the dominant realities of his day than the ethereal and illusory one that can be inferred from the cultural activities of such relative intellectual innocents as Bigelow and Howe. But our interest in Morse derives precisely from his lack of genuine critical independence of the world on which he was empowered to comment. By his intellectual exuberance and his sheer volubility, Morse constitutes himself as much more fully and richly representative than anyone else in Marlborough of what was involved in the secularization of Puritanism under the auspices of capitalism. In brief, Morse's very considerable intellectual gifts and vitalities came to be devoted to a competitive struggle for cultural supremacy, and to the purveying of attractively packaged but groundless opinions.[1] _____

At the outset of Chapter 3, I spoke briefly of how the Protestant ethic was in part an expression of Protestantism's commitment to bring the secular realm into more perfect conformity with God's will. It was held both that the accumulation of wealth and the acquisition of power by the godly in itself constituted sanctification and reform, and also that, as in the doctrine of stewardship, the wealth thus piously accumulated would sooner or later be diverted to good works and worthy public projects, such as those stipulated by Robert Keayne in his will. During the era we are now considering, the former principle continued to be articulated, as when Carroll D. Wright, the commissioner of the Massachusetts Bureau of Labor Statistics, declared in 1882 that the factory

[1] *MT*, Apr. 26, 1877. For intellectual empowerment in Colonial New England, see above, chap. 4, nn. 33–42.

"outstrips the pulpit in the actual work of the gospel, that is, in the work of humanity." But the latter idea was the source of the dominant form of Protestant sanctification in nineteenth-century New England. It was no accident that the period of great capitalist transformation beginning in the second decade of the century was also a period of causes and reform movements, of agitation for the abolition of slavery and war, for temperance, for changes in the status of women and criminals, for the establishment of public libraries and the drastic alteration of the public shools. The same sanctifying energies were being poured into economic and more directly moral transformations. The doctrine of the antebellum academic moralists quoted in Chapter 8, that "as a nation grows [wealthy], so does its capacity for doing good," was thus but an acknowledgment of what had indeed been happening.[2]

Although reform was not as prominent a strain in American culture after the Civil War as it had been before it, it did survive in various quarters, such as among those professionals and intellectuals of New England and the Northeast who had cast their lot with Radical Republicanism in the 1850s and 1860s, but in the 1870s through the 1890s formed the backbone of the anti–U. S. Grant, Liberal Republican and the Mugwump–Cleveland Democrat movements. Detaching themselves, as they supposed, from parties and vested interests, reformers of this stripe sought to extend the tradition of top-down Puritan moral stewardship on into the era of big business and mass democracy. Political venality and the more conspicuous forms of capitalist exploitation and consumption had to be curbed, they insisted, by the reimposition of a higher moral law. Charles F. Morse was among the less illustrious members of this group (among the more illustrious were E. L. Godkin, Samuel Bowles, Henry and Brooks Adams, Henry Cabot Lodge, and President Charles William Eliot of Harvard). He consistently advocated its favorite projects, such as tariff and civil service reform and accommodation with the "natural rulers" of the South, and he was a vocal supporter of Grover Cleveland from 1884 onward. In 1891 he gave expression to what he and most of the rest of these latter-day reformers regarded as their core identity when he linked the causes and movements to which he was committed to the

[2]Alan Dawley, *Class and Community: The Industrial Revolution in Lynn* (Cambridge, Mass.: Harvard University Press, 1976), p. 150; D. H. Meyer, *The Instructed Conscience: The Shaping of the American National Ethic* (Philadelphia: University of Pennsylvania Press, 1972), pp. 105–6. The standard surveys of antebellum reform are Alice Felt Tyler, *Freedom's Ferment: Phases of American Social History from the Colonial Period to the Outbreak of the Civil War* (New York: Harper Torchbooks, 1962; orig. 1944); and Russel Blaine Nye, *Society and Culture in America, 1830–1860* (New York: Harper and Row, 1974), pp. 32–70.

central traditions of New England moral and social activism. "Did it ever occur to you," he rhetorically asked his readers, "that nearly all the sons of the old Abolitionists and Free Soilers that amount to anything are tariff reformers, civil service reformers and habitual voters of the democratic ticket?"[3]

In general, Morse liked to think of himself as a lonely and courageous crusader for unpopular causes. "We are all alone in our opposition" to an ill-considered and sentimental scheme for a home for impoverished Civil War veterans, he proudly proclaimed in 1883, "as we have been all alone in some previous controversies. But we are not afraid of solitude." His goals as a reformer were perhaps best summarized in the definition of the true scholar he quoted approvingly from Ralph Waldo Emerson's journal in 1889: "The scholar is bound to stand for all the virtues and all the liberties—liberty of trade, liberty of press, liberty of religion—and he should open all the prizes of success, and all the roads of nature to free competition." Morse was a nineteenth-century liberal, someone who placed his ultimate trust in a universe of autonomous individual beings. In the words of Emerson, from his essay "Wealth," which Morse also quoted in the same 1889 issue of the *Times:* "Give no bounties, make equal laws, and you need not give alms. Open the doors of opportunity to talent and virtue and they will do themselves justice." Another essential aspect of Morse's posture was that he believed himself to be a rational reformer, unlike, for example, those extremists and fanatics who agitated for prohibition of the liquor traffic. The issue of temperance engaged Morse continuously throughout his editorial tenure at the *Times.* Like most other Independents, he regarded legislated suppression of intoxicating liquors as both unjust in principle (a violation of human freedom) and unworkable in practice. Prohibition fostered drinking on the sly in "club rooms and low dives," he argued, surroundings in which a person's consumption was less likely to be restrained by neighborly public scrutiny, and in which the probability of obtaining such relatively harmless beverages as wine and beer was very low and that of being served the true demon rum was correspondingly high. As an alternative to such quixotic endeavors after total

---

[3]David Montgomery, *Beyond Equality: Labor and the Radical Republicans, 1862–1872* (New York: Knopf, 1967), pp. 368, 385; Geoffrey Blodgett, *The Gentle Reformers: Massachusetts Democrats in the Cleveland Era* (Cambridge, Mass.: Harvard University Press, 1966), pp. 19–22; John G. Sproat, *"The Best Men": Liberal Reformers in the Gilded Age* (New York: Oxford University Press, 1968), pp. 20–28, 61–63, 101; *MT*, Oct. 8, 1891. See also David D. Hall, "The Victorian Connection," in *Victorian America*, ed. Daniel Walker Howe (Philadelphia: University of Pennsylvania Press, 1976), pp. 81–94.

elimination of what was indeed a major social evil, Morse favored regulating the sale of liquor by a system of licensing, which was an option the Massachusetts legislature had made available to the towns of the commonwealth through a law passed in 1875.[4]

As in most communities, the most vocal advocates of prohibition in Marlborough were the evangelically inclined clergy—in the 1870s the Reverend J. T. Burhoe of the First Baptist Church; in the 1880s the Reverend A. F. Newton of the Union Congregational Church, which had been the town's established church in Colonial times. In debate with Burhoe and Newton, Morse made full use of those gestures of urbane ridicule which had been developed by such earlier New England antienthusiasts as eighteenth-century Arminians and nineteenth-century Unitarians. "We are always prepared for anything in the line of extravagance when Mr. Burhoe gets to going on temperance or any other subject before the general public, because he is so excitable," Morse commented in 1879 à propos of a remark Burhoe had made which many interpreted as anti–Roman Catholic. A week later, Morse added that Burhoe's subsequent disavowal of anti-Catholic sentiment would be believable, "were it not for that unfortunate habit of his . . . of getting intoxicated with the exuberance of his own eloquence. The habit which leads him to say things which he doesn't really mean, and is perhaps sorry for after, may also cause him to say things he doesn't remember, when the ecstacy of the occasion has passed." As for Reverend Newton, Morse was wont to accuse him of indulging in "intemperate speech," and of being "drunk with zeal," interested primarily in "sensation and sky-rocketism." All this terminology—extravagance, ecstasy, being drunk with zeal, sky-rocketism—derived from the same frame of reference as Jonathan Mayhew had been working within when he had remarked of the evangelists of the Great Awakening of the 1740s: "[They] think themselves *converted,* when the poor, unhappy creatures are *only out of their wits.*" And Morse was merely making use of another utterly traditional antienthusiastic rhetorical gambit when, in 1885, in rejoinder to Newton's attributing the birth of more than thirty illegitimate children in Marlborough the previous year to the fact that the town had voted against prohibition at the 1884 town meeting, he coolly stated: "It would be an easy enough task to show that the Christian religion of Mr. New-

[4]*MT*, Dec. 30, 1880; Mar. 29, 1883; July 18, 1889; Sproat, *Best Men*, p. 212; Michael H. Frisch, *Town into City: Springfield, Massachusetts, and the Meaning of Community, 1840–1880* (Cambridge, Mass.: Harvard University Press, 1972), p. 162.

ton's brand was the cause of a great deal of illegitimacy, but it is a fact too well known to need demonstration."[5]

So in his presentation of his views on the temperance question, Morse was bringing together two of the most venerable sets of conventions and responses in New England culture: those relating to the conflict between order and enthusiasm, and those relating to the deep-seated urge to reform and sanctify. As long as the editor remained contained within such conventions, the actual point and purpose of polemical endeavor—in this case the promulgation of a more realistic yet also more efficacious policy for the regulation of appetite—remained in the rhetorical foreground. Yet Morse found it impossible to remain so contained. Again and again, his advocacy of "rational" temperance reform degenerated into sheer ad hominem abuse. In his treatment of Reverend Newton, for example, the familiar association between religious enthusiasm and sexual license became the endlessly repeated insinuation that the Congregationalist minister was, à la Henry Ward Beecher, "a corrupter of women." This was communicated by such means as calling Newton an "obscene and nasty little preacher," and speculating that if he "should ever slip through the legs of St. Peter . . . what a scuttling and scurrying to hide there would be among the decent female denizens of the place." Morse constantly threatened and boasted that he would run Newton out of town, a result he believed he had accomplished in the case of Reverend Burhoe and a number of other prohibitionist spokesmen. It seemed that he was engaged in an effort less to sanctify than to dominate and destroy whoever or whatever presumed to resist him— indeed there was never a time between 1877 and 1892 when the editor of the *Times* was not in the combative posture illustrated by his response in 1882 to the rumor that a Hudson shoe manufacturer intended to sue him for libel: "This big mogul, whose [adulterous] proclivities we seem to have exposed, has intimated that he will seek his revenge through the legal channels, and has instituted inquiries as to our responsibility pecuniarily. All right; he is a free burgess and the law is open to him; let him come on."[6]

Editor Morse's tendency to engulf his own reform impulses and ideological preferences in his lust for cultural warfare was shown most fully in the course of his relationship with Father Peter McKen-

[5]*MT*, May 15, 1879; May 22, 1879; Mar. 15, 1883; Oct. 2, 1884; Feb. 26, 1885; July 16, 1886; Alan Heimert, *Religion and the American Mind from the Great Awakening to the Revolution* (Cambridge, Mass.: Harvard University Press, 1966), p. 177.

[6]*MT*, Apr. 7, 1881; Jan. 5, 1882; Oct. 22, 1885; Apr. 22, 1886; Mar. 8, 1888.

na of the Church of the Immaculate Conception, which served Marlborough's Irish-Americans. By several measures—such as numbers of people serving in public office, disposition to form or expand voluntary associations and have them display themselves in public— the second half of the 1880s was the time when the Irish and French-Canadian people of Marlborough began to assert themselves more definitely, and as they did, it was Father McKenna who provided them with their most vigorous leadership. Within a year of his commencing his duties as parish priest in 1886, McKenna had, by the addition of a steeple, chimes, and stained-glass windows, transformed the Church of the Immaculate Conception into a fittingly imposing structure; he had obtained pledges from the licensed liquor dealers of Marlborough, most of them Roman Catholics, not to sell to minors or to remain open on Sundays; he had established, under the sponsorship of the Catholic Lyceum, a newspaper, the *Marlborough Star;* and he had become the principal spokesman in town for the cause of Irish nationalism.

That McKenna's intent was to lead the Irish and French-Canadian people toward a position in which they would participate fully in community life, while at the same time not abandoning but rather affirming their own distinct ethnic traditions, was brought out in May 1887. It had become customary that a special service in honor of the Grand Army of the Republic (G.A.R.), the organization of Civil War veterans, be held the Sunday before Memorial Day. Heretofore, this observance had always taken place in one of the Protestant churches. But this year it was to be held, at Father McKenna's instigation, at the Church of the Immaculate Conception. But McKenna was not going to allow this overture to be interpreted as a sign of Irish subservience. Plans went ahead for the Irish union picnic, which had become an established tradition for Memorial Day, and McKenna chose to augment the display of Irish presence this particular year by inviting all the Catholic Total Abstinence societies of the Archdiocese of Boston to hold their annual convention in Marlborough. At the very same hour that the G.A.R. and the Protestant clergy were conducting the official Memorial Day service, the streets of Marlborough were enlivened by a mammoth ex-immigrant parade. Contingents from all the Catholic Total Abstinence societies, the Catholic Lyceum, the Grattan, Emmet, and Everett societies, the Hoop-La Club, the Cadet Band, the Holy Name Society, and the St. Stephen's Mission of Framingham were all to be seen, along with carriages filled with priests. Furthermore, the Irish were joined for the occasion by the St. Jean Baptiste Society and all the other French-Canadian organizations of

Marlborough. Under revitalized leadership, the new citizens of Marlborough were making it known that they had indeed come to stay.[7]

Until 1888 the leadership of Marlborough's native Protestant
culture, in both its Unitarian or lapsed-Unitarian and its evangelical
Methodist, Baptist, and Congregationalist guises, reacted tolerantly, if
a trifle condescendingly, to the new sociocultural potency of its Irish
and French-Canadian neighbors. But in June of that year the hoary
tradition of "no popery" was revived throughout eastern Massachusetts, as a result of an incident in the Boston public schools in
which, it was believed, school policy had been dictated by Roman
Catholic pressure. In Marlborough it was Charles F. Morse's principal
foe of the moment, the Reverend A. F. Newton, who most assiduously
and aggressively peddled anti-Catholic demonology, in the pages of
Morse's journalistic competitors, the *Mirror-Journal* and the *Daily Mirror*. One of Newton's typical contributions reads: "CHRISTIAN WOMEN
OF MARLBORO! This day God calls you to your duty to the public
schools of Marlboro, by registration. It is the last opportunity you may
ever have to hold the public schools along the American line. . . . Our
public schools may from this day pass into the hands of the Roman
priests for a generation. . . . Let the baking go today. Better your
families live on crackers for a little than to let the children of Marlboro for all the coming years receive their mental pabulum at the
parochial schools and at so called public schools run in accordance
with the schemes of the Romish priests."[8]

But the Protestant liberals of Marlborough did not support the
anti-Catholic crusade of 1888 and 1889. Indeed, they made their
opposition to it quite clear. In May 1888, before the controversy had
come to a head, R. A. Griffin and his Universalist colleague had
refused to sign a resolution circulated among the Protestant ministers
of the town condemning Father McKenna for raising money for his
church by means of a lottery. Doubtless they concurred in the sentiments expressed by the Unitarian Reverend W. H. Thomas of
Worcester: "I am not in harmony with the un-Christian, un-Ameri-
can, discourteous assault upon the Roman Catholic Church now so
popular about Boston. I am endeavoring to educate my people to

---

[7]*MT*, Aug. 19, 1886; Dec. 9, 1886; Mar. 3, 1887; Apr. 28, 1887; May 12, 1887; May
26, 1887; June 2, 1887; Sept. 22, 1887; Oct. 13, 1887; Nov. 24, 1887. The "ethnic"
population of Springfield was also making itself more visible during the mid- and
late-1880s; see Frisch, *Town into City*, pp. 195–96.

[8]Robert H. Lord, John E. Sexton, and Edward T. Harrington, *History of the Archdiocese of Boston*, 3 vols. (New York: Sheed and Ward, 1944), 3:118–21; *MT*, Oct. 4,
1888.

higher things." In November 1888 E. L. Bigelow and the two other Unitarian trustees of the public library acquiesced in the demand of the four Roman Catholic trustees that the library cancel its subscription to the *Daily Mirror*. In effect, the library had joined in the boycott of the *Daily Mirror* which Father McKenna had organized some months earlier.

As for Marlborough's other leading liberal institution, the *Times* spoke out in January 1889:

> We have heard of children who had got so accustomed to hearing tales of ghosts, giants and hobgoblins, that they couldn't go to sleep at night, without having some horrible story told them. The people of the Orthodox [i.e., Congregational] church, in this town, seem to have got into some such morbid and excited condition, and they are as uneasy as a dog with a burdock under its tail unless they are listening to some new tale of horror. And parson Littlebreeches [Morse's favorite nickname for Newton] seems to be able to supply them with all the dreadfulness they need, his particular bugaboo and blunderbore being the Pope, who, his deluded hearers seem to believe, is on his way over here, to destroy the country, break up our school system, and carry us all away captives. Deacon Goodale has got so full of this terrible raw-head and bloody-bones, that he is rarely seen out of his own doors after dark. Deacon Curtis [a shoe factory superintendent] wants to get rid of the papists now in his employ, and probably would if unrestrained by higher power. Deacon Rufus Howe, one of the best men ever raised here, tucks his head under the bed clothes at night and prays that papistry may not get the better of him in his old age. The Curtis brothers, devout and obsequious followers of the disgruntled Littlebreeches [who ran a butcher shop], are debating with themselves whether they ought not to refuse to furnish meat to Catholic customers, as thereon they might grow fat and strong to the overthrow of our institutions and the bringing in of popery. But outside of that church, the world is tolerably calm and unscared, and most people don't care whether other people worship God after the Catholic or Protestant formula, or whether they don't worship any God at all, or whether there is, or is not any God to worship.

In every respect, Morse was for a moment fulfilling what he had defined back in 1877 as his journalistic purpose. He was viewing things "with broad day light shining in on a cool head," coming forward as "a friendly voice saying to [the people of the Orthodox church] in the paper, 'don't be absurd.'" Not only does Morse here not fall beneath the conventional framework of order's controversy with enthusiasm, he even manages to rise humanely above that framework: as he holds the distortions and fanaticisms of evangelicalism up for public scrutiny, he speaks not in the usual tone of judgmental ridicule, classifying the various specimens of subrationality of which evangelicalism is purportedly composed, but rather in one of deft, good-humored cajolery, as though his subjects were indeed capable of changing, recovering their wonted postures of upright good sense. It was an unusually well-focused gesture of liberalizing sanctification.[9]

By mid-1889 the no-popery hysteria in Marlborough had been brought under control, as the newspaper that had principally disseminated it had been driven out of business by the McKenna-led boycott. We may be sure that Morse felt no hesitation whatsoever about the position he had taken in this matter, for he had always held McKenna in the highest esteem, in distinct contrast to his belittling perspective on most Protestant clergymen and especially to his abusive treatment of Newton. Morse felt an affinity with McKenna that was both ideological and temperamental. He appreciated the energetic, can-do spirit evidenced in the priest's various plans for improving his physical plant: "He is a whole team, with a horse tied behind, and a dog under the wagon, at putting things through." Moreover, McKenna was an excellent speaker and writer, talents that were in short supply everywhere, but especially among the clergy: "[He] slings the Queen's English with tremendous vigor, and is as eloquent and entertaining in print as in speech." Moreover, McKenna had joined with Morse in opposing such absurdities of late nineteenth-century evangelicalism as prohibition and sabbatarianism. All in all, Morse discerned in McKenna the anomaly of a down-to-earth liberal (exactly like himself) wearing a clerical collar: "For a man who gets his living by the alleged service of God, our Rev. Father McKenna is the level headedest individual we know of. He tells the young people of his flock they must come to church once on Sunday, in the morning, and then they may go where they please and have a good time, resting or recreating, riding, playing ball and enjoying themselves as best they can, always with the condition that they are not to disturb other people. Such liberality and horse sense almost makes us religious."[10]

The association between Morse and McKenna seemed to be an unusually full exemplification of liberal principle. When a Roman Catholic priest and a freethinking, ex-Unitarian atheist could find common ground in "liberality and horse sense," it appeared that the

[9]*MT*, Apr. 26, 1877; May 10, 1888; Nov. 8, 1888; Dec. 6, 1888; Jan. 10, 1889.
[10]*MT*, July 1, 1886; Oct. 20, 1887; Aug. 9, 1888; May 16, 1889. In lauding McKenna for slinging "the Queen's English with tremendous vigor," Morse was alluding to his mild criticisms of the priest for having played an active part in the Irish nationalist protest against the Victoria Jubilee; see *MT*, June 23, 1887.

narrower ethnic and sectarian sources of identity and belief had been entirely transcended. How striking it was, therefore, that by August 1890, with the only outward erosion of the relationship McKenna's switch the previous March to advocacy of prohibition, McKenna was lambasting Morse as a "nihilist, outlaw, nothingarian, Prince of Mountebanks, carrion, mud, dyed in the wool bigot," and calling for a boycott of the *Times*. Morse immediately took up the gauntlet thus flung down, replying with a stale, dyed-in-the-wool no-popery bigot's bit of snickering about priestly celibacy: "A Catholic priest is fortunate in one respect. If we were mean and cowardly enough to attack his private character on account of his public utterances, we couldn't possibly descend to the blackguardism of assailing him through the medium of his wife and children, since priests are denied those blessings." Where there had previously been harmonious public cooperation, there was now, abruptly, a no-holds-barred brawl.

In December Morse took another roundhouse swing. In the course of informing his readers that he suspected that the Irish nationalist leader Charles Stewart Parnell was indeed guilty as charged of adultery, Morse gave McKenna a piece of advice: "If he would take truthfulness, temperance, and chastity for his themes, working in a little personal experience by way of illustration, he would be very interesting." The leader of Irish nationalism and Roman Catholicism in Marlborough had ample reason to exhibit "fellow feeling" for Parnell, Morse concluded. The immediate result of Morse's continuing to dabble in such utterly trite anti-Catholic sexual titillation and slander was that a mass meeting of well over a thousand of Marlborough's Irish Catholics committed itself to a serious implementation of the boycott of the *Times* which McKenna had called for the previous summer. And the ultimate result—as Morse persisted week after week in such tactics as smirking about how McKenna was "kissing and caressing the young ladies of his flock without regard to their reciprocation or acquiescence"—was that Morse was compelled to resign from the editorship of the *Times* in March 1892. The tables had been turned on the man who had always bragged about his success in wiping out all opposition to his power as a moral and cultural arbiter.[11]

Why was Editor Morse's stewardship of his position of journalistic trust so openly and flagrantly contentious, so apt to turn into pointless, empty competition? The peculiarities of Morse's particular character and temperament no doubt had a great deal to do with it. But as

[11]*MT*, Mar. 6, 1890; Aug. 21, 1890; Aug. 28, 1890; Nov. 20, 1890; Dec. 4, 1890; Dec. 11, 1890; Feb. 26, 1891; Mar. 15, 1892.

in the case of the troubled interactions between Ebenezer Parkman and his Westborough parishioners, it seems likely that Morse's behavior and experience are also representative of the larger culture. It is suggestive, for example, that Morse's great journalistic exemplar, Samuel Bowles, was, according to his otherwise adulatory biographer, someone whose "faults lay almost wholly on the side of self-will and pride. He was by nature masterful—fond of having his own way and the first place. His life as a journalist in some respects confirmed that disposition. The *Republican*'s attitude of entire independence sometimes ran into excess and caprice. It was never servile, but it was sometimes arrogant."

To say that the nineteenth century was an era that subscribed to an ethos of unrestrained competition among self-willed, proud, masterful free agents is only to take note of what is common knowledge. It was believed that economic, social, political, and cultural competition was what fueled the constant progress upward in morality and virtue believed to be taking place. The competition caused the progress, and the progress justified the competition. Yet as we have seen, competition had pretty much come to an end in the Marlborough shoe industry by the 1860s, and the image of the Marlborough manufacturers that emerges from the surviving documents of the 1870s and 1880s is not one of competing individual economic agents, but rather one of class solidarity, a cohesive, harmonious ruling group, unified around a consensus, both ungrounded and unchallenged, regarding the justice of existing property relations and the continuing offer of upward mobility for those who were for the time being going without. Yet although competition had ceased to be a daily, lived reality for those controlling Marlborough's economy, it continued to be honored in the culture as an expression of energy and virtue and a source of unfolding justice and fulfillment, and it therefore continued to be manifested. But since competition now had little connection with the most fundamental realities of the economy and society (these had attained to a condition of relative equilibrium), and since it could concern itself only with relatively peripheral issues such as temperance, not with questions of fundamental value (these had for the time being been resolved), it could not but be thin and superficial in its matter and increasingly rancorous and violent in its manner.

The situation was well summarized by Editor Morse himself in his response to the Irish Catholic mass meeting of December 1890 which had resolved to boycott him and destroy him. He wrote defiantly: "We are living in a tolerably free country, in which no man's religion or political belief is sacred from attack, and in which the weakest must go to the wall, and in which no church or sect or party can make war on others and be safe from reprisal." As Morse seemed to grasp, in a capitalist age, in which energies had been both liberated and provided with only the most insubstantial visions and purposes, competitive intellectual freedom was apt to amount in very great part to no more than a Hobbesian war of all upon all, a Darwinian struggle for existence. Such a sense of things readily reminds us of the Satan who, in Book VI of *Paradise Lost*, bases his conduct on the hope that the war in Heaven would persist for "eternal days."[12]

Morse's career exemplifies much that is unpleasant to contemplate about the cultural realities that seem to have developed in conjunction with an industrial capitalist economy and social order. In contrast to the contention of the Colonial era, nineteenth-century competition did not know how to control itself, was not restrained and focused by an ultimate sense of organic communal intimacy and collaborative endeavor. Yet Morse's very candor, in the passage just quoted, concerning the unrelieved belligerence of nineteenth-century cultural conflict, may indicate that at least he was not trapped in avoidance and fantasy to the same extent as were his colleagues E. L. Bigelow, S. H. Howe, and their spokesman, Unitarian Reverend R. A. Griffin. He may have been prone to a rhetorical violence that was so indiscriminately aggressive as to be in the end self-destructive, but at least he remained capable of telling the truth. The remainder of this chapter consists of a demonstration both of the validity of these propositions and of their very definite limits.

As the reader will have by this point gathered, the editor of the *Times* was what Reverend Griffin called, in an 1882 sermon doubtless composed with this former member of his church in mind, a "New England Infidel." Morse could not believe in the Christian God because, as he searched the Scriptures daily with all the diligence and concentration of his New England Puritan forebears, he found those writings to be nothing but a tissue of ludicrously obvious inconsistencies and contradictions. For example, in one place the Lord "pretended to have the G. Washington complaint, so that he could not tell a lie, for he says, 'God is not a man that he should lie,' but he knew how to get his lying done for him, it would seem, for, 'The Lord hath put a lying spirit in the mouth of all these, thy prophets.' And again, 'If the prophet be deceived when he hath spoken a thing, I the Lord

[12]George S. Merriam, *The Life and Times of Samuel Bowles*, 2 vols. (New York, 1885), 1:213; *MT*, Dec. 11, 1890; above, chap. 3, nn. 20–23.

have deceived that prophet.'" Such particular absurdities and irrationalities were but aspects, however, of the manifestly unreal, the grotesquely fantastic nature of the overarching scheme of Calvinist Protestantism:

> First, [God] undertook to create the universe and make mankind in his own image. He had good luck in that, and finished the contract inside of a week. Then he undertook to find an excuse for tormenting everybody, who might ever live, in endless hell fire. He found the pretext in the sin of a woman only a day old, and with no one but the devil to tell her the difference betwixt good and evil. Then he essayed the work of saving his own children from his senseless and ridiculous wrath. This was the great and wonderful scheme of salvation. His only son, mother unknown, was to come down on earth, loaf round thirty odd years, be betrayed and crucified and then, presto, the thing was done.

Except that it wasn't done, for as Morse had pointed out many years before, "with all his Godly attributes of power and wisdom, that son after thirty years' residence on earth had only about a dozen disciples, one of whom betrayed him and another denied him, and now after 1800 years of experiment, only about one man out of a thousand is saved by that scheme, while nine hundred and ninety-nine go to hell."[13]

Morse's posture of skepticism and realism regarding Christian myth and theology arose from a perspective that was in some respects a latter-day reconstitution of the Miltonic synthesis of antinomianism and Arminianism (described above in Chapter 1). It was a secularization of the traditional Arminian emphasis on works that led him to object repeatedly and vehemently to the versions of "the great doctrine of justification by faith alone" propounded by nineteenth-century evangelicalism: "We have no faith whatever in [a] future state of existence . . . where those who have lived wicked and shameful lives here, can, by a few hours of repentance and profession of faith in the efficacy of the blood of Christ to cleanse them from their foulness, go straight up to glory with Moses and the Lamb, while men and women who have lived pure and holy lives here, must suffer everlasting torment, because too honest to profess belief in what seemed to them

---

[13]*MT*, Dec. 1, 1881; Nov. 23, 1882; Aug. 28, 1890; Mar. 12, 1891. The evidence that Morse was a lapsed Unitarian is that in 1861 he served as the moderator of the annual Unitarian parish meeting; see *Marlborough Mirror*, Mar. 30, 1861. According to Hall, "Victorian Connection," p. 83, many late nineteenth-century agnostics came from Puritan backgrounds and had for a time been Unitarians.

wholly improbable." A similar moralizing Arminianism lay behind Morse's declaring that to thank God for the Union victory in the Civil War, as had the 1882 Memorial Day orator, was to show disrespect for the "human valor, energy, endurance, and pluck" that had really won the war. And it also lay behind the unambiguous opposition Morse was fond of presenting between, on the one hand, such needful traits of a person formed by the Protestant ethic as "industry, enterprise, frugality, and temperance," and on the other, the character of Christ and his disciples, who had been "a lazy, shiftless, improvident set of tramps."[14]

Morse's other set of Miltonic inclinations, his secularized antinomianism, was expressed most explicitly in connection with his views on the afterlife, which amounted to a recognizable permutation of the radical Protestant tradition of materialism and mortalism: "We never saw any man who could describe a purely spiritual condition of happiness, or who could explain to us how mind could exist without matter. Until we meet such a one we fear we shall have to grope along in the belief that as we never had a soul or a mind until we had a body, that as whatever we have of soul or mind or spirit, grew in us with the growth of our body, so when our body dies, we die altogether." Nor did Morse fail to draw the traditional antiascetic conclusions from these doctrines: "The Bible tells us that when God breathed the breath of life into Adam's nostrils he became a living soul, not that he put the soul within the man to be evicted at the time of his death. The fact is, if people would only live in this world, so as to get the most enjoyment out of life, and to give others the greatest amount of pleasure, they need not care whether there is any future life for them, but people who are all the time fretting about what is to become of their souls, after death, are in no condition to half enjoy life, and might about as well die." In *Christian Doctrine*, Milton draws from this same text (Gen. 2:7) exactly the conclusion drawn by Morse, that a human being "is not double or separable: not, as is commonly thought, produced from and composed of two different and distinct elements, soul and body. On the contrary, the whole man is the soul, and the soul the man: a body, in other words, or individual substance, animated, sensitive, and rational."[15]

Just as the dualistic Unitarian aspiration to be "loftily elevated above [the world] of sense and appetite" showed itself, in ongoing life, in such

---

[14]*MT*, Jan. 26, 1882; June 1, 1882; Nov. 2, 1882.

[15]*MT*, Jan. 19, 1882; June 2, 1887; *CPW*, VI, 318. For mortalism and materialism as key tenets of Puritan antinomianism, see Christopher Hill, *Milton and the English Revolution* (New York: Viking, 1978), pp. 317–33.

things as the ethereality of the Bigelow family's cultural enterprises, so the contrasting antinomian convictions of Marlborough's atheistic, ex-Unitarian country editor, that "whatever we have of mind or soul or spirit, grew in us with the growth of our body," were manifested in a contrasting earthiness in his prose style and general bearing. But Morse's distinctiveness can be shown most fully by comparing him once again with Samuel Bowles. Morse and Bowles were both descended from families that had been settled in New England since the seventeenth century, and they both belonged (being born in 1833 and 1826, respectively) to what Bowles's nineteenth-century biographer called "the generation in which New England broke through the sheath of Puritanism, and flowered into broader and more various life." Both became forceful commentators and intellectual presences without the benefit (or the hindrance) of college instruction. Moreover, there seems to have been a certain proportionality between the professional achievements of these two secularized Puritans of the press. Just as Bowles took a provincial weekly, situated in a place that would never be more than a medium-sized city, and turned it into a daily paper of national fame and influence, so Morse started up a weekly in what would never be more than a minor mill town and made it into a publication that was known, appreciated, and respected statewide. In 1883 the *Somerville Truth* noted the parallel between the two men, calling Morse "this would-be successor to Sam Bowles." The year before the *Boston Globe* had stated that the *Times* was "the champion country paper" in Massachusetts. Referring to his religious infidelity, two other papers bestowed upon Morse, to his delight, the title of "the wickedest editor in Massachusetts." And the *Worcester West Chronicle* declared: "The *Times* is as smart and brilliant as any weekly in the Commonwealth, and is highly esteemed by the press throughout the State. There is about it a spirit of free-and-easy independence that captivates the reader."[16]

But if Morse exhibited "a spirit of free-and-easy independence," then he was quite different from Samuel Bowles and the other secularized Puritans and Independents with whom he identified himself. Like them, he was committed to independence, both as a specific postwar political movement and as the raison d'être of a liberal social order. But as we have seen in Chapter 7, Bowles was the opposite of free and easy in his discursive manner; he was ever staking out the high ground and gazing upward at the sublime. The high-brow tem-

---

[16]Merriam, *Bowles*, 1:1–21; *MT*, Dec. 14, 1882; July 26, 1883; Aug. 2, 1883; Jan. 10, 1884; Jan. 15, 1885.

perament exemplified by Bowles was exactly the sort of thing Morse often delighted in deflating. In 1860, when Marlborough celebrated and took solemn note of its bicentennial, he chaired a committee that organized a sort of antimasque for the occasion, a procession of "Antiques and Horribles" that was "not a part of the Committee's programme." Twenty-one years later, older but happily not much wiser, Morse was a member of the committee putting together another "Antiques and Horribles" pageant, this time a burlesque Fourth of July parade. One feature of the mock parade seemed to suggest that many in Marlborough appreciated their editor's weekly display of "free-and-easy independence." A float dubbed "Associated Press" depicted Morse's local competitor as a donkey and himself as the devil.

As far as Morse's prose style is concerned, the *Boston Evening Transcript,* that ultimate in journalistic gentility, spoke of Morse as "this wordy jester of Marlboro, whose extraordinary productions are at once the perplexity and delight of his readers. . . . Like Touchstone and some of the rest of Shakespeare's professional funny men, he has a fantastical tendency to play with big words." In 1888 the *Boston Evening Record* paid Morse the compliment of accepting his invitation to a game of parodic banter:

> We wish the customarily good tempered Boston *Record* would tell the public what it is that stirs its protervity and agitates its spinosity whenever it has occasion to mention the Boston Water Commissioners.—*Marlboro Times*

> If the esteemed *Times* would kindly let up on its absonous gallimaufry of palaeocrystic orisinology, and express its exacerbation in less catachrestical terms, its enthymemes might have more anchylosis. Brother Morse is too much of a linguistic scaramouche to be entirely apodictic.—*Evening Record*

> Whatever the *Record* may think of the various water meters, it evidently has no use for a language meter, but we really think it ought to use a filter when such verbal enormities are coming along. Such a torrential flow of moideric multiloquence ought to be dammed, but we don't feel equal to its coarctation.—*Marlboro Times*

Obviously Morse was as fond of rhetorical as he was of ceremonial burlesques. But this aspect of his literary mien was not seen only on those occasions when he was manifestly clowning around. Even when he was being serious and sincere, his discourse always hovered not far from parody of the rounded and long-winded orotundity to which

the secularized Puritans of nineteenth-century New England were
addicted:

> For ourselves, who have always been ready to welcome and applaud
> woman in any vocation which her natural talents or acquired accomplish-
> ments fitted her to fill, it was an easy matter to get over the unusualness
> of seeing a woman breaking through the supposed restrictions of the
> Pauline thearchy, but we are full of the belief that almost any of the
> conservative and hunkerish old adherents to the doctrine that women
> should keep silent in the churches, would have had his crust of conser-
> vatism softened and dissolved by habitually listening to the clean, pure
> and forcible utterances which have been the ruling characteristics, mark-
> ing and distinguishing all the public efforts of Miss Haynes, to which it
> has been our good fortune to listen.

This was what Morse had to say in praise of Marlborough's woman
Universalist minister, the Reverend Lorenza Haynes, when she left
her position in 1878. The impression made by this and many other
such polysyllabic and syntactically ornamented and gargoyled utterances found in the pages of the *Times* is not that Morse was essaying,
with less than complete success, to write as Samuel Bowles had written
in his 1851 editorial on the role of the modern press. Rather, he
sounds as though he is laughing discreetly up his sleeve at the pom-
posities in which Bowles and other elevated and moralistic Independents seemed often to be trapped. There was a saving element of self-
deprecation in Morse's always slightly lugubrious style.[17]

In 1883, while Morse was away on what he claimed was his first
vacation ever, those of his subordinates to whom he had entrusted the
Times in his absence also paid him the compliment of teasing him
about his style: "The Somerville *Truth* likes short editorials. We do
too. They are better. Best. We object to long sentences. So do other
criminals. Put in plenty of periods. Easier. This is a thundering editorial. We think Gen. Butler is the best governor the Commonwealth
ever had." The final sentence was an allusion to the fact that Morse
had in the course of 1883 come to inveigh with increasing ferocity
against the way Benjamin Butler had been conducting himself in the
State House office to which he had finally been elected in the autumn
of 1882. Morse's hearty disapproval of Butler was not new and it was
not unique to him. Samuel Bowles and all the other latter-day Pu-

---

[17]*Marlborough Mirror*, Apr. 21, 1860; June 16, 1860; *MT*, Nov. 28, 1878; July 7,
1881; Nov. 17, 1887; Apr. 5, 1888. For Samuel Bowles and the high style, see above,
chap. 7, n. 14.

ritans of Massachusetts regarded Butler with fear and loathing as, in David Montgomery's words, "the image of the Caesar—the wealthy demagogue who seized power by catering to the ignorance and vice of the rabble." Morse often spoke in the typical Independent mode of frantic excoriation of Butler, as when Butler was scheduled to make a campaign stop in Marlborough, in the course of an unsuccessful re-election effort in the autumn of 1883: "Go and hear this vain, bombastic, vulgar old man, who keeps up the ridiculous pretense of being the friend of the laboring man, and the especial patron saint of the poor, and who has become a millionaire by grinding down the faces of the poor laborers employed in his enormously profitable mills."

Yet because the Marlborough editor did not aspire, either by temperament or belief, to the typical secularized Puritan posture of lofty elevation, he could also achieve a more complex response to Butler, could go beyond one-dimensional moralizing and savor, in a manner that was almost Dickensian, the man's energy and audacity:

> That staunch, copper fastened, A1, broad sterned and capacious holded vessel, B. F. Butler, which has been cruising in Southern waters for some time past, is now at moorings in East Cambridge court house, engaged in the case of Lemon vs. the city of Newton. The old craft shows signs of age and weatherbeatenness, especially about the prow and figure-head, and there is a sort of crankiness about the motion of the walking beams that indicates breaking up, but we rather think the old cutter is good for another voyage and will be seen yet with a Beacon hill boom on, bound for the state house.

Morse's prose could radiate the same cheerful appreciation of wily resourcefulness and cheek when it was contemplating more commonplace scoundrels:

> A couple of citizens, not unknown in criminal circles, were confined in the lock-up under Town Hall last Sunday night, and didn't like it. One of them wanted to go home, and the other, like the late Otis Rice when he got lost in Boston, wanted to go 'anywhere by —— to get out of this —— hole.' They wanted a writ of *habeas corpus Christi* to get out on, but there was nothing of the kind to be found, so in lieu thereof they took the stove wrench and part of an old bedstead and rigged a derrick with which to lift the heavy iron door off the hinges and so escaped. They haven't been arrested yet, but they are liable to be any time.

Morse was able to get a kick out of the maneuvers of a disreputable political rogue and two anonymous vagrants because he could recognize in them the same subversive impulses as he himself expressed when he engaged, as he regularly did, in sly and subtle ridicule of moral and literary pretension. In very great part, Morse was a cultural democrat in a way that most other Independents and secularized Puritans were not. Unlike those such as the Adams brothers who were born into the Brahmin aristocracy, or those such as Samuel Bowles and Horace Mann who struggled up to enjoy, and to be constrained by, the prerogatives of eminence, Morse lived his life down on the plains of mid-nineteenth-century democratic opportunity. He tried this line of work, then he tried that one, rising to middling success and fulfillment in whatever he took up, but always feeling free to move on to something else when the spirit so moved him: retail employee, independent retail tradesman, army volunteer and officer, insurance salesman, deputy sheriff, auctioneer, real estate speculator, country editor. From his own experience of the leveled openness of American society, he learned to speak in a journalistic voice that was at once thoughtful, amusing, self-mocking, and negatively, democratically capable. That the words and deeds of most nineteenth-century secularized Puritans were glaringly deficient in those last three qualities was one of the principal reasons they had such difficulty functioning effectively as political and cultural leaders in a democracy. They might have done worse than to pay more serious attention to this relatively obscure spear carrier in their own ranks.[18]

Morse's insistence on the dignity and value of the realm of "sense and appetite," and his corresponding earthiness of style and manner, seem to hold out the promise of a more adequate engagement with late nineteenth-century social reality than was achieved by those of the loftily elevated persuasion. But when we turn to Morse's utterances on the central issue of the time, that of the relations between capital and labor, this unfortunately is not what we find. Instead, there is an avoidance that seems, precisely to the extent that it constitutes a be-

[18]*MT*, Dec. 18, 1879; Apr. 28, 1881; June 14, 1883; Oct. 25, 1883; Montgomery, *Beyond Equality*, p. 367. Their political opponents sneered at the secularized Puritans as the "God and Morality Party"; see Irwin Unger, *The Greenback Era: A Social and Political History of American Finance, 1865–1879* (Princeton, N.J.: Princeton University Press, 1964), p. 72. Morse's occupational history has been gleaned from the following sources: Ella A. Bigelow, *Historical Reminiscences of the Early Times in Marlborough, Massachusetts,* . . . (Marlborough, 1910), pp. 212–13; *Annual Visitor and Lyceum Journal*, Feb. 17, 1858; *Marlborough Mirror*, Oct. 27, 1860; Mar. 30, 1861; Dec. 23, 1865; Dec. 30, 1865; May 30, 1868; Sept. 30, 1874; 9th U.S. Census (1870), manuscript returns for Marlborough, p. 363. His activities as real estate agent and deputy sheriff were mentioned in virtually every issue of the *Times*.

trayal of fundamental inclinations and energies, even more willful than that of E. L. Bigelow's and S. H. Howe's spokesman, R. A. Griffin. Like Griffin, Morse claimed to be in sympathy with the efforts of labor unions to gain for their members the modern equivalent of the just price: "Every man who gets a living by the labor of his hands desires and ought to have, the highest possible wages the employer of labor can afford to pay, and we are heartily in favor of every combination, cooperation and union by which those who do the hard work in this world can secure a fairer share of the results of their labor." Yet, along with every other Independent, Mugwump, Cleveland Democrat, and other bourgeois spokesman of the day, Morse thus affirmed in general the right of labor to organize, while at the same time denying it the right to make its organizing meaningful and effective. As he stated the operative principle during the strike of 1878, "No man has a right to interfere with another man's right to work when he has a chance and wants to do it." If labor unions were to be allowed to prevent people from working, except on terms set by the unions, Morse was saying more vehemently than ever in 1889, then the great American dream of life, liberty, and the pursuit of happiness "is only a 'glittering and sounding generality.'" Possibly so, but by the same token, such an abstracting of the "right to work" from the only context in which that right could be exercised, that of emergent corporate capitalism, likewise turned Morse's acknowledgment of the legitimacy of unions into no more than a "glittering and sounding generality."

Nor was this all there was to Morse's flight from reality in this area. In the late 1880s Morse's indignation at union infringements on the right to work was focused on the "walking delegates" whom the Knights of Labor had sent out to bargain on behalf of the workers in such factory towns as Marlborough, and who thus had been given the authority to make decisions about such matters as strikes. The walking delegate system, the editor irately pronounced, "which takes from any man the right to work for whom he pleases and for what wages he pleases, and puts it into the power of a stranger and alien . . . makes our boasted liberties something less than a name and is too utterly despicable to be fully described by any words we know how to use." Furthermore, he depicted the delegates themselves as monsters of deceit and greed. Commenting in 1887 on a meeting held in Marlborough to raise funds in support of a strike in neighboring Worcester County, he alleged that "whoever watches the walking delegates—who never walk when hacks and herdics can be hired, by the way—who sees how they dress, how much they spend for good cigars, fine liquor, theatres, &c.. and how recklessly they bet at poker and pitch, will get an idea of where the bulk of the money goes." Walking delegates were "loud-mouthed, lazy and drunken blatherskites, who join the [union] only from the hope of seeing a chance to live without work."

In these litanies of abuse, we can hear distinct echoes of the opprobrium traditionally heaped upon the heads of itinerant preachers and enthusiasts by the anointed representatives of New England ecclesiastical order. The manufacturers, and the institutions and resources they controlled, did occupy the same central position in nineteenth-century New England culture as the established churches had occupied in the seventeenth and eighteenth centuries, so there is no reason to be surprised that the appointed literary representative of the Marlborough manufacturers devoted himself to anathematizing rootless subversives with all the energy at his command. But we ought nevertheless to spell out the intellectual consequences of this predictable phenomenon. In retaliating against a movement he considered guilty of demagoguery with the most childishly demagogic, cartoonlike representations of sportily dressed, cigar-puffing, whiskey-swilling "blatherskites," Morse was refusing to extend himself into that posture of sociocultural negative capability which, as we have just seen, he did on occasion achieve.

The same refusal was contained in his response in 1888 to the declaration in the constitution of the new Central Labor Union of Marlborough that "complete independence can be obtained only when the laborer is no longer dependent on other individuals for the right to work." Morse allowed himself to imagine that he had turned in an elegant piece of debating when he pretended that the inordinate power being referred to was not that of the manufacturers, but rather that of labor's own walking delegates. Whatever may have been the intellectual and moral deficiencies of the late nineteenth-century labor movement, it at least managed to read the signs of the times and identify a trend that ought to have been of prime interest and concern to such an apostle of independence as Charles F. Morse: that the increasingly massive and coercive power of capital was emptying the great nineteenth-century ideal of independence of any meaningful social content. On this crucial subject, Morse drew back, objectified and absolutized his opinions instead of submitting them to encounters with new social realities, and to the attendant intellectual challenges and possibilities of dialectical development and transformation.[19]

[19]*MT*, Jan. 24, 1878; Sept. 24, 1885; Mar. 18, 1886; May 26, 1887; Jan. 19, 1888; Feb. 2, 1888; Feb. 7, 1889. For other contemporary statements accepting unions in theory while denying to them any power to work their will, see Blodgett, *Gentle Reformers*, pp. 36–37; Montgomery, *Beyond Equality*, pp. 146, 231, 247, 294; Sproat, *Best Men*, pp. 206–8, 229. And for an account of the many others besides Morse who regarded walking delegates as "vampires that live and fatten on . . . honest labor," see Daniel T.

Morse's tendency to jump to superficial conclusions and devote himself to the mere bustling embroidery of them was not confined to this one fundamental question of the relations of capital and labor. On issue after issue, he settled into his fixed position and that was that. Criminology? "You cannot successfully control hardened criminals with sentiment. Morbid sympathy and mince pie are very well in their place but in order to keep murderous villains in subjection there must be arbitrary rules and enforced obedience to them." Women's suffrage? "We used to be pretty strongly in favor of the theory of female suffrage, but have found it was something the great bulk of femininity didn't want, and we'll be goll darned, if we are going to force her to take it." In 1886 Morse pointed out the intellectual slackness that was implicit in a remark made by his local competitor— "It is the fashion now-a-days for all well-regulated newspaper factories to open an opinion shop for the display of their intellectual bric-a-brac." Yet in fact, since Morse refused to develop his observations and perceptions into thoughts, and a thought-through perspective, since he insisted instead on articulating a collection of opinions, each of which took on through repetition a thinglike distinctness and solidity, the running of a "newspaper factory" and "an opinion shop for the display of . . . intellectual bric-a-brac" came to constitute an accurate description of his own intellectual functioning. With his bright and splashy dogmatism, Morse was accomplishing in the intellectual realm what the manufacturing and mercantile stockholders in the *Times* were accomplishing in the material realm: just as they were producing and distributing consumer goods, so he was producing and distributing items and articles of public opinion. His maneuvers suggest that in the respect of reification and commodification, the phrase "free marketplace of ideas" was in the late nineteenth century becoming as much literal description as trite metaphor.[20]

The validity of these observations can be demonstrated more fully by a brief examination of Morse's views on the question of tariff reform. As Geoffrey Blodgett, John G. Sproat, and Daniel T. Rodgers have shown, the reduction of protectionist import duties was a key article of faith for the Independent and Mugwump reformers with whom Morse chose to be associated. In his and their view, the protective tariff constituted a wholly unwarranted interference with the

---

Rodgers, *The Work Ethic in Industrial America, 1850–1920* (Chicago: University of Chicago Press, 1978), pp. 221–22. The consequences for the ethos of independence of the emergence of corporate capitalism in the late nineteenth century is the principal subject of Rodgers's book.

[20]*MT*, Sept. 13, 1883; Feb. 4, 1886; Aug. 14, 1890.

workings of the free market. It was a "'socialistic' contrivance, that enabled a few to get rich without working," growled E. L. Godkin. Worse, it legitimized other forms of interference with the free market, such as strikes and worker demands for government regulation of wages and hours. And by encouraging "combination" and ultimately monopoly, it insured that strikes and other forms of labor radicalism would indeed be called forth. The tariff reformers imagined that the problems of industrial capitalism were being caused not by the intrinsic functioning of the system, but rather by this "artificial, external encumbrance. . . . Remove the encumbrance and the nightmare of labor violence would dissolve with the dawn. Remove the encumbrance and monopoly would disappear." Independent and Mugwump advocates of tariff reduction were hearkening back to the antebellum ideal (most Radical Republicans had indeed been free traders) of "the autonomous American individual standing free of his government, asking no favors, a single citizen among equal millions." Or as Morse put it: "Give the laboring man the chance to sell his labor where it will bring the highest price, and let him buy his goods where he can get the most for his money, and he doesn't need any other 'protection' to his industry."[21]

So tariff reform proceeded from as superficial and deluded an understanding of the status of independence in late nineteenth-century society as did the fulminations of Morse and others against the "despotism" of labor unions and their walking delegates. Nevertheless, as the focus of his perception that some degree of reform of industrial capitalism was indeed required, this cause repeatedly propelled Morse into radical-sounding rhetoric and even into what looked like systemic analysis. "Protection protects the capitalist at the expense of the working people always and inevitably," he categorically declared in 1882. "Every high tariffite in the country will tell you he wants a protective tariff for the benefit of the wage earners, but, mind you, he is never in favor of a tariff on imported laborers. He wants his cheap labor to come free, but on everything the poor man eats or wears he wants protection, so as to make him pay double what it would cost him otherwise, and a large proportion of which increased price goes into the hands of the soft-speeched but iron-hearted and India-rubber-conscienced manufacturer." This argument was apt to degenerate into ethnic slurs, as when the *Boston*

[21]Blodgett, *Gentle Reformers*, pp. 79–80; Sproat, *Best Men*, pp. 158, 172, 175, 213; Rodgers, *Work Ethic*, p. 221; Eric Foner, *Free Soil, Free Labor, Free Men: The Ideology of the Republican Party before the Civil War* (New York: Oxford University Press, 1970), p. 105; *MT*, Jan. 31, 1884.

Evening Record stated in 1888: "The New England village, with its intelligence, its restless aspiration, has become a Kanuck settlement—alien in thought, barren of ambition and of all the elements which have made up New England civilization." Morse quoted this remark with approval, but he went on to shift the emphasis away from group antagonism, back toward an apprehension of the remorseless inner logic of the system of buying cheap and selling dear:

> Precisely; and when the Kanucks get intelligent enough to see that their labor is worth more than they are receiving for it, and demand higher pay, out they'll go and their places will be supplied by Poles, Hungarians or Chinese. For there is no tariff on labor, you know. There is no protection for the man who has his labor to sell, and he must compete with the pauper labor, not only of Europe, but of Asia and Africa, while everything his labor buys is outrageously taxed for the benefit of somebody else, and that somebody the rich employer, who is constantly cutting down his wages under the threat of filling his place with imported labor.[22]

This was the view of "imported labor" taken by Morse when he was arguing most strenuously for tariff reform. Yet when he was arguing against the labor movement's own demand for an eight-hour day, which was the most "jackassically stupid" thing he had yet seen, a violation of the sacred imperatives of the Protestant work ethic, he portrayed the foreign worker in a rather different light:

> Probably not one man in ten of all in this country is able to take sixteen hours out of the twenty-four for refreshment and sleep. Nor are there many who want to, for the natural inclination is to be busy about something useful, and the loafers are a small minority. The mechanics of this country, as a body, cannot accomplish all there is for them to do by working eight hours out of every twenty-four, and if they will not do all that is to be done, others will come from Canada, from Europe, and even from Asia, to help them, for the work has got to be done.

The duty-free pauper labor of the entire world, held by capital in readiness to destroy the livelihood of the American worker, is now inexplicably, magically transformed into a worldwide brotherhood of industrious "mechanics" (Morse's choice of the old-fashioned term is appropriate and revealing), eager to lend a helping hand. What is of greatest interest about this rhetorical about-face is not that, in re-

[22]*MT*, May 25, 1882; May 17, 1888.

sponse to a key item on the working-class agenda, Morse's editorial ink flows so readily into the channels well worn by the familiar mythology of energetic capitalist enterprise and harmonious capitalist social relations. It is, rather, that Morse does not pause to acknowledge, or probably even to notice, that he is contradicting himself.

A similar contradiction was involved in the editor's insisting that the maintenance of Marlborough's streets and roads, and the work on its urban improvements of the 1880s, such as the waterworks and the sewer system, be accomplished not by the employment of day-laboring residents of the town, but rather by the cheaper method of hiring a contractor who brought with him an imported, immigrant (usually Italian) crew of workers. In 1887 the Irish Catholic paper, the *Star*, pointed out this particular contradiction to Morse, but he simply dissolved the objection with a wave of his editorial wand, gliding nimbly by the key consequence that in the broader context of the overall tariff reform debate he was so eager to stress—the depression of wages and the elimination of jobs:

> We have always vehemently opposed the keeping of a high protective tariff on everything the laboring man in America eats, wears, or uses, and yet allowing cheap laborers to be imported unrestrictedly. But that has nothing to do with the manner in which our roads shall be made. If a prudent man has a cellar or a well to be dug, or a house to be built, he looks about to see who will undertake the job for the least money, and when he finds the lowest he can get the job done for by a reliable man, he makes a contract with him for the work. Why should not the town do likewise?[23]

Morse's blithe unconsciousness or cavalier dismissal of the obvious contradictions to be found in his various opinionated utterances on pauper labor, helpful foreign mechanics, and reliable men who would contract for the work at the lowest price, no questions asked, reveal that for him the intellectual world, like the economic, consisted of a random collection of readily separable parts. As far as he was concerned, a phenomenon such as the eagerness of capital to disregard national boundaries in its procurement of labor did not exist as a solid fact, to be integrated into a process of thought which aimed at an apprehension of reality as a whole. Explicit apprehension of a totalized reality was not what Morse's mind worked from and toward. Rather, he began and ended in the definite, settled position on the

[23]*MT*, May 13, 1886; July 21, 1887.

isolated, atomized issue, just as the capitalism of his day assumed not an interrelated matrix of polity, society, and ecoenvironment, but rather the atomized individual consumer and the equally atomized single commodity. Consequently, the internationalism of capital's purchase of labor could in Morse's prose take on whatever shape, hue, and coloration would contribute the most to the sharpening and polishing up of whichever position on whichever issue it was that had for the time being come to the fore.

It was a disregard for consistency which closely resembled that "incessant intellectual activity" of Satan's in which, as in Book IV of *Paradise Lost,* he proceeds swiftly and nimbly from an exalted and respectful to a reduced and condescending view of Adam and Eve.[24] Like the archfiend, our country editor was steeped in the spirit of capitalism much more thoroughly than is indicated simply by the fact that he invariably sided against labor and with capital whenever a real choice had to be made. Not only were his views those of a proponent of the industrial capitalist order, his method of argumentation was capitalist in its form and tone. As in energetic capitalism so in the exuberant mind of Charles F. Morse, everything is treated as raw material, to be expropriated and improved at will, without regard for the wider reverberations and longer-range consequences.

In "Brother Morse," the developments we have been chronicling are brought to a certain fulfillment. With his reformist impulses and allegiances, Morse was a late participant in the efforts made throughout the nineteenth century by a variety of New Englanders to preserve Puritan idealism and make it viable for a secular age. As argued in Chapters 7 and 8, those efforts were epistemologically as well as morally idealistic. Nineteenth-century New England was marked by the achievement of hegemonic dominance of the Protestant ethic's sanctioning not only of material, but also of intellectual enterprise, its bestowal of the gift of hermeneutic freedom along with that of economic improvement and reward. By the Protestant ethic's ultimate standard of inner motive, outer reality was constantly available for reassessment and reinterpretation, and in practice this meant that outer reality came to be enclosed in and obscured by ever more elaborate constructs of desire and aspiration. Brother Morse's experience of the actualities thus obscured—its opportunities and informalities, but also its limits, pressures, and struggles—was rather more direct and close up than that of most other secularized Puritans, and he thus

[24]See above, chap. 3, n. 28.

in some respects raises the intriguing prospect of the secularizing of that form of Puritanism which had not been epistemologically idealistic, that of Quakers, Diggers, and *Paradise Lost.*

However, since Morse was not moved by any serious degree of critical detachment from capitalism, a system committed to coercive transformations of the given in both the material and intellectual realms, his eathier mode of apprehension amounted in the end not to an alternative to nineteenth-century idealism, but rather to a further development of it. Where Samuel Bowles or R. A. Griffin give the impression of struggling to get away from and get above a solid, unyielding world the presence of which the reader nevertheless continues to feel in the very laboriousness of the struggle, the result of the combination of Brother Morse's breezy familiarity with that real world and his unperturbed juggling of contradictory views of it is, in Marx's phrase, that "all that is solid melts into air," and the reader is left floating in realms of pure rhetorical invention. It is certainly no coincidence that Morse and his newspaper flourished at the time when mass advertising, in which "facility with language rather than the quality of the commodity sold manufactured goods," became established as a major American institution.[25] The same capitalist imperatives that were bringing mass advertising into existence were remolding the floridity of Samuel Bowles into the facility of Brother Morse. And the movement of secularized Puritan discourse from Bowles to Morse, from soaring grandiloquence to fast-talking conjurations, is, as we have seen, the intellectual and rhetorical movement made by Satan, as he proceeds from his magnificent entrance into *Paradise Lost* to his ignominious exit from it.

[25]Burton J. Bledstein, *The Culture of Professionalism: The Middle Class and the Development of Higher Education in America* (New York: Norton, 1976), p. 70.

Conclusion:
The Loss of Paradise

The period in which Charles F. Morse flourished and fell has recently been identified as a watershed in American cultural history. T. J. Jackson Lears has shown that the end of the nineteenth century and the beginning of the twentieth witnessed the emergence, among a wide variety of New England and northeastern figures who were far more influential than Morse, of an ideology of "antimodernism," in reaction against precisely that "pattern of evasive banality" by which Morse and other apologists for the modernist hegemony of capitalism and liberal rationalism strove to conceal its manifest contradictions. "Disparate as their odysseys were," writes Lears, "[the antimodernists] shared a common view that modern culture had narrowed the range and diffused the intensity of human existence. They longed to rekindle possibilities for authentic experience, physical or spiritual—possibilities they felt had existed once before, long ago." The story Lears has to tell about this movement of dissent is primarily one of incorporation and co-optation, as the inherent psychologism of a quest for intensity and authenticity has developed into a sophisticated form of consumerism ideally suited to an economy and society of corporate capitalist abundance. Antimodernists have in great part been seeking what Satan makes available to Eve in the dream he induces in her in *Paradise Lost:* "Forthwith up to the clouds / With him I flew, and underneath beheld / The earth outstretched immense, a prospect wide / And various: wondering at my flight and change / To this high exaltation" (V, 86–90).[1]

[1] T. J. Jackson Lears, *No Place of Grace: Antimodernism and the Transformation of American Culture, 1880–1920* (New York: Pantheon, 1981), pp. 57–58. Lears also repeatedly stresses that there is a residue of antimodernism that remains unincorporated.

But if our culture has thus been significantly modified during the past century, those of its constitutive components which have developed out of the dialectics of Protestantism and Puritanism remain nevertheless basically intact. We continue to inhabit a world defined by the constant and ever more hectic material and intellectual manipulations of capitalism, and also by experiences of uneasiness within in our semiegalitarian, semihierarchical domestic, educational, and occupational surroundings. Of the two of these, it is the former, the dimension of modernism I have associated with Satan, which for the most part shapes our larger environment, while the latter, that part of the modern situation Milton represents in Adam and Eve, determines what transpires for us on a more direct, day-to-day level. So we find our capitalist roots in an old newspaper and the sources of our convoluted psychosocial experience in an old diary. And so, in the final three books of *Paradise Lost*, Milton depicts a great world of cosmic maneuvering and historical panorama which remains dominated by satanic values, alongside a more intimate realm in which we see Adam and Eve, "two ordinary human beings in despair, divided, and then coming together in ordinary human decency."[2] Just as *Paradise Lost* has throughout this book provided us with a paradigm for our downward historical spiral, so it now points our way forward, in a manner that ignores none of the realities that have caused us to fall "such a pernicious highth" (I, 282).

As E. M. W. Tillyard notes and Joseph Summers emphasizes, it is Eve who in Book X makes the first crucial initiatives toward repentance and reconciliation.[3] This development is foreshadowed in the divergent responses of Adam and Eve to being summoned before God to give an account of themselves. Adam is all tortuous intellectual sophistication: "but strict necessity / Subdues me, and calamitous constraint / Lest on my head both sin and punishment, / However insupportable, be all / Devolved; though should I hold my peace, yet thou / Wouldst easily detect what I conceal" (X, 131–36). An acknowledgment of what he in particular did he allows to escape his lips only with the utmost reluctance, after he has managed to insinuate that perhaps it is God himself who is ultimately at fault: "This woman whom thou madest to be my help, / And gavest me as thy perfect gift, so good, / So fit, so acceptable, so divine, / That from her hand I could suspect no ill, / And what she did, whatever in it self, / Her doing seemed to

---

[2] E. M. W. Tillyard, *Studies in Milton* (London: Chatto & Windus, 1951), p. 43.
[3] Ibid., pp. 39–40; Joseph Summers, *The Muse's Method: An Introduction to* Paradise Lost (New York: Norton, 1968; orig. 1962), pp. 108, 176–78.

justify the deed; / She gave me of the tree, and I did eat" (137–43). Eve, in obvious and pointed contrast, "with shame nigh overwhelmed, / Confessing soon, yet not before her judge / Bold or loquacious, thus abashed replied. / The serpent me beguiled and I did eat" (159–62).

But in contemplating the events of Book X, it is more helpful to attend to the continued sociological and psychological appropriateness of Milton's portrayal of our first parents than to make invidious comparisons. Boyd Berry says of the final three books of *Paradise Lost:* "[They] wonderfully catch the ebb and flow of human consciousness and everyday spirituality . . . in contrast to a systematic Puritan treatment of spiritual growth, with its neat categories and implicit sense of steady progress, this drama records the real vicissitudes of human existence."[4] We are now in a position to extend this insight. A large part of what is compelling about the recovery from the Fall is that, like the Fall itself, it records the real vicissitudes of specifically Puritan existence. Without engaging in the least little bit of wishful thinking, it shows how those enmeshed in uneasiness within and without might just begin to go beyond it, might just succeed in coping positively with extreme duress.

Thus, both Adam and Eve behave here at the moment of judgment in ways that we might expect, in view of what we know about the forms of uneasiness within characteristic of each of them. Eve has not won through to a selfless humility. Rather, she is "with shame nigh overwhelmed," struck virtually dumb by the thoroughness with which she has evidently undone herself, her husband, and her community. Having felt (as she was meant to) empowered, having, accordingly, taken a major initiative, having been propelled in the course of implementing it into a touchy self-defensiveness, and having been forced to see the apparently unqualified disaster she has brought about by being thus bold, Eve retreats precipitously from boldness to a thunderstruck, mute timidity. It is the style of remorse which, we may well imagine, might have been manifested by Eunice Andrews if her confrontation with Parkman had resulted, say, in his falling dead of a stroke. Similarly, Adam is not being merely self-serving in his response to divine interrogation. He is indeed making excuses for himself ("You and this woman tricked me into it"), but at the same time he is also beginning to struggle, for perhaps the first time in his life, with an anomaly: "That between this benevolent deity and this breathtaking femininity, things should have come to such a pass!" Even as he

[4]Boyd M. Berry, *Process of Speech: Puritan Religious Writing and* Paradise Lost (Baltimore, Md.: Johns Hopkins University Press, 1976), p. 262.

endeavors to protect himself just as he always has in his superior Puritan learnedness, Adam is taking his first baby steps toward that posture of exploratory intellectual groping amidst the new and unexpected which he so conspicuously failed to adopt at the moment when he had to decide how to deal with Eve's having eaten the forbidden fruit.

The subsequent behavior of both Adam and Eve is consistent with these first extremely tentative stirrings toward bringing their vain contest to an end. In a long, tortured soliloquy, Adam proceeds to involve himself more definitely in this new, experientially rooted mode of intellection. In Ebenezer Parkman's case, a sense of affliction which might have brought him to the point of suffering a fortunate intellectual fall was indeed experienced, but it was kept out of sight. In the course of both the Andrews and the Bolton affairs, he had a number of "most unusually troublesome and distressing" dreams,[5] but these remained confined in the nighttime realm of mere emotion and individuality. They had no impact on his daylight social and rational presence, which thus never consisted of anything more than the repetition of establishmentarian precepts. Adam's soliloquy amounts to the endeavor that eluded Parkman, the bringing of most unusually troubling and distressing dreams to bear on the style of a Puritan leader's rationality and sociality. No longer can Adam merely invoke the overall structure of things, as he did in dealing with Eve's dream, with her gesture toward greater autonomy, and with her transgression. He must now raise questions, rather than give answers, about the relationship of particular experience to general order:

> Did I request thee, Maker, from my clay
> To mould me man, did I solicit thee
> From darkness to promote me, or here place
> In this delicious garden? As my will
> Concurred not to my being, it were but right
> And equal to reduce me to my dust,
> Desirous to resign, and render back
> All I received, unable to perform
> Thy terms too hard, by which I was to hold
> The good I sought not. To the loss of that,
> Sufficient penalty, why hast thou added
> The sense of endless woes? Inexplicable
> Thy justice seems; yet to say truth, too late,
> I thus contest; then should have been refused

---

[5]See above, chap. 6, nn. 10, 12, 22.

> Those terms whatever, when they were proposed:
> Thou didst accept them; wilt thou enjoy the good,
> Then cavil the conditions? And though God
> Made thee without thy leave, what if thy son
> Prove disobedient, and reproved, retort,
> Wherefore didst thou beget me? I sought it not:
> Wouldst thou admit for his contempt of thee
> That proud excuse? (743–64)

It is as though the necessity of asking such urgent questions mobilizes an energy that propels the intellect, almost in spite of itself, beyond the illusory orderliness of the dogmatic and syllogistic mode. Adam places his trouble within a neat, logical construct ("As my will / Concurred not to my being, it were but right / And equal to reduce me to my dust"), only to press on to a recognition of its inadequacy. And this leads in turn to something we have never before seen from him—he puts himself in the place of the one he is arguing against: "And though God / Made thee without thy leave, what if thy son / Prove disobedient, and reproved, retort, / Wherefore didst thou beget me?" Willy-nilly, in the midst of his prolonged "evasions vain, / And reasonings" (829–30), Adam stumbles on a moment of intellectual empathy, in which he stops managing and controlling and starts participating and exploring.

The process by which Puritans might have begun to climb out of the pit of contention into which they repeatedly plunged themselves continues, however, to be depicted as a painfully gradual one. Adam's soliloquy eventually comes to the correct Puritan conclusion that he must convict himself of sin: "first and last / On me, me only, as the source and spring / Of all corruption, all the blame lights due" (831–33). Yet just as Ebenezer Parkman concluded many a diary entry both regretting "what was amiss in me at this critical juncture" and persisting in his certainty that the layperson he was dealing with was someone who "deserv'd Correction," so Adam here combines an awareness of himself as an anguished sinner with a perception of Eve as a merely hardened one, "that bad woman" (837).[6] Given the stubborn strength of the Puritan character and the depth of the contradictions that drove Puritans into confrontations with one another, recovery and reconciliation cannot but be extremely difficult. And so this blinkered, misogynist view of Eve as a bad woman is what governs Adam's initial response to Eve's attempt to assay "soft words to his fierce passion" (865):

---

[6]See PD, Apr. 30, 1750; and Summers, *Muse's Method*, pp. 182–83.

Out of my sight, thou serpent, that name best
Befits thee with him leagued, thy self as false
And hateful; nothing wants, but that thy shape,
Like his, and colour serpentine may show
Thy inward fraud, to warn all creatures from thee
Henceforth.   (867–72)

This is in many ways the low point in Adam's and Eve's dealings
with each other, and our understanding of it as such can only deepen
when we take in the view Milton provides of Eve "desolate where she
sat" just before making her overture. If Adam in his soliloquy has
been moving fitfully toward vulnerability and intellectual openness,
so Eve has evidently been immersing herself all this time in her "overwhelmed" sense of shame and guilt. For Adam to reply to her "soft
words" with the hardest words he has ever spoken to anyone is for
him to kick his wife when she is, of her own volition, down. Yet this
very brutality may be a sign that we are in the presence of real instead
of cosmetic change. Adam has been brought to a point to which
Ebenezer Parkman was never brought, that of entirely losing his intellectual and sociopolitical composure. The guardian of order has fall-
en into a disorderly rage of a sort he had avoided even when the
seemingly endless "vain contest" had been at its height at the close of
Book IX.

Such a temporary razing of the relational status quo is fundamental
to the plausibility of Milton's imagining of how reconciliation might
transpire. The equivalent moment, as far as Eve is concerned, is her
response to this speech of Adam's:

He added not, and from her turned, but Eve
Not so repulsed, with tears that ceased not flowing,
And tresses all disordered, at his feet
Fell humble, and embracing them, besought
His peace.   (909–13)

Joseph Summers notes the connection between these actions and the
earlier time when, as we have seen, Eve "silently a gentle tear let fall /
From either eye, and wiped them with her hair" (V, 130–31) after
Adam has consoled her about her strange dream.[7] But what seems
most significant is the difference between the two situations. Adam is
himself so distressed, so overthrown from his wonted position as the
guide and governor, that he does not now do what he did before in that

[7]Ibid., p. 74; above, chap. 2, nn. 6–7.

capacity. He does not make Eve stop crying, does not manage and confine her emotions. And she, "with tears that ceased not flowing, / And tresses all disordered," is therefore able to become what she had been inhibited from becoming before, a richly penitent woman like the one in the story from Luke to which both this and the earlier episode allude, one who stands a chance of moving her husband away from the posture of the Pharisee and toward that of Jesus. An opening to change and growth is thus created by the fact that Adam and Eve are now both "all disordered." In large part, the reason the peace ceremony consummated during the Andrews controversy seems hollow is that it was so carefully structured. It embodied the desire for peace, to be sure, but it also appears to have been designed to contain that desire within the established order. The most substantial peacemaking gesture made in the course of Ebenezer Parkman's ministry in Westborough, it will be recalled, was the one made spontaneously by Cornelius Cook after the prearranged, formal peace conference had come to an unavailing conclusion.[8] Milton insists here in Book X that a breaking through toward peace must also in some significant sense be a breaking beyond the patterns by which relations have hitherto been ordered.

Yet Milton also continues to insist, in all realism and sobriety, that while the true peace is revolutionary, it is not revolutionary in any simple or immediate sense. As our first parents proceed to become reconciled to each other, it appears outwardly that little has changed. Having been thoroughly humbled does not prevent Eve from continuing to manifest her urge toward autonomy, offering as before the Fall and at its verge her own thoughts and ideas on the circumstances confronting them. First, she suggests that she sacrifice herself, return "to the place of judgment . . . / There with my cries importune heaven, that all / The sentence from thy head removed may light / On me" (932–35). After this plan is rejected, she is not abashed and henceforth submissive. On the contrary, she responds attentively to Adam's musings regarding the question of original sin ("A long day's dying to augment our pain, / And to our seed (O hapless seed!) derived" [964–65]), coming up with the programmatic solutions of sexual abstinence or suicide just as she had earlier suggested, after hearkening unto Adam's worries about gardening, a program of altered work organization.

For Adam's part, his having lost control of himself and the situation does not mean that he does not readily regain control once the point of severest crisis is past. It again becomes his habit and role to lecture

---

[8]See above, chap. 5, n. 22; chap. 6, n. 13.

and generalize and to define Eve's initiatives as impulsive and ill considered: "Unwary, and too desirous, as before, / So now of what thou know'st not" (947–48). Moreover, in the overall sequence leading from the picture of Eve's "lowly plight / Immovable" at Adam's feet (937–38) to that of both of them praying "in lowliest plight" to God (XI, 1–2), Adam betrays a distinct tendency to expropriate, while at the same time criticizing and minimizing, the decisive contributions to the healing of the situation which Milton by this verbal echo acknowledges to have been Eve's very own. As we have just seen, Eve was the one who had first raised the possibility of propitiating God, in the course of her crucial propitiation of Adam. At that point, Adam had appreciated the generosity of Eve's willingness to sacrifice herself only obliquely, by stating that he would do the same thing, were it not for his dogmatic, semi-Calvinist certainty that prayers cannot "alter high decrees" (953). Yet later on, after he rejects Eve's next suggestion of suicide as yet another sign of her intellectual limitations, he decides on prayer as the best course to pursue after all, without conceding in the slightest that he is following not only this general idea of Eve's, but even her intuitive sense that the place where the Son had passed judgment on them would be the most appropriate place to implement it: "What better can we do, than to the place / Repairing where he judged us, prostrate fall / Before him reverent, and there confess / Humbly our faults, and pardon beg" (1086–89). The irony here seems too clear and pointed, too noticeable a part of a narrative and spiritual turning point, not to be seen as Milton's shrewd recognition that change does not happen all at once, that the practices and patterns of the old order will endure long after the new order has begun to be born.

It may seem perverse to claim that *Paradise Lost* offers a prospect of anything even remotely resembling a new order of justice and love. For in the two books that succeed the reconciliation and repentance of Adam and Eve, and in which the historical and prophetic dimension of the poem becomes explicit, Adam learns that the history of the human race will be a chronicle in which "violence / Proceeded, and oppression, and sword-law / Through all the plain, and refuge none was found" (XI, 671–73). And while we, the heirs of "that system which had promised order and progress and yet produced the twentieth century,"[9] with its enduring, resourceful, and diversified sys-

9Raymond Williams, *Problems in Materialism and Culture* (London: Verso Editions, 1980), p. 102.

tems of oppression whose power has reached apocalyptic proportions, and its dreary pattern of failed revolutions, may find that the
grim vistas of Books XI and XII amount to yet another way in which
Paradise Lost continues to tell us about ourselves, we can scarcely be
consoled by such an awareness.

But if *Paradise Lost* concludes by insisting that we harbor no great
expectations about the overall logic of history, it also requires that we
live nevertheless as though our actions might make a difference, as
though the new order intimated in Adam's and Eve's reconciliation
might indeed be built. These are books filled with oppression and
sword-law, with a consciousness of necessity, but they are also books
filled with the freedom such a consciousness makes possible. They
show us a Noah who, like Milton after his years of revolutionary
activism, responds to the failure of his direct action and agitation not
by sinking into quietism, but rather by constructing "a vessel of huge
bulk" (XI, 729) stocked like *Paradise Lost* with generous provision for
the forms of life. They show us the Israelites, proceeding toward
Canaan after their miraculous rescue from Pharaoh's pursuing army

> Through the wild desert, not the readiest way,
> Lest entering on the Canaanite alarmed
> War terrify them inexpert, and fear
> Return them back to Egypt, choosing rather
> Inglorious life with servitude.   (XII, 216–20)

Here again is a reference to Milton's own political work, his participation in the effort to make England into a latter-day Promised Land.
Specifically, there are two allusions to Milton's final, desperate political gesture, his *Readie and Easie Way to Establish a Free Commonwealth*,
which had concluded by bitterly likening the impending Restoration
to the Chosen People "chusing them a captain back for *Egypt*" (*CPW*,
VII, 462). In contrast to what Milton had previously advocated, that
is, the Chosen People are here seen to be proceeding in "not the
readiest way," in order to avoid being driven "back to Egypt."

This is partly a matter of accepting the need for indirection and
revolutionary patience. For we are soon informed that "by their delay
/ In the wide wilderness," the Israelites succeed in founding "their
government, and their great senate choose / Through the twelve
tribes, to rule by laws ordained . . . / Thus laws and rites / Established,
such delight hath God in men / Obedient to his will, that he vouch-
safes / Among them to set up his tabernacle, / The holy one with
mortal men to dwell" (223–26, 244–48). What Milton had proposed

in *The Readie and Easie Way,* a free commonwealth presided over by a "great senate" and consecrating itself to godliness, is here established not in the land flowing with milk and honey, but rather in the wild desert, the wide wilderness. Once this is accomplished, the actual conquest of the Promised Land becomes a thing of no significance whatever: "the rest / Were long to tell, how many battles fought, / How many kings destroyed, and kingdoms won" (260–62). As before with Noah, what is involved is not a disavowal of active political labor on behalf of the kingdom of God, but rather a recasting of its form and a redirection of its focus. The task at hand is not to seize the state and inaugurate a new era that will sooner or later turn into yet another version of the old era. It is, rather, to build the kingdom day by day, as best we can, in the wide wilderness where, as far as we can meaningfully see, we always are. It is not only from the example of Jesus, but also from those of Noah and the Chosen People wandering in the desert that Adam wins through to his understanding of what, as E. M. W. Tillyard notes, he and Eve had already experienced, that the committed, laboring life is one of "by small / Accomplishing great things, by things deemed weak / Subverting worldly strong, and worldly wise / By simply meek" (XII, 566–69).[10]

Milton's demand that we labor on in good faith though deprived of most of the sources of hope has also been articulated by those writers of our own troubled century who have managed to remain both thoughtful and politically committed. For example, in Nadine Gordimer's novel *Burger's Daughter,* the protagonist is the child of two leading South African Communists who have been heroes and martyrs in the struggle against apartheid. In the course of her endeavors to establish her own autonomous identity, Rosa Burger manages to escape for a time from the imprisonment, pressure, and darkness of South Africa to the freedom, relaxation, and bright sunlight of the south of France. It is like the movement in the first four books of Milton's epic from Hell to Paradise. The further possibility emerges of remaining permanently in this privately liberating and nurturant

---

[10]Tillyard, *Studies in Milton,* p. 44. The belief that the church had been languishing in the wilderness since apostolic times, and would remain in that condition for the foreseeable future, was entertained by many of the defeated mid-century revolutionaries. Isaac Penington wrote in the 1650s: "When God redeems his people out of Babylon, he brings them not immediately unto Sion . . . but into the Wilderness where the church lies unbuilt. . . . There is a long travel from Babylon to Sion." See Christopher Hill, *The Experience of Defeat: Milton and Some Contemporaries* (New York: Viking, 1984), pp. 123, 297–303. Hill suggests the possibility that there is the same fruitful ambiguity in Penington's "travel," which might alternatively be read as "travail," as there is in the "wayfaring/warfaring" crux in Milton's *Areopagitica.*

air, for Rosa falls in love with a French leftist whose commitment to her includes an understanding of her psychopolitical heritage and predicament. However, through an encounter with a black South African exile who had lived with her family when he and she were both children, she is eventually brought to recognize the extent of her own complicity in a system that denies freedom, release from pressure, bright sunlight, and the delights of intimacy to most people. For her to remain in Europe with her lover, taking advantage of the facts that she is white and that her father had been a left-wing celebrity, would be for her to opt for "un paradis inventé." She chooses instead to expel herself from Paradise and return home to South Africa, where, "like anyone else, I do what I can. I am teaching [children] to walk again, at Baragwanath Hospital. They put one foot before the other." Knowing that her actions will have no discernible effect on the apartheid regime (at the novel's end, she has been imprisoned), and knowing in addition that her parents' politics of an overall vision of "the Future" have, at the least, done as much harm as good, Rosa nevertheless commits herself to the loss of Paradise, to the humdrum political labor of daily enablement of those denied access to the fulfillments that our life on this earth can make available to us. Like anyone else, like Noah or the Chosen People, she does what she can to build a kingdom of justice and love in what will remain, for all we know, a desert and a wilderness.[11]

The posture of Noah, of the Chosen People journeying toward the Promised Land but never reaching it, of Nadine Gordimer's Rosa Burger, is the posture in which Milton brings his story of human origins and Puritan vicissitudes to an end:

> whereat
> In either hand the hastening angel caught
> Our lingering parents, and to the eastern gate
> Led them direct, and down the cliff as fast
> To the subjected plain; then disappeared.
> They looking back, all the eastern side beheld
> Of Paradise, so late their happy seat,
> Waved over by that flaming brand, the gate
> With dreadful faces thronged and fiery arms:

[11]Nadine Gordimer, *Burger's Daughter* (New York: Viking, 1979), pp. 287, 332. I find a similar significance in *Homage to Catalonia*, George Orwell's great book about the Spanish Civil War. And Andrew Delbanco finds it in the life and work of a central New England figure, in *William Ellery Channing: An Essay on the Liberal Spirit in America* (Cambridge, Mass.: Harvard University Press, 1981); see esp. chap. 4.

> Some natural tears they dropped, but wiped them soon;
> The world was all before them, where to choose
> Their place of rest, and providence their guide:
> They hand in hand with wandering steps and slow,
> Through Eden took their solitary way.
>
> (636–49)

No matter how sobering and transformative their experiences, how careful their preparation and instruction, Adam and Eve are going to feel a jolt when they are left all alone on the subjected plain, with no one but themselves and nothing but their memories to guide them safely out beyond a throng of dreadful faces and fiery arms. They hesitate and they cry, fully united here at last in the shedding of tears and the wiping of them. And then they venture forth. Confronting what they know will be, they nevertheless hold fast to the bounty of the world's body that has been and will also yet be, in spite of everything. The world is all before them. They look into the distance to their ultimate place of rest, homeward returning, but they do not gaze fixedly upon it. Instead they proceed, with wandering steps and slow, by not the readiest way, across the subjected plain. Like anyone else, they do what they can. They join hands and put one foot before the other.

Index

Index

Index

Index

Liberal Republican movement (*cont.*) *See also* Independents (nineteenth-century)

Light imagery: in *Paradise Lost*, 22–23, 26, 28, 30, 82, 89–90; in seventeenth-century antinomianism, 22, 23n

Literacy, 127; and Westborough Andrews controversy, 180–85

Literary criticism: antisatanist school, 62; feminist and *Paradise Lost*, 37n; and Milton's Puritanism, 1–2; and Milton's social views, 19, 32, 69; poststructuralist school, 8–9n, 54n; satanist school, 62, 90, 242

Literature: social function in nineteenth-century New England, 215–16

Locke, Samuel, 192

Lodge, Henry Cabot, 246

Lyceums, 215

Lynn, Mass., 110; and labor militance, 240; shoe industry, 220–21, 226

Lyon, Josiah: and Ebenezer Parkman, 151

McKenna, Peter F.: Charles F. Morse and, 253–54; and Marlborough Irish Americans, 249–52

Malden, Mass., 113

Mammon, 82–85, 241–42

Manchester, Mass., 169

Mann, Horace: and evangelicalism, 210–11; and Protestant ethic, 211–14; and public school movement, 211–13; Satan and, 219

Manufacturers: and competition, 255; and intellectual autonomy, 244; social role, 13, 265. *See also* Shoe industry

Marlborough Association, 125–26; and Bolton controversy, 191; and Great Awakening, 126; and Westborough controversies, 179, 193

Marlborough, Mass., 13; in Colonial era, 138–41; in nineteenth century, 220–41, 244–71

Martyn, John, 148

Marx, Karl, 92, 271

Mather, Cotton, 127; *Magnalia Christi Americana*, 97, 194

Mather, Increase, 139, 194

Matthews, Marmaduke, 113

Mayhew, Jonathan, 248

Mechanick preaching. *See* Formal education

Mechanization: and intellectual development, 211–12. *See also* Shoe industry

Merchants, Colonial: and Quakers, 115;

and toleration, 111. *See also* Keayne, Robert

Military traditions: in Puritan culture, 86; Satan and, 78, 86–88

Milton, John: church-outed question, 5, 6n. *See also names of individual works*

Ministerial associations: and incorporation, 125–26

Ministerial conventions: and Bolton controversy, 192; Ebenezer Parkman's sermon to, 143; Westborough Bolton controversy and, 193–94

Moloch, 84

Morse, Charles F., 244–71; career and role summarized, 13; and S. H. Howe, 234; and shoe worker income, 227; social connections, 232. *See also* Competition; Sanctification; Subjectivity

Morse, Frederick L., 240–41

Mortalism: Charles F. Morse and, 258

Muggletonians, 121

Mugwumps, 246, 264, 267. *See also* Independents (nineteenth-century)

Native Americans in *Paradise Lost*, 26

Nayler, James, 70, 122–23

Negative capability: Charles F. Morse and, 262–63, 265

Negative voice: and incorporation, 125; promulgated, 110–11; in Westborough Bolton controversy, 193–95

Newbury, Mass., 117, 121

New Lights. *See* Great Awakening

New Model Army, 37–39

Newspapers: *Boston Evening Record*, 260, 267–68; *Boston Evening Transcript*, 260; *Boston Globe*, 259; and capitalist development, 13, 215–18; *Marlborough Daily Mirror*, 251–52; *Marlborough Mirror-Journal*, 251; *Marlborough Star*, 250, 269; *Marlborough Times*, 227, 232, 239, 244–71; *Somerville Truth*, 259; *Springfield Republican*, 216–18; *Worcester West Chronicle*, 259

Newton, A. F.: and anti-Catholic agitation, 251–53; Charles F. Morse and, 248–49

Nisroc, 88–89

Noah in *Paradise Lost*, 280

Nonconformists, 85

Non-Importation Covenant: Ebenezer Parkman and, 167–68

Northampton, Mass., 121, 123

Northborough, Mass., 148

Norton, John, 114

Norwich, Conn., 133–34

Index

Index

Library of Congress Cataloging-in-Publication Data

Stavely, Keith W. F., 1942–
  Puritan legacies.

  Includes index.
  1. Puritanism—New England. 2. New England—Civilization.
3. Marlborough (Mass.)—Civilization. 4. Westborough (Mass.)—
Civilization. 5. Puritanism—Massachusetts—Marlborough.
6. Puritanism—Massachusetts—Westborough. 7. Milton, John, 1608–
1674. Paradise Lost. 8. Milton, John, 1608–1674—Influence. I. Title.
F7.S83 1987   974   87-47551
ISBN 0-8014-2016-4

DATE DUE

	FGL NOV 2 3 1988	
FGL R1 1 0888		
	UGL SEP 2 8 1991	
	UGL R SEP 2 7 1991	
UGL NOV 0 7 1991		
MAR 2 6 1997	1997	
UGL DEC 1 8 1998		
FGL DEC 1 2 1998		
2 5 2004		
UGL R NOV 0 8 2004		